COMPUTER STUDIES

C S FRENCH, BSc.(Hons), M.Sc., Grad.Cert.Ed.,
AFIMA, FBCS, C.Eng.

Carl French currently works in the financial sector of the computer industry where, in recent years, he has been involved in the design and implementation of a number of large database systems. He was previously employed as a Principal Lecturer in Computer Science at The Hatfield Polytechnic following several years' experience of teaching on a wide variety of computer courses.

3rd Edition

DP PUBLICATIONS LTD
Aldine Place
142/144 Uxbridge Road
Shepherds Bush Green
London W12 8AW
Tel: (081) 746 0044

1990

ACKNOWLEDGEMENTS

I wish to express my thanks to the following:
Mr. P. Ashurst who contributed significantly to this edition both by suggesting various improvements at the planning stage and by providing draft copies of some of the new material.
Messrs. P. Harrison and J. A. Moffat for their help in the preparation of the manuscript of the first edition.
Messrs. E. C. Oliver and R. J. Chapman for permission to use material from their book "Data Processing".
IBM UK Ltd. for permission to use a number of illustrations and photographs within the text. (Separate acknowledgements are given in each case.)
DRS Data and Research Services Ltd for permission to reproduce specimen OCR character fonts and for permission to reproduce photographs of a their high speed OCR system.
Apple Computers UK Ltd, CalComp Ltd, Compaq Computer Ltd, Digital Equipment Corporation (DEC), FACIT data products, Feedback Data Ltd, Kennedy International Inc., NCR Ltd, PHILIPS, Rediffusion Computers Ltd, Research Machines Ltd, Sun Microsystems Ltd, and Toshiba for permission to reproduce photographs of their products.
The Associated Examining Board (AEB), the East Anglian Examination Board (EAEB), the University of London University Entrance and School Examination Council (London), The Oxford Delegacy of Local Examinations (OLE) , the Royal Society of Arts (RSA) and the South-East Regional Examination Board (SREB) for permission to reproduce past examination questions.

Carl French 1990

First Edition   1982   Reprinted 1983   Reprinted 1984   Reprinted 1985
Second Edition   1986   Reprinted 1987   Reprinted 1988   Reprinted 1989
Third Edition   1990   Reprinted with corrections 1991

ISBN 1 870941 41 1

Copyright C. S. French © 1990

Printed in Great Britain by
The Guernsey Press Co. Ltd,
Guernsey, Channel Islands.

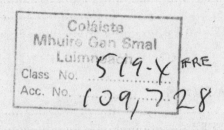

Contents

COMPUTERS IN PERSPECTIVE

Preface

INTRODUCTION AND AIMS OF THE MANUAL

1. There is an ever growing demand for individuals who are at ease with computer technology and familiar with how to use computer based systems. Public awareness of this has perhaps given rise to the increasing numbers of *examination courses in Computer Studies* and a growing number of candidates for such courses.

2. This book is aimed at such courses and and provides a sound foundation in Computer Studies to meet the needs of introductory examinations in Computer Studies. In particular, the text is intended to suit courses leading to the following examinations.

    a.   GCSE Computer Studies. The national criteria were taken into account when the very first edition of this book was produced. In particular, the questions set at the end of chapters are carefully graded to support differential assessment.

    b.   BTEC specialist courses in Computer Studies and option courses in Computer Studies on BTEC courses in Business or Technology.

    c.   RSA examinations in Computer Studies.

    e.   City and Guilds courses in Computing.

Where appropriate, questions in the text have been taken from examination papers for the above.

3. The text may also prove useful on introductory courses in Information Technology, as an introductory text in Information Technology, *and indeed as a text for preliminary reading for any one about to embark upon a first course in Computing*.

APPROACH

4. The text has been designed for use in independent study or as a text to be used in conjunction with tuition at school, college, etc. Practical examples are incorporated throughout the text so as to enable the reader to grasp the new concepts more easily, and in order to stress the relevant practical applications of each new topic.

QUESTIONS ASSIGNMENTS AND ANSWERS

5. In order to satisfy a variety of uses; as an instructional manual, course text book, revision text, etc., the following types of coursework have been included:

    a.   Questions at the end of each chapter with answers in each appendix.

    b.   Questions at the end of each chapter but with no answers given. Teachers and lecturers may obtain a free copy, if they send a written request to the publishers using school or college stationery.

    c.   Small assignments are given at the ends of selected chapters where it is thought helpful for the student to do such work at that point.

    d.   Rather longer assignments are provided at the end of the text. They are aimed primarily at BTEC students but may also be useful, as a basis for projects, to those studying on other courses.

    e.   A set of revision questions is provided at the end of the text.

END OF CHAPTER

6. At the end of chapters is found:

    a.   Summary of chapter.

    b.   Points to note. These are used for purposes of emphasis or clarification.

    c.   Questions. (as described above)

APPENDICES

7. Use has been made of appendices and the reader should note carefully the purpose of each.

- a. **Appendix I** contains revision test questions with and without answers.
- b. **Appendix II** contains answers to questions and specimen solutions to revision test questions.
- c. **Appendix III** contains notes on projects, coursework and other study followed by assignments suitable for BTEC courses.
- d. **Appendix IV** contains details that have been excluded from the text in the interests of clarity or details which need to be referred to at different stages in the text.

HOW TO USE THE MANUAL

8. Students are advised to read the manual chapter by chapter since subsequent work often builds on topics covered earlier.

9. The layout of the chapters has been standardised so as to present information in a simple form that is easy to assimilate. To ensure the assimilation is complete students are advised to attempt questions as they come to them, and to check their answers in the appendix before reading further.

NOTATION AND TERMINOLOGY

10. The terminology used within this manual is consistent with the more widely accepted definitions and, in particular, it is consistent with the booklet containing "A glossary of computer terms" published by the BCS. Where other equivalent terms are also in common use in examinations they have been mentioned. Notation is defined as it is introduced.

FURTHER READING AND REFERENCES

11. This text may be regarded as an introduction to the following two specialist text also available from DP Publications Ltd.

- a. Oliver and Chapmans' Data Processing and Information Technology by C. S. French.
- b. Computer Studies by C. S. French.

These two texts have some material in common but the former is oriented towards Business and Accountancy courses whereas the latter is oriented towards A level. City and Guilds, BTEC and BCS Part 1 courses.

Both texts may serve as a reference works for Computer Studies.

SUGGESTIONS AND CRITICISM

12. The author would welcome any suggestions or criticism from students or lecturers.

I would like to take this opportunity to thank all those who have written to me with their comments and suggestions.

NOTE TO THE THIRD EDITION

13 The contents of the text have been systematically revised and brought up to date. For topics concerning hardware and its uses this has required a significant change in emphasis reflecting the growing importance of workstations and more modern forms of human-computer interfaces. The treatment of programming has also been revised to reflect the more up to date methods which have fortunately now found there way into the examinations.

New material has also been introduced in the areas of databases, 4GLs, software packages and methods of applications development.

Carl French. 1990.

INTRODUCTION

1.   What is Computer Studies? If you want an answer to this question please read the rest of this book! If you want a short answer to be going on with then Computer Studies deals with the features of computers, and the ways and methods of using computers, so as to provide a basis for understanding the impact of computers on individuals, organisations and society.

2.   How is Computer Studies related to other subjects? There are many activities associated with handling information including its manipulation, location, modification and production, for example, using a library, answering an examination question or producing a bill. All such activities fall under the general subject category of **Information Processing (IP)**. Computers have been developed to **automate** *some* Information Processing activities. The telephone and television have automated other Information Processing activities. Computers, telecommunications equipment (eg, telephone and telex), and other technology associated with automation come under the general heading of **Information Technology (IT)**.

3.   Definition. Information Technology is the technology which supports activities involving the creation, storage, manipulation and communication of information, together with their related methods, management and applications.

**4.   **Although Computer Studies is part of IT it is not sensible to thing of Computer Studies as being in a watertight compartment and therefore it is important to realise that many of the topics we look at in Computer Studies are also important in other subjects which are regarded as part of IT eg, telecommunications. The difference will be that we will look at the topics from a Computer Studies point of view. For example, electronic communications equipment and video technology are important in Computer Studies because of the ways they are used in conjunction with computers, but we are not particularly concerned with their technological details. An electronic engineering student would be interested in such detail but might only be interested in some parts of Computer Studies.

**5.   **In the first chapter of this text the reader is introduce to some of the basic ideas of Computer Studies including how a computer may be used, what a computer is and how it works.

1 Using Computers

INTRODUCTION

1.1   The purpose of this chapter is to help the reader to start using a computer. The chapter also gives some basic information about what a computer is. We will be looking at one simplified example of an application of a computer and we will be taking the view of a computer user rather than that of a computer specialist. Specialist topics come later in the text.

1.2   This chapter first examines an organisation whose work the computer could be used for but which is currently being carried out manually. Then we will look at the computer and the way in which it can be used for the organisation's work.

AN ORGANISATION AND ITS WORK

1.3   A small organisation, which we shall call the "A - Z Music Club", is able to obtain records and cassettes for its members at discount prices. Members pay an enrolment fee. In return they are sent the club's latest catalogue four times a year. The members also receive details of special offers at various other times.

1.4   Provided a member places at least one order during the year his or her enrolment is renewed without charge for the following year. Otherwise, the membership lapses unless the member pays a re-enrolment fee.

1.5   The club currently uses a set of membership record cards to maintain a list of its member's details (fig. 1.1). You will see from figure 1.1. that each member has a membership number. The membership number is used because, unlike many common names, it is unique.

1.6   The cards are used to provide the names and addresses from which the envelopes for mailing can be typed. Also, the cards are used to record the date of each member's last order. This information is used to keep the membership up to date, by identifying members who either need membership re-enrolment reminders or need to be deleted having failed to re-enrol.

1.7   Orders are handled separately from the tasks just described, with the exception of updating "date of last order" details on the card, and we will not consider them further here.

1.8   The system works satisfactorily but the task of preparing the various mail shorts is laborious, slightly error prone, and time consuming. There are occasional problems too, when individuals change address or make mistakes with their membership number.

1.9   It appears that a small computer system may be useful in overcoming these problems because computers are good at doing simple repetitive tasks accurately and quickly.

A WORD OF CAUTION

1.10   Whilst it is true that computers can be used very effectively to perform all kinds of tasks, particularly now they are available at prices that most organisations can afford, it is all too common to find examples where computers have been introduced to make things better and have only made things worse! The reason for this are in some ways quite simple. A computer will only succeed when those using it have taken the trouble to determine:

    a.   WHAT they require the computer to do.

    b.   HOW the computers can best do it.

    c.   Whether the BENEFITS are worth the COSTS.

    d.   Whether those involved are ready, willing and able to work with the computer.

Miss any of these and there is every chance of introducing a computer which does the wrong job in the wrong way, has caused extra expense and provided no savings, and which nobody enjoys using.

```
┌─────────────────────────────────────────────────┐
│         Membership Number:  _____      │
│                                                   │
│              A-Z MUSIC CLUB                       │
│              MEMBERSHIP RECORD                    │
│                                                   │
│   Title (Mr, Mrs, Miss, Ms, Dr.):  _____  │
│                                                   │
│                                                   │
│   Initials:  _____ │
│                                                   │
│                                                   │
│   Surname:  _____ │
│                                                   │
│                                                   │
│   Address:  _____ │
│                                                   │
│             _____ │
│                                                   │
│             _____ │
│                                                   │
│   Postcode:  _____ │
│                                                   │
│                                                   │
│   Date of last order:  _____ │
│                                                   │
│             _____ │
│                                                   │
└─────────────────────────────────────────────────┘
```

Figure 1.1. A - Z Membership Record Card.

1.11 In later chapters we will look at how such problems can be avoided. In this chapter we will assume that all the necessary questions have been asked and answered satisfactorily. The outcome has been the decision to use a computer in the way now to be described.

A SMALL COMPUTER SYSTEM

1.12 The computer to be used by the A - Z Music Club is that shown in figure 1.2. It is an example of a **"Personal Computer (PC)"** which is a name commonly given to a small computer used primarily by an individual at work or at home but mostly for business use. Small computers, such as PCs and the computers used for playing computer games, belong to a class of computers known as **microcomputers**. The name microcomputer need not concern us here. We will look at it and the classification of computers more closely in later chapters.

3

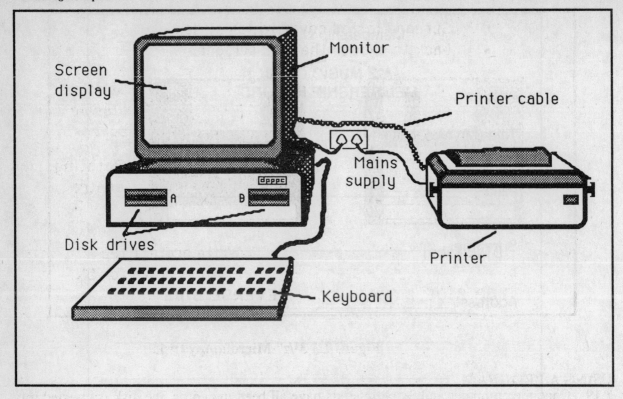

Figure 1.2. A Personal Computer (PC).

1.13 Examine fig 1.2. You will see that there are several items of equipment in the figure. Strictly speaking, what we are looking is not just a computer but a computer system. The computer itself is contained within the same cabinet as the disk drives. Connected to it by various cables are devices such as the printer, keyboard, monitor and disk drives.

1.14 Peripherals. The devices connected to the computer are called its **peripherals.**

1.15 Hardware. The general name for all the equipment, including both the computer and its peripherals is **hardware.**

1.16 By itself, the hardware is of as much use as a cassette player without cassettes. The computer hardware is capable of carrying out a wide variety of decisions and tasks but to do so it needs to be given a set of instructions in a form which it can understand.

1.17 A set of instructions written in the language of the computer is called a **program.** (Note the spelling.) The general name used to describe *all* the programs which may be used on a computer is **software.**

1.18 When a computer carries out the instructions in a program we say the program is being "run" or "executed" by the computer. Before the program can be executed by the computer it must be fed into the computer in some way. The program to deal with the membership of the A - Z music club is recorded on an object called a **microfloppy disk** or **microdiskette** (fig. 1.3). The program is recorded onto the disk surface which is coated with a magnetic material similar to that used on the surface of domestic audio or video cassettes. The program can be read from the disk by the computer once the disk has been inserted in a slots in the front of a disk drive (fig 1.2) We will not consider how this program is used.

4

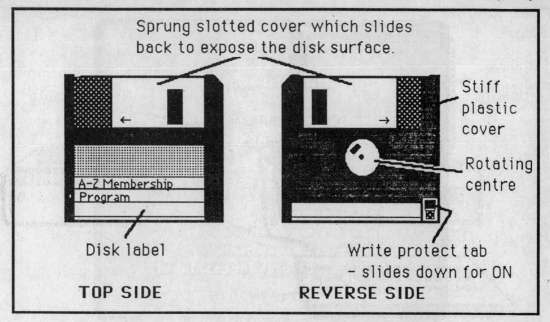

Figure 1.3 3½" Microfloppy Disk.

USING A PROGRAM

1.19   Once the computer and its peripherals have all been turned on, the disk is inserted into the disk drive labelled "A" (fig 1.2). In general, a number of possible things can take place at this stage. We will assume that on being switched on the computer automatically reads from the disk in drive "A" and that the disk contains programs which cause the computer immediately to place a display on the monitor screen like that shown in figure 1.4.

1.20   The display in fig 1.4 is an example of a **"menu"**. It lists a set of options for the computer user to choose from. As you can see from the figure there are seven options. The first option is that of adding a new member to the club. If the computer users presses the "A" key on the keyboard the computer responds by sending a new display to the monitor screen like that shown in fig 1.5a. Each of the other options will give rise to a different display, except the "E" option which can be used to end the program.

1.21   Note how the keyboard is used to feed **data** (ie. facts such as names or numbers) into the computer. It is a common example of an **input device** (see fig 1.6). The monitor and printer are examples of **output devices** since data is fed out to them by the computer. The disk drives are **storage devices.** The disk placed in them are able to retain recorded programs or data. The computer is able both to *store* (ie. record) data or programs on the diskettes and to *retrieve* copies of the stored data or programs. In this example we will assume that data corresponding to that on the membership records (fig. 1.1.) is stored on a disk which is placed in disk drive "B".

1.22   Let us assume that the key "A" is pressed by the user when the main menu (fig 1.4) is displayed so that the display of fig 1.5a appears on the screen. You will notice that there is white square on the display just to the right of "Title (Mr, Mrs..):". This square is known as the **cursor.** If you were watching a real monitor screen you would see the cursor flashing on and off. It is used to signify the position on the screen at which data typed in on the keyboard will be displayed. In this case it is also indicating to the user that the title of the new member is to be typed in.

5

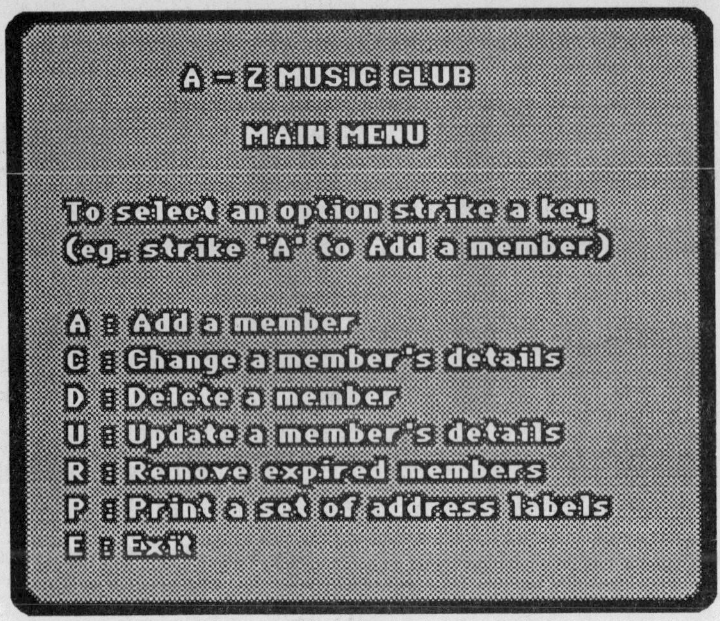

Figure 1.4. A Monitor Screen Display.

Figure 1.5a

A - Z MUSIC CLUB

ADD NEW MEMBER
MEMBERSHIP NUMBER : 3576281

Title (Mr,Mrs...): Mr___ Initials: P___

Surname: ▮————————————————

Address: ————————————————

————————————————

Postcode: _____

Figure 1.5b

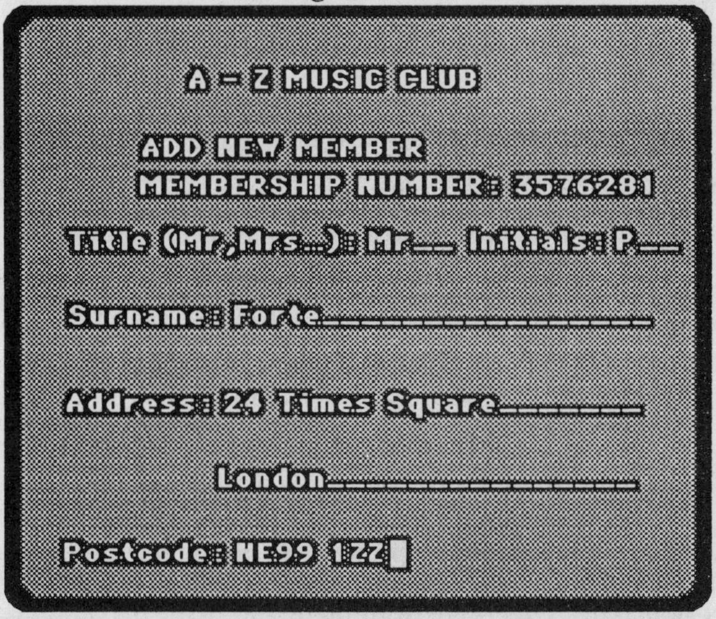

A - Z MUSIC CLUB

ADD NEW MEMBER
MEMBERSHIP NUMBER : 3576281

Title (Mr,Mrs...): Mr___ Initials: P___

Surname: Forte————————————

Address: 24 Times Square————

London————————————

Postcode: NE99 1ZZ▮

Figure 1.5c

Figure 1.5. Steps in Entering Some Data.

7

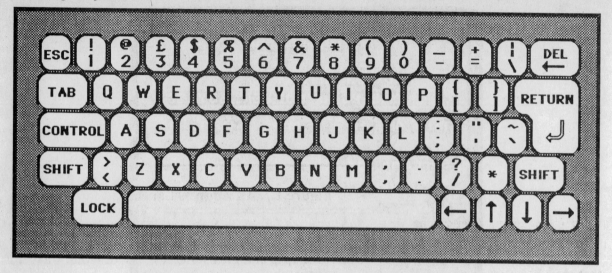

Figure 1.6. A computer keyboard.

1.23 The user can type in the item of data, "Mr" in this case, and as each letter is typed and gets displayed on the screen the cursor moves forward one letter position. The user indicates that the data item is complete by pressing the "RETURN" key (see fig 1.6). The computer records the title and causes the cursor to be moved to the first letter position of the "Initials". If the user types "P" and again presses the "RETURN" key the computer again records the input data and causes the cursor to be moved to the next data item. At this stage the display will look like that shown in fig 1.5b. Again the user types in the data until the last letter of the postcode is typed. The display then looks like that shown in fig 1.5c. Once the "RETURN" key is pressed the input of new member information will have been completed and the display of figure 1.4 will appear again.

1.24 This time the user might press the "P" key and the computer will respond with another menu. This time the menu will give the user a choice of what labels to print:

    a.   Labels for all members.
    b.   Labels to remind members who need to re-enrol.
    c.   Labels to selected members.

The label for the member whose details were shown on figure 1.5 might appear as shown in figure 1.7. Each label is sticky and can be peeled off a backing paper and stuck on an envelope.

1.25 Once the required labels have been printed the computer will again display the main menu (fig 1.4) from which the user may make a selection. The user will be able to carry on in this manner repeatedly making selections from the menu, with the computer carrying out the necessary actions in each case, until finally the "Exit" option, "E", is selected from the main menu. Once "E" is typed the execution of the program will be brought to an end. In general there are several things which can happen at this stage. We will assume that the computer clears the screens, ejects the disks from their drives and then waits for other disks to be inserted or until it is switched off.

```
MR   P       Forte
24 Times Square
London
NE99 1ZZ


Membership No. 3576281
```

Figure 1.7. An Address Label.

THE COMPUTER ITSELF

1.26 Now for some basic information about what a computer is.

1.27 Computers come in so many different shapes and forms that it is not obvious what it is that they have in common. Neither is it always obvious when we are using a computer. For instance, when we look at a digital watch we seldom give a moment's thought to the fact that there is a small special purpose computer inside it. Similarly, the customer at the bank or in a large supermarket is unlikely to give much thought to the fact that the services being provided depend greatly upon computers. What characteristics do these various computers have in common? We will now consider this matter.

THE CHARACTERISTICS OF A COMPUTER

1.28 Computers display the following characteristics to a greater or lesser extend dependent on their type and application:

a. The ability to perform calculations at very high speeds .

b. The ability to take in information and to store that information for future retrieval or use.

c. The ability to take in and store a sequence of instructions for the computer to obey. Such a sequence of instructions is called a **program** and must be written in the language of the computer. (Note the spelling: Program not programme).

d. The ability to obey a sequence of program instructions, provided the instructions are stored within the computer. The program instructions will be obeyed in sequence, automatically, without the need for manual intervention at each step. This is very different from the operation of a typical pocket calculation which needs buttons to be pressed for each operation, and where the person using the calculator controls the sequence of operations.

e. The ability to use simple logical rules to make decisions for their own internal control, or for the control of some external activity eg, to take over the role of the calculator operator.

f. The ability to communicate with other systems.

g. The ability to exploit a complex internal structure of microelectronic circuitry in a variety of ways.

These characteristics will all be described, explained and illustrated in detail in later chapters. In the remainder of this chapter the more important characteristics will be introduced and illustrated by suitable examples.

The Apple Macintosh computer model IIci.
An advanced type of personal computer.
Picture courtesy of Apple Computers Ltd.

COMPUTER CALCULATIONS

1.29   The ability of computers to perform calculations at high speed can be illustrated by these examples:

    a. How long do you think it would take you to count up to one million? Well, if you count *very* quickly you might be able to count up to 200 in a minute. Try it if you like. Keeping up that speed it would take 5000 minutes to count to 1 million, which is over 83 hours or about 3 $1/2$ days. A typical modern computer would the ability to do the same tasks in about a second if used solely for that task, and some computers could complete the tasks in a small fraction of one second!

    b. Computers are not quite so fast at addition and subtraction as they are at counting, yet if a million numbers had already been fed into a typical modern computer it would have the ability to calculate the total in very few seconds or so if used solely for that task.

    c. Even multiplication and division which take longer than addition and subtraction are incredibly fast when performed by computer. A million divisions or multiplications might only   take about a minute to perform. The same tasks performed manually would take weeks or months to complete and would probably include many wrong answers, whereas the computer results would all be correct if the computer was used properly.

1.30   So, once the numbers have been fed into the computer they can be handled very quickly. There is, therefore, a need for quick and efficient ways of feeding in the numbers and getting out the results, so that this fast processing speed can be used effectively. This means that efficient input and output is very important.

INFORMATION INPUT AND OUTPUT

1.31   The examples given in 1.29 showed how computers can operate at extremely high speeds on data which is already stored within them, but getting data into the computer and out again poses certain problems.

    The problems arise because humans communicate less quickly than computers and in a different way ie. by speech writings etc. A computer's internal communication is based upon codes formed from high frequency electronic pulses. The problems are:

    a. How to design suitable codes into which we can convert our data, which the computer can   then use, and which can be converted back again.

    b. How to make the coding and decoding system fast and efficient enough eg. by the

design of suitable devices.
c. What to do about slow communication at the human end.

Fig. 1.8 summarises the situation.
(NB. Other problems of human/machine communication are covered later).

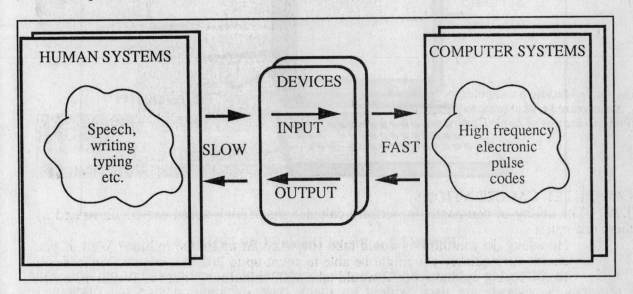

Figure 1.8 Human Computer Communication.

1.32 It is necessary, therefore, to present data to the computer in a way which provides easy conversion into the electronic forms used by the computer. These electronic forms consists of codes made from combinations of different kinds of electronic pulses. The details need not concern us here.

1.33 A wide variety of computer **input devices** have been developed to do this work. One example, the computer keyboard was introduced previously in fig 1.6. A number of **output devices** have also been developed, each with the ability to convert the computer's electronic pulse codes into forms which are intelligible to us, eg. printed documents, pictures and graphs. Two output devices were introduced earlier in the chapter, namely, the monitor and the printer (fig 1.2). The process of input and output can be illustrated by the **Visual Display Unit (VDU)** which has a keyboard and monitor built into it.

1.34 The VDU. A device able to perform both the task of input and output is the VDU (Visual Display Unit) See figure 1.9 and illustrations. It is really two devices; one for input, one for output. Data is fed in via a Keyboard (fig. 1.6) which is like a typewriter keyboard.

Keys are marked with individual letters A-Z, digits 0-9, or other symbols eg. +, 0 * ( ). This set of letters, digits and symbols is called a **character set.** We recognise the individual characters by their appearance: the computer recognises a character from the unique electronic pulse code assigned to it. When for example the key for the letter "A" is pressed, the VDU generates and transmits the computer's electronic pulse, code for "A" along a cable to the computer. The pulse coded form of "A" is echoed back to the screen display by either the device or the computer. The computer can output information by transmitting the electronic pulse codes of characters and displays the appropriate characters on the screen. The speed of input is limited by the typing speed of the VDU operator. Most VDUs can receive and display data at speeds up to about 900 characters per second. Details of other devices will be given in later chapters.

11

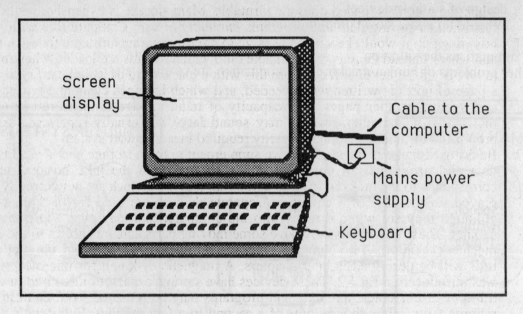

Figure 2.2 A Visual Display Unit (VDU)

1.35 The difference between human and computer communication is not the only input problem. Keyboards are used widely on many types of input device but often cause "bottlenecks" in the flow of information because the computer can handle data at speeds hundreds of times faster than the data can be typed in. In some applications this is turned to advantage by connecting many VDUs to one computer and thereby allow many individuals to use the computer at the same time. The computer can work so quickly that it can meet the demands of all the users at once. In other applications different approaches may be adopted. For example the measuring instruments and regulating controls inside a power station or chemical factory may be connected directly to the computer so that the computer can monitor and control the process automatically and at speeds which could not be matched by humans. this provides examples of several characteristics of the computer:

    a. Automatic operation under the control of a stored program without the need for manual intervention.

    b. Control of an external activity requiring decision making.

    c. Communication with another system.

INFORMATION STORAGE AND RETRIEVAL

1.36 The uses of computers for information storage and retrieval are in many respects more important than uses in numerical work. For example, roughly 80% of all computer usage is commercial, and commercial computing is mainly concerned with manipulating stored information including some simple arithmetic and less concern with complex computations.

1.37 Details of computer storage will be given in later chapters. At this stage only general features will be mentioned. The two basic types of storage are **main storage** and **backing storage.** The distinguishing characteristics are as follows:

    a. **Main Storage** is a wholly electronic miniaturised part of the computer from which data and program instructions are accessible at extremely high speed. For example a number may be retrieved from main storage in much less than one millionth of one second! Data and program instructions are only *immediately usable* when held within main storage, just as music can only be heard from a record in a juke box when the record is loaded onto the turntable. Main storage is expensive so its use is restricted to storing data and programs *currently in use*. Compare this with a juke box in which it would be very expensive to have a separate turntable for each record and where instead there is one turntable onto which records are loaded when they are to be played, or better still compare this with a blackboard or whiteboard onto which a page of notes is written when needed, and which is wiped clean and reused again and again for other pages. The capacity of main storage is measured in tens of thousands of characters, which may sound large but usually represents a small, proportion of the total storage capacity required in a computer system.

b. **Backing Storage** is a less expensive supplement to main storage and is used to hold data and programs not currently in use. In terms of the juke box example, it corresponds to the racks of records within the juke box which are not currently being played. In the case of a computer, separate devices are used for backing storage although they are wired directly into the computer and may even share the same cabinet. These devices usually have some moving parts and are subject to the risk of mechanical failure. Two common types the **magnetic disk unit** and **magnetic tape unit** will be described in later chapters. A magnetic disk unit for microfloppy disk was introduced in fig 1.2. These devices have storage capacities measured in tens of millions of characters and data and programs may be retrieved from them in times ranging from a few thousandths of a second to a few minutes. Full details will be given in chapter 14.

1.38 There are many computer applications which exploit the computer's impressive storage and retrieval facilities. For example: manufactures of suppliers of goods often use computers to store details of customers, products or suppliers. Details of customers could be held on backing storage and viewed via a VDU. Programs held within main storage would be able to handle the VDU inputs and outputs and to handle the flow of data between the VDU and backing storage. This data flow would be via main memory. The VDU operator could type in a request eg. for details of a particular customer. Within a few seconds the details could be retrieved from backing storage, pass through main storage and appear on the VDU screen. Other facilities could allow new details to be added, or allow existing details to be changed or deleted.

1.39 Now that we have looked at the characteristics of a computer it is time to bring together a number of definitions.

SOME DEFINITIONS

1.40 The previous paragraphs should have provided you with an introduction to the following terms which will now be given precise definition.

1.41 Data and Information

a. "Data" is the name given to basic *facts* eg. numbers of items sold by a business or the numerical values used in some mathematical calculation.

b. When "data" has been processed into a *more useful or intelligible form* (eg. by a computer) it is called "information". eg. "SMITH, 48" is data "the examination result for   Mr Smith is 48% and a pass" is information.

1.42 Program. A program is a *set of instructions* which is written in the language of the computer. A program is used to make the computer perform a specific task such as adding up a set of numbers.

1.43 Computer. A computer is a device which works under the control of a stored program, automatically accepting and processing data to produce information which is the result of that processing.

1.44 Hardware and Software.

a. **Hardware** is a general term used to describe *all* computer equipment.

b. **Software** is a general term used to describe *all* the various programs which may be used on a computer system.

SUMMARY

1.45 a. The reader has been shown how the computer may be used for a simple application.

b. The various component of a small computer system have been introduced. These include:

    i. an **input device - the keyboard**

    ii. **output devices - monitor screen and printer**

    iii a **storage device - disk drive for microfloppy disks**

    iv. the **computer** itself

c. **Hardware** and **Software** have been defined.

d. The terms **menu**, **data**, **peripheral** and **cursor** have been explained.

e. This chapter has also given some basic information about what a computer is.

f. A number of important concepts and terms have been introduced:

    i. **Program.** A set of program instructions written in the language of the computer.

    ii. **Character Set.** A set of letters, digits and symbols as found on keyboards.

    iii. **VDU.** Visual Display Unit. (An input and output device).

    iv. **Main Storage.** A wholly electronic miniaturised internal component of the computer used for storing data and programs.

    v. **Backing Storage.** A supplement to mains storage able to hold larger volumes of data but slightly less accessible. Common secondary storage media are *magnetic tape* and *magnetic disk.*

POINTS TO NOTE

1.46 a. A computer is a device which can accept data, process data and output data. A more precise definition will be given in later chapters.

b. There are many different types of computer hardware. The examples given in the chapter are typical of the kinds which the reader is most likely to use on his or her course. Other types of hardware will be discussed in later chapters.

c. Although this chapter should help the reader to use a computer there is no substitute for first hand practical experience. Therefore the reader should, whenever possible, accompany the reading of the text with practical exercises.

d. The characteristics introduced in this chapter will be examined in more detail in later chapters.

e. Main Storage is also called **main memory**, and **immediate access store(IAS)**.

f. Backing Storage is also called **auxiliary storage**.

g. Computers come in different sizes. A broad classification from smallest to largest is: **microcomputer, minicomputer, mainframe computer**.

QUESTIONS A *(Answers in Appendix II)*

1. *a.* *What is **hardware**?*

    b. *Given an example of what each of the following items of hardware used for:*

      i. *Monitor*

      ii. *Keyboard*

      iii. *Disk drive and microfloppy disk*

      iv. *Printer*

2. *What is software?*

3.   *What is the purpose of a cursor?*

4.   *Distinguish between main storage and backing storage.*

5.   *What are the basic problems presented by getting data into the computer and out again? How are these problems overcome?*

QUESTIONS B *(Without Answers)*
1.   *What is a peripheral? Give examples.*

2.   *Explain how a computer user might use a* **menu***.*

3.   *Microfloppy disks can be used to store data. What else can they be used to store?*

4.   *Why do VDU keyboards cause "bottlenecks" in the flow of information? Suggest a way in which this can be overcome.*

5   *Refer to a computer keyboard which you use and describe its character set. Also explain the purpose of any special keys.*

ASSIGNMENTS
1.   Produce a list and brief description of all the main items of hardware and software which are used at the school or college at which you are studying this course.

15

APPLICATIONS OF COMPUTERS

1. In this Part we look at a wide variety of different applications of the computer. The material is introductory in nature because this is not the only place in this text where we examine uses of the computer. Indeed, throughout the remainder of the text every opportunity is taken to illustrate the material by practical examples. Also, in the Part entitled "Further Applications" towards the end of this text, we make use of the material covered earlier to examine a number of specific applications in detail.

2. Chapter 2 provides a practical illustrations of how the computer may be applied to calculations on **spreadsheets** by means of software in the form of what is called a "computer package".

3. Chapter 3 provides another practical illustration of how the computer may be applied but this time the emphasis is on the computers capabilities of **information storage and retrieval.**

4. Chapter 4 rounds of the practical illustration of how the computer may be applied by examining how the computer may be used for **document processing**.

5. Chapter 5 concludes this Part of the text by examining the general criteria for using a computer and then surveys the various areas in which computers can be applied. The areas covered include science, commerce and education.

2 Spreadsheets

INTRODUCTION

2.1 A "**spreadsheet**" is nothing more than a simple table in which individual elements are identified by column and row references, rather like squares on a street map (see Fig 2.1). However, the term "spreadsheet" is now most commonly used in connection with software that provides computerised forms of spreadsheets, more correctly called "**spreadsheet packages**". This chapter examines spreadsheet packages in some detail in order to provide a practical example of a common use of computers for calculations. Having introduced the term **"package"** here, this is a good point at which to explain what a package is.

	A	B	C	D	E	F	G	H	I	J
1		1.2	5	6.0						
2		1.4	4	5.6						
3		1.1	3	3.3						
4		1.7	2	3.4						
5		1.0	7	7.0						
6			21	25.3	1.20					
7										

Figure 2.1 A simple spreadsheet

COMPUTER PACKAGES

2.2 In chapter one we saw an example of a program which had been written to carry out a particular job, namely, maintaining the membership details of the A - Z Music Club. It can be very expensive and time consuming to write new programs for each new job the computer is required to do. One answer is to write the programs in such a way that it is possible for them to be used for a variety of similar jobs instead of merely one. For example, a program could be written so that a number of different clubs could use it to maintain their membership details. This is the idea behind the **computer package**.

2.3 **Definition.** A **computer package** consists of a set of programs and associated documentation designed to be used for a specific type of problem. Many computer packages are produced for particular applications, for example payroll, and are then called **applications packages.** Other computer packages provide facilities for dealing with a particular type of processing, the **spreadsheet package** is one example, another is the **database package.** The former deals with computations involving inter-related rows and columns of data, the latter deals with the creation and maintenance of data for enquiry and reporting purposes.

SPREADSHEETS

2.4 Consider the following problem which a spreadsheet package can solve easily. In order to give a more accurate representation of how data would appear on a VDU screen a different typeface has been use in the following figures.

2.5 In figure 2.2 you will see the results obtained from the assessment of a group of students. The results have not yet been arranged into any particular order and various pieces of information are still needed. These include the overall mark for each student and the average marks. A pocket calculator would be useful in doing this job but a spreadsheet package will be even better.

```
------------------------------------------------------------
NAME                EXAMINATION %        COURSEWORK %
------------------------------------------------------------

S     Smith         35.00                49.00
J     Brown         56.00                52.00
G W   Jones         72.00                88.00
A S   Robinson      48.00                66.00
R J   Harris        63.00                58.00
N     Johnson       51.00                75.00
------------------------------------------------------------
```

Note. The group is small for simplicity's sake

Figure 2.2 Results of Student Assessment.

2.6 We will now consider how a typical spreadsheet package may be used for this problem. In figure 2.3 you can see a spreadsheet into which the data of figure 2.2 has been inserted. You will notice that the spreadsheet comprises a grid of numbered rows and lettered columns. A typical spreadsheet may have as many as 256 rows and 8192 columns. Each grid position is called a **cell** and can contain either text or numerical values. For example, in figure 2.3 the cell C1 contains the word of text "RESULT" and the cell D5 contains the numerical value 52.00.

```
COL>      :A           :B           :C        :D            :E
ROW+------------------------------------------------------------------
   1|                                RESULTS
   2|      Surname      Initial (s)  Exam' %  Coursework %
   3|      ============ ============ ======== =============
   4|      Smith        S            35.00    49.00
   5|      Brown        J            56.00    52.00
   6|      Jones        G W          72.00    88.00
   7|      Robinson     A S          48.00    66.00
   8|      Harris       R J          63.00    58.00
   9|      Johnson      N            51.00    75.00
  10|      ============ ============ ======== =============
  11|
  12|
  13|
```

Figure 2.3. Part of a Spreadsheet.

2.7 When using a spreadsheet package on a computer the user sees only part of the spreadsheet at any one time. The section of the screen displaying the spreadsheet is called a **window** (see Figs 2.4 and 2.5). In addition to the window the user also sees other information. In these examples this information is shown as two other displays. In the top section of the screen there is a display which provides a summary of the functions and commands which can be used. We will see how they are used later. The bottom section of the screen displays details about the status of the one cell currently being worked upon. A

18

cell to be worked on is selected by moving the cursor about the screen until it is at the cell's position. The cursor is moved either by using the arrowed keys on the keyboard (see Fig 1.6) or by means of device called a "**mouse**" (details in later chapters). In figure 2.5 cell C1 has been selected and this is indicated to the user by the presence of the two symbols ">" and "<" on either side of the cell.

```
     FUNCTIONS                | COMMANDS
ON VALUE:ABS,SQRT,EXP,LOG     | C Copy D Delete      I Insert F Format
ON RANGE OR LIST:MAX,MIN,CNT  | S Sort R Recalculate P Print
                 SUM, AVG     | L Load K Keep        Q Quit
COL>  :A        :B      :C         :D           :E
ROW+------------------------------------------------------------------
  1|    >            <
  2|
  3|
  4|
  5|
  6|
  7|
  8|
  9|
 10|
   +------------------------------------------------------------------
     PRESENT CELL POSITION:   A1
            CELL TYPE:
            CELL CONTENTS:
            CELL VALUE:
     ENTER COMMAND OR VALUE: _____
```

Figure 2.4. An Empty Spreadsheet Display.

2.8 Data is entered into the spreadsheet by moving the cursor to selected cells and then typing in the data. The data first appears on the line at the bottom of the screen labelled "ENTER COMMAND OR VALUE _____" and gets inserted into the cell when the "RETURN" key is pressed. Notice how column headings can be inserted as well as the data itself. For example, in figure 2.6 you can see what the spreadsheet looked like just after the main heading, "RESULTS" had been typed in.

19

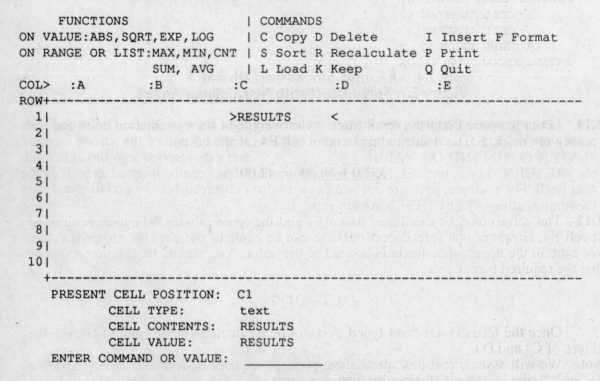

```
      FUNCTIONS                    | COMMANDS
ON VALUE:ABS,SQRT,EXP,LOG          | C Copy D Delete       I Insert F Format
ON RANGE OR LIST:MAX,MIN,CNT       | S Sort R Recalculate P Print
                SUM, AVG           | L Load K Keep          Q Quit
COL>  :A          :B          :C              :D           :E
ROW+-------------------------------------------------------------------------
  1|                      >RESULTS        <
  2|    Surname     Initial(s) Exam %       Coursework %
  3|    ========== ========== ============= =============
  4|    Smith      S                 35.00         49.00
  5|    Brown      J                 56.00         52.00
  6|    Jones      G W               72.00         88.00
  7|    Robinson   A S               48.00         66.00
  8|    Harris     R J               63.00         58.00
  9|    Johnson    N                 51.00         75.00
 10|    ========== ========== ============= =============
   +-------------------------------------------------------------------------
    PRESENT CELL POSITION:   C1
           CELL TYPE:        text
           CELL CONTENTS:    RESULTS
           CELL VALUE:       RESULTS
    ENTER COMMAND OR VALUE:  _____
```

Figure 2.5. A Spreadsheet Display.

```
      FUNCTIONS                    | COMMANDS
ON VALUE:ABS,SQRT,EXP,LOG          | C Copy D Delete       I Insert F Format
ON RANGE OR LIST:MAX,MIN,CNT       | S Sort R Recalculate P Print
                SUM, AVG           | L Load K Keep          Q Quit
COL>  :A          :B          :C              :D           :E
ROW+-------------------------------------------------------------------------
  1|                      >RESULTS        <
  2|
  3|
  4|
  5|
  6|
  7|
  8|
  9|
 10|
   +-------------------------------------------------------------------------
    PRESENT CELL POSITION:   C1
           CELL TYPE:        text
           CELL CONTENTS:    RESULTS
           CELL VALUE:       RESULTS
    ENTER COMMAND OR VALUE:  _____
```

Figure 2.6. Entering a Heading into the Spreadsheet.

SPREADSHEET CALCULATING

2.9   The spreadsheet shown in figure 2.5 merely displays the information shown in the original table (Fig. 2.2). The spreadsheet package is particularly useful because it can be used to perform calculations on the values displayed. For example, it can be used to calculate the overall mark for each student, as follows.

2.10   First, we may add a further column heading to the spreadsheet, in the same way as the "RESULT" heading was added, so that the spreadsheet appears as shown in figure 2.7.

```
      FUNCTIONS                 | COMMANDS
ON VALUE:ABS,SQRT,EXP,LOG       | C Copy D Delete      I Insert F Format
ON RANGE OR LIST:MAX,MIN,CNT    | S Sort R Recalculate P Print
               SUM, AVG         | L Load K Keep        Q Quit
COL>  :A        :B        :C                  :D           :E
ROW+-------------------------------------------------------------------
  1|                        RESULTS
  2|  Surname    Initial(s) Exam %        Coursework % Overall %
  3|  ========== ========== ============  ============ ==========
  4|  Smith      S              35.00          49.00>              <
  5|  Brown      J              56.00          52.00
  6|  Jones      G W            72.00          88.00
  7|  Robinson   A S            48.00          66.00
  8|  Harris     R J            63.00          58.00
  9|  Johnson    N              51.00          75.00
 10|  ========== ========== ============  ============ ==========
   +-------------------------------------------------------------------
   PRESENT CELL POSITION:  E9
         CELL TYPE:
         CELL CONTENTS:
         CELL VALUE:
   ENTER COMMAND OR VALUE:  _____
```

Figure 2.7. Spreadsheet with New Column Added.

2.11   Let us suppose that the overall mark is the average of the examination mark and the coursework mark. So, the value to be placed in cell E4 calculated as:

$$\frac{35.00 + 49.00}{2} = 42.00$$

2.12   The value could be calculated manually and the typed in with the cursor positioned at cell E4. However, the spreadsheet package can be made to calculate the required value. We type in the appropriate formula instead of the value. You should be able to recognise that the required formula is:

$$+ (C4 + D4)/2$$

Once the formula has been typed in it can be recalculated if we need to change the values of C4 and D4.

Note. We will assume that this spreadsheet package requires all formulae to begin with a "+" or "-" sign in order to distinguish them from text.

2.13 Once the formula has been typed in the spreadsheet appears as shown in figure 2.8.

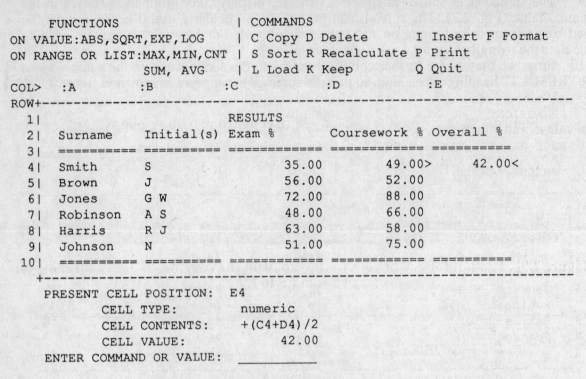

```
      FUNCTIONS                | COMMANDS
ON VALUE:ABS,SQRT,EXP,LOG      | C Copy D Delete      I Insert F Format
ON RANGE OR LIST:MAX,MIN,CNT   | S Sort R Recalculate P Print
                SUM, AVG       | L Load K Keep        Q Quit
COL>  :A         :B        :C              :D           :E
ROW+----------------------------------------------------------------------
  1|                         RESULTS
  2|  Surname    Initial(s) Exam %      Coursework % Overall %
  3|  ========== ========== =========== ============ ===========
  4|  Smith      S               35.00        49.00>     42.00<
  5|  Brown      J               56.00        52.00
  6|  Jones      G W             72.00        88.00
  7|  Robinson   A S             48.00        66.00
  8|  Harris     R J             63.00        58.00
  9|  Johnson    N               51.00        75.00
 10|  ========== ========== =========== ============ ===========
   +----------------------------------------------------------------------
     PRESENT CELL POSITION:  E4
             CELL TYPE:      numeric
             CELL CONTENTS:  +(C4+D4)/2
             CELL VALUE:        42.00
     ENTER COMMAND OR VALUE:  _____
```

Figure 2.8. Using Spreadsheet Formulae.

2.14 Similar formulae can be entered into cells E5, E6, E7, E8 and E9. These formulae are the same except for the row numbers which they contain. Since it would be rather time consuming to type in almost the same formula again and again, especially if there were lots of rows, the spreadsheet package usually provides a *copy command*. Formulae can be copied and adjusted accordingly. We will assume that in this spreadsheet a command consists of a "!" followed by the appropriate letter selected from the table of commands summarised at the top of the display. The initial "!" is used to distinguish the command from text, just as the "+" and "-" are used to distinguish formulae from text. In response to the copy command the spreadsheet may prompt the user to type in further information. The sequence of prompts, at the foot of the screen may be shown in figure 2.9.

```
+----------------------------------------------------------------------
  PRESENT CELL POSITION:   E4
          CELL TYPE:         numeric
          CELL CONTENTS:     +(C4+D4)/2
          CELL VALUE:            42.00
  ENTER COMMAND OR VALUE:   !C_____  CELL TO COPY? =E4
```

Figure 2.9a. A prompt for which cell to copy from, with response "E4".

```
+----------------------------------------------------------------------
  PRESENT CELL POSITION:   E4
          CELL TYPE:         numeric
          CELL CONTENTS:     +(C4+D4)/2
          CELL VALUE:            42.00
  ENTER COMMAND OR VALUE:   !C_____  COPY TO CELL(S)? E5:E9
```

Figure 2.9b. Prompt for cell or cells to copy to, with the response "E5:E9" meaning all cells from E5 to E9.

```
+----------------------------------------------------------------------
  PRESENT CELL POSITION:   E4
          CELL TYPE:         numeric
          CELL CONTENTS:     +(C4+D4)/2
          CELL VALUE:            42.00
  ENTER COMMAND OR VALUE:   !C_____  ADJUST FORMULA Y/N? Y
```

Figure 2.9c. Prompt whether to adjust the formula to allow for the changes in row number, with response "Y" for "yes".

Figure 2.9. A Series of Prompts for the Copy Command "!C".

2.15   After the command prompts have been answered the spreadsheet will *automatically* copy the adjusted formula into each of the cells and calculate the appropriate values. When this is completed the spreadsheet will appear as in figure 2.10.

2.16   Having seen the way commands may be used we will now look at the use of functions. The average of each column can be calculated using the function called "AVG". A new row for these averages can be added to the spreadsheet. When the cursor is moved down below row 10 in order to add further rows the window is automatically altered by the spreadsheet package. Once the necessary formulae have been added the spreadsheet will appear as shown in figure 2.11.

```
      FUNCTIONS                   | COMMANDS
ON VALUE:ABS,SQRT,EXP,LOG         | C Copy D Delete     I Insert F Format
ON RANGE OR LIST:MAX,MIN,CNT      | S Sort R Recalculate P Print
                SUM, AVG          | L Load K Keep          Q Quit
COL>  :A        :B        :C              :D            :E
ROW+-----------------------------------------------------------------------
  1|                            RESULTS
  2|  Surname    Initial(s) Exam %      Coursework % Overall %
  3|  ========== ========== ============ ============ ==========
  4|  Smith      S              35.00        49.00        42.00
  5|  Brown      J              56.00        52.00        54.00
  6|  Jones      G W            72.00        88.00        80.00
  7|  Robinson   A·S            48.00        66.00        57.00
  8|  Harris     R J            63.00        58.00        60.50
  9|  Johnson    N              51.00        75.00>       63.00<
 10|  ========== ========== ============ ============ ==========
   +-----------------------------------------------------------------------
     PRESENT CELL POSITION:  E9
            CELL TYPE:         numeric
            CELL CONTENTS:     +(C9+D9)/2
            CELL VALUE:            63.00
     ENTER COMMAND OR VALUE:  _____
```

Figure 2.10. The spreadsheet with the new calulated column values included.

```
      FUNCTIONS                   | COMMANDS
ON VALUE:ABS,SQRT,EXP,LOG         | C Copy D Delete     I Insert F Format
ON RANGE OR LIST:MAX,MIN,CNT      | S Sort R Recalculate P Print
                SUM, AVG          | L Load K Keep          Q Quit
COL>  :A        :B        :C              :D            :E
ROW+-----------------------------------------------------------------------
  3|  ========== ========== ============ ============ ==========
  4|  Smith      S              35.00        49.00        42.00
  5|  Brown      J              56.00        52.00        54.00
  6|  Jones      G W            72.00        88.00        80.00
  7|  Robinson   A S            48.00        66.00        57.00
  8|  Harris     R J            63.00        58.00        60.50
  9|  Johnson    N              51.00        75.00        63.00
 10|  ========== ========== ============ ============ ==========
 11|             AVERAGES        54.16        64.66>       59.41<
 12|  ========== ========== ============ ============ ==========
   +-----------------------------------------------------------------------
     PRESENT CELL POSITION:  E11
            CELL TYPE:         numeric
            CELL CONTENTS:     +AVG(E4:E9)
            CELL VALUE:            59.41
     ENTER COMMAND OR VALUE:  _____
```

Figure 2.11. The spreadsheet with column averages included.

2.17 The data in the spreadsheet may be sorted into order using the sort command. We need not worry about the details of how this is done but it will involve a series of prompts and responses like those used with the copy command. Rows 4 to 9 may be sorted into alphabetic order on column A, to give the spreadsheet shown in figure 2.12, or sorted into rank order (descending numerically) on column E, to give the spreadsheet shown in figure 2.13.

```
       FUNCTIONS                 | COMMANDS
ON VALUE:ABS,SQRT,EXP,LOG        | C Copy D Delete      I Insert F Format
ON RANGE OR LIST:MAX,MIN,CNT     | S Sort R Recalculate P Print
                   SUM, AVG      | L Load K Keep           Q Quit
COL>   :A          :B         :C               :D            :E
ROW+-----------------------------------------------------------------------
  3|   ========== ========== ============= ============= ==========
  4|   Brown      J             56.00         52.00         54.00
  5|   Harris     R J           63.00         58.00         60.50
  6|   Johnson    N             51.00         75.00         63.00
  7|   Jones      G W           72.00         88.00         80.00
  8|   Robinson   A S           48.00         66.00         57.00
  9|   Smith      S             35.00         49.00         42.00
 10|   ========== ========== ============= ============= ==========
 11|              AVERAGES      54.16         64.66>        59.41<
 12|   ========== ========== ============= ============= ==========
   +-----------------------------------------------------------------------
   PRESENT CELL POSITION:   E11
          CELL TYPE:        numeric
          CELL CONTENTS:    +AVG(E4:E9)
          CELL VALUE:       59.41
   ENTER COMMAND OR VALUE:  _____
```

Figure 2.12. Spreadsheet with Results in Alphabetic Order.

2.18 The user of the spreadsheet may wish to have a printed copy of the all or part of the spreadsheet. A print command is usually provided for the purpose. When printed out the spreadsheet of figure 2.13 could appear as shown in figure 2.14

```
     FUNCTIONS                  | COMMANDS
ON VALUE:ABS,SQRT,EXP,LOG       | C Copy D Delete      I Insert F Format
ON RANGE OR LIST:MAX,MIN,CNT    | S Sort R Recalculate P Print
               SUM, AVG         | L Load K Keep        Q Quit
COL>    :A        :B        :C              :D            :E
ROW+----------------------------------------------------------------------
   3|  ========== ========== ============ ============ ==========
   4|  Jones     G W              72.00        88.00        80.00
   5|  Johnson   N                51.00        75.00        63.00
   6|  Harris    R J              63.00        58.00        60.50
   7|  Robinson  A S              48.00        66.00        57.00
   8|  Brown     J                56.00        52.00        54.00
   9|  Smith     S                35.00        49.00        42.00
  10|  ========== ========== ============ ============ ==========
  11|            AVERAGES         54.16        64.66>       59.41<
  12|  ========== ========== ============ ============ ==========
   +----------------------------------------------------------------------
      PRESENT CELL POSITION:   E11
            CELL TYPE:         numeric
            CELL CONTENTS:     +AVG(E4:E9)
            CELL VALUE:            59.41
      ENTER COMMAND OR VALUE:   _____
```

Figure 2.13. Spreadsheet with Results in Rank Order.

```
                    RESULTS SHEET
                    RANKED ORDER
                       RESULTS
        Surname     Initial(s) Exam %      Coursework % Overall %
        ========== ========== ============ ============ ==========
        Jones      G W              72.00        88.00        80.00
        Johnson    N                51.00        75.00        63.00
        Harris     R J              63.00        58.00        60.50
        Robinson   A S              48.00        66.00        57.00
        Brown      J                56.00        52.00        54.00
        Smith      S                35.00        49.00        42.00
        ========== ========== ============ ============ ==========
                   AVERAGES         54.16        64.66>       59.41<
        ========== ========== ============ ============ ==========
```

Figure 2.14. Information Printed by the Spreadsheet Package.

2.19 There is no need for us to go through detailed examples of all the other functions and commands but here is a brief summary of some of the more important ones:

a. FUNCTIONS
   i.   SQRT   the square root function
   ii. MAX   The maximum value of a range of cells
   iii. CNT   Counting the number of cells in a range of cell
   iv. SUM   The sum of the values in a range of cells

b. COMMANDS
   i. Delete and insert - whole rows or columns
   ii. Format - change the width of a column
   iii. Keep - save a copy of the spreadsheet data on a disk
   iv. Load - get saved data back from a disk
   v. Recalculate - used on formula after data has been changed
   vi. Quit - finish using the spreadsheet package

2.20. By now you should have quite a good idea of what a spreadsheet is and how a spreadsheet package can be used. Try to use a real spreadsheet package if you possibly can. It will not be exactly the same as the simplified one described here but it will be quite similar and should be fairly easy for you to use if you have followed these examples. Two of the most popular products are **"Lotus 1-2-3"** and **"Microsoft Excel"**. Both are straightforward to use for basic work although mastering them completely can take some time.

SPREADSHEET PRODUCTS
2.21 The examples given in this chapter have emphasised the basics of using a spreadsheet by means of a simplified spreadsheet package. The spreadsheet packages commonly sold are rather more sophisticated than the one described here although the basic techniques still apply. To complete the picture, here are further details of the most common feature found in the modern spreadsheet packages.

2.21 Further details of spreadsheet package features.
   a. A large number of cells eg, 8192 rows (numbered 1,2,3...) and 256 columns (labelled A,B, C.. AA, AB, AC...).
   b. Search and replace facilities.
   c. Colour.
   d. Charting facilities, for example providing Pie Charts or Bar Charts from the data in the spreadsheets.
   e. Macros - ie, more complex forms of named formulae which can be saved and re-used in a number of different spreadsheets.
   f. Multi-dimension capabilities.

SUMMARY
2.22 a. Computer packages have been defined.
   b. Spreadsheet packages have been explained by means of practical examples.
   c. Spreadsheet terminology was introduced, including the use of cells, windows, functions and commands.

POINTS TO NOTE
2.23 a. There are lots of different kinds of computer package. This chapter has merely given an example of a spreadsheet package. A general discussion about what kinds of packages there are, when to use them and how to select them will be given in later chapters.
   b. It is often simpler, cheaper, easier and generally better to use a computer package than it is to write a program especially for an application.

QUESTIONS A *(Answers in Appendix II)*
1. What is an application's package?

2. Describe three sections which you might expect to see on the screen when using a spreadsheet package.

QUESTIONS B *(Without Answers)*
1. What is a spreadsheet cursor and how is it moved?

2. What are the different things a spreadsheet cell can contain?

ASSIGNMENTS
1. Use computer magazines, newspapers, adverts and any other useful sources of information to find out about the computer packages available, for example at your school or college. Produce a brief summary of what each package is supposed to do.

2. Gain access to suitable packages and work through the examples given in this chapter. Seek the guidance of your teacher or lecturer in doing this.

3 Information Storage and Retrieval

INTRODUCTION

3.1 The previous chapter, on spreadsheet packages, emphasised the use of the computer's ability to manipulate data and do calculations on it. In this chapter the use of the computer for the storage and retrieval of information is the theme. As in the previous chapter the ideas will be illustrated by a simplified example of a software package. Packages used for information storage and retrieval are most commonly called "**database packages**". The term "**database**" is often used to describe a complete set of data being used for a particular application or by a particular organisation. When we examine databases in detail later in the text we will see that the term "database" really has a more specific meaning.

3.2 Database packages have facilities which allow the user to store data in an organised way, use the data, and keep it up to date. The following example should make these ideas clearer.

USING STORED DATA

3.3 In chapter 2 we looked at how the overall examination results for a group of students could be produced with the aid of a spreadsheet package. Such results usually need to be kept along with other results for future reference. This data will be stored using some form of backing storage (1.37). In this example we will assume that there is a need to store the following data so that it can be used as a source of information.

    a. The surname of each student.
    b. The initials of each student.
    c. The data of birth of each student.
    d. The list of subjects available.
    e. The list of subjects taken by each student.
    f. The overall grade for individual subjects taken by each student.

3.4 Examples of typical data are given in the set of tables shown in figures 3.1, 3.2 and 3.3.

Again, as in chapter 2, a different typeface is used in the figures so that the data appears more like it would on a VDU screen.

STUDENT NUMBER	SURNAME	INITIAL	DATE OF BIRTH
2100	Brown	J	22-JUN-1970
2101	Foster	C R	20-SEP-1969
2102	Granger	P	03-DEC-1969
2103	Harris	R J	19-MAY-1970
2104	Johnson	N	14-FEB-1970
2105	Jones	G W	24-OCT-1969
2106	Phillips	H D	12-JAN-1970
2107	Robinson	A S	25-FEB-1970
2108	Smith	S	01-APR-1970
2109	Wilson	M A	04-NOV-1969

Figure 3.1. Students.

```
------------------
SUBJECT NAME
------------------
Computer Studies
English
French
Geography
History
Maths
Science
------------------
```

Figure 3.2. Subjects.

```
---------------------------------
STUDENT NUMBER   OVERALL MARK
---------------------------------
    2100             54.00
    2103             60.50
    2104             63.00
    2105             80.00
    2107             57.00
    2108             42.00
---------------------------------
```

Figure 3.3. Results for Computer Studies.

3.5   The database package should enable us to do the following:
  a.   Define what data is to be stored and how it is to be stored and kept up to date
  b.   Define the ways in which the data is to be retrieved from storage and presented to the user.
  c.   Enter data or update data.
  d.   Obtain answers to questions about the data. The answers being either displayed on the screen or printed out.

DEFINING DATA
3.6   Examine the table shown in figure 3.1. There are ten lines of data in the table. All the data on a given line is about one particular student and may therefore be treated as a single unit. Such a single unit of related data items is called **record**. So, the ten lines in the table represent ten student records. The individual data items in a record are called its **fields**. Each student record contains the four fields shown in figure 3.4.

```
-------------------------------------------------
FIELD NUMBER      FIELD NAME       FIELD TYPE
-------------------------------------------------
      1           Student Number   Numeric
      2           Surname          Text
      3           Initials         Text
      4           Date of Birth    Text
-------------------------------------------------
```

Figure 3.4. Student Record Fields.

3.7   The final column in figure 3.4 indicates the type of data to be found in the field (ie Numeric or text). You may remember that the cells of the spreadsheet were classified in the same way. Each student has been given his or her own unique student number and this number is placed in the first field. It can be used to identify each student's record. A field used for such a purpose is called a **key field**. A combination of the student surname and initial could have been used for the key instead of the student number but would have been less suitable because there is no guarantee that a surname plus initial will always be unique, for example, there could be more than one "S Smith".

3.8   The database package will enable the user to define records and their fields and keys. For example, the package may present the user with a menu of possible things to define. If the user selects the "DEFINE RECORD" option the package may then respond with a series of prompts to which the user types appropriate responses (See Fig. 3.5).

STORING AND RETRIEVING DATA

3.9   Once records have been defined data can be entered into them or retrieved from them. In fact, there is likely to be a whole series of options available to the user including:

    a.   Add a new record
    b.   Delete an existing record
    c.   Display a record
    d.   Print a record
    e.   Change a record
    f.   Display or print data selected from a number of records.

3.10   There is no need to look at all these options in detail. The reader can probably guess what most of them might be like. However, there is some value in looking at the last option on the list since it illustrates value of a database package in answering queries about the data.

3.11   Suppose that the data shown in figures 3.1, 3.2 and 3.3 has been entered into the database package and that option "f" (3.9) has been selected. Let us see how we can get an answer to a question about the data.

```
               DEFINE RECORD

RECORD NAME =? Student

FIELD  1.  FIELD NAME =? Student Number
FIELD TYPE (N FOR NUMERIC OR T FOR TEXT) =? N
USED AS KEY (Y/N) =? Y

ANY MORE FIELDS (Y/N) =? Y

FIELD  2.  FIELD NAME =? Surname
FIELD TYPE (N FOR NUMERIC OR T FOR TEXT) =? T
USED AS KEY (Y/N) =? N

ANY MORE FIELDS (Y/N) =? Y

FIELD  3.  FIELD NAME =? Initials
FIELD TYPE (N FOR NUMERIC OR T FOR TEXT) =? T
USED AS KEY (Y/N) =? N

ANY MORE FIELDS (Y/N) =? Y

FIELD  4.  FIELD NAME =? Date of Birth
FIELD TYPE (N FOR NUMERIC OR T FOR TEXT) =? T
USED AS KEY (Y/N) =? N

ANY MORE FIELDS (Y/N) =? N
```

Figure 3.5 Defining a Record.

3.12 To get a printed list of all students who took Computer Studies and obtained an **overall grade of more than 60%** Fig 3.6 shows the prompts and responses which might take place.
3.13 When the query of figure 3.6 is processed it will give rise to the output shown in figure 3.7.

```
              DISPLAY OR PRINT SELECTED DATA

  SELECT (1. DISPLAY 2. PRINT 3. PRINT & DISPLAY)  =? 2

  SELECT RECORD AND FIELD ( TYPE Record Name . Field name )
      OUTPUT FIELD  1.  =? Student . Student number

      ANOTHER FIELD ( Y/N)  =? Y

      OUTPUT FIELD  2.  =? Student . Initial

      ANOTHER FIELD ( Y/N)  =? Y

      OUTPUT FIELD  3.  =? Student . Surname

      ANOTHER FIELD ( Y/N  =? Y

      OUTPUT FIELD  4.  =? Computer Studies . Overall Mark

      ANOTHER FIELD ( Y/N)  =? N


  SELECTION RULE (Y/N)  =? Y

  TYPE THE RULE ON THE FOLLOWING LINES, END WITH A BLANK LIN

  Student . Student Number = Computer Studies . Student
  Number AND
  Computer Studies . Student Number > 60

  PROCESSING QUERY...

NB. The first line of the rule requires the student numbers
in the student records to be matched with the student
 numbers in the Computer Studies record.  The second line
 of the rule selects only those students with marks greater
than 60%.
```

Figure 3.6. Setting Up a Query.

Student Number	Initial	Surname	Overall Mark
2103	R J	Harris	60.50
2104	N	Johnson	63.00
2105	G W	Jones	80.00

Figure 3.7. Output Resulting from Processing Query.

FORMS INTERFACES

3.14 So far the examples of how the user would be able use the package have been based upon a simple dialogue between the user and the computer involving little more than prompts and responses. This interaction between the user and the computer is called the **user interface**. Many packages use a superior type of user interface which mimics paper based forms and is therefore called a **forms interface**. An example is provided by figures 3.8 and 3.9.

3.15 Figure 3.8 shows a VDU screen on which a "form" has been displayed. The screen contains text headers and boxes for data. Such information on forms is called "**trim**", to distinguish it from data. Along the bottom of the screen a series of options is displayed for the user to choose from. For example, if the user wants to print what is on the screen he or she must press a function key on the keyboard labelled "F3". Of course, this assumes that a suitable keyboard is available. The form shows a query typed in by the user, who wants to find out information about all students with surnames beginning with "J" who have passed (the pass mark is 40). You will notice that the line on the form just below the titles the contain "J*" in the "Surname" column and ">=40" in the "Overall Marks" column. The "J*" means all names beginning with J and followed by any other letters. The symbol used to stand for any letters, as "*" is used in this case, is called a "**wild card**". The ">=40" means all values greater than or equal to 40. When the user presses the function key for "SELECT" (key F1) the data which satisfies the query will be retrieved onto the form. The result of pressing key F1 is shown in figure 3.9.

3.16 By now you should have quite a good idea of what a database package can do. As was recommended for the spreadsheet, try to get practical experience with a real package. In the first place, however, try to use a package for an application which has already been set up for you.

STUDENT MARKS ENQUIRIES FORM

Student Number	Initial	Surname	Overall Mar
		J*	>=40

SELECT (F1)   DISPLAY (F2)   PRINT (F3)   END (F4)

Figure 3.8. A simple enquiry on a form.

STUDENT MARKS ENQUIRIES FORM

Student Number	Initial	Surname	Overall Mar
2104	N	Johnson	63.00
2105	G W	Jones	80.00

SELECT (F1)   DISPLAY (F2)   PRINT (F3)   END (F4)

Figure 3.9. The result of the enquiry in Fig 3.8.

INTEGRATED PACKAGES
3.17   If you look back at the examples given in this and the previous chapter you can see

that it would be useful to take results from the spreadsheet package and feed them into the database package. This kind of data transfer is often possible in practice. The idea can be taken a stage further by designing one single large package which consists of a spreadsheet, a database and possibly some other packages all rolled into one. Such packages are usually called **integrated packages.** One popular example of an integrated package is Lotus Framework

SUMMARY
3.18   a. The general idea of a database was introduced.
        b. The terms **record, field** and **key** were defined.
        c. A **forms interface** was explained by means of a simple example.
        d. The term **integrated package** was defined.

POINTS TO NOTE
3.19   a   There are legal requirements governing the way in which computers can be used to store   information about individuals. It is therefore advisable to seek advice if intending to use database packages to hold information like that given in the examples used in this chapter. This matter will be discussed in a later chapter under the heading of **the data protection act.**

QUESTIONS A *(Answers in Appendix II)*
1.   *Explain the following terms:*

    a.   *Record*

    b.   *Field*

    c.   *Key*

QUESTIONS B *(Without Answers)*
1   *Why is it not always a good idea to use a person's name as a key and what might be a better choice?*

ASSIGNMENT
1.   Gain access to a suitable package and work through the examples given in this chapter. Seek the guidance of your teacher or lecturer in doing this.

4 Document Processing

INTRODUCTION

4.1   Computers are not only very good at processing numerical data, as illustrated by the spreadsheet package, they also have the ability to manipulate non-numeric data such as text. The user of a VDU or PC is able to create and modify documents with ease. The simplest kinds of programs which allow users to write and modify text are called **text editors**. Text editors first became widely used in the 1970s when the hardware needed to perform text editing became cost effective to use for this purpose. It became common for programmers to enter their programs directly into the computer by this means. Prior to that programs and data had most commonly been input in the form of punched cards. Punched cards are now obsolete.

4.2   It was realised that the same principles could be applied to the preparation of any text document such as a memo or letter or even a book, and not just to program writing. So, more sophisticated text editors called "**Word processing programs**" were developed.

4.3   Word processing software packages are now the most widely used application for personal computers. Many owners of PC's use their machines solely for word processing and there are probably more word processing packages available in the marketplace than any other type of software.

4.4   More recent developments in software have seen the introduction of **desk-top publishing (DTP)** packages. Whereas word processing programs are aimed at producing documents which contain solely text, DTP software allows the user to incorporate images and pictures into the document and to design the layout for publication.

4.5   The first part of this chapter is concerned with word processing and the later part with desk-top publishing: collectively these two activities are referred to as **document processing**.

WORD PROCESSING

4.6   A word processing program allows the user to create, edit, format, store and print text documents. A text document is anything that can be typed: a memo, a letter, a report or a book.

4.7   In offices and businesses word processing has virtually replaced typing as the means of producing these documents. Compared with using a typewriter, word processing has a number of advantages which include:

    a.   The ability to store typed words in the computer's memory,
    b.   The ability to view the document on screen before printing,
    c.   The ability to correct mistakes,
    d.   The ability to insert or delete words, sentences or paragraphs,
    e.   The ability to move sections of text to another part of the document,
    f.   The ability to store documents on backing store for later recall,
    g.   The ability to incorporate other text without having to retype it,
    h.   The ability to change the layout of the document,
    i.   The ability to print the document more than once.

4.8   The term word processor is sometimes used to describe a complete system, rather than just the software. Many office suppliers have in the past produced what are in effect dedicated computers with a printer which run only word processing software. Although there are certain advantages in this, the advent of low cost personal computers which are able to run a number of different application packages has dented the market for dedicated word processors.

HOW WORD PROCESSING WORKS

4.9   The computer's screen can be thought of as a page of typing paper. As characters are typed in, these are displayed on the screen just like a typewriter. It is important to realise, however, that you are not typing onto the screen: the screen merely displays what you are entering into the computer's memory (see Fig 4.1).

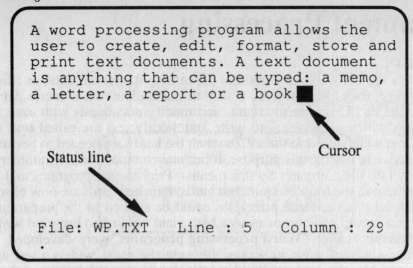

Figure 4.1. A word processor screen display .

4.10 The word processing program also displays a **cursor** to show where the next character will appear on the screen - this is usually a flashing dash or rectangle.

4.11 This cursor can be moved around the screen by means of special **cursor keys**, allowing an up/down/left or right movement of one character position. Other special keys, or combinations of keys pressed simultaneously, allow the cursor to be moved in larger increments, for example a whole screen's worth or a whole page worth at a time.

4.12 The computer's memory can hold far more characters than can fit onto one printed page. Many word processing programs indicate where a page break occurs by means of a row of dashes on screen, though these are not printed.

4.13 The screen itself can only display about 24 lines of text (slightly less than half of a printed page) and also displays some **status information** such as number of words typed and even typing speed. The document size is not limited to this size, however: as more lines of text are typed, the earlier lines move off the top of the screen, but although they have disappeared from view they are still retained within the computer's memory.

4.14 The screen thus acts like a **window** on the text, which can be moved up or down by means of the cursor keys. The printed material is like text on a scroll, only a small part of which can be seen at any one time through the window (see Fig. 4.2). The scroll is rolled up or down by moving the cursor, a process referred to as **scrolling**.

4.15 As characters are typed across the screen there comes a point when a new line is required. A typist has to decide if the word about to be typed will fit on to that line, but this is catered for automatically by a word processing package: it counts the number of spaces remaining and forces the word onto a new line if necessary. This feature is called **word wrap**. The carriage return key is thus used only to indicate the end of a paragraph or to force a blank line.

4.16 If a word has been typed incorrectly it is quite easy to move the cursor to the offending word and correct the mistake. This is the process referred to as **editing**. A word processing program allows single characters, whole words or even several lines to be deleted from the text, and the text that follows will automatically be moved to take the place of the deleted items.

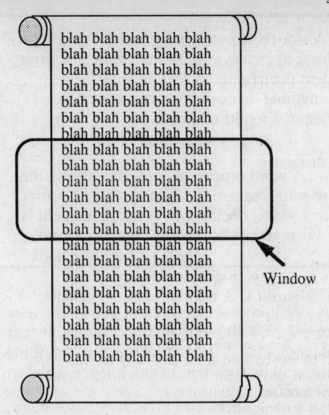

Window

Figure 4.2. Scrolling text seen through a window.

4.17 New characters, words or several lines can also be inserted into existing text. The cursor is moved to the appropriate point and the new characters typed; they will automatically be inserted into the text, the following text being moved along to accommodate the changes.

4.18 Word processing packages also incorporate "**cut and paste**" facilities whereby a section of text can be selected and moved to a different part of the document. A variation on this is to copy the selected section of text, without removing it from its original position.

4.19 A **search and replace** facility is frequently provided in these packages: this allows the user to replace a single word or phrase wherever it occurs in the document with another word or phrase. A report containing several references to "Mr. Smith", for example, could be changed quite easily to refer to "Mr. Reginald Smith".

4.20 The document is viewed on screen before printing and changes to the layout or **format** of the document (rather than content) can also be made. These changes in format include adjustment to the width of the left-hand or right-hand margins and the top and bottom space on the paper, setting the page numbering style and position, and also changing the printing style and size. Another common formatting technique is **text justification** which means the alignment of text against a margin. **Left-justification** means alignment against the the left margin, **right-justification** means alignment against the right margin and **full-justification** means both left and right justification (see Fig. 4.3). For full-justification, extra spaces are inserted by the program into lines of text to ensure a straight right hand edge to the document. Other examples include centring of text, underlining of text, and emboldening of text. Adjusting these formatting parameters is often achieved by means of special function keys on the computer keyboard.

A word processing program allows the user to create, edit, format, store and print text documents. A text document is anything that can be typed: a memo, a letter, a report or a book.

a. Left-justified

A word processing program allows the user to create, edit, format, store and print text documents. A text document is anything that can be typed: a memo, a letter, a report or a book.

b. Right justified

A word processing program allows the user to create, edit, format, store and print text documents. A text document is anything that can be typed: a memo, a letter, a report or a book.

c. Fully justified

Figure 4.3. Examples of text justification.

4.21   Many packages now claim to be "**WYSIWYG**" or "what you see is what you get". This means that the representation of the document on screen is very close to how it will appear when printed. Assuming that a printer is connected to the computer, the document can be printed out at any time and indeed as often as is required.

4.22   The contents of the computer's memory can be **saved** for long term storage onto **backing store** (eg, floppy disk - see Fig. 1.3) as a "**file**". This represents what has been typed and it means that the same document can be **loaded** back into the word processing program at a later time without it needing to be retyped. Further corrections or amendments can then be made.

4.23   This facility also allows other files to be merged into a new document, for example a file containing a document of current price list can be added to a letter to be sent out to a potential client - only the letter needs to be typed. The technique of building up a document from standard paragraphs, such as clauses in a contract, is known as **boilerplating**.

4.24   Word processing packages continue to be developed and extra facilities are constantly being introduced. There are also a number of ancillary programs which can be used in conjunction with word processed documents to enhance the standard facilities.

4.25   One such facility is the process known as **mail-merge**. In this it is possible to produce a standard letter into which the name and address (and other details) of a number of clients in turn are merged and a series of individual letters printed. Each recipient of the letter receives an original print.

4.26   Many word processing packages now include **spell check** facilities. The spell check program comes with its own dictionary of from 20,000 to 100,000 words and is able to scan through the document and report wherever a word is found which does not exist in its dictionary. The user is then able to correct the word or leave it as it was originally spelt. Unless they have facilities for adding new words to the dictionary spell checkers have difficulty recognising people's names and postcodes as correct "words".

4.27   Some spell checking programs can be left to search through a document and mark every doubtful word for later checking by the user (useful for very long documents) rather than provide interactive facilities. Others can check against their dictionary of words so quickly that they can provide immediate feedback to the user as each word is typed in.

4.28   Many spell checkers provide the user with a list of alternative words which are similar in spelling or sound to the doubtful word. Some also allow the user to create and maintain their own dictionary of words, which is very useful if the user constantly refers to specialised or "jargon" words in a particular subject area (eg, chemical compounds).

4.29   Some professional writers (journalists, authors, novelists etc.) use word processing packages and a **thesaurus** is a very useful addition. This is a program which allows the user to choose an alternative word to a selected word. A thesaurus is basically a dictionary of synonyms (similar words) and antonyms (dissimilar words), and the user points to a particular word and is presented with a list of alternatives.

4.30   It should be pointed out that spell checking programs cannot guarantee that every spelling mistake will be detected in a document. The words "there" and "their", for example, are correctly spelt only if used in the correct context. The words "fore examples" are both correctly spelt in themselves, but are incorrect if "for example" was intended. Another common mistake in documents is double-typing of the the same word, as in this sentence. Programs aimed at detecting these types of mistakes are often referred to as **grammar and style** programs.

4.31   Style analysis also helps to identify unnecessary words or wordy phrases which appear in the document. To help eliminate repetition, these programs can check to see if particular patterns of words appear again and again in the document, and they can also indicate if sentences seem too long.

4.32   Many text documents also need to include tables and charts, and some word processing packages incorporate limited **graphics capability** to allow lines and fancy borders to be drawn around such tables. There is often a need to bring data into a document which has been produced on another application package such as a spreadsheet, for example a table of numbers, and many word processing packages allow for this **importing** of data files from other packages.

4.33   Other enhancements that have appeared recently allow for many different type faces or **fonts** to be used in the printed document. The size of each printed character in these fonts can also be changed.

4.34   Although it has been assumed so far that the keyboard will be used as the means of entering the text into the document when word processing, this is not the only form of input device that could be used. In some situations, particularly where the text has already been printed, an **optical character recognition** or **OCR** device may be used.

4.35   This is a scanning device which is able to "read" printed documents by recognising the shape of characters and changing them into codes which can be used by the word processing software, without the document needing to be typed in manually. Only certain typefaces and sizes can be recognised by the OCR device and software, and this coupled with the relatively high cost of the equipment, means that its use is not widespread. In situations where a large volume of pre-printed material needs to be word processed, however, it is probably the only practical solution.

PRODUCING THE DOCUMENT

4.36 Obviously, the main aim of word processing is to produce documents which are to be printed. A variety of printers are available, and it is important to choose one to suit the particular situation. Printers are described in more detail in Chapter 13, but it is worthwhile here making a few relevant points to compare them.

4.37 A **dot matrix printer** is very useful for printing out different drafts of the document, as it is fast, inexpensive and can support a variety of different type styles. The quality of output is not very high, however, as it tends to have a "dotty" appearance. Manufacturers have recently introduced print heads with more pins (24) which are claimed to give **near letter quality (NLQ)** and these work by printing the dots more closely together so that the character formed appears continuous. Printers with fewer pins in the print head (ie 9) can also achieve NLQ by overprinting the characters many times, but this obviously slows down the rate of printing.

4.38 A **daisywheel** printer mimics a typewriter in that a complete character is printed. This type of printer is relatively slow and noisy and is limited to the typeface on the daisywheel, but as this gives a better quality finish to business correspondence it was the preferred choice of printer in offices until recently.

4.39 The cost of **laser printers** has reduced considerably in recent years and these have become very popular in word processing applications.

4.40 These work along similar lines to photocopiers in that a whole page is printed: an image is built up on an internal drum which is transferred to the paper, and this image can include graphics as well as text. They are quiet in operation and typically produce 6 to 8 pages per minute. The image is formed from minute dots (about 300 dots per inch) which gives a high quality output.

4.41 The output from word processing need not be limited solely to printers, however. In order to cut down on huge values of paper, one solution is to miniaturise output by recording it on microfilm. **Computer output on microfilm**, or **COM**, is too expensive for small businesses at present, but large companies use COM to maintain backup records of invoices or copies of purchase orders. It is also used instead of carbon copies of letters sent to clients.

4.42 Most professional printing is typeset: it looks better and is easier to read than typewritten material. It is also far cheaper for documents that are produced in large quantities. Typesetting machines produce output in the form of very minute dots, so small that individual dots cannot be seen even with a magnifying glass (typically, 1200 to 2540 dots per inch).

4.43 Because of the similarities between typesetters and word processors, they can be linked together through software. The output from a word processing package may be aimed at a typesetter, rather than a printer as listed above: files produced from the package can be read by a typesetting machine, with which it is possible to insert special formatting commands to suit the planned output.

DESKTOP PUBLISHING

4.44 Desk top publishing fills the gap between word processing and professional typesetting. Unlike word processing, **desktop publishing (DTP)** offers the user of a personal computer the ability to carry out **page composition**.

4.45 This means that the user can decide where text and pictures should appear on the page, what typefaces should be used and the size of these typefaces, in a much more flexible way than a word processing package allows.

4.46 Coupled with a low cost laser printer, it is possible to produce professional quality documents quickly without the cost and delay of using professional printing services.

4.47 DTP software is generally made up of a word processing program, a graphics program and a page composition program. The publishing process can be thought of as a number of cycles:

      a. Writing cycle, where the manuscript is written and preliminary suggestions for illustrations can be made;

b. Editing cycle, where the manuscript is edited, illustrations are selected, and the manuscript is prepared for production and design;

c. Design cycle, where the total length of the manuscript is estimated, pages are designed, the typeface is chosen, other page elements are designed, colours are chosen, sample pages are produced, and illustrations are generated;

d. Production cycle, where the text is typeset, the text is proof-read, the text is placed on pages, illustrations are incorporated onto the pages, and finishing touches applied;

e. Printing cycle, where halftones are stripped in and four-colour separations are made, printing plates are made, documents are printed, and the documents are bound if necessary.

4.48 The writing cycle is usually carried out on a word processing package. Illustrations can be generated by graphics application packages, some of which allow the user to make the illustration, others allow pictures and photographs to be copied into the computer's memory. DTP packages allow the user to complete the editing, design and production cycles using a personal computer. DTP also eliminates the time-consuming measuring, cutting and pasting involved in traditional production techniques.

4.49 Page composition is concerned with the appearance of the printed page. Headlines are planned not just in terms of what they say but also in terms of where they appear, the size of typeface, or **point (pt.)**, and the spacing between the letters. **Kerning** is a term relating to the spacing between characters, which may need to be adjusted to take account of the shape of the characters, for example in the word WAVE.

4.50 One design consideration concerns where a particular drawing should be placed, and how large it should be: page makeup programs allow the user to reposition marked areas on the screen and to scale them up or down to fit. Other design issues include whether text should be in columns, and if so then how many and how wide, and should there be lines between the columns and of what style and width. The spacing between lines, or **leading** also needs to be considered. All of these things can be changed with ease on the screen to see what the effect is.

4.51 Several different typefaces are provided in DTP packages, and these are often selected via a system of menus. A **typeface** is a set of characters of the same design, and these can be printed in a specific **weight**, such as **boldface** which is extra dark, and in a specific style, such as *italic*. (see Fig 4.4) Alternative typefaces on disk are also provided by third parties. Standard graphic images produced by professional artists can also be obtained for inclusion in documents: these collections of images are referred to as **clip art**.

4.52 A page layout program allows text to be imported from a file prepared on a word processing package. The text can be made to flow around an area on the page: this area may be reserved for an illustration, or maybe for a section of text to be highlighted in some way.

4.53 Some editing facilities to the text are often incorporated, but these are not as extensive as in a word processing package.

Having the means to design pages does not necessarily turn the user into a graphic designer. It is, in fact, a lot easier to use page composition programs than it is to create a page that looks attractive. Some companies produce **templates** for novices: these are page layouts from professional designers that can be used with the user's own text and graphics.

This font is Times Roman 12pt .

This font is Times Roman 14pt .

This font is Times Roman 14pt bold

This font is Times Roman 14pt italic

Times Roman is a proportional font which
means that the width of the letters varies
so that it is easier to read.

```
This font is Courier 12pt. It is not
proportionally spaced.
```

Figure 4.4. Examples of different fonts and styles.

HARDWARE

4.54 The hardware needed for DTP is more extensive than for word processing. In addition to the keyboard for input of text and commands, a **mouse** is often used to make menu selections and to manipulate areas of text and graphics on screen. A **scanner** or **digitiser** may be used for capturing images from existing pictures. These devices mentioned here will be described more fully later.

4.55 The quality of the **monitor** (eg,, screen for VDU or PC) is very important in DTP. The pages to be displayed must be very clear, so a high resolution monitor is needed, and clearly this should have graphics capability. A colour monitor will obviously be needed for colour work, although a monochrome monitor is sufficient for most applications. Paper white monitors, which have a high brilliance white phosphor, are favoured for DTP work, and some of these are capable of displaying two pages side by side. The ability to display a complete sheet of paper on screen which can be read clearly is an obvious advantage.

4.56 The quality of the printer is one of the most important aspects of desktop publishing. Laser printers give acceptable results, especially for low volume work, but if clearer, sharper text is required an alternative is to send the output file from the DTP package to be typeset. Either way, the printout will be camera-ready, which means that it is ready to be photographed to make a plate for printing.

4.57 In many businesses the cost of publications is second only to personnel costs. Many newsletters, advertising leaflets, technical manuals and in-house business publications do not need to be of the finest quality. They can be designed, produced and printed with desk top publishing. Even when the volume of publications or quality required dictates the services of a professional printer, DTP can still be used effectively in the design and production, offering speed, flexibility, and low-cost.

SUMMARY

4.58 a. **Word processing, desktop publishing** and **document processing** were introduced and described.

      b. The operation of a word processor and word processing terms were defined including: cursor, scrolling, word wrap, editing, "cut and paste", text justification, WYSIWYG, boilerplating, mail-merge, fonts, point size, typeface and clip art.

c. The hardware needed for document processing was described.

POINTS TO NOTE
4.59 a. This chapter was introductory in nature and has therefore avoided going into the finer points of the terminology relating to typefaces, fonts and point sizes. The reader will not be expected to master such terminology for examination purposes although it could be useful in an examination, for example, when asked to providing examples of an application.

b. A number of items of hardware have been introduced in this chapter. Where appropriate, they will be described in more detail later.

ASSIGNMENT
1. Ask for access to a word processing package and find out what features it provides.

5 Applications Areas

INTRODUCTION

5.1 Computers can be employed for a wide variety of purposes but they are particularly suited to certain kinds of work. It may be possible to use a computer for a particular application if certain criteria are met. Whether or not a computer is used will depend on other factors. This chapter considers these criteria and factors and then deals with a variety of particular applications which illustrate the general principles.

CRITERIA FOR USING COMPUTERS

5.2 The following are the criteria by which to judge an application's possible suitability to the use of computers:-

   a. **Volume.** The computer is particularly suited to handling large amounts of data.
   b. **Accuracy.** The need for a high degree of accuracy is satisfied by the computer and its consistency can be relied upon.
   c. **Repetitiveness.** Processing cycles that repeat themselves over and over again are ideally suited to computers. Once programmed the computer happily goes on and on automatically performing as many cycles as required.
   d. **Complexity.** The computer can perform the most complex calculations. As long as the application can be programmed then the computer can provide the answers required.
   e. **Speed.** Computers work at phenomenal speeds. This combined with their ability to *communicate* with other systems, even those at remote locations, enables them to respond very quickly to given situations.
   f. **Common data.** One item of data on a computer system may be involved in several different procedures, or accessed, updated or inspected by a number of different users. In manual systems data is often accessible to a limited number of people for particular purposes. This can hinder the work of others who need access to the data.

5.3 It is usually the combination of two or more of the criteria listed which will indicate the suitability of an application to computer use. The criteria that have been described will be used by those who carry out a **Preliminary Survey** in order to judge the suitability of applications for computerisation.

OTHER FACTORS

5.4 If the general criteria for using a computer suggest that a particular application may be suitable for computerisation, then there are a number of questions which will require satisfactory answers before any decision to computerise is taken. The main questions will be:-

   a. Is the use of a computer for this application **technically feasible?** ie can it be done with the computer technology currently available?
   b. Would the use of a computer be **cost effective?** ie. would the computer pay for itself in terms of the benefits it would provide?
   c. would the use of a computer be **socially acceptable?** ie. would the impact of the computer on people's work, jobs or general lifestyle be acceptable?

5.5 The answers to questions such as those just mentioned, change with changing circumstances. For example many computer applications which were mere science fiction a few years ago, are now technically feasible. eg. the use of simple robots. Developments in microelectronics have reduced prices so that applications which have been technically feasible for twenty years or more, are only now becoming cost effective. People's willingness to accept computers depends on previous experience, general attitudes, and on how well or badly they have been informed.

LEVELS OF COMPUTERISATION
5.6 The extent to which an application may be computerised will be determined by the nature of the work involved. Three basic levels of computerisation may be identified:-
  a. **Complete computerisation.** Simple well defined and repetitive tasks can often be completely computerised eg. basic clerical functions or control of simple machines.
  b. **Partial computerisation.** Computers can often be applied to applications which require the control of operations under some agreed plan or strategy. The computer may take over routine control but may be monitored by humans, who will also deal with exceptional cases, eg. the day to day operation of a stock control system or a computerised production line.
  c. **Computer aided applications.** Computers may be used in many applications to aid management or decision making, by the timely provision of accurate results or information, eg. the computer can be used to analyse problems or simulate systems in order to aid designing or planning.

MAIN AREAS OF APPLICATION
5.7 Two main areas of computer application may be identified:
  a. **Commercial applications.** This covers the use of computers for clerical, administrative and business uses, in private and public organisations, ie. the emphasis is on data processing (ie. Collecting, maintaining and manipulating volumes of data to produce information).
  b. **Scientific, Engineering and Research Applications.** This covers the use of computers for complex calculations, the design, analysis and control of physical systems and the analysis of experimental data or results, that is, the emphasis is on Scientific Processing (ie. the rapid processing of data relating to complex problems).

There are other minor areas which do not fall into either of the two main categories eg. "Personal Computing" ie. computing done as a hobby. One could argue that it falls into either category.

5.8 Many organisations use computers for a variety of applications. For example a manufacturer may use computers for data processing, scientific research and engineering development work.

COMMON APPLICATIONS
5.9 **Payroll.** This is a well established computer application normally handled by batch processing. The production of the weekly wages or monthly salary payments of employees is a regular repetitive clerical task on sizable volumes of data and ideal for computerisation.

5.10 **Office Automation.** In contrast with payroll which is a long standing computer application, office automation is a relatively new area of computerisation.

In automated offices many of the routine clerical and secretarial tasks are taken over by computer based equipment which exploits developments in microelectronics.

5.11   Elements of such systems include:-
- a. Modern computer systems.
- b. Document processing systems (see chapter 3.).
- c. Modern methods of displaying and copying data electronically
- d. Modern communication links able to interconnect all elements in the system to one another and to other systems eg. by networks or electronic mail (details later).

5.12 **Stock Control.** This application will be discussed in chapter 28. The control of stock is important in both public and private organisation.

5.13 **Production and labour control.** The success of an organisation depends on how well it manages its resources. People, machines, materials, money and buildings all need careful management. Computers are used to control production and labour, just as they are used to control stock.

5.14 **Accounting.** There are many routine clerical tasks associated with recording details of financial transactions made by an organisation. This has given rise to the frequent use of computer for such accounting functions, particularly in larger organisations.

EXTENDING AND INTEGRATING APPLICATIONS

5.15 Many basic applications can be extended to give useful information for management purposes eg. using a stock control system to provide reports to management.

5.16 Further benefits can be obtained by integrating different applications eg. linking the payroll system to the labour or production control system.

PARTICULAR APPLICATIONS AREAS

5.17 In this section a number of particular applications areas are described because of their importance and interest.

5.18 **Applications exploiting the full computational power of computers.** Many of these applications have a scientific bias. They include:-
- a. **Weather forecasting systems.** Reliable weather forecasting demands vast computational powers. This is an area for the super computers (ie. computers with exceptionally fast processors).
- b. **Mathematical and Statistical Analysis.** This includes large calculations and the solution of mathematical problems. The applications requiring this include research in physics, chemistry, geology, archaeology, medicine, astronomy etc. Some commercial problems also have a mathematical bias eg, those that require mathematical analysis to determine the optimum use of resources.
- c. **Design work.** Computers can be exploited as a design tool in engineering and other disciplines. **CAD** (Computer Aided Design) is growing in importance in Electronic, Electrical, Mechanical and Aeronautical Engineering and in Architecture. This application often also exploits **computer graphics.**

5.19 **Analog Computing.** Most computers in everyday use today are *digital computers*. That is, they are computers which carry out operations on distinct data values in discrete steps. **Analog computers,** in contrast to digital computers carry out operations on data which can vary continuously.

5.20 **Financial Applications.** The banks and insurance companies are major users of commercial computer systems. Here is an indication of some of the ways in which banks use computers.

a. **Automatic cheque clearing.** Since the late 1950s banks in Britain have used a computerised system for handling cheques which ensures that payments by cheque are cleared within three days.

b. **Standing Orders and Direct Debit.** Regular payments may be made automatically by banks as part of a computerised system called **BACS** (Bankers' Automatic Clearing Services Ltd.). Magnetic tape is used to store details of the transactions for a particular day.

c. **General uses.** Bank customer accounts are largely computerised and some details, eg. current balance, may be available on-line.

d. **Newer uses.** Within the last ten years or so a number of special purpose cash dispensing machines have been introduced for use outside banks even when the banks are not open. This is a computerised service.

5.21 The cashless society. The success of computers in banking and in supporting credit card systems such as BARCLAYCARD or ACCESS has led many people to predict that we will eventually have a "cashless society" in which credit cards and special tills will cater for all "money" transactions. At present over 90% of all payments are in cash.

5.22 Retailing. The use of computers in the retail trades is now widespread. There have been numerous developments particularly in the area of data capture.

5.23 Some large supermarket chains have large and sophisticated stock control systems in which tills, using laser scanners, provide on-line data capture, and also have warehouses which are fully computerised.

5.24 Medical Applications. There are numerous applications of computers in medicine. Here are some examples:-

a. Computers can be used as an aid to medical research by analysing data produced from experiments eg. in the trial of drugs.

b. Computers can be used to aid diagnosis. The computer acts as a large bank of data about known medical conditions. Once the computer system has been set up by medical experts an ordinary doctor can be taken through a question and answer session by the computer until a correct diagnosis is made.

c. Computers can be used to hold details of dentists' or GPs' patients. Small computer systems have been used for this purpose in increasing numbers since the late 70's.

d. Computerised children's health records for immunisation have been used by local health authorities for a number of years. These records are used by medical officers, health visitors etc.

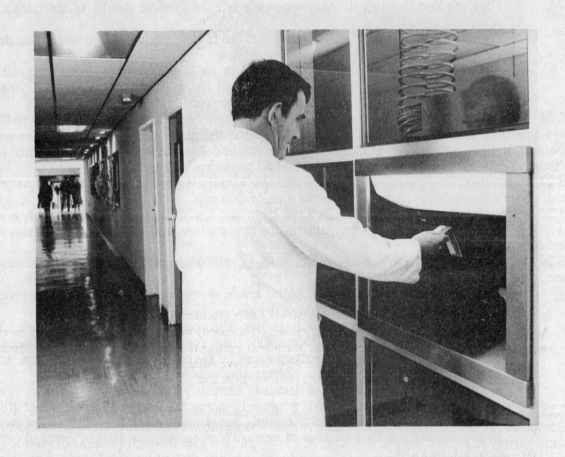

NCR 5080 ATM (Automatic Teller Machine)
Installed at Johnson Wax Ltd. factory for staff use
(Photograph courtesy NCR Ltd.)

Testing NCR Automated Teller Machines.
At NCR's manufacturing plant in Dundee, a robot continuously makes withdrawals and other service requests from the ATMs (Automated Teller Machines), putting them through the equivalent of several years transactions to ensure reliability.
(Picture courtesy NCR Ltd.)

5.25 Education. Computers are not only used extensively as part of a specialist study in Computer Studies, they are used as an extremely versatile way of aiding the understanding of a wide variety of other subjects. The computer can guide a user through a course of instruction at a VDU. the computer can provide instructions and ask questions of the user. This kind of activity is called **CAL** (Computer Aided Learning) or **CAI** (Computer Aided Instruction)

5.26 Computers are also used for a number of other applications in Education eg. the marking of multiple choice examination papers and processing examination results for many examination boards.

5.27 Manufacturing. Some aspects of computer use in manufacturing have already been covered eg. stock and production control, and engineering design. The design, manufacturing and testing processes are all becoming increasingly computerised, hence the terms **CAD** (Computer Aided Design), **CAM** (Computer Aided Manufacture) and **CADMAT** (Computer Aided Design Manufacture and Testing).

5.28 Robots. The word "Robot" comes from a Czech word meaning "to labour" and first appeared in a play written by Karel Capek in 1920. For many years the term "robot" was associated with science fiction rather than science fact. That association is now changing. Even so, modern industrial robots do not resemble people!) (see Fig. 5.1).

5.29 The main difference between modern industrial robots and other automated machines is that a robot can be programmed to carry out a complex task and then reprogrammed to carry out another complex task. Each complex task is a series of actions involving multi-way mechanical manipulation.

5.30 The majority of robots in current use, eg, in car assembly lines, are "blind" and lack a "sense of touch". The next generation of robots will probably be able to find and locate objects or detect their presence by touch and a light sense mechanism.

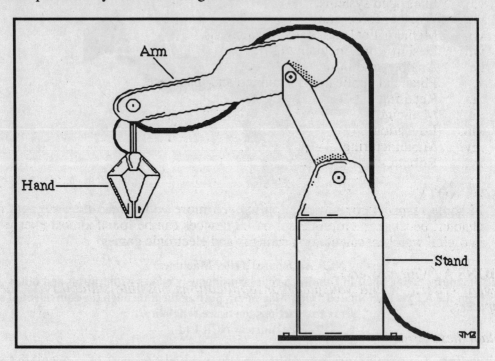

Figure 5.1 An Industrial Robot.

SUMMARY

5.31 a. The criteria for using computers were considered:
     i.   Volume
     ii. Accuracy
     iii. Repetitiveness
     iv. Complexity
     v.   Speed
     vi. Common data.

  b. Other factors affecting the decision to computerise were explained:-
     i.   Technical feasibility.
     ii. Cost effectiveness.
     iii. Acceptability

  c. Various levels of computerisation were described.
  d. The main areas of application were described:-

i.   Commercial applications.
ii.   Scientific, Engineering and Research applications.
e. Many common applications were discussed:-
i.   Payroll
ii.   Office automation
iii.   Stock, production and labour control
iv.   Accounting
v.   Integrated systems.
vi.   Weather forecasting
vii.   Mathematical and Statistical analysis.
viii.   Design work, including CAD
ix.   Analog computing.
x.   Financial applications: Banking and Insurance
xi.   Retailing
xii.   Medicine
xiii.   Education
xiv.   Manufacturing
xv.   Robotics

POINTS TO NOTE
5.32 a. In some respects computerisation is even more widespread than suggested in this chapter, because microprocessor based devices can be found almost everywhere eg. in digital watches, calculators, cameras and electronic games.

QUESTIONS A *(With answers)*
1. *By what criteria would you judge an applications possible suitability to the use of computers?*

2. *Explain these terms:-*

a. *"technically feasible".*

b. *"cost effective".*

3. *What kind of work is suited to complete computerisation?*

4. *In what general ways can computers aid management?*

5. *What are the two main areas of computer application? Which area represents the most widespread use?*

6. *Give the meanings of the following acronyms:-*

a. *CAD*
b. *BACS*
c. *CAL*

    d.   CAM

    e.   CAI

    f.   CADMAT

7.   *What type of computer is a combination of analog and digital? Where might such a computer be used?*

8.   *Give one example of each of the following:*

    a.   An application which exploits the computer's ability to store large quantities of data and retrieve individual data items quickly.

    b.   An application which exploits the computational powers of large computers.

    c.   An application which aids a decision making process.

QUESTIONS B *(Without answers)*

1.   *When an application is suitable for computerisation what main factors will determine whether or not computerisation will take place?*

2.   *Suggest as many ways as you can, in which computers could be used by a manufacturer.*

DATA AND PROGRAMS

1. The value of information is demonstrated by the way in which we use it to guide our actions (eg, using the weather forecast in deciding what clothes to wear).

The sounds coming out of the Radio or TV when we hear the weather forecaster speaking are *not* information in themselves. Information is the *meaning* which we attach to those sounds. By transferring information to us which we understand the weather forecaster has communicated information. The *methods* of communication involve the use of language and language transmission (eg. we get information from the weather forecaster by the use of English and Radio transmitters and receivers.) The following four chapters deal with those methods of communications which are important in Computer Studies.

2. Chapter 6 starts by drawing an important distinction between "Information" and "Data" and goes on to deal with various aspects of data.

3. Chapter 7 deals with various conventions for representing numerical data relating to number bases.

4. Chapter 8 is on designing small programs. The methods covered are an important part of an expressing our requirements in a language which a computer can interpret and use to control its own actions.

5. Chapter 9 is on data structures and files and looks at methods of organising data.

6. Chapter 10 introduces simple logic as used by the computer.

6   Data Types and Data Representation

INTRODUCTION
6.1   This chapter deals with data in a variety of ways. It draws a distinction between data and information and the different types of data. It also deals with the representation of stored and transmitted data.

DATA AND INFORMATION
6.2   In everyday speech the terms "data" and "information" are often interchanged but in Computer Studies it proves useful to distinguish between them.

6.3   **"Data"** is the name given to basic *facts* such as names and numbers. Examples are:- times, dates, weights, prices, costs, numbers of items sold, employee names, product names, addresses, tax codes, registration marks etc.

6.4   "Information" is data which has been converted into a more *useful* or *intelligible* form. Examples are:- headed tables, printed documents, pay slips, receipts, reports etc. So a set of words would be data but text would be information. eg. "SMITH, BROWN, JONES, ROBINSON" is data. "DAVID BROWN SCORED THE HIGHEST EXAMINATION MARK" is information. Information may be processed or manipulated further of course eg. a printed text may be reorganised.

Note. There is a tendency to use the term "**communication**" for the transfer of information and the term "**transmission**" for the transfer of data.

6.5   **Data Processing and Scientific Processing.**

   a.   **Data Processing (DP)** is the term given to the process of collecting data together and converting them into information. The methods of doing this may be manual, semi-manual   (eg. aided by a calculator), mechanical or electronic. **Electronic Data Processing (EDP)**   involves substituting a computer for machines and/or human labour.

   "Data Processing" is a Term mostly associated with business and commercial work. Since the use of computers for such applications is now widespread the term DP is often taken to imply EDP. In commercial DP the emphasis is normally on the volume of data processed with perhaps only small amounts of processing on each item of data. These features of EDP are summarised in figure 6.1.

   Note.   A company might hold details of its employees, names, addresses, rates of pay, pay to date, tax code etc. etc. on backing storage. (This is the maintained semi-permanent data). Each week the details of the hours worked by employees that week could be input. By using the newly input data and data from backing storage the computer could process all the relevant data to produce a set of payslips for each employee, and to bring the pay to date details up to date. The latter would be an "update" of maintained data.

   b.   **Scientific Processing.** Scientific applications of the computer conform to the same basic pattern as DP ie. INPUT OF DATA, PROCESS, OUTPUT OF INFORMATION, but the emphasis is on the processing stage and the volumes of data input may be small. These features of scientific processing are summarised in figure 6.2.

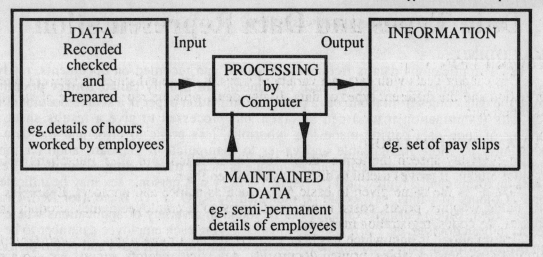

Figure 6.1.   Features of Electronic Data Processing (EDP).

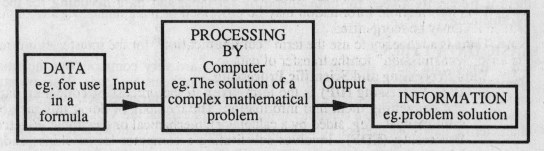

Figure 6.2.   Features of Scientific Processing.

Note.   Having made a distinction between the features of Data Processing and Scientific Processing it must be said that the basic principles are the same for all types of processing, only the emphasis changes.

QUALITATIVE AND QUANTITATIVE DATA

6.6   a.   **Qualitative data** is data which indicates the classification characteristics or nature of things eg. good, average, bad, hot, warm, cold, red, orange, green, yellow, blue, long, short.

   b.   **Quantitative data** is data which is expressed in terms of measurable quantities, for example, 100°, 50°, 0°, 1500^oC, 30^oC, -273^oC; 1000m, 2mm. Data expressed in quantitative form has the advantage of being largely free of the *subjective* bias of the observer, eg. one person might say a room was *hot,* whilst another said it was only *warm* which would provide conflicting qualitative data. A thermometer in the same room might display a quantitative reading of 30^oC which would provide *objectively* measured data. Quantitative data may not always be more informative however. Would you rather be told a colour had a wavelength of 5890 Ångstrom units or would you prefer to be told it was yellow?

DATA CODING

6.7   In DP applications data is frequently collected and recorded on documents, ready for input to the computer. Incidentally such documents are usually called **source documents** because the data comes from them, eg. a pupil's examination paper is a source document from which data (examination marks) can be taken and processed to give a results sheet. The recording of such data can be made less laborious, less prone to error and the data will subsequently be more manageable and easier to manipulate if standard abbreviations or simplified representations are used. This technique is called **data coding**. Examples:- Yes/No answers on forms can be represented by single Y's or N's. A person's sex may be indicated by M or F. Colours of paints, say, could be indicated by R, O, Y, G, B etc. (for Red, Orange, Yellow, Green, Blue.) Further examples can be found in a variety of applications where long codes have been devised. eg. car registration marks; giving each employee a number to be used when dealing with the payroll; using postal codes to indicate postal town and postal district; or introducing codes for parts or spare parts of manufactured items; and so on. Note that data coding is particularly useful with qualitative data. Data is less intelligible in coded forms, so there is frequently a need for **data encoding** for input and **data decoding** for the output of information.

BASIC DATA TYPES

6.8   Basic data items such as names or numbers are very common, but the smallest data elements are the letters or digits from which these data items are made. A set of letters, digits and other symbols used for representing data is called a **character set.** In 1.34 it was shown how data could be fed into a computer using the characters on the VDU keyboard. A very basic character set like those used on some computer input devices is shown here in Figure 6.3.

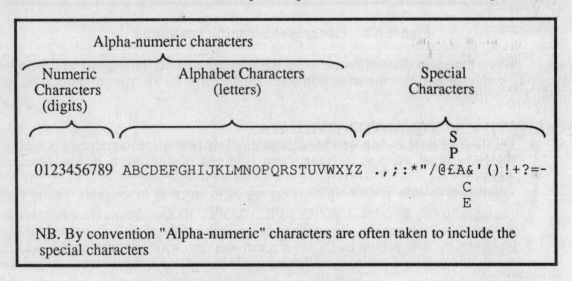

Figure 6.3. A Simple Character Set.

There are 56 characters in the set shown in Figure 6.3. Most sets in actual use have at least 64 characters, including some for control of the device eg. "RETURN" to the start of the line as shown in figure 1.6. Most larger character sets provide for both uppercase letters (capitals) and lower case letters (small) as shown here in Figure 6.4.

```
0123456789ABCDEFGHIJKLMNOPQRSTUVWXY
                                  S
                                  P
abcdefghijklmnopqrstuvwxyz.,;:*"/@£A&'()+?=-
                                  C
                                  E
```

Figure 6.4 An Extended Character Set.

CHARACTER TYPES AND DATA TYPES

6.9   a.   Figure 6.3 shows the basic classification of character types:-
          i.   Numeric (digits) also "Alphanumeric"
          ii. Alphabetic (letters) also "Alphanumeric"
          iii. Special
    b.   The same basic classification can be extended to data types:-
          i.   Numeric eg. 37.64   a number
          ii. Alphabetic eg. SMITH   a name
          iii. Alphanumeric eg. VLU910X a car registration mark
Various further sub-classifications are possible particularly for numeric data items.

NUMERIC DATA TYPES

6.10   a.   **Integers.** These are the positive and negative whole numbers, and zero, ie (0, 1, +2, +3, +4, ...). When integers are being processed a number of further points are of interest:
          i.   The positive whole numbers are called the **Natural numbers** ie. (1, 2, 3, 4.....). It is common practice to represent these numbers without the "+" sign in front of them in many situations. In practical work you can expect to come across the term **unsigned integers** eg. 1, 2, 3 and **signed integers** eg. +1, +2, +3. Negative integers *must* be signed to distinguish them from positive integers.
          ii. The **Numerical Value** (or magnitude) of an integer is its value disregarding its sign eg. +3 and -3 have the *same* numerical value. Another term for numerical value is **absolute value.**
          iii. The integers can be represented on a numerical scale thus:

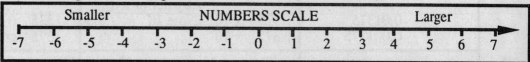

Integers to the right hand side are larger than those to the left hand side. Therefore **+3 is larger than -6** but **+3 has a smaller numerical value than -6.** Great care must therefore be taken when using the words "larger" and "smaller".

iv. The lefthand end digit of an integer is called the **most significant digit** and the righthand end digit of an integer is called the **least significant digit**.
Example.

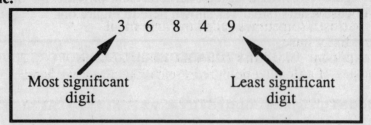

b. **Real Numbers.** These are **all** the numbers on the number scale shown in (aiii) above (ie including those between the integers). Real numbers include *all* the integers and *all* the fractions. These are all real numbers: 0, -0.5, 3+, 9, -1 1/7, 39.864, 1/8. The points regarding integers made in (a) above also apply to real numbers.

ALTERNATIVE REPRESENTATIONS OF NUMBERS

6.11 a. **Fixed Point Representation.** The usual way of representing numbers is to write the number with the decimal point **fixed** in its correct position between the two appropriate digits eg. 13.75 or 3862.4. This is **fixed point representation** and it proves very useful in data processing for example where sums of money are to be processed or printed. However this representation becomes laborious and cumbersome when dealing with several very large or very small numbers eg. 1375000000, 386240000, 0.0000001375, 0.00000038624. The answer is to use floating point representation.

b. **Floating Point Representation.** Here are some examples.

Fixed Point Representation	Floating point Representation	
	Notation used in Science	Notation used in Computing
13.75	1.375×10^1 (Note $10^1 = 10$)	$.1375 \times 10^2$
137.5	1.375×10^2 (Note $10^2 = 100$)	$.1375 \times 10^3$
1375.	1.375×10^3 (Note $10^3 = 1000$)	$.1375 \times 10^4$
1375000000.	1.375×10^9	$.1375 \times 10^{10}$
1.375	1.375×10^0 (Note $10^0 = 1$ by definition)	$.1375 \times 10^1$
0.1375	1.375×10^{-1} (Note $10^{-1} = {}^1/10$ by definition)	$.1375 \times 10^0$
0.01375	1.375×10^{-2} (Note $10^{-2} = {}^1/100$)	$.1375 \times 10^{-1}$
0.001375	1.375×10^{-3}	$.1375 \times 10^{-2}$
3862.4	3.8624×10^3	$.38624 \times 10^4$
386240000.	3.8624×10^8	$.38624 \times 10^9$
.00000038624	3.8624×10^{-7}	$.38624 \times 10^{-6}$

In each of the floating point representations just given in the table the decimal points have been moved or *floated* along the digits to a position in between the first and second non zero most significant digits. There are three components to a floating point representation:

i.   the **mantissa** sometimes called the **argument**,

ii. the **radix** or **base**,

iii. the **exponent** sometimes called the **characteristic**.

The components of a floating point representation are shown here:

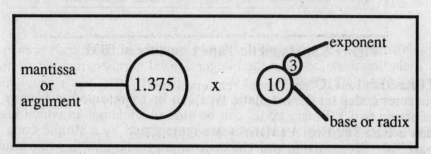

Note
i.   The exponent takes integer values.

ii. 13.75 x 102, 0.01375 x 105 and 1.375 x 103 are *all* floating point representation of the fixed point number 1375 but the last of the three like those in the table is in a **standard form** with the point between the first and second non zero most significant digits.

iii. In some applications computer input and output of floating point numbers is printed on one line as shown here:

Handwritten floating point representation	Computerised version
1.375×10^3	$+ 1.375E + 3$
3.8624×10^{-7}	$+ 3.8624E - 7$

The "E" separates the exponent from the mantissa and base 10 is assumed.

DATA REPRESENTATION S FOR COMPUTER DEVICES

6.12   The idea of **data coding** was introduced in paragraph 6.7 but here we deal with a completely different type of data coding; the coding of characters so that data can be handled by computer. Ideally we would like to communicate with computers in the spoken or written form of our everyday language. In practice we have to convert data to forms more readily acceptable to a machine. Magnetic tape is considered here to illustrate the general principles of data coding. For convenience, other features of this medium are left for discussion in chapter 11.

6.13   Magnetic Tape Coding. In this medium invisible "spots" of magnetism are created in the magnetic surface of the tape. These "spots", can each be magnetised in one of two directions corresponding to magnetic North or South.

Figure 6.5. Magnetic Tape Courtesy of IBM.

BINARY REPRESENTATIONS

6.14 The character codes on the magnetic tape can be represented in **binary** form (binary meaning "numbering two"). Binary codes can be used in situations in which just *two* possible alternatives can occur. The two alternatives are represented by a simple code using the two symbols "O" and "1". For example, with the code on magnetic tape this rule could be adopted: "1" stands for a spot magnetised in one direction (left to right, say) and "0" stands for a spot magnetised in the opposite direction (right to left)". Such a code is called a **binary code.** When using binary codes the two symbols "O" and "1" are called **BITS** which is short for **B**inary Dig**ITS.**

6.15 Binary codes are applied to numerous situations which can be used as the basis of character codes and data representations. Some simple examples are given in figure 6.6 In figure 6.7 you can see some examples of the binary codes used for the magnetic tape shown in figure 6.5.

6.16 The code used on the magnetic tape shown in figure 6.5. is known as BCD (Binary Coded Decimal). An even more popular code than BCD is the ASCII code. ASCII is short for American Standard Code for Information Interchange. The ASCII code is given in figure 6.8.

BINARY CODE TRANSMISSION

6.17 Remember (6.12) that coding is used in order that data may be handled by a computer. Converting data into the binary codes used for magnetic tape of disk is an important step towards this goal, but data on disk is **outside** the computer and data must be stored **inside** the computer in order that it may be processed. This transfer of data into the computer is done by input devices which convert the data codes on the various input media (eg. tape) into electrical signals which are transmitted through wires into the computer's central processing unit or main memory. As these transmitted signals enter the computer the circuitry within the processor converts them into stored forms of the codes eg. sets of charged "memory" cells. The output of data occurs in reverse fashion. Figure 6.9 summarises the process.

Coded as binary " 0 "	Coded as binary " 1 "	Comment
Spot of magnetism on magnetic medium magnetised one way ———▶ N	Spot magnetised the other way N◀———	Used for data storage on magnetic tape and magnetic disk
Electrical Switch OFF	Electrical Switch ON	
Electric light OFF	Electric light ON	Can be used to display the binary states of an electronic device
Transistor (A simple electronic switch) b OFF c e	Current in b switches current ON b from c to e ON c e	Basis of the computer's electronic switching circuitry
Electronic storage " cell " discharged OFF	charged ON + -	Basis of modern main storage

Figure 6.6 The Use of Binary Code

CHARACTER	J	K	L
MAGNETIC TAPE CODE	- -	- -	-- --
BINARY REPRESENTATION	0100001	0100010	1100011

Figure 6.7. Examples of Binary Coded Characters on Magnetic Tape.

BINARY CODE	ASCII CHARACTER	BINARY CODE	ASCII CHARACTER	BINARY CODE	ASCII CHARACTER
00100000	SPACE	00110000	0	01000000	@
00100001	!	00110001	1	01000001	A
00100010	"	00110010	2	01000010	B
00100011	#	00110011	3	01000011	C
00100100	$	00110100	4	01000100	D
00100101	%	00110101	5	01000101	E
00100110	&	00110110	6	01000110	F
00100111	.	00110111	7	01000111	G
00101000	(	00111000	8	01001000	H
00101001	)	00111001	9	01001001	I
00101001	*	00111010	:	01001010	J
00101011	+	00111011	;	01001011	K
00101100	.	00111100	<	01001100	L
00101101	-	00111101	=	01001101	M
00101110	.	00111110	,	01001110	N
00101111	/	00111111	?	01001111	0
01010000	P	01100000		01110000	p
01010001	Q	01100001	a	01110001	q
01010010	R	01100010	b	01110001	r
01010011	S	01100011	c	01110011	s
01010100	T	01100100	d	01110100	t
01010101	U	01100101	e	01110101	u
01010110	V	01100110	f	01110110	v
01010111	W	01100111	g	01110111	w
01011000	X	01101000	h	01111000	x
01011001	Y	01101001	i	01111001	y
01011010	Z	01101010	j	01111010	z
01011011	[	01101100	k	01111011	{
01011100	\	01101100	l	01111100	|
01011101	]	01101101	m	01111101	}
01011110	^	01101110	n	01111110	~
01011111	-	01101111	o	01111111	DEL

Figure 6.8. The ASCII Character Set.

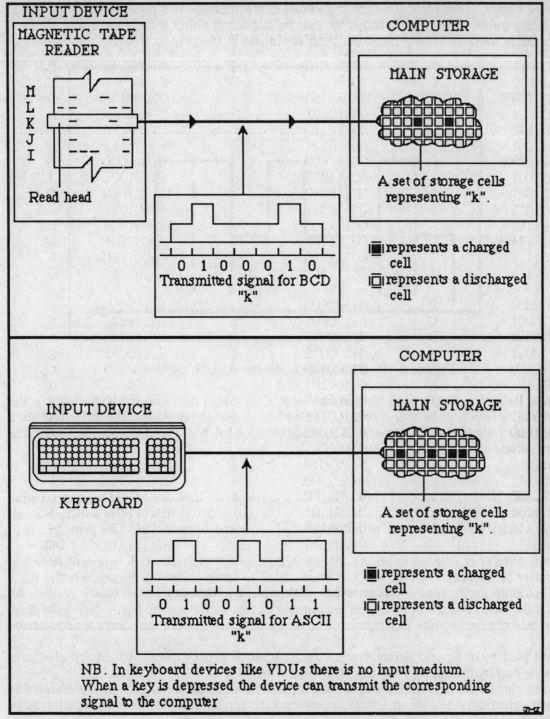

Figure 6.9.   Data Code Transmission.

6.18 Pulse Trains. The signal for each individual character code is a rapid series of electrical pulses called a pulse train. During transmissions pulses are at either a high level or low level, the former being used for binary 1 and the latter for binary 0. (see Fig. 6.10).

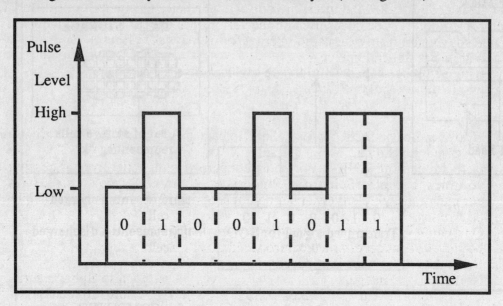

Figure 6.10. The pulse train for ASCII "K".

6.19 Uses. Pulse trains are used to transmit both data codes and control codes within the computer and between computer devices. The pulses occur at very high speed eg. within a microprocessor pulses may be generated at frequencies of 4 MHz (megahertz) ie. 4 million cycles per second with two pulses per cycle.

PARITY

6.20 You may have noticed the "check bits" on the magnetic tape codes and wondered what was their purpose. They are extra bits added to the code in order to detect errors such as those caused by a faulty tape write head which might fail to record some codes. The principle is as follows.

6.21 Even parity. If you examine the magnetic tape codes of figure 6.5. you will discover that the parity bit ("check" in Fig. 6.5) has been added to some codes on the tape so that the 6 bit code *including* parity always has an even number of bits. This is an even parity system. As each character code is read from the tape the number of bits including the parity bit, is checked. Should an odd number of bits be discovered in an even parity system then an error must have occurred.

6.22 Odd parity. In an odd parity system the number of bits in the tape for each character code is made odd by the appropriate use of the parity bit.

6.23 Parity checks are also important in code transmission. A device receiving a transmission with a parity error may be able to signal the error to the sender causing the transmission to be retransmitted correctly.

INTERNAL AND EXTERNAL CHARACTER CODES

6.24   Data may be presented to the input devices in a variety of binary codes according to the media used, but it is common practice to use one particular binary code for all data within the computer. This code is called the **internal code** and the choice of internal code differs from one manufacturer to another. The codes used on the various peripherals are called **external codes.**

6.25   Code conversion from external to internal forms may take place:
   a.   within a peripheral device,
   b.   within a device called an **interface** as data enters the computer,
   c.   within the computer itself.

SUMMARY

6.26   a.   "Data" are basic facts, "Information" is data arranged into an intelligible form so as to convey meaning.
   b.   Data Processing (DP) is normally concerned with repetitive processing of large volumes of data. Scientific Processing is normally concerned with lengthy computations on relatively small columns of data. The same basic principles apply to both cases.
   c.   Qualitative data and quantitative data were distinguished.
   d.   Methods of data coding were introduced.
   e.   Basic data types were introduced:-

Numeric:	Integers		also alphanumeric
	Real	Fixed point	also alphanumeric
	Real	Floating point	also alphanumeric
Alphabetic			also alphanumeric
Special			

   f.   Computer data codes were introduced eg. ASCII
   g.   Binary codes were introduced
   h.   Code transmission was explained.

POINTS TO NOTE

6.27   a.   This chapter has concentrated on various aspects of what data is. Later chapters use this material when considering how to manipulate and process data.
   b.   One "data type" which has not been considered in this chapter is the "picture". In the future we may expect computers to be used in the storage and retrieval of pictures and a few examples will be given in later chapters. If you look very closely at a newspaper picture or colour TV screen you will see it is represented in rows and columns of dots. A binary representation of these can be used by computers.

QUESTIONS A *(With answers)*

1.   What is the main difference between data processing and scientific processing?

2.   Describe, giving examples, the use of a parity bit in magnetic tape codes.

3.   Distinguish between "data" and "information".

4.   Consider the signed integer - 3625.

Write down its

i. absolute value
ii.   most significant digit
iii.   least significant digit

QUESTIONS B *(Without answers)*

1. What is the purpose of data coding? Give three examples of data coding which are in common use.

2. By reference to the magnetic tape in figure 6.5 write down the binary codes for the characters "7", "C" and "X".

3. Convert the following fixed point numbers to floating point numbers as used in Computer Studies:-

    a.   456.25

    b.   0.000345

    c.-   0.267

    In each case state which part of the number is the mantissa and which part is the exponent.

4. Suggest suitable ways of coding the following types of data. If you know a method already in use describe that method.

    a.   shoe sizes.

    b.   book classification eg. in a library or by publishers,

    c.   colours,

    d.   bus routes,

    e.   Classification of films for age suitability,

    f.   major and minor routes on maps,

    g.   paper sizes.

7 Number Bases

INTRODUCTION

7.1 The previous chapter introduced binary codes. This chapter extends the topic by introducing numbers to base two, called binary numbers. The importance of binary numbers lies in their use by digital computers in the storage and processing of data. Some other number bases also have uses in computing and so they are introduced in this chapter together with the methods needed for converting from one base to another. It is important to distinguish between binary numbers and binary codes. The binary symbols 0 and 1 can be used to produce a wide variety of codes. If these symbols are used to produce the particular codes specified in paragraph 7.3 then they represent binary numbers.

7.2 **Decimal Numbers** are the numbers in everyday use, and are also known as **Denary** numbers, or numbers to **base 10**, because ten is the basis of the number system. To write a number in decimal we make use of the ten **digit** symbols 0, 1, 2, 3, 4, 5, 6, 7, 8 and 9 and also use the method of **place value** (ie. the position of a digit affects its meaning).

Example. The number "235" in decimals is made up thus:

PLACE VALUE	10^3 (1000)	10^2 (100)	10^1 (10)	10^0 (1)		10^2 (100)	10^1 (10)	10^0 (1)
Digit '5' in position 10^0				5	$= 5 \times 10^0$	0	0	5
Digit '3' in position 10^1			3		$= 3 \times 10^1$	0	3	0
Digit '2' in position 10^2		2			$= 2 \times 10^2$	2	0	0
					TOTAL	2	3	5

Figure 7.1 A decimal number's representation.

BINARY NUMBERS

7.3 **Binary Numbers** are numbers to base 2. The binary number system uses just *two* symbols, 0 and 1, and place values increasing in powers of *two*.

Examples. (You should memorise these first 8 values for future use).

BINARY NUMBERS	$2^3 = 8$ $2^2 = 4$ $2^1 = 2$ $2^0 = 1$	DECIMAL EQUIVALENTS
0 0 0 1	$= (0 \times 2^3) + (0 \times 2^2) + (0 \times 2^1) + (1 \times 2^0)$ =	1
0 0 1 0	$= (0 \times 2^3) + (0 \times 2^2) + (1 \times 2^1) + (0 \times 2^0)$ =	2
0 0 1 1	$= (0 \times 2^3) + (0 \times 2^2) + (1 \times 2^1) + (1 \times 2^0)$ =	3
0 1 0 0	$= (0 \times 2^3) + (1 \times 2^2) + (0 \times 2^1) + (0 \times 2^0)$ =	4
0 1 0 1	$= (0 \times 2^3) + (1 \times 2^2) + (0 \times 2^1) + (1 \times 2^0)$ =	5
0 1 1 0	$= (0 \times 2^3) + (1 \times 2^2) + (1 \times 2^1) + (0 \times 2^0)$ =	6
0 1 1 1	$= (0 \times 2^3) + (1 \times 2^2) + (1 \times 2^1) + (1 \times 2^0)$ =	7
1 0 0 0	$= (1 \times 2^3) + (0 \times 2^2) + (0 \times 2^1) + (0 \times 2^0)$ =	8

Figure 7.2. The first eight binary numbers.

7.4   Subscripts are used to indicate the base of a number in its written form. For example when we see 101_2 the subscript 2 tells us we are looking at a binary number, which from our table we identify as being equivalent to 5 in decimal. Without the subscript we would probably read 101 as meaning one hundred and one in decimal. So *at all times use subscripts* to indicate the base used if there is any risk of confusion without them. The subscript itself is always in decimal.

7.5   Conversion from Binary to Decimal.

Example Convert 1101101_2 to Decimal

Place Values	2^6 (64)	2^5 (32)	2^4 (16)	2^3 (8)	2^2 (4)	2^1 (2)	2^0 (1)	Decimal Value
Binary Numbers	1	1	0	1	1	0	1	
Conversion	$(1 \times 64) + (1 \times 32) + (0 \times 16) + (1 \times 8) + (1 \times 4) + (0 \times 2) + (1 \times 1)$							= 109

Figure 7.3. Conversion from Binary to Decimal.

7.6   Conversion from Decimal to Binary. We use repeated *division* by 2.

Example. Convert 109 Decimal to Binary. *Arrows* are used here to emphasis the direction in which the Binary Number should be read.

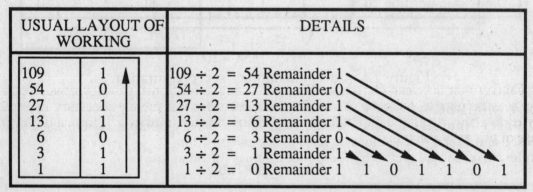

USUAL LAYOUT OF WORKING		DETAILS
109	1	$109 \div 2 = 54$ Remainder 1
54	0	$54 \div 2 = 27$ Remainder 0
27	1	$27 \div 2 = 13$ Remainder 1
13	1	$13 \div 2 = 6$ Remainder 1
6	0	$6 \div 2 = 3$ Remainder 0
3	1	$3 \div 2 = 1$ Remainder 1
1	1	$1 \div 2 = 0$ Remainder 1 1 0 1 1 0 1

Figure 7.4. Conversion from Decimal to Binary.

We have thus checked our previous result, $109_{10} = 0010010_2$

OCTAL NUMBERS

7.7   Octal numbers are numbers to **base 8.** There are eight symbols used in the octal system (0, 1, 2, 3, 4, 5, 6 and 7) and place values increase in powers of 8.

70

7.8. Conversions between Octal and Decimal.

Example. Convert 109_{10} to octal and convert back to decimal as a check.

a. Conversion to Octal is done by repeated division by 8.
In other respects the method is the same as conversion from Decimal to Binary.

WORKING		DETAILS
105	5 ↑	$109 \div 8 = 13$ Remainder 5
13	5	$13 \div 8 = 1$ Remainder 5
1	1	$1 \div 8 = 0$ Remainder 1

Thus, $109_{10} = 155_8$

b. Conversion *to* Decimal *from* Octal

PLACE VALUES	8^2 (64)	8^1 (8)	8^0 (1)	DECIMAL
OCTAL NUMBER	1	5	5	VALUE
CONVERSION	$(1 \times 64) + (5 \times 8) + (5 \times 1)$			$= 109$

Thus, $155_8 = 109_{10}$

7.9 Conversion between Octal and Binary.

A simple relationship exists between octal and binary, because eight is the cube of two. To do conversions it is merely necessary to remember binary equivalents for the eight octal symbols. Octal is often used as a "shorthand" for binary because of this easy conversion.

Conversion Table

OCTAL NUMBERS	0	1	2	3	4	5	6	7
BINARY EQUIVALENTS	0 0 0	0 0 1	0 1 0	0 1 1	1 0 0	1 0 1	1 1 0	1 1 1

Example a.   Convert 155_8 to Binary

OCTAL NUMBER		1		5			5		
BINARY EQUIVALENTS FROM THE CONVERSION TABLE	0	0	1	1	0	1	1	0	1

Thus $155_8 = 001\ 101\ 101_2$

Example b. Convert 1110111000010_2 to octal. In order to use the conversion table we group the binary digits into threes working from right to left, adding extra zeros at the left end if necessary.

GROUPED BINARY DIGITS	0	0	1	1	1	0	1	1	1	0	0	0	0	1	0
OCTAL EQUIVALENT FROM THE CONVERSION TABLE	1			6			7			0			2		

Thus $1110111000010_2 = 16702_8$

Note. Conversions between Decimal and Binary are often quicker via Octal, ie. using Binary to Octal to Decimal, or Decimal to Octal to Binary.

HEXADECIMAL NUMBERS

7.10 Hexadecimal numbers, usually abbreviated to **"Hex"**, are numbers to **base 16**. The sixteen symbols used in the Hex system are 0, 1, 2, 3, 4, 5, 6, 7, 8, 9, A, B, C, D, E and F, and place values increase in powers of sixteen. We need to remember that A, B, C, D, E and F are equivalent to 10, 11, 12, 13, 14, and 15 DECIMAL.

7.11 Conversions between Hexadecimal and Decimal follow the same pattern used for Binary and Octal.

Example. Convert 109_{10} to Hex and back again.

a.   Conversion *to* Hex *from* Decimal.

WORKING		DETAILS
109	$13 = D_{16}$ ↑	$109 \div 16 = 6$ Remainder 13
6	$6 = 6_{16}$	$6 \div 16 = 0$ Remainder 6

Thus $109_{10} = 6D_{16}$

b.   Conversion *to* Decimal *from* Hex.

PLACE VALUES	16^2 (256)	16^1 (16)	16^0 (1)	
HEX NUMBERS	0	6	D	DECIMAL VALUES
CONVERSION	(0 X 256) + (6 X 16) + (13 X 1)			= 109

Thus $6D_{16} = 109_{10}$

7.12   Conversion between Hex and other bases. Conversion between Hex, Octal and Binary is done in much the same way as the Octal/Binary conversions in paragraph 7.9. A conversion table is given in the following table.

Conversion Table

DECIMAL	0	1	2	3	4	5	6	7
HEX	0	1	2	3	4	5	6	7
BINARY	0000	0001	0010	0011	0100	0101	0110	0111
OCTAL	0	1	2	3	4	5	6	7

DECIMAL	8	9	10	11	12	13	14	15
HEX	8	9	A	B	C	D	E	F
BINARY	1000	1001	1010	1011	1100	1101	1110	1111
OCTAL	10	11	12	13	14	15	16	17

Example a.   Convert $6D_{16}$ to Binary and Octal. A conversion between Hex and Octal is most easily made via Binary.

Stage 1 (Hex to Binary)

HEX NUMBER	6				D			
BINARY EQUIVALENT FROM THE TABLE	0	1	1	0	1	1	0	1

Stage 2 (Binary to Octal)

BINARY	0	0	1	1	0	1	1	0	1
OCTAL		1			5			5	

Example b. Convert 11101110000010_2 to Hex. We group binary digits into fours from the right, then use the conversion table.

GROUPED BINARY DIGITS	0	0	0	1	1	1	0	1	1	1	0	0	0	0	1	0
HEX EQUIVALENT FROM THE CONVERSION TABLE		1				D				C				2		

BINARY FRACTIONS

7.13   Examples of Binary fractions are given in this table

BINARY FRACTION	$2^{-1}=\frac{1}{2}$ $2^{-2}=\frac{1}{4}$ $2^{-3}=\frac{1}{8}$ $2^{-4}=\frac{1}{16}$	DECIMAL EQUIVALENT
.1 0 0 0	$= (1 \times \frac{1}{2}) + (0 \times \frac{1}{4}) + (0 \times \frac{1}{8}) + (0 \times \frac{1}{16})$	$= \frac{1}{2} = 0.5$
.0 1 0 0	$= (0 \times \frac{1}{2}) + (1 \times \frac{1}{4}) + (0 \times \frac{1}{8}) + (0 \times \frac{1}{16})$	$= \frac{1}{4} = 0.25$
.0 0 1 0	$= (0 \times \frac{1}{2}) + (0 \times \frac{1}{4}) + (1 \times \frac{1}{8}) + (0 \times \frac{1}{16})$	$= \frac{1}{8} = 0.125$
.0 0 0 1	$= (0 \times \frac{1}{2}) + (0 \times \frac{1}{4}) + (0 \times \frac{1}{8}) + (1 \times \frac{1}{16})$	$= \frac{1}{16} = 0.0625$

7.14   **Conversion from Binary to Decimal.**
   Example. Convert 11.101_2 to a decimal value

PLACE VALUE	2^1 (2)	2^0 (1)	.	2^{-1} ($\frac{1}{2}$)	2^{-2} ($\frac{1}{4}$)	2^{-3} ($\frac{1}{8}$)	DECIMAL VALUE
BINARY NUMBER	1	1	.	1	0	1	
CONVERSION							

PLACE VALUE	2^1 (2) 2^0 (1) . 2^{-1} ($\frac{1}{2}$) 2^{-2} ($\frac{1}{4}$) 2^{-3} ($\frac{1}{8}$)	DECIMAL VALUE
BINARY NUMBER	1 1 . 1 0 1	
CONVERSION	$(1 \times 2) + (1 \times 1) + (1 \times \frac{1}{2}) + (0 \times \frac{1}{4}) + (1 \times \frac{1}{8})$	$3\frac{5}{8} = 3.625$

7.15   **Decimal to Binary Conversion.** (The whole number part is converted as in 7.6).
   Example 1. Convert 0.625_{10} to binary.

WORKING	COMMENT
.625 x 2 1.25 .25 x 2 0.5 .5 x 2 1.0 .0 x 2 .1 0 1	Multiply by 2 and write result beneath. Remove digit before the point to form the binary fraction. Repeat process until a zero fraction value occurs, or the required accuracy is reached.

7.16   Example 2.   Convert 1/3 to binary using 5 bits for your representation.

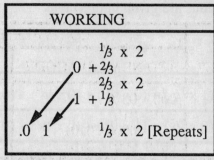

ie. 1/3 is 0.0101_2

BINARY CODED DECIMAL (BCD)

7.17   Details of this code are included here because it is important to distinguish this method of number representation from the binary numbers detailed in this chapter.

The standard form of BCD numeric code (strictly speaking called 8421 weighted BCD) represents the decimal digits 0, 1...9 by the corresponding 4 bit binary numbers. Here are the ten BCD codes:-

DECIMAL DIGIT	0	1	2	3	4	5	6	7	8	9
BCD CODE	0000	0001	0010	0011	0100	0101	0110	0111	1000	1001

Example. The number 2039_{10} would be coded thus:

DECIMAL NUMBER	2	0	3	9
BCD CODE	0010	0000	0011	1001

Note that each digit is coded separately

7.18   Note that the representation of a decimal number in BCD is usually different from the representation obtained by converting the number to binary as shown in paragraphs 7.6 and 7.15. The latter representation is known as **pure binary** in order to distinguish it from BCD.

7.19 Examples. To illustrate the different between pure binary and BCD representations of decimal numbers here are a few examples:-

DECIMAL NUMBER	EQUIVALENTS	
	BCD NUMERIC CODE	PURE BINARY
12	0001 0010	1100
25	0010 0101	11000
0.5	0000 . 0101	0 . 1
21.5	0010 0001 . 0101	10101 . 1

7.20 The BCD numeric code may be extended by adding an extra 2 bits to form a 6 bit code which is just called BCD code instead of BCD numeric code. The magnetic tape code shown in figure 6.5 is in BCD. If you inspect the diagram closely you will notice that zero is coded differently in the 6 bit code for reasons which need not concern us here.

EXTENDED BINARY CODED DECIMAL INTERCHANGE CODE (EBCDIC)
7.21 This code (pronounced "Eb–see–dick") was developed by IBM. It uses 8 bits to provide 2^8 (ie 256) individual codes. See appendix (IV.3).

SUMMARY
7.22 a. A Numbering system is characterised by the base and symbols used. The table summarises those considered.

NUMBER SYSTEM	BASE	SYMBOLS USED
Binary	2	0,1.
Octal	8	0,1,2,3,4,5,6,7.
Decimal or Denary	10	0,1,2,3,4,5,6,7,8,9.
Hexadecimal or Hex	16	0,1,2,3,4,5,6,7,8,9,A,B,C,D,E,F.

   b. The base of a number is indicated by a subscript.

POINTS TO NOTE
7.23 a. Another name sometimes used instead of a "base" is **"radix"**.
   b. Octal and Hex numbers can be used as "shorthands" for binary.
   c. You will need to use the methods described in this chapter, so practice on the questions given here.
   d. The simplest sequences to adopt when converting between bases are shown here:-

   i. Decimal ⇔ Octal ⇔ Binary

   ii. Hexadecimal ⇔ Binary ⇔ Octal

   e. When converting a number with both a whole number part and a fractional part remember to convert the two parts separately.

QUESTIONS A *(With answers)*

1. Convert these decimal numbers to
   a. Octal
   b. Binary
   c. Hex'
i.	18	ii.	26	iii.	44	v.	50
v	111	iv.	173	vii.	196	viii.	236
ix.	298	x.	331	xi.	382	xii.	515

2. Convert these Octal numbers to:
   a. Decimal
   b. Hex'
   c. Binary
   i. 47 ii. 65 iii. 125 iv. 210 v 235 vi. 536

3. Convert these Hexadecimal numbers to decimal and octal
   i. 8B ii. E4 iii. 148 iv. IBO v 1EB

4. Express this binary number in Octal and Hex:
   11011101010110101011_2

5. Convert these binary numbers to decimal
i.	0.101	ii.	0.1101	iii.	0.0011
iv.	101.011	v.	1011.1111	vi.	1101.0101

6. Convert these decimal numbers to binary.
i.	0.75	ii.	0.6875	iii.	0.65625
iv.	3.875	v.	13.4375	vi.	2.4

7. a. Given that you can convert octal fractions to binary by writing down the binary equivalent of each octal digit, convert these octal fractions to binary (eg. $0.3_8 = 0.011_2$).
   i. 0.153 ii. 0.672 iii. 0.405

   b. Using a similar rule for hexadecimal fractions (eg. $0.3_{16} = 0.0011_2$) convert these Hex' fractions to binary.
   i. 0.872 ii. 0.A3E iii. 0.BFD

8. Convert the following decimal numbers into
   a. Pure Binary
   and
   b. BCD numeric code.
   i. 34 ii. 325 iii. 17

QUESTIONS B *(Without answers)*
1. *Convert these decimal numbers to*
   a. Octal
   b. Binary
   c. Hex'.
      i. 304   ii. 330   iii 500

2. *Convert these Octal numbers to*
   a. Decimal
   b. Hex',
   c. Binary
      i. 352   ii. 416   iii. 733

3. *Convert these Hexadecimal numbers to*
   a. Decimal
   and
   b. Octal
      i. IFE   ii. 10B   iii 123

4. *Convert these binary numbers to decimal*
      i. 11101.0111 i. 10111.1001 iii. 10101.1111

5. *Convert these decimal numbers to binary.*
      i. 21.9375   ii. 13/16 iii. 7.8

6. *Convert the following decimal numbers into*
   a. pure binary
   b. BCD numeric code.
      i. 19   ii. 286.

8 Designing Small Programs

INTRODUCTION
8.1 The aim of this chapter is to introduce the reader to program design, the stages in programming and the principles and techniques of programming. The chapter introduces the use of **pseudocode** and then uses it extensively. The chapter also briefly deals with **program flowcharts** which are an alternative to pseudocode still in common use even though they are somewhat dated. The reader should regard this chapter as one to be read and reread several times as part of learning practical programming skills.

ALGORITHMS, PROCEDURES AND PROGRAMMING
8.2 A set of instructions which describe the steps to be followed in order to carry out an activity is called an **algorithm** or **procedure.** If the algorithm is written in the computer's language then the set of instructions is called a program. The task of writing a computer program involves going through several stages only one of which requires instructions to be written in the computer's own language. So programming requires more than just *writing* programs. The stages in programming will be discussed in this chapter.

THE IMPORTANCE OF GOOD PROGRAMMING METHODS
8.3 Computers are only machines and will slavishly follow the instructions given them. Great care must therefore be taken when writing a program to ensure that the computer which uses the program does what is is intended to do. This point may not seem too serious to a user in education for whom a dud program may just be an irritation, but we all rely very heavily on computers for such things as national defence, banking, government administration, insurance etc. A faulty program in such cases could be disastrous!

GENERAL POINTS ABOUT PROGRAMMING METHOD
8.4 Here are two obvious points which some over eager novice programmers sadly ignore.
We cannot instruct a computer to do a task if
  a.   we are not clear in our own minds exactly what we are trying to do

and   b.   we have not already worked out for ourselves how the task should be done.

How to deal with these two points forms the first two stages in programming ie. **understanding the problem** and **planning the solution.**

For the pupil or student, understanding the problem often involves understanding a question set by a teacher or lecturer, or maybe understanding an examination question. This can be rather artificial because the problems may be short, whereas many real programming problems are too complicated for just one person to deal with. Also the professional programmer will often need to go back and ask further questions of the person who set the problem, whereas the student in an examination will just have to carry on and make whatever assumptions seem appropriate.

8.5 Once a method of solution has been decided upon the programmer must then break the method down into a manageable set of tasks. This involves identifying procedures performed on data ie, asking the questions "What information is required?", "What data is to be used?" and "What do I do to the data to get the required information?" This is similar to the elements of a cook's recipe. The cook must pay attention to what is being produced, the ingredients, and the method. The programmer must pay attention to the output, the data and the procedures.

8.6   The cooking method given in a recipe is normally written in English and English is a good starting point for the programmer. However, writing instructions in English can be troublesome for a variety of reasons, for example:

a. English is a "natural" language and it is easy to convey the wrong meaning by mistake. There are lots of old jokes about recipes which illustrate the point eg. the cook with blue face and teeth chattering who followed the instruction "stir the mixture well and then stand in the fridge for 5 minutes."

b. Now for some more precise points. Descriptions in English may be vague unless further definition is given eg "...continue cutting until the ingredients are roughly chopped." What is meant by "roughly chopped?" It's easy to find other examples eg. What is a "good" examination result.

c. It is easy to accidentally write statements in English which are ambiguous (ie. which have more than one meaning). This is the basis of most puns, *not always obvious* but funny when we see them eg. In the film AIRPLANE one scene included lines something like this:
Man: "Surely you don't mean that Doctor?"
Doctor: "I do, and don't call me Shirley."

d. There are many pitfalls when we try to express logic in natural English. For example, what is the difference between these two rules?

Rule 1.
You will be allowed to study Spanish if you have passed English and have started to study French or if you have passed English and have not started to study German.

Rule 2.
You will be allowed to study Spanish provided you have both passed your English and you have not both started to study German and, not started to study French.
You may decide that the rules are the same. They are meant to be but they are both rather clumsy.

8.7   At the third stage in programming, English is abandoned in favour of alternative means of expressing procedures. These include Flowcharts, diagrams, tables and a rather strict and limited form of words which may be called, **"Pseudocode"**, **"Structured English"** or **"Tight English"** according to the version used.

Further details of this and the other stages in programming, and details of the methods come later in this chapter.

PROGRAMMING AIMS

8.8   In the early days of computing, and indeed into the seventies computer main memory was expensive and therefore an important aim for the programmer was to write programs which used as little memory as possible. This is seldom an important factor today except for the user of very small computers. Other factors have become far more important. The general aims when writing a program may include:-

a. **Reliability.** ie. the program can be depended upon always to do what it is supposed to do.

b. **Maintainability.** ie. the program will be easy to change or modify when the need arises.

c. **Portability.** ie. the program will be transferable to a different computer with a minimum of modification.

d. **Readability.** ie. the program will be easy for a programmer to read and understand (this can aid (a), (b) and (c).
e. **Performance.** ie . the program causes the tasks to be done quickly and efficiently.
f. **Storage saving.** ie. the program is not allowed to be unnecessarily long.

Some of these aims are in conflict with others.

The costs of computer hardware have fallen, but the costs of paying programmers have risen. Add to this the fact that badly written programs will be unreliable, perhaps leading to costly errors, troublesome to maintain, hard to read and difficult to transfer to other computers. The need for good quality programming is higher than ever but there is also a need to keep costs down because people are reluctant to pay more for programs than they pay for hardware. Experience has shown that it pays to put greater effort into program design, and design effort will be used more economically if greater effort is concentrated in the early stages of programming. So try to meet aims (a) to (d) first and satisfy aims (e) and (f) later.

STAGES IN PROGRAMMING

8.9   In the process of producing the necessary instructions making up a program, the following stages can be recognised:-

a.   Understanding the problem.
b.   Planning the method of solution.
c.   Developing the methods by using suitable pseudocodes, flowcharts, tables etc.
d.   Transcribing the instructions into "machine-sensible" form.
f.   Testing the program components in turn and the program as a whole.
g.   Documenting all the work involved in producing the program.

If during testing the program an error is discovered then *it is important to go back to earlier stages* in order to correct the error. If the error comes from misunderstanding the problem it will probably be better to start again from the beginning. An outline of what happens at each programming stage now follows.

8.10   Understanding the problem. The programmer needs to know exactly what the program is required to do and normally works from a detailed "System Specification" which lays down the *inputs, processing* and *outputs* required. Examples will be given later.

8.11   Planning the method of solution. Depending upon the extent of the task, the program preparation may be shared amongst many programmers. Such cooperation requires an overall plan. Large programs may require each programmer to write a separate part of the program. These separate parts are often called modules or segments. The modules may be prepared and tested separately, then linked together to be tested as a whole.

8.12   Developing the method by using suitable pseudocode, flowcharts, tables, etc. Modern approaches to programming recognise the fact that complicated problems can be solved most easily if they are broken down into simpler more manageable tasks in a step by step fashion. At each step the problem is broken down further and consideration of details is put off as long as possible. This general approach is known as **Top Down Programming.** Details follow shortly along with details of how to use pseudocode etc.

8.13   Writing the instructions in a programming language. This may be regarded as the last step in top down programming. The instructions given in the pseudocode or flowchart are written as instructions in a programming language. There are different types of programming "languages" and details will be given in later chapters. At one time programs were written on special forms called "Coding Sheets" for subsequent input to the computer. These days the programmer normally types the program using a text editor of the kind discussed in chapter 4.

So, this combines the writing with the next step.

8.14   Transcribing instructions into "machine-sensible" form. Programs can be input to the computer in the same way as data. eg. via a VDU Keyboard.

8.15   Testing the program. Once written a program has to be subjected to various tests to check that it has been written and entered correctly, and does what it is supposed to do. These tests invariably reveal errors which have to be corrected. This can be quite a lengthy, and expensive process. Careful and thorough design in the early stages of programming will help to minimise these errors. The later an error is discovered the more expensive and troublesome it will be to get rid of.

8.16   Documentation. It is very important that the work of the programmer in producing a finished program is fully documented. This documentation will include a statement of the problem (System Specification), pseudocode, flowcharts (if used), tables, coding sheets (if used), test data and results, technical details, details and instruction for the user etc. Producing these documents should be done as part of each stage in programming and not as an afterthought. If this is done the documentation will aid the programmer in programming and good documentation will aid the maintenance of a program during its lifetime. Some programs have very long lives. For example some programs written during the 1960's are still in use today, although they may have been subjected to *regular maintenance* ie. modification or bringing up to date.

USING PSEUDOCODE

8.17   The examples given here show how to use pseudocode. Its use in programming follows shortly. A different typeface is used in the examples to make the pseudocode appear more like it would on the screen of a VDU or PC. Special words belonging to the pseudocode are in bold type. Other words are in plain type.

8.18   Opening a locked door. This is a simple **sequence** of instructions.

Note.   Even in this simple example certain assumptions have been made, eg. the door must be pushed open not pulled.

```
BEGIN
Put Key in Lock
Turn Key
Remove Key
Turn Handle and push door open
END
```

8.19 Addressing and stamping an envelope. A simple sequence with a **selection** in the middle.

```
BEGIN
Write Address on envelope
IF
     the letter is urgent
THEN
      stick first class stamp on envelope
ELSE
      stick second class stamp on envelope
ENDIF
fold letter
place letter in envelope
lick gum on envelope
seal envelope
END
```

8.20 Knocking a nail into a block of wood.
The opportunity is taken here to show two stages in a top-down process.

This uses: a hammer, a nail, a block of wood.
Step 1.

```
BEGIN
get the nail started
knock the nail right into the block
END
```

Step 2. The details are refined.

```
BEGIN
hold nail in position
hit nail with hammer
let go of nail
REPEAT
     hit nail with hammer
UNTIL
     the nail is completely in
END
```

Note.
i. The three steps "hold nail in position" "hit nail with hammer" and "let go of nail" are a refinement of "get the nail started".
ii. The repetition of "hit nail with hammer" until "the nail is completely in" is a

refinement of "knock the nail right into the block".

ii. The repetition in this example is just one form of repetition. Here we repeat "HIT THE NAIL" **UNTIL** we finish and HIT THE NAIL *at least once* after the "get the nail started" which we assume does not achieve "nail completely in". If the first hit could knock the nail completely in it would be better to express the repetition using "**WHILE**", as shown below.

Alternative Step 2. The details are refined.

```
BEGIN
hold nail in position
hit nail with hammer
let go of nail
WHILE
    the nail is not completely in
DO
    hit nail with hammer
ENDWHILE
END
```

PROGRAMMING METHODS

8.21 The sections which follow look at several practical methods used in programming. Don't be put off by their names, the methods themselves are simple.

There are three main areas to concentrate on:

a. **Data.** eg. types of data, data layout, restrictions on data etc.
b. **Processing method and their representation.** eg. by pseudocode.
c. **Top-down design.** eg. as introduced in paragraph 8.20.

DATA

8.22 The background information needed here has been covered in chapters 6 and 7.

Data must be given careful consideration in the early stages of programming as part of **understanding the problem.** Only once the input data, output data, and processing requirements of data are understood can a method of solving the problem by suitable procedures be worked out.

8.23 The following two specimen document figures 8.1 and 8.2 are used to illustrate several points about the data.

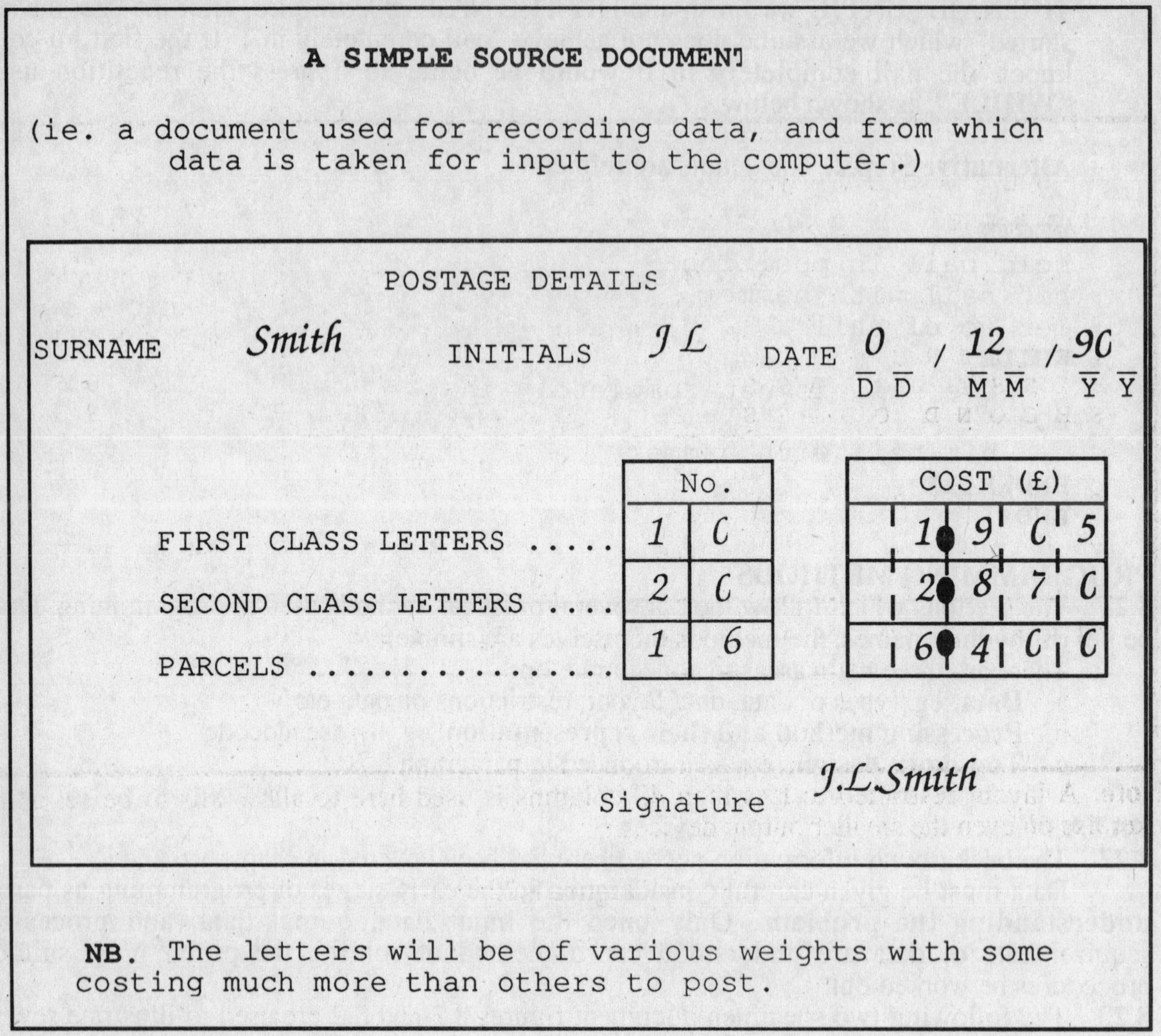

A SIMPLE SOURCE DOCUMENT

(ie. a document used for recording data, and from which
data is taken for input to the computer.)

POSTAGE DETAILS

SURNAME   *Smith*   INITIALS   *J L*   DATE $\frac{0}{\overline{D} \ \overline{D}}$ / $\frac{12}{\overline{M} \ \overline{M}}$ / $\frac{90}{\overline{Y} \ \overline{Y}}$

	No.		COST (£)			
FIRST CLASS LETTERS	1	0	1	9	0	5
SECOND CLASS LETTERS	2	0	2	8	7	0
PARCELS	1	6	6	4	0	0

Signature   *J.L Smith*

NB. The letters will be of various weights with some
costing much more than others to post.

Figure 8.1. A source document

```
                P O S T A G E    D E T A I L S
    D E T A I L S   F O R   J L    S M I T H
    D A T E       0 6 / 1 2 / 8 2

                    N U M B E R      C O S T    :   A V E R A G E
                        O F                     :      C O S T
                    I T E M S   ( P O U N D S ) :    ( P E N C E )
    L E T T E R S
    F I R S T      C L A S S    10       1 . 9 0 5  :    1 9 . 0 5
    S E C O N D  C L A S S      20       2 . 8 7 0  :    1 4 . 3 5
                                ─ ─ ─ ─ ─ ─ ─ ─ ─
              T O T A L         30       4 . 7 5 5  :    1 5 . 8 5
    P A R C E L S                                   :
                                                    :
                                16       6 . 4 0 0  :    4 0 . 0 0
    ─ ─ ─ ─ ─ ─ ─ ─ ─ ─ ─ ─ ─ ─ ─ ─ ─ ─ ─         :
    G R A N D   T O T A L       46      1 1 . 1 5 5  :   2 4 . 2 5
    ─ ─ ─ ─ ─ ─ ─ ─ ─ ─ ─ ─ ─ ─ ─ ─ ─ ─ ─         :
                                                    :
```

Note. A layout restricted to less than 40 columns is used here to allow this to be set as an exercise on even the smaller output devices.

Figure 8.2.

8.24 Identifying data items and data types. From figure 8.1 we can identify these features of the input data.

Data Item	Data Type
Surname ⎯⎯⎯ Initials {	Alphabetic characters or alphanumeric(6.9) to allow for commas, full stops, hyphens and spaces.
Date	May be treated as a single 6 digit integer numeric, (6.10) or possibly as three 2 digit integer numeric data items: day number, month number and year number.
Number of First Class Letters	2 digit Integer numeric (6.10)
Number of Second Class Letters	2 digit Integer numeric (6.10)
Number of Parcels	2 digit Integer numeric (6.10)
Cost of First Class Letters	5 digit Real numeric (6.10)
Cost of Second Class Letters	5 digit Real numeric (6.10)
Cost of Parcels	5 digit Real numeric (6.10)

A similar exercise may be performed for figure 8.2. Some data items are common to figure 8.1 and figure 8.2 whilst others only occur in figure 8.2.

8.25 Processing requirements. There is sufficient detail in figure 8.1 and figure 8.2 for us to recognise the way in which the output data is obtained from the input data. In more complicated problems this will not be the case and the System Specification should provide the necessary information.

8.26 Input format. Figure 8.1 is a "source document" from which data may be taken and *transcribed* (ie. copied across) onto an input medium eg. magnetic tape. Alternatively the data may be entered directly via a VDU or PC. This is by far the most common method today and is illustrated in figure 8.3.

```
                    VDU OR PC INPUT

   SURNAME       = ?  SMITH

   INITIALS      = ?  J.L.


   DATE (DDMMYY)   = ?  061282

   FIRST CLASS LETTERS

                        NUMBER    = ? 10
                        COST      = ? 1.905


   SECOND CLASS LETTERS

                        NUMBER    = ? 20
                        COST      = ? 2.87


   PARCELS

                        NUMBER    = ? 16
                        COST      = ? 6.4
```

NB.
Bold type indicates the prompt displayed by the computer.
Normal type indicates data input by the VDU user.

Figure 8.3.

8.27 Output format. Figure 8.2 showed a specimen output document. The system specification and program documentation would normally include the design for the output (see Fig. 8.4). In figure 8.4 the programmer has designed the output for figure 8.2. Underlined items will be printed as shown. X's show the positions of alphanumeric characters and 9's show the positions of numeric characters.

8.28 Restrictions on data. The programmer must deal with any restrictions on the data. For example it may well be desirable to ensure that a date is not accepted if it has a month number greater than 12 or a day number greater than 31. Such checks performed on input data are called **validation checks.** The provision of validation checks is another job for the programmer. Validation checks will be dealt with in more detail later in this book.

PRINT LAYOUT CHART

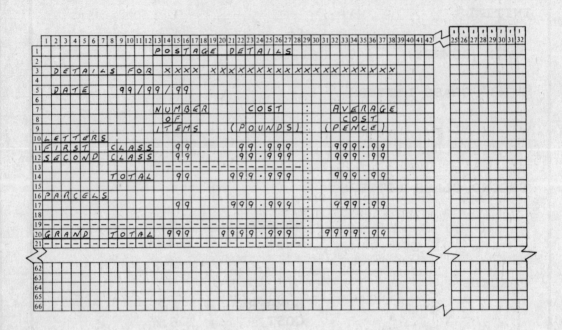

Figure 8.4. A print Layout chart.

8.29 Operations on Data. Operations on data will be dealt with in detail in chapter 9. For the time being we need to recognise the fact that operations are related to data types. For example the operations add, subtract, multiply and divide commonly refer to numeric data ie. they are arithmetic operations. We usually signify the operation to be performed by special symbols called **operators** eg. the most common arithmetic operators are +, −, × and ÷. Some alternative operator symbols are frequently used in computer languages as we shall see later.

There are other operators which are commonly used in programming including those called **relational logic operators** given here.

OPERATOR	MEANING
=	equal to
≠ or < >	not equal
<	less than
>	greater than
≤ or < =	less than or equal to
≥ or > =	greater than or equal to

Figure 8.5. Operators and their meanings.

For example, is $2 \times 5 < 3 \times 4$? Answer YES ie. 10 is less than 12.

8.30 Identifiers, Constants and Variables. When handling data we often find it convenient to associate names or letters with data values, eg. letting N stand for the Number to be stored. In such a case N is called an **identifier** ie. a name or letter by which a data value can be identified. An identifier is a **"constant"** if it is always associated with the same data value and it is a **"variable"** if its associated data value is allowed to vary or change.

8.31 Literals. When referring to letters or names we must be careful to specify whether we mean them to be taken *literally* or to be treated as identifiers. When names or letters are used literally we call them **literals,** and we enable them to be distinguished from identifiers by placing them within quotation marks. So the instruction PRINT "N" means print the letter N, and the instruction PRINT N means print the value associated with N. Numeric values need not be written within quotation marks, however, since we always take numeric values literally eg. 15 means "15".

TOWARDS STRUCTURED PROGRAMMING

8.32 The section which follows this one deals with a technique called structured programming. At first sight it may appear that the word "structured" placed in front of the word "programming" means something harder or more complicated than just "programming". This is the exact opposite of what is really the case. If you compare structured programming to building a house, say, then just programming ie. unstructured programming is like building the house and drawing the plans at the same time. Here is a slightly longer explanation about the ideas behind structured programming.

8.33 Which of these two cases would you say was preferable?

    a. Building a house from scratch to your own design and designing and making your own bricks, window frames, doors etc.

    b. Using standard ready made bricks, window frames, doors etc. in a standard design method.

You did pick (b) didn't you? We could rule (a) out because it is lengthy, troublesome, probably involves trial and error and stands a very good chance of resulting in a strange or badly built job.

8.34 There are also some more general points which might lie behind our choice of (b) rather than (a). Here they are:

i.   If a job can be done well by using what is already available and known to be well tried and tested than trying out something new for the sake of it is a waste of effort. Also what is produced will be untried and may have some, as yet hidden faults.

ii. It is easier to develop skills and produce better quality work if the materials used conform to some pattern or standard. eg. using bricks of standard sizes leads to better bricklaying.

iii. Standard materials and methods are more easily dealt with by others. If a house built by method (a) needs repair or alteration who will be able to do it? It is no surprise then, that the idea of using standard methods and materials or components has found widespread favour. Apart from our building example there are other examples to be found in a variety of places eg. standard components in cars, and electrical goods. Standard sizes of paper, envelopes etc. The list seems endless. This same idea when applied to program design is called **structured programming.** The details now follow.

STRUCTURED PROGRAMMING

8.35 The term "**structured programming**" was first used by Professor E. Dijkstra in the mid 1960's. The methods were tried out by computer manufacturers such as IBM in the late sixties with considerable success and have now been widely adopted in the computer industry. Sadly, some unstructured and even trial and error methods of programming are still to be found. Such methods may be the result of outdated knowledge or the non awareness of the amateur.

8.36 The basic theory behind structured programming was established in two Italian Computer Scientists, C Bohm and G Jacopini, in 1966. This theory is of no concern to us except that Bohm and Jacopini provided a result which proves to be very useful. It is quite simply this: "The pseudocode for any program can be built from a combination of just the following three basic pseudocode forms , the **sequence (BEGIN...END),** the **selection (IF...THEN... ELSE...ENDIF),** and the **repetition (WHILE...DO...ENDWHILE) .**" The same rule can be expressed in terms of flowcharts as: "The flowchart for any program procedure can be built from a combination of just the following three basic kinds of flowchart. (Fig. 8.6)."

Please see appendix 3 for an explanation of flowchart symbols.

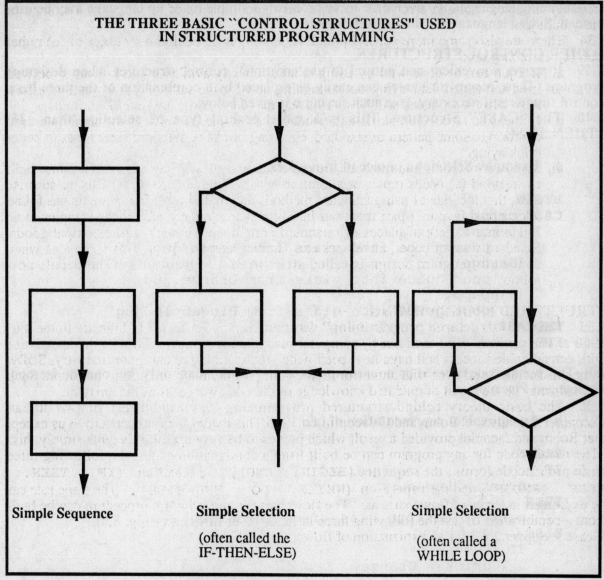

Figure 8.6. Control Structures.

8.37 The three basic kinds of **"control structures"** shown in figure 8.6 are easy to use because:-

    a. They are easy to recognise when looking for solutions to programming problems.

    b. They are simple to deal with because they have just one entry point and just one exit point.

    c. They are free of the complications of any particular programming language.

8.38 Pseudocode. Although flowcharts tend to be easy to follow they are not such a natural way of expressing procedures as writing instructions in English nor are they similar to programming languages. To overcome these problems a simple made up language may be used instead. Such a language is called a **pseudocode**.

OTHER CONTROL STRUCTURES

8.39 It proves convenient and natural to use additional control structures when designing programs. These control structures can easily be replaced by a combination of the three basic control structures if necessary. One such structure is given below.

8.40 The "CASE" Structure. This is a more general type of selection than **IF ..THEN..ELSE.**

a. **Example:** Selecting a choice of fruit juices.

```
BEGIN
CASE drink
    (Lemon)
        pour juice into glass from Lemon jug
    (Orange)
        pour juice into glass from Orange jug
    (Pineapple)
        pour juice into glass from Pineapple jug
ENDCASE
END
```

NB. This pseudocode is based on an assumption that "drink" can only be one of Lemon, Orange and Pineapple

b. **An equivalent representation of (a).**

```
BEGIN
IF
    drink = Lemon
THEN
    pour juice into glass from Lemon jug
ELSE
    IF
        drink = Orange
    THEN
        pour juice into glass from Orange jug
    ELSE
        pour juice into glass from Pineapple jug
    ENDIF
ENDIF
END
```

8.41 Checking that all cases have been considered. When dealing with problems where there are a number of possible alternative actions it can help to work out all the possible alternatives before writing pseudocode or drawing flowcharts. For example, at an early stage in preparing figure 8.8 the following layout could be sketched out.

a. A simple "Decision Tree".

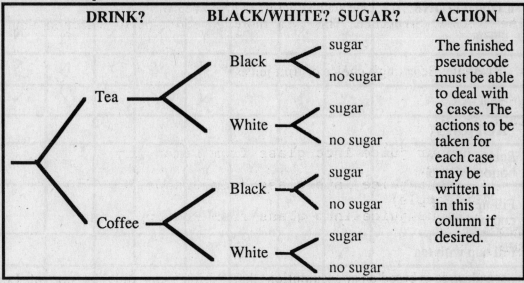

Figure 8.7.

b. **A simple "Decision Table".**

Y means Yes   N means No

CONDITIONS	Here are the 8 cases (N against TEA means COFFEE) (N against BLACK means WHITE)							
TEA	Y	Y	Y	Y	N	N	N	N
BLACK	Y	Y	N	N	Y	Y	N	N
SUGAR	Y	N	Y	N	Y	N	Y	N
ACTIONS								
Pour milk into bottom of cup			√	√				
Fill up rest of cup with tea			√	√				
Fill cup with tea	√	√						
Pour normal amount of coffee into cup							√	√
Top up cup with milk							√	√
Fill cup with coffee					√	√		
Add sugar	√		√		√		√	
Stir cup	√		√	√	√		√	√

Figure 8.8

The decision table and decision tree have been included because of their possible practical value to the reader. Questions on these methods would not be expected in examinations at this level.

8.42   In concluding this section the general picture can be presented in figure 8.24 which follows on the next page.

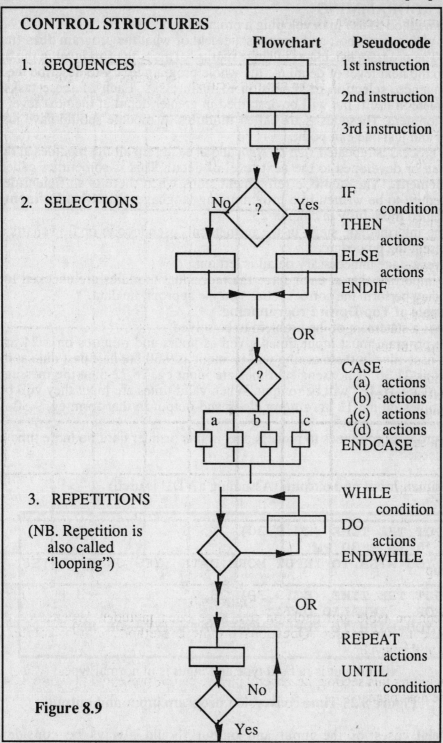

Figure 8.9

TOP-DOWN PROGRAMMING
8.43 Here is a method to use in developing a program procedure.

a. Start with a very short and simple statement of what the program **does** (not its name) eg. "The program calculates average marks." This is the **top level** in the design.

b. Go to the next level of detail for the whole program ie. try to describe the program as a sequence, selection or repetition of main tasks. Each of these tasks should be complete in itself but will be described in greater detail at the next level of program development. These tasks are called **modules.** A module should have just one entry point and just one exit point.

c. This process is repeated *step by step,* and at each step all the modules at that level are *refined* or developed to the next level of detail. This is sometimes called **stepwise refinement.** The stepwise refinement stops when there is sufficient detail for the procedure to be written in a programming language. **Stepwise Refinement** will be explained more fully in chapter 23.

d. At the intermediate steps in the refinement, pseudocode or flowcharts are used to represent the procedure.

e. At every stage unnecessary detail is left out.

f. It is important that at each stage the individual modules are checked to make sure that they perform the correct actions on the appropriate data.

8.44 An example of Top-Down Programming.

a. Here is a statement of the problem to be solved:-
"The program must input times given as hours and minutes on a 24 hr. clock. eg. Half past nine in the morning will be input as 9.30 but half past nine at night will be input as 21.30. If nonsensical times are input eg. 28.72 then the message "ERROR INVALID TIME" will be output. When valid times are input they will be converted into times on the 12 hr. am/pm clock and output in that form eg. 9.30 AM or 9.30 PM.
The program continues to process data in this manner until no more time conversions are needed".

b. **Specimen input and output.** (Assuming a VDU is used).

```
INPUT THE TIME (EG.9,30) 21,30
21,30 IS 9:30 PM
DO YOU WISH TO INPUT MORE DATA (YES OR NO)? YES

INPUT THE TIME (EG.9,30) 28,72
ERROR - INVALID DATA
DO YOU WISH TO INPUT MORE DATA (YES OR NO)?
```

NB. Output is in bold type and input is in normal type.

Figure 8.25 Time conversion program input and output.

c. **Special cases** of the input and output should always be considered by the programmer, but should really be given to the programmer as part of the problem specification. We may note here that 00.00 hours is 12 midnight (neither am nor pm) and 12.00 hrs. is 12 noon (neither am or pm.)

SOLUTION

8.45   Step 1. (See paragraph 8.43a).

A Program to **process time details. All steps are written in pseudocode**

```
BEGIN
Process time details
END
```

8.46   Step 2.

Now we **refine** "PROCESS TIME DETAILS" which is clearly a **repetition** of "PROCESS A TIME DETAIL". What sort of repetition? Well from the problem and specimen output it is apparent that *at least one* time detail is processed and the processing is repeated *until* there is no more data, we therefore use **REPEAT..UNTIL**:

```
BEGIN
REPEAT
     Process a time detail
UNTIL
     No more data
END
```

8.47   Step 3.

"PROCESS A TIME DETAIL" must now be refined further. There appears to be a sequence of actions on each time detail namely "INPUT THE TIME DETAIL", "CHECK THE TIME DETAIL", "DEAL WITH TIME DETAIL". There is a temptation to go into more detail about "DEAL WITH TIME DETAIL" because we can see that there is an exception in the case of nonsensical data. The temptation should be resisted (paragraph 8.43e).

```
BEGIN
REPEAT
     Input time detail
     Check time detail
     Deal with time detail
UNTIL
     No more data
END
```

8.48   Step 4.

a.   At this stage the data must be given closer attention eg. What is a "time detail?" It is appropriate to introduce some identifiers (8.30) ie. names for our data items. From the information given in the problem and specimen input/output we see that hour details and minute details need to be handled separately and that there are hour details both for the 24 hr. clock and the 12 hr. clock. These three identifiers (data names) can be used:

hours-in, hours-out, minutes

(all three are integers)

Always use data names which have reasonably clear meaning. Hyphenated names often prove useful. Unfortunately you may be forced to use short data names when writing in some programming languages eg, in the language BASIC you might use the names H1, H2, and M for this problem.

b. Refinement of INPUT TIME DETAILS
This *must* be refined as far as dealing with the individual data items. Treatment of finer detail *can* be postponed.

```
input hours-in
input minutes
```

c. Refinement of CHECK TIME DETAILS
This refinement highlights several practical points as follows:
i. In following the basic method laid down in paragraph 8.43 we have separated "CHECK TIME DETAIL" and "DEAL WITH TIME DETAIL". When we consider "DEAL WITH TIME DETAIL" we will need to consider the case of valid and invalid data. We might decide therefore to deal with "CHECK TIME DETAIL" and "DEAL WITH TIME DETAIL" as one big module. Such a decision is usually a mistake because it leads to more complicated and less manageable procedures. The answer is a simple one. We make "CHECK TIME DETAIL" produce information about the validity of the time details so that "DEAL WITH TIME DETAIL" can use the information when it needs it.
ii. We introduce another data item into "CHECK TIME DETAIL" and call this data item "VALID-TIME". This data item will be allowed to have just two possible values such that:
When the time detail is valid VALID-TIME will be given the value 1.
When the time detail is invalid VALID-TIME will be given the value 0.
iii. We should ensure that "CHECK TIME DETAIL" has one entry point and one exit point (paragraph 8.43b) and the VALID-TIME has the appropriate value (1 or 0) at the exit point.

Note.

i. Data items used in the way VALID-TIME is are called **Flags** or **Switches**.
ii. The symbol combination := is called an **assignment operator**. For example, "valid-time := 1" means assign (ie. give) valid-time the value 1. Similarly, "Total := Total + 1" would mean replace the value associated with "Total" by its current value + 1.

100

```
IF
    hours-in > 23
    OR
    minutes > 59
THEN
    valid-time := 0
ELSE
    valid-time := 1
ENDIF
```

d. Refinement of "DEAL WITH TIME DETAIL".
   In this module we may recognise a selection between actions for valid and invalid times as follows:

```
IF
    valid-time = 0
THEN
    output error message
ELSE
    produce output information
ENDIF
```

That completes Step 4.

8.49 Step 5. "INPUT TIME DETAIL" is simpler than "CHECK TIME DETAIL" and "DEAL WITH TIME DETAIL" so we delay its refinement and concentrate on the other two at this stage.

a. Continuing from paragraph 8.47b we can split the selection question into two simple YES/No questions thus:

```
IF
    hours-in > 23
THEN
    valid-time := 0
ELSE    IF
            minute > 59
        THEN
            valid-time := 0
        ELSE
            valid-time := 1
        ENDIF
ENDIF
```

b. Continuing from paragraph 8.48c. "PRODUCE OUTPUT INFORMATION" can be refined further. First refer to paragraphs 8.44b and 8.44c to remind yourself of the details of the specified problem. First consider the various cases to be dealt with. They are tabulated here:

101

INPUT	OUTPUT	COMMENTS
00,00	12:00 MIDNIGHT	Special Case
00,01 to 00,59	12:01 am to 12:59 am	12 added to hours - in giving hours - out $\Big\}$ am
01,01 to 11,59	01:01 am to 11:59 am	
12,00	12:00 NOON	Special case
12,01 to 12,59	12:01 pm to 12:59 pm	
13,01 to 23,59	01:01 pm to 11:59 pm	12 subtracted from hours - in giving hours - out $\Big\}$ pm

Note that each output ends with "AM", "PM", "MIDNIGHT", or "NOON". The data name(identifier) "time-name" will be used for these.

```
IF
     hours-in = 0
     AND
     minutes = 0
THEN
     hours-out := 12
     time-name := "MIDNIGHT"
ELSE IF
     hours-in = 0
     AND
     minutes > 0
THEN
     hours-out := 12
     time-name := "am"
ELSE IF
     hours-in > 0
     AND
     hours-in < 12
THEN
     hours-out := hours-in
     time-name := "am"
ELSE IF
     hours-in = 12
```

```
    AND
    minutes = 0
THEN
    hours-out := 12
    time-name := "NOON"
ELSE IF
    hours-in = 12
    AND
    minutes > 0
THEN
    hours-out := 12
    time-name := "pm"
ELSE
    hours-out := hours-in - 12
    time-name := "pm"
ENDIF ENDIF ENDIF ENDIF ENDIF
PRINT hours-out, ":", minutes, time-name
```

8.50 This stage could be refined further but the example has been taken far enough to illustrate the method. Details of the later stages in programming will be introduced in the chapters which follow. Before we leave this example just look at a copy of the whole program **which is highly reduced in size so as to fit onto one page and thereby highlight its complexity** (figure 8.24). You are not mean to try and read it, although you should be able to recognise the structures within it. It shows how the step by step approach has turned a large unmanageable problem into a set of small manageable problems.

```
BEGIN
REPEAT
    input hours-in
    input minutes
    IF
        hours-in > 23
    THEN
        valid-time := 0
    ELSE    IF
                minute > 59
            THEN
                valid-time := 0
            ELSE
                valid-time := 1
            ENDIF
    ENDIF
    IF
        valid-time = 0
    THEN
        output error message
    ELSE
        IF
            hours-in = 0
            AND
            minutes = 0
        THEN
            hours-out := 12
            time-name := "MIDNIGHT"
        ELSE IF
            hours-in = 0
            AND
            minutes > 0
        THEN
            hours-out := 12
            time-name := "am"
        ELSE IF
            hours-in > 0
            AND
            hours-in < 12
        THEN
            hours-out := hours-in
            time-name := "am"
        ELSE IF
            hours-in = 12
            AND
            minutes = 0
        THEN
            hours-out := 12
            time-name := "NOON"
        ELSE IF
            hours-in = 12
            AND
            minutes > 0
        THEN
            hours-out := 12
            time-name := "pm"
        ELSE
            hours-out := hours-in - 12
            time-name := "pm"
        ENDIF ENDIF ENDIF ENDIF ENDIF
        PRINT hours-out, ":", minutes, time-name
    ENDIF
UNTIL
    no more data
END
```

Figure 8.25. The program as a whole intentionally reduced in size(8.50).

SUMMARY

8.51 a. **Flowcharts** and **Pseudocode** were introduced together with the methods of using them.

b. The general aims in programming were introduced:-
Reliability, Maintainability, Portability, Readability, Performance and storage saving, of which the first four are normally the primary aims.
The stages in programming were introduced and explained:
i.   Understanding the problem.
ii. Planning the method of solution.
iii. Developing a method using eg. flowcharts or pseudocode.
iv. Writing the instructions in a programming language.
v.   Transcribing the instructions into "machine-sensible" form.
vi. Testing the program and **returning to earlier stages in programming when errors are discovered.**
vii. Documenting all the work involved in producing the program.

d. The ideas behind **Structured Programming** were introduced.

e. A method of **top down programming** was explained by examples.

POINTS TO NOTE

8.52 a. Good programs only come from good program design and good program design only comes from giving sufficient thought and effort in the early stages in programming.

b. The programmer cannot solve a programming problem satisfactorily if the problem has not been properly staged.

c. Further examples of flowcharts and pseudocode will be found in many of the following chapters.

d. Top down programming by stepwise refinement will be explained more fully in chapter 23.

QUESTIONS A *(With answers)*

1. *Consider each of the following and state whether it is true or false.*

   a. $3 < 7$

   b. $8 \times 5 = 5 \times 2 \times 4$

   c. $5 \times 7 > 4 \times 9$

   d. $5 \times 4 \geq 11 \times 3$

   e. $8 \times 9 \leq 12 \times 6$

   f. $6 \times 4 <> 2 \times 12$

2. *List the stages in programming.*

3. *What is the difference between a REPEAT loop and a WHILE loop?*

4. *Write pseudocode which gives the steps in making a cheese sandwich. Assume that butter, a knife, slices of cheese and bread etc. are all available and ready for use.*

5. *Write pseudocode which gives the steps in making one sandwich where the person eating is given a choice between having a cheese sandwich or a ham sandwich. Again assume that all things required to do the job are available and ready for use.*

6. Write pseudocode which gives the steps in cutting a whole loaf of bread into slices, given that the bread, a bread knife and a bread board are available and ready for use.

7. A group of students run a small refreshment stall in break times and lunchtimes in order to raise money for a students' club. They sell such things as biscuits, soft drinks, sweets etc. Each Friday they work out how much money they have made that week and also work out what items to purchase over the weekend ready for the next week. What data will they need to record and use and what activities will need to be carried out with the data?

   NB. You are not required to work out detailed procedures in the form of pseudocode.

8. Consider each of the following and state whether it is true or false.
   a. $4 \times 6 \leq 3 \times 8$ b. $-5 > 3$
   c. $6^2 <> 9 \times 4$ d. $16_8 + 13_8 < 29_{10}$

9. Distinguish between constants and variables.

10. Bohm and Jacopini proved that any program procedure can be built from a combination of just three flowchart structures. What are they? What are their forms in pseudocode?

11. Here are six sets of data:
    a. $A = 7, B = 5, C = 1$ b. $A = 8, B = 2, C = 4$
    c. $A = 2, B = 9, C = 5$ d. $A = 4, B = 8, C = 2$
    e. $A = 6, B = 3, C = 9$ f. $A = 1, B = 4, C = 6$

    Use each set of data with the following pseudocode and state the output in each case.

    What does this procedure do?

    What happens if all the numbers are the same (ie. $A = B = C$)?

```
BEGIN
IF
    A > B
THEN
    IF
        A > C
    THEN
        PRINT A
    ELSE
        PRINT C
    ENDIF
ELSE
    IF
        B > C
    THEN
        PRINT B
    ELSE
        PRINT C
    ENDIF
ENDIF
END
```

12. Produce the output generated by the following pseudocode. What is the value of POWER at the end of the program and how is it related to the final output?

```
BEGIN
    Power := 0
    Number := 1
    WHILE
        Power < 10
    DO
        Number := Number * 2
        Power := Power + 1
        PRINT Number
    ENDWHILE
END
```

13. This pseudocode should find the smallest value of 2^P which is greater than 5000 and then print P and 2^P. Fill in the missing details where you see "?????".

```
BEGIN
    ?????  .........  (a) P := 0     or P := 1
    Number := 1
    REPEAT
        Number := Number * 2
        P   := P + 1
    UNTIL
        ?????  ........(b) Number > 5000   or   Number < 5000
    PRINT   ?????  (c)
    PRINT   ?????   (d)
END
```

14. Produce pseudocode for a procedure which will input an examination mark as a percentage and output a corresponding result according to the following table.

Examination Mark (%)	Result
60 - 100	Credit
40 -	Pass
0 -	Fail

How many items of test data are needed to test all cases?
Suggest suitable values for such items.

15. In this question there is a set of examination marks. Each mark must be processed in the way described in question 14. The set of marks is terminated by the rogue value 999. Produce pseudocode for this procedure. Give test data and the the corresponding results.

QUESTIONS B *(Without answers)*

1. Why is program documentation necessary? List the documents to be included in documentation.

2. Given that there is available a loaf of bread, sufficient slices of ham and cheese, sufficient butter and a breadboard, breadknife and ordinary knife plus a plate etc. produce a pseudocode for the following procedure.

Sandwiches are to be made from a whole loaf of bread. The whole loaf is to be cut into slices first. Then slices are taken in pairs and sandwiches are made from each pair of slices. Before each sandwich is made a request is input for "ham" or "cheese". As the sandwiches are made they are to be placed on a plate. (ie. one plate for all the sandwiches).

Note: Since pairs of slices are needed for sandwiches an odd slice may be left over.

3.   Produce pseudocode for a procedure which inputs three numbers and which then:

    a. Determines the number which is the middle one in order of magnitude (ie, neither the largest nor the smallest) and prints it.
    b. Finds the average and prints it.
    c. Compares the number found in (a) with the number found in (b) and prints either "AVERAGE IS LARGER" or "AVERAGE IS SMALLER" as appropriate.

4.   Here is a slow but simple method of converting numbers from decimal to octal. In this example the method is limited to converting numbers less than 64_{10} but could be extended.

METHOD
Subtract 8 from the decimal number repeatedly, counting how many times you do it, until the number left is less than 8. The octal equivalent of the decimal number you started with will be a 2 digit octal number whose first digit is the number of subtractions made and whose second digit is the number left when subtraction stops.

Example:- Converting 29_{10} to Octal

```
 29
 -8..........1st  subtraction
 21
 -8..........2nd  subtraction
 13
 -8..........3rd  subtraction
  5                     Thus 29₁₀ = 35₈
```

Thus $29_{10} = 35_8$

Present this method in the form of pseudocode.

9 Data Structures and Files

INTRODUCTION

9.1 When individual data items are arranged or organised together as one unit we call such an organised collection of data a **data structure**. This chapter looks at some common data structures notably **arrays** and **files**, but starts with some methods which apply to individual data items and to data structures.

9.2 The previous chapter drew attention to the fact that many programming problems involve the *repetition* of the same action many times *while* or *until* some condition is met. Such repetitions frequently require the data being processed to be organised into a suitable sequence ready for processing. Some organised sequences of data have special names and they will be dealt with later in this chapter. First, by way of simple introduction, this chapter considers repetitive processing of sequences of individual data items.

9.3 In the following example numbers are input and added to a total one at a time until all the numbers have been input. The end of the sequence of numbers is signified by the input of the number 999. The number 999 is NOT one of the numbers to be added to the total. A value used in this way is called a *sentinel* or *rogue value*. The sentinel value 999 would not be suitable in practice if it could be one of the number to be added together. For the sake of simplicity, it is assumed here that *999 is outside the range of normal values to be input*.

9.4 Example. Assume a set of examination marks is to be input and totalled. A simple program which carries out this task is shown in the following pseudocode (Fig. 9.1).

```
Step 1 (outline)          Step 2 (refined)
BEGIN                     BEGIN
set up                    total := 0
                          sentinel := 999
                          INPUT mark

WHILE                     WHILE
    mark <> sentinel          mark <> sentinel
DO                        DO
    add mark to total     total := total + mark
    get next mark         INPUT mark
ENDWHILE                  ENDWHILE
PRINT total               PRINT total
END                       END
```

Figure 9.1

9.5 Counting. Very often when performing repetitions it is necessary to count the number of times a particular process is repeated. For example in the problem just given it might be desirable to know the number of marks input and the average mark. In this, and other examples, care must be taken to count at the right time eg, the sentinel must *not* be counted. Remember too, that we must watch out for special cases (8.44c). *The average mark is the total of the marks divided* by the number of marks making the total. **When performing divisions by computer always watch out for cases of division by zero.** (Division by zero gives an infinite or undefined result.) To avoid the problem in this example (Fig 9.2) when no marks are input, ie. if the first number input is 999, the program stops indicating "no data".

```
BEGIN
     total := 0
     count := 0
     sentinel := 999
  INPUT mark
     IF
        mark = sentinel
     THEN
        PRINT "NO DATA"
     ELSE
        WHILE
           mark <> sentinel
        DO
           count := count + 1
           total := total + mark
           INPUT mark
        ENDWHILE
        average := total/count
        PRINT count, total, average
     ENDIF
  PRINT total
END
```

                                    Figure 9.2.

9.6   Counting fixed number of repetitions.

In many programming problems the number of repetitions to be performed is known in advance. In such cases the following method may be used. In figure 9.3) the number of marks is input at the beginning and then the marks are counted as they are entered until the required number has been input.

9.7   In the example just given (Fig 9.2) the set of marks was processed satisfactorily by dealing with them in turn one at a time. In many problems, however, it is necessary to keep all the data together and then refer to individual data items. A common example of this is the use of **arrays**.

ARRAYS (OR TABLES)

9.8   In many situations, sets of data items, such as the set of examination marks for a class, may be conveniently arranged into a sequence and referred to by a single identifier eg.

MARKS = (56 42 89 65 48)

Such an *arrangement* is a data structure called an ARRAY.

An array in a single sequence like this may also be called a LIST

111

```
            BEGIN
                total := 0
                count := 0
                sentinel := 999
            INPUT mark
                IF
                    mark = sentinel
                THEN
                    PRINT "NO DATA"
                ELSE
                    WHILE
                        mark <> sentinel
                    DO
                        count := count + 1
                        total := total + mark
                        INPUT mark
                    ENDWHILE
                    average := total/count
                    PRINT count, total, average
                ENDIF
            PRINT total
            END
```

Figure 9.3.

9.9   Individual data items in the array may be referred to separately by stating their position in the array. Thus MARKS (1) refers to 56, MARKS (2) refers to 42, MARKS (3) refers to 89, and so on. The position numbers given in parentheses are called subscripts. Variables may be used as subscripts eg. MARKS (N), so when N = 2 we are referring to MARKS (2) ie. 42 and when N = 4 we are referring to MARKS (4) ie. 65

9.10   Array Input. Before an array can be processed in any way it must have data input to it. In this example (Fig 9.4) an array of marks, "MARKS" is filled with data. The number of items in the array "NUM" is input first. The subscript indicating the position number in MARKS is called "POSN".

Note that in figure 9.3 the count took place *after* each input here (Fig 9.4) the count is *ahead* of each input.

```
            BEGIN
            INPUT num
            posn := 1
            REPEAT
                INPUT MARKS(POSN)
                posn := posn + 1
            UNTIL posn > num
            process array
            etc...
```

Figure 9.4.

9.11 FOR...TO..ENDFOR. The example just given used a common type of repetition in which a procedure is repeated from an initial value (posn = 1) with "posn" being increased in steps until a final value "num" is reached. This is so common that it pays to use a pseudocode abbreviation for it as illustrated by the following example (Fig 9.5).

(Using REPEAT..UNTIL)	(Equivalent using FOR..TO..ENDFOR)
BEGIN	BEGIN
posn := 1	FOR posn 1 **TO** num
REPEAT	process
process	ENDFOR
posn := posn + 1 etc.	etc...
UNTIL posn > num	
etc...	

Figure 9.5.

FURTHER ARRAY HANDLING

9.12 In the following example (Fig 9.7) individual examination marks are placed into an array one at a time *to be used later*. As the data is input a cumulative total "Tot" is produced from which the average mark "Aver" is calculated at the end. The highest mark "Large", lowest mark "Small" and number of marks greater than the pass mark of 45 "Npass" are also found. Marks are percentages.

SUCCESSIVE VALUES

Num	Tot	Npass	Large	Small	Posn	Marks(1)	Marks(2)	Marks(3)	Marks(4)	Marks(5)
5	0	0	0	100	1	56				
	56	1	56	56	2		42			
	98	1	89	42	3			89		
	187	2			4				65	
	252	3			5					48
	300	4			6					

Figure 9.6.

To use this table (Fig. 9.6) follow the pseudocode (Fig 9.7) and tick values in the table as you come to them. This method can be used to test the pseudocode is correct.

9.13 Array Elements. The individual data items in an array are often called its **elements.** Strictly speaking however, a data item *occupies* an element, ie. elements rather like pigeonholes, are regarded as locations into which data items may be placed and removed.

9.14 In paragraph 9.12 it stated that data was to be placed into the MARKS array *to be used later*. One possible later use would be to go back and look at the data in the array in order to find the number of marks above the average. The important points to note here are that this could not be done as the marks were input because at that stage the average was not known, and the data must be held in the array so that it can be used again later.

```
                    BEGIN
                    Input Num
                    IF
                         Num < 1
                    THEN
                         PRINT
                         "No Data"
                    ELSE
                         TOT    := 0
                         Npass := 0
                         Large := 0
                         Small := 100
                         FOR Posn 1 TO Num
                              INPUT Marks(Posn)
                              Tot := Tot + Marks(Posn)
                              IF
                                   Marks(Posn) > 45
                              THEN
                                   Npass := Npass + 1
                              ENDIF
                              IF
                                   Marks(Posn) > Large
                              THEN
                                   Large :=  Marks(Posn)
                              ENDIF
                              IF
                                   Marks(Posn) < Small
                              THEN
                                   Small := Marks(Posn)
                              ENDIF
                         ENDFOR
                         Aver := Tot/Num
                         PRINT Aver, Large, Small, Npass
                    ENDIF
                    END
```

Figure 9.7.

9.15   Two dimensional arrays or tables have elements arranged into rows and columns and are used for a variety of data tables. For example the examination marks of a class for several subjects could be placed in a two dimensional array as shown in figure 9.8.

Pupil or Row Number	English Column 1	Maths Column 2	This table can be represented in an array called
1	A(1,1) = 56	A(1,2) = 44	56 44
2	A(2,1) = 42	A(2,2) = 36	42 36
3	A(3,1) = 89	A(3,2) = 73	A = 89 73
4	A(4,1) = 65	A(4,2) = 86	65 86
5	A(5,1) = 48	A(5,2) = 51	48 51

Figure 9.8.

Individual elements can be specified by two subscripts used like a map reference **Row** 1st, **Column** 2nd. (To remember this order think of **R**hubarb and **Custard**) eg. A(3, 1) = 89, A(4,2) = 86. Again subscripts may be variable, as for a one dimensional array, so for A(Rpos, Cpos) if Rpos = 3 and Cpos = 2 we are referring to A(3, 2) = 73.

9.16   2D Array handling (Table Handling).

In this example(Fig 9.9) the data is entered row by row. This pseudocode has two "loops" ie. *steps are repeated until* each row is read, and *steps are repeated until* each column is read. A loop within a loop is called a "**nested loop**". Follow the pseudocode filling in array A as you go through it.

SORTING A ONE DIMENSIONAL ARRAY

9.17   There are many situations in which data items need to be arranged into sequence eg. alphabetic order or numerical order. The order may be ascending or descending as required eg.

    a.   3, 6, 15, 20, 46. (Five same numbers in descending order).

    b.   46, 20, 15, 6, 3. (The same numbers in descending order).

    c.   Ann, Bill, Charles, David. (Four names in ascending alphabetic order).

9.18   The process of getting data items into order is called **sorting**. There are many sorting methods available. This section deals with just one method called **The Straight Insertion Sort.** It is not the fastest method available, fast methods are too complicated to include in a book at this level, but the reader should get an understanding of how to sort from the following example. The reader may leave the rest of this section for a later reading if he or she prefers since the details of this method are not needed later.

```
                    Variables:
                    Rnum  Number of rows
                    Cnum  Number of columns
                    Rpos  Row position ie, row subscript
                    Cpos  Column position ie, column subscript
                    A     Array


                    BEGIN
                    INPUT Rnum, Cnum
                    IF
                        (Rnum < 1)
                        OR
                        (Cnum < 1)
                    THEN
                        PRINT "NO DATA"
                    ELSE
                        FOR Rpos := 1 TO Rnum
                            FOR Cpos := 1 TO Cnum
                                INPUT A(Rpos,Cpos)
                            ENDFOR
                        ENDFOR
                    ENDIF
                    END
```

                    Figure 9.9

9.19 Example. Arranging a set of marks into ascending numerical order.

The method is explained by using pseudocode and the complete method will be shown in pseudocode at the end. Assume that the marks are in an array called MARKS and the number of marks is NUM.

a. **Overview.**

```
IF
    Marks array contains more than one data item
THEN
    Sort-Marks-Array
ELSE
    no sort is required for just one element
ENDIF
```

    eg. i.   Starting with MARKS = (89) no sorting is required.

      ii.   Starting with MARKS = (56 42 89 65 48)

         MARKS must be sorted into this order:-

            MARKS = (42 48 56 65 89)

116

b. i.   Details of **Sort-Marks-Array**

```
BEGIN
Start at position 2 in the marks array
REPEAT
     Put the element value into its correct
     position relative to values in the
     present and lower elements.(Details of to do this
     come later)
     Increase the element position value by 1
UNTIL
     all element values have been dealt with.
END
```

   ii. **Example** of Sort-Marks-Array are shown in figure 9.10.

c.   i.   Details of how to put the element value into its correct position relative to values in the present and lower elements.

```
BEGIN
Set a point to the present position.
WHILE
     (point > 1)
     AND
     (Value < value position one down from the pointer)
DO
     Copy value at (pointer position - 1) up to pointer
     position
     Move pointer position down one.
ENDWHILE
Place value into the element specified by the pointer.
END
```

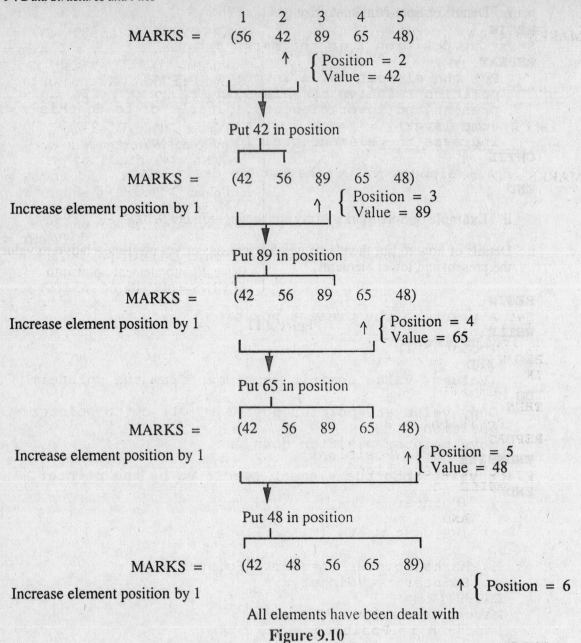

All elements have been dealt with

Figure 9.10

ii. **Example** based upon "put 48 in position" from (bii)

MARKS = (42 56 65 89 48)

↑

Put 48 in position

MARKS = (42 48 56 65 89)

Position = 5
Value = 48

DETAILS

MARKS = (42 56 65 89 48)
↑ Pointer = 5
(Pointer > 1) AND (48 < 89)
Copy 89 up. Move pointer down.
MARKS = (42 56 65 89 89)
↑ Pointer = 4
(Pointer > 1) AND (48 < 65)
Copy 65 up. Move pointer down.
MARKS = (42 56 65 65 89)
↑ Pointer = 3
(Pointer > 1) AND (48 < 56)
Copy 56 up. Move pointer down.
MARKS = (42 56 56 65 89)
↑ Pointer = 2
(Pointer > 1) BUT (48 > 42)
Place 48 into element pointed to
MARKS = (42 48 56 65 89)

Figure 9.11

d. **The Complete Sort.**

```
BEGIN
IF
    Num > 1
THEN
    Position := 2
REPEAT
    Value Marks(Position)
    Pointer Position
    WHILE
        (Pointer > 1)
        AND
        (Value < Marks (Pointer - 1)
    DO
        Marks(Pointer) := Marks(Pointer - 1)
        Pointer := Pointer - 1
    ENDWHILE
    Marks(Pointer) :=  Value
    Position := Position + 1
UNTIL
    Position > Num
ELSE
    PRINT "No sort is required for just one element."
ENDIF
END
```

Figure 9.12

9 of Data Structures and Files

STRINGS

9.20 We now turn our attention to data structures which are used for text handling and related problems. A sequence of characters handled as a single unit of data is called a string eg. "ABC21-,3" and "THE CAT SAT ON THE MAT." are literal strings. A common notation for string identifiers is one in which the string is denoted by a letters followed by a $ sign.

NAME$ = "ALEX" or NAME$ = "JAMES"

9.21 String Arrays. Individual strings can be used as elements of an array. For example the names of pupils in a class could be placed in this string array:

NAME$ = ("John Smith" "David Brown" "Mary Jones")

        Here NAME$ (1) = "John Smith", NAME$ (2) = "David Brown" and NAME$ (3) = "Mary Jones".

9.22   Example. In order to process a set of examination marks for a class the following two arrays are to be input first.

Pupil Name	Pupil Mark
John Smith	45
David Brown	78
Mary Jones	63

Figure 9.13

```
BEGIN
INPUT Num
IF
     Num < 1
THEN
     PRINT "NO DATA"
ELSE
     FOR Posn 1 TO Num
          INPUT NAMES (Posn)
          INPUT MARKS (Posn)
     ENDFOR
etc...
```

Key Num   :   Number of Marks
     Posn   :   Counter
     Name$:   Names array
     Marks :   Marks array

Figure 9.14

OPERATIONS ON STRINGS

9.23 Substrings. Strings may be split into smaller strings called **substrings** eg. Given NAME$ = "JOHN SMITH" FORE$ = "JOHN" and FAMILY$ = "SMITH" are substrings of NAME$

9.24 Concatenation. When strings are joined together they are said to be **concatenated.** eg. NAME$ may also be regarded as the concatenation of FORE$ and FAMILY$.

9.25 String manipulation. Some programming languages provide facilities for handling substrings. To specify a substring it is necessary to state the string of which it is a substring plus sufficient information to determine its position in the string and the substring length. Some dialects of the programming language BASIC provide these facilities and use "functions" called eg. MID$, LEFT$ and RIGHT$. Details of these functions can be found in books on BASIC programming eg. BASIC programming by B.J. Holmes, Pub. DP publications. String manipulation can also be handled well in some other programming languages eg. in Pascal.

FILES

9.26 A file holds data which is required for providing information. Files are normally held on backing storage media because they tend to be too large to fit into main storage all at once. Some files are processed at regular intervals to provide information (eg. a payroll file may be processed each week in order to produce employees' wages). Other files will hold data which is required at irregular intervals (eg. a file containing medical details of a doctor's patients).

ELEMENTS OF A COMPUTER FILE

9.27 A file consists of a number of *records*. Each record is made up of a number of *fields* and each field consists of a number of *characters*.

  a. **Characters.** A character is the smallest element in a file and can be alphabetic, numeric or special.
  b. **Field.** An item of data within a *record* is called a field - it is made up of a number of *characters,* eg. a name, a date, or an amount.
  c. **Record.** A record is made up of a number of related fields, eg. a student record, or an employee payroll record (see Fig 9.15)

STUDENT NUMBER	STUDENT NAME	DATE OF BIRTH	SEX	EXAM MARK
1201	JOHN SMITH	6 12 72	M	45

Characters   Field   Note Student number is the **Key field.**

Figure 9.15. Student Record (Part only).

9.28 At this stage you may find it easier to think of such a file in *non computer form* as set of cards with each card holding the details of one student record.

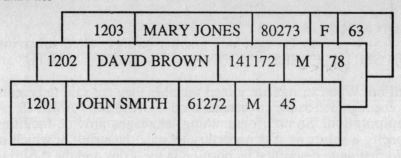

3 records in a file

Figure 9.16

ACCESS TO FILES

9.29 Key field. Once having created a file one must have the means of access to particular records within the file. In *general* terms this is usually done by giving each record a "Key" field and the record will be recognised or identified by that particular key.

In the example just given the student number was the key field.

9.30 Not only does the key field assist in accessing records but the records themselves can, if required, be *sorted* into the sequence indicated by the key. A file which has been sorted into the sequence of its key fields is called a **sequential file.**

9.31 The basic method of processing a single sequential file is quite simple and so it is illustrated here by an example. Other methods of file processing will be dealt with in later chapters. In this example the non-computer file set of cards is used to make the method simpler to understand. (See Figure 9.17). The basic method is described below and again in more detail in the pseudocode of figure 9.18.

In this example a sequential file of pupil details is processed to produce a results sheet. The records are read into memory one at a time in sequence. For each pupil's record the pupils number and name are printed on a report together with a grade. The grade is a FAIL for marks below 45, a PASS for marks between 45 and 69 and a CREDIT for marks of 70 or above. Note that reading a record from a file gets the record into memory which then allows all the fields within the record to be used. In the pseudocode shown in figure 9.18 use is made of **"comments"** which can be recognised because they appear between a "/*" and a "*/". A comment is not a pseudocode instruction but merely additional information to make the pseudocode easier to follow. Comments are used extensively in programming to make programs easier to read. They are a form of "self-documentation". Code yet to be refined can also be written as comments, for example, in figure 9.18 "/* print Results Sheet headings */" is a comment which will need to be expanded into a number of different PRINT instructions.

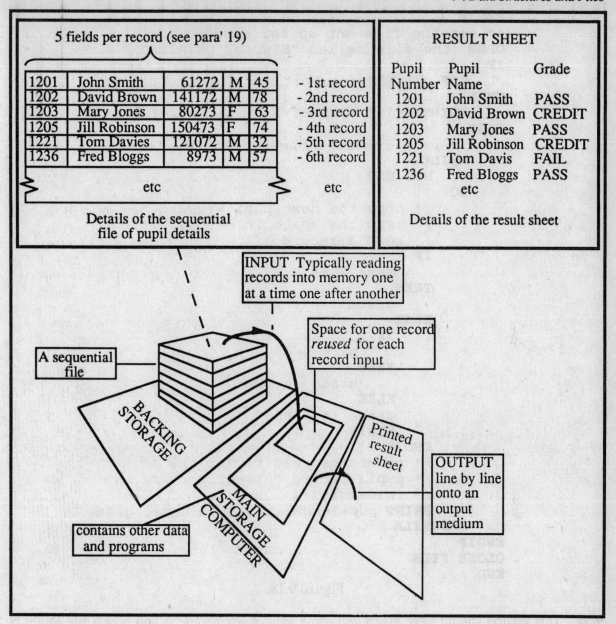

5 fields per record (see para' 19)					
1201	John Smith	61272	M	45	- 1st record
1202	David Brown	141172	M	78	- 2nd record
1203	Mary Jones	80273	F	63	- 3rd record
1205	Jill Robinson	150473	F	74	- 4th record
1221	Tom Davies	121072	M	32	- 5th record
1236	Fred Bloggs	8973	M	57	- 6th record

etc   etc

Details of the sequential
file of pupil details

RESULT SHEET

Pupil Number	Pupil Name	Grade
1201	John Smith	PASS
1202	David Brown	CREDIT
1203	Mary Jones	PASS
1205	Jill Robinson	CREDIT
1221	Tom Davis	FAIL
1236	Fred Bloggs	PASS

etc

Details of the result sheet

INPUT Typically reading records into memory one at a time one after another

Space for one record *reused* for each record input

A sequential file

BACKING STORAGE

Printed result sheet

OUTPUT line by line onto an output medium

MAIN STORAGE COMPUTER

contains other data and programs

Figure 9.17.

```
            BEGIN
            /* get the file set up for reading */
            OPEN  the file called "STUDENT DETAILS"
            IF
                EOF  /* EOF is short for End Of File */
            THEN
                PRINT "FILE IS EMPTY"
            ELSE
                /* print Results Sheet headings */
                WHILE
                    NOT EOF
                DO
                    /* copy the next pupil record */
                    /* into the space in memory.  */
                    /* read a record */
                    IF
                        mark > 69
                    THEN
                        grade := "CREDIT"
                    ELSE
                        IF
                            mark < 45
                        THEN
                            grade := "FAIL"
                        ELSE
                        grade := "PASS"
                        ENDIF
                    ENDIF
                    /* print the results for the */
                    /* pupil record currently    */
                    /* in memory */
                    PRINT pupil-number, pupil-name, grade
                ENDWHILE
            ENDIF
            CLOSE FILE
            END
```

Figure 9.18.

9.32 This section should have given you some idea of what a file is and how a file might be used. The various types of file and a variety of file processing methods will be dealt with in later chapters. At this stage it is worth noting that in very basic terms files may be regarded as **Data Files** (eg. like the file of pupil records just given) or as **Program Files,** ie, a file on which the "data" held on the file is a computer program. Program files contain programs which may be read into main memory from backing storage when the program is to be used.

SUMMARY
9.33 a. An **array** is a **data structure** in which data is placed in **elements** arranged in sequence and numbered by **subscripts.** 2D arrays (Tables) have subscripts for rows and columns.

    b. A **string** is a sequence of characters placed in order.

    c. A file is a collection of **related** records.

    d. A file is made up of **records**, which are made up of **fields**, which are made up of characters.

    e. A record is recognised or identified by the record **key field.**

    f. A **sequential file** is one which has been sorted so that it is in the sequence of its key fields.

POINTS TO NOTE
9.34 a. Arrays are also called tables. Arrays containing numbers only are also called **matrices.** (one **matrix**, many **matrices**).

    b. One dimensional matrices are sometimes called **vectors.**

    c. A one dimensional array is sometimes called a **list.**

    d. To specify a particular data item in a data file requires that the file **name**, record name (number) and field name all be stated.

    e. When a program is stored as a file the program's name is a file name.

    f. Greater understanding of files will come once you have reached and read the chapter on data storage devices and media.

QUESTIONS A *(with answers)*

1. What is a "data structure"?

2. What is an "array" and how is a particular element in a two dimensional array specified?

3. What is a "string"?

4. What are the elements of a computer file and how are the elements related to one another?

5. What is a "key field" and what is a key field used for?

6. What is a "sequential file"?

7. Explain the difference between a "data file" and a "program file".

NB. The remaining questions in this chapter are intended for students who do practical programming as an important part of their course.

8. In EUROBURG the postal service is slow and expensive. First class letters can be expected to arrive at their destination within one week and second class letters usually arrive within one month! The postal charges shown in the following table are in EUROBURG pounds (E).

Produce pseudocode for a procedure which takes in the mass of the parcel (in grammes), and the postal class required (1 or 2), and prints out the postal charge due. Make use of an array to hold the postal charges.

Table of postal charges

MASS	CLASS 1	CLASS 2
0 -	5	2
100 -	8	3
150 -	12	6
200 -	26	15
1000-2000	50	28

You may assume that the postal charges data has already been input to an array but state how you assume it has been stored.

QUESTIONS B (Without answers)

1. In the student marks example would a student surname be a good key field? Give reasons for your answer.

2. In chapter 7 it suggested that readability of programs was a desirable aim. In what ways can you achieve this aim in the programming language which you use for your coursework?

3. Briefly explain how program readability might affect program maintainability. Bear in mind that the maintenance programmer may not be the original programmer.

4. Show how to produce the three flowchart structures of figure 8.24 in the programming language you use.

5. Produce pseudocode for a procedure which does the following.
   a.   A set of results from throwing a 6 side die are input in the order in which they occur, erminated by the rogue value 7.eg 2, 1, 3, 6, 5, 1, 3, 5, 3, 5, 7.
   b.   The number of times each score occurs is recorded in an array ready for output at the end (ie. when all scores have been input).
   c.   As each result is input, one is added to the appropriate array element. (eg. when 2 is input a 1 is added to array element 2). With the values given in (a) the final form of the array will be:-

ELEMENT NUMBER	1	2	3	4	5	6
CONTENTS	2	1	3	0	3	1

6.   Extend the example given in paragraph 9.16 so that the totals for rows are calculated and stored in one array and the totals for columns are calculated and stored in another array. (ie. one total for each row and one total for each column). The grand total of all elements should also be calculated. When all totals have been found they should then be printed out with the row totals first, the column totals next and then the grand total.

7.   Produce pseudocode for a procedure which
   a.   Inputs data to a one dimensional array "A".
   b.   Inputs data to a one dimensional array "B" of the same length as A.
   c.   Multiplies corresponding elements of A and B placing the results in an array "C" (eg C(1)   A(1) * B(1)).
   d.   Prints the elements of the three arrays in sequence ie. A(1), B(1), C(1) then A(2), B(2), C(2) etc.

8.   Produce pseudocode for a procedure which reads through a sequential file like the one in Figure 9.18 and produces a list of pupils who have gained marks between 30% and 40% inclusive and who will be asked to retake the examination.

10 Simple Logic

INTRODUCTION

10.1 This chapter deals with a topic which has importance both in programming, and in the understanding of the internal operation of the computer. Some of the points covered here were introduced in chapter 8. This chapter extends those ideas and lays the foundations for the material covered in later chapters, particularly chapter 28. Although the subject of this chapter is simple logic it is helpful to begin by examining one or two aspects of arithmetic related to the logic operations which are to be introduced.

ARITHMETIC OPERATIONS

10.2 The arithmetic operations on numerical data were introduced in 8.29. The basic terminology will now be restated and enlarged upon.

10.3 It is important to be able to distinguish between the terms "**Operation**", "**Operator**" and "**Operand.**" For example when we perform 4 + 3, the operation is addition, the operator is "+" an the operands are 4 and 3. The **result** of the operation is 7.

The arithmetic operations of addition, subtraction, multiplication and division are normally indicated by the use of the operators +, -, x and -. However, in computing other operator symbols are more commonly used in a variety of programming languages. Other arithmetic operations are also represented by special symbols:-

Normal Representation	Symbols used in the programming language BASIC	Symbols used in the Programming language Pascal
+ - x $\frac{}{3}2$	+ - * / 3 ↑ 2 or 3 ** 2	+ - * / for real numbers **div** for integers no symbol

Note In Pascal arithmetic operations on integers give integer results so for example 9 div 4 has the result 2 not 2.25. (9 divided by 4 is 2 remainder 1). The remainder is given by mod eg. 9 mod 4 has result 1.

10.4 Assignment Operations. Results of operations may be given names by using an assignment operation. For example we may call "X" the result of A + B by using an appropriate **assignment operator.** Here are three common alternative assignment operations.

$$X := A + B \quad \text{(as used in flowcharts and in pseudocode)}$$
$$\text{LET} \quad X = A + B \quad \text{(as used in the programming language BASIC)}$$
$$X := A + B \quad \text{(as used in the programming language Pascal)}$$

10.5 Functions. Functions are used greatly in computing particularly in scientific applications. A commonly found example is the square root function shown here:-

$$Y := \text{SQRT}(X) \quad \text{(eg. when X is 9, Y will be 3)}$$

Given a value X the square root function performs a "hidden" procedure to produce a result Y, a positive number which has the property, $Y \times Y = X$. The value taken by the function, X in this case, appears to be treated rather like an **operand** in an operation, but is called a function **parameter** or **argument**.

10.6   Relational Logic Operators. These were introduced in 8.29 and are repeated here for completeness.

OPERATOR	MEANING
=	equal to
$\neq$ or < >	not equal
<	less than
>	greater than
$\leq$ or < =	less than or equal to
$\geq$ or > =	greater than or equal to

Although these operators clearly apply to numerical data eg. $3 < 9$ is true, the operators also apply to any data set which has an order eg. using alphabetic order "B"< "D" is true and "Y"< "M" is false.

PROPOSITIONS AND LOGIC

10.7   Propositions. A proposition is a statement which can either be **true** or **false**.

Examples

	STATEMENTS OR PROPOSITION	LOGICAL VALUE
a.	``You are reading this book"	(TRUE)
b.	$3_{10} + 4_{10} = 10_{10}$	(FALSE)

Questions and exclamations are **not** propositions.

Examples
   a.   "who are you?" (NOT A PROPOSITION)
   b.   "oh what a hot day!" (NOT A PROPOSITION)
   c.   "Is $410 > 310$?" (NOT A PROPOSITION)

10.8   Propositions appear frequently in programming and form the basis of decision making.

Example

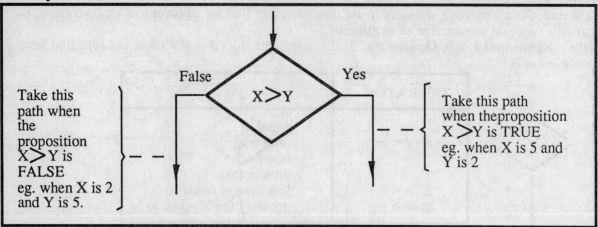

10.9 Combining propositions. In the previous chapter it proved useful to combine propositions into single expressions eg. (X > Y) OR (Z < 9). This too, can be represented by a flowchart:-

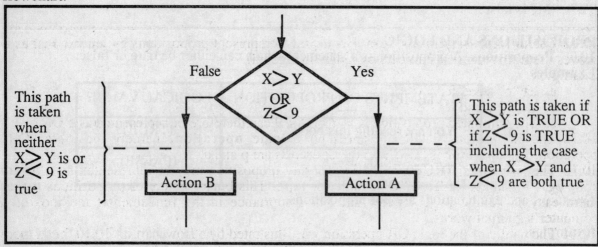

10.10 This situation is made clearer if we split the condition (X > Y) OR (Z < 9) into two separate ones thus:-

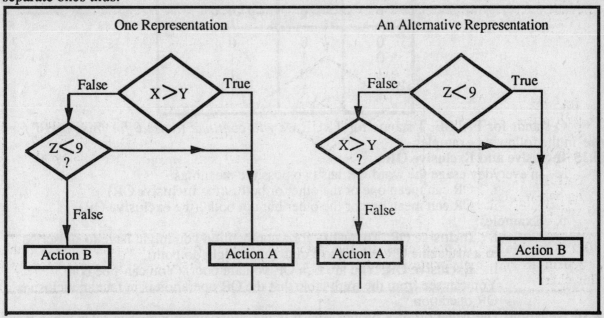

10.11 Useful Representations. It proves useful to represent propositions by letters(Just as it proves useful to represent numbers by letters in algebra).

Examples

 a. let "p" stand for "X > Y"

 b. let "q" stand for "Z < 9"

 c. The combined proposition X > Y or Z < 9 can therefore be represented as p OR q.

10.12 The expression "p OR q" represents a **logic operation,** namely the logic "OR" operation. The **operator** is "OR" and the **operands** are p and q.

10.13 The **two** cases, TRUE or FALSE, for any proposition may be represented by a binary code eg. "1" stands for True "O" stands for false. This binary nature of propositions makes them easy to handle by computer and has importance in the fundamental methods of a computer's internal works.

10.14 The nature of the logic OR operation was illustrated by a flowchart in 10.10, but a more common method of defining a logic operation is by means of a truth table.

Example.

 a. Using the previous example.

X > Y	Z < 9	(X > Y)OR(Z < 9)
False (eg. X is 2, Y is 5) False True (eg. X is 5, Y is 2) True	False (eg. Z is 12) True (eg. Z is 4) False True	False True True True

b. A simpler representation of the truth table defining the "OR" OPERATION

p	q	p OR q
0	0	0
0	1	1
1	0	1
1	1	1

O stands for FALSE, 1 stands for TRUE *we will continue to use 0 for false and 1 for true* in the following examples.

10.15 Inclusive and Exclusive ORs.

a. In everyday usage the word OR has two possible meanings:-
   - i.   OR can mean one or the other or both> (the **inclusive** OR)
   - ii. OR can mean one or the other but not both. (the **exclusive** OR).

b. **Examples.**
   - i.   **Inclusive** OR. To qualify for a competition you might have to subscribe to a magazine OR belong to a club (You might do both).
   - ii. **Exclusive** OR. You are rich OR you are poor. (You can't be both.)
   You can see from the truth table that the OR operation is in fact an inclusive OR operation.

10.16 Negation. The negation of a proposition p is the proposition which is false when p is true, and true when p is false. The negation of "p" may be written "NOT p".

Example.

"p" is the proposition "You are reading this book"

"NOT p" is the proposition. "You are not reading this book".

10.17 Truth Tables. The table shown below is a **truth table**. It shows the possible value of p and NOT p. It also serves as concise definition of NOT p in terms of p.

p	NOT p
0	1
1	0

When p is true, NOT p is false
When p is false, NOT p is true

The corresponding flowchart looks like this:-

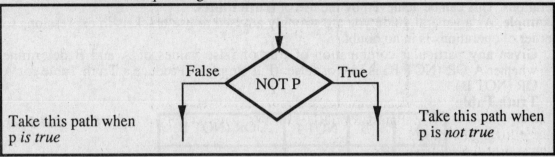

False   NOT P   True

Take this path when
p *is true*

Take this path when
p is *not true*

10.18 The AND Operation is defined in the truth table given below.

p	q	p AND q
0	0	0
0	1	0
1	0	0
1	1	1

Note:

a. All possible combinations of p and q are given. Only one combination gives p AND q true.

b. The AND operation may also be called the **logical product, intersection** or **conjunction.**

10.19 The corresponding flowchart looks like this:

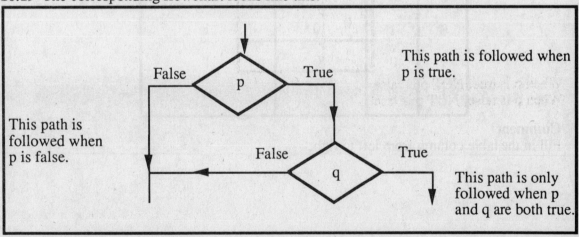

False   p   True

This path is followed when
p is true.

This path is
followed when
p is false.

False   q   True

This path is only
followed when p
and q are both true.

10.20 Boolean Algebra. A set of rules exists which govern the way in which logic expressions can be formed and manipulated. This "Algebra of logic" is called **Boolean Algebra** after its pioneer **George Boole.** It is beyond the scope of this book to go into the details of Boolean Algebra but for practical purposes we do need a basic method of handling combinations of logic operations. This can be achieved by the use of **truth tables.**

10.21 Example. As a general guide you are strongly advised to use brackets in expressions so that the order of operations is in no doubt.

a. Given any particular combination of true of false values of A and B determine whether A OR (NOT B) is true or false. (Put simply: - Produce a Truth Table for A OR (NOT B).

Truth Table

A	B	NOT B	A OR (NOT B)
0	0	1	1
0	1	0	0
1	0	1	1
1	1	0	1

Comments

i. First write out the complete set of combinations of A and B values as in the first two columns

ii. Fill in NOT B (change B's 1s to 0s and o's to 1s as in paragraph 10.17).

iii. Fill in A OR (NOT B) using the table in paragraph 14 as a guide ie. treat A like p and (NOT B) like q.

b. Produce a Truth Table for NOT (A AND B)

A	B	A AND B	NOT (A AND B)
0	0	0	1
0	1	0	1
1	0	0	1
1	1	1	0

Comment

Fill in the table column from left to right

c. Produce a Truth Table for NOT (A OR B).

A	B	A OR B	NOT (A OR B)
0	0	0	1
0	1	1	0
1	0	1	0
1	1	1	0

d. Produce a Truth Table for (A OR B) AND (A OR C)

A	B	C	A OR B	A OR C	(A OR B) AND (A OR C)
0	0	0	0	0	0
0	0	1	0	1	0
0	1	0	1	0	0
0	1	1	1	1	1
1	0	0	1	1	1
1	0	1	1	1	1
1	1	0	1	1	1
1	1	1	1	1	1

Note.
  i. The columns for A, B and C correspond to the pattern of bits for the binary number representing the decimal numbers 0, 1, 2, 3, 4, 5, 6, 7.
  ii. The other columns are filled in from left to right
  iii. Operations within brackets are dealt with first.

10.22 Logic operations are also of importance in the material to be covered on the CPU in later chapters but **"logic circuits"** is a topic which is left till chapter 18.

SUMMARY
10.23 a. The terms **operation, operand** and **operator** were explained.
  b. Alternative arithmetic operators were introduced eg. +, -, *, /,
  c. These assignment operators were given: , LET =, : =
  d. **Functions** and function **parameters** were introduced.
  e. These relational logic operators were explained: =, =, <>,. <, >, < =, >=
  f. Propositions were defined.
  g. The logic operations **AND, OR, NOT** were defined by the use of **Truth Tables**.

P	NOT P
0	1
1	0

P	Q	P AND Q	P FOR Q
0	0	0	0
0	1	0	1
1	0	0	1
1	1	1	1

POINT TO NOTE
10.24 a. The operation and operators introduced in this chapter will be needed later so commit them to memory now.

QUESTIONS A *(With answers)*

1. *Which of the following are propositions?*
    i.   Are blue and red the same?
    ii. Red and blue are different
    iii. 13 + 5 = 91
    iv. What a looney song!
    v.   Leaves are brown and bark is green
    vi. Dogs are faster than vacuum cleaners.

2. *Consider the expression 8 - 5 and identify the operation, operator and operands.*

3. *Write down relational logic operators which have these meanings:*
    a. greater than
    b. less than or equal to
    c. not equal to
    d. greater than or equal to
    e. equal to
    f. less than

4. *Which of these propositions is true?*
    a. (5 > 4) AND (3 < 7)
    b. (8 < 12) OR (6 < 2)
    c. (5 <> 8) AND (15 > 15)
    d. (5 < 2) OR (26 < 21)
    e. (3 = 8) AND (5 > 1)
    f. (-8 < 1) AND (128 < 12 10)

5. *Construct a truth table for each of these expressions.*
    a. (NOT A) AND B
    b. A AND (NOT B)

    c. *(NOT A) AND (NOT B)*
    d. *NOT (A OR B)*
    e. *NOT (A AND B)*
    f. *(A AND C) OR (B AND C)*

QUESTIONS B *(Without answers)*

1. *Which of the following are propositions?*

    a. $3 \times 9 + 5 = 32$
    b. 1024_{10} *is the tenth power of two*
    c.   *What is an integer?*
    d.   *Oh what a surprise!*
    e.   *This parrot talks, can you fly?*
    f.   *Black is not a colour*
    g. $(3 \times 8) > (4 \times 5)$
    h. $15. < (4 + 3)$

2. *Which of the following propositions are true if $X = 3$, $Y = 4$ and $Z = 5$?*
    a.   *(X < Y) AND (H > Z)*
    b.   *(X * Y) > (Y + Z)*
    c.   *NOT (X > Z) OR (Y << Z)*
    d.   *(Z > X) and (NOT (Z < Y))*

3. *Construct a truth table for the following expressions.*
    a.   *(X AND Y) OR ((NOT X) AND (NOT Y))*
    b.   *((NOT X) AND Y) OR (A OR (NOT B))*
    c.   *((NOT A) OR B) OR ((NOT B) AND C)*

HARDWARE FEATURES AND USES

1. This part of the book takes a detailed look at computer hardware. There are many reasons why we might want to examine computer hardware in detail, eg:

   a. It is nice to know how sophisticated equipment works.
   b. Understanding hardware helps us to understand how complete computer systems work.
   c. Understanding hardware helps us to know the possible uses and probable limitations of computers so that we know how computers should and should not be used.

   The last reason given is clearly a very important one.

2. This section of the book is divided into the following chapters.

   a. Chapter 11 provides an overview and gives the background to many developments covered in detail in the following chapters.
   b. Chapter 12 describes input devices, methods, media and their uses.
   c. Chapter 13 describes output devices, methods, media and their uses.
   d. Chapter 14 describes storage devices, methods, media and their uses.
   e. Chapter 15 serves as a summary for the previous four chapters and considers choices of devices, methods and media.
   f. Chapter 16 describes communications systems and their uses.

11 Hardware Overview

INTRODUCTION

11.1 Modern computers tend to have a fascination for most people. This fascination is at least partly caused by the impressive speeds at which computers perform, and by computer behaviour which at times can appear like actions made by an intelligent being, although of course they are not. Computers certainly have been developed remarkably over a relatively short period of time, and much of this development has been based upon big improvements to all aspects of hardware.

11.2 Although computers are impressive we might ask whether or not they can do all we would like then to do. the answer is a definite "NO!". There are two other questions which often need to be asked about computer hardware:

    a. What would we ideally like computers to do?

    b. Which of the currently available hardware is best suited to our specific needs.

    This chapter takes a broad view of the development of all elements of computer hardware to meet general and specific needs.

11.3 An ideal computer. What would an ideal computer be like? Perhaps it would be an inexpensive, compact, robust, reliable machine which was easy to communicate with and which at our request would use its own powerful capacity to memorise, calculate and reason for us. Perhaps it would be mobile and skillful too; a kind of obedient super robot? Well whatever it might be, we won't see one for a very long time to come if ever. But, how far we have moved towards that goal is well worth considering. The topics covered in this chapter should help in providing an answer.

11.4 In this chapter the functional elements of computer systems are considered in turn in terms of the developments which have taken place in hardware. These elements are:

    a. Input

    b. Output

    c. Storage

    d. Processing.

11.5 Before looking at these elements in detail we will consider an example which explains what they all do to make the computer work. We can get a quite a good idea of what the basic elements of a computer do if we compare a computer with a person *performing tasks under instructions*. Human features like feeling, emotion or imagination have no computer counterpart so don't try to take this comparison too far!

A PERSON AS A COMPUTER

11.6 In the following examples, just consider human actions carried out under orders eg. adding up a set of numbers in a prescribed way. Study the following diagrams and pictures which introduce the elements of the computer, then go on to the next paragraph for a practical exercise to explain and demonstrate the elements featured here.

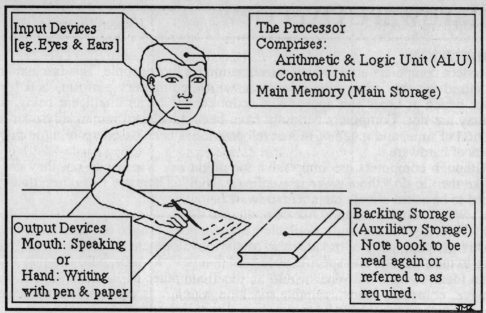

Figure 11.1 A Human Example to illustrate Computer Terminology.

Computer Elements	Purpose	Human Example
INPUT	To take in data (facts) and instructions via a suitable device, in a suitable form for the device.	Using Eyes or Ears
OUTPUT	To give out information via a suitable device eg.a printer. The information is fed to the device from main storage - see below.	Using mouth - for speech Using hands - writing with pen and pad
STORAGE:- (a) Main Storage (Main Memory)	To hold data and instructions after input until needed.Also to hold information awaiting output. The instructions will dictate the action to be taken on the data.	Memorising the data and instructions and recalling them when needed. Also remembering results.
(b) Backing Storage (Auxiliary Storage)	To supplement main storage. A less costly supplement to main storage for mass storage.	Using a notebook to record data or intructions too long to memorise. Subsequent use to read back or reference contents.
ARITHMETIC & LOGIC UNIT (ALU)	To obey specific instructions when required. eg. adding two numbers or checking whether two data items match.	same examples apply.
CONTROL UNIT	To take stored instructions in sequence one at a time. To intrpret each instruction and prompt its execution by one of the other units input, output, storage or addition.	Following a set of instructions by controlling ones own mental or bodily actions. These actions could be looking,listening, memorising, recalling, adding, writing etc.

Figure 11.2.The Elements of a Computer System
ON THE NEXT PAGE IS Figure 11.3. A Computer System

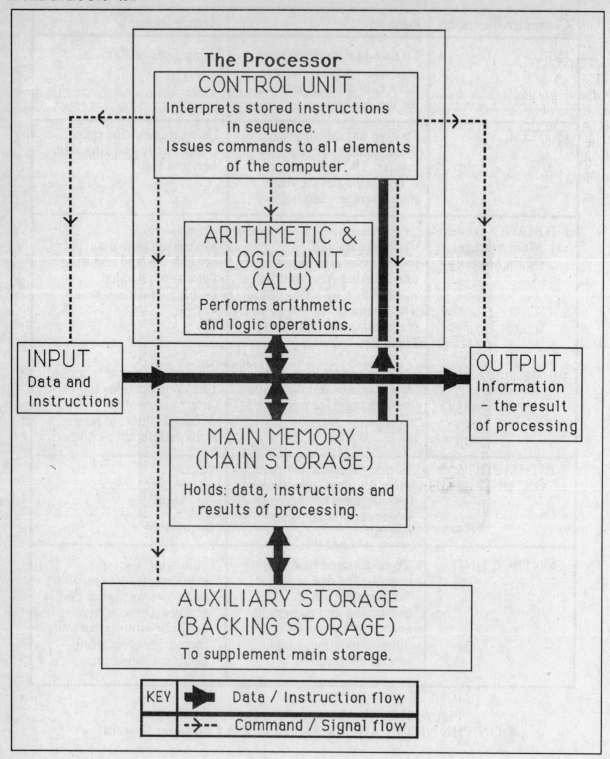

A PRACTICAL EXERCISE TO EXPLAIN HOW A COMPUTER OPERATES

11.7   In order to understand the operation of a computer *the reader should take part in the following exercise*. The exercise is based upon the program whose output is shown in fig 11.4. In fig 11.4a you will see the first screen of information displayed by the program. Please read it. As you can see it tells you that the program adds up a set of numbers typed in by the user. The second screen display (fig 11.4b) shows what happens when the user types in the numbers 5, 4, 7 and 1 followed by 999 to indicate that he or she has finished. The program finally displays the total which is 17 in this example.

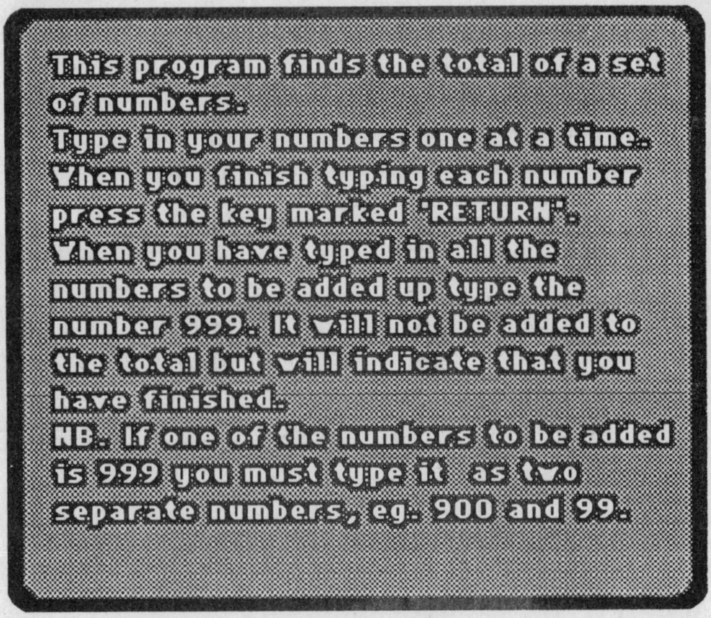

This program finds the total of a set
of numbers.
Type in your numbers one at a time.
When you finish typing each number
press the key marked 'RETURN'.
When you have typed in all the
numbers to be added up type the
number 999. It will not be added to
the total but will indicate that you
have finished.
NB. If one of the numbers to be added
is 999 you must type it as two
separate numbers, eg. 900 and 99.

Figure 11.4a.

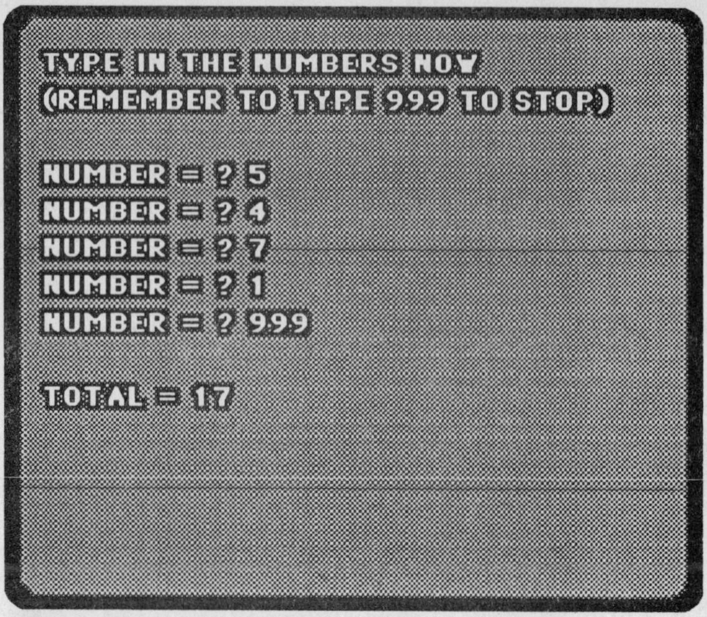

Figure 11.4b.

Figure 11.4. Screen Displays for a Simple Program

11.8 In the following exercise *you play the part of the computer*. You may "input" numbers by reading them from the book ie. the "input device" will be your eyes. Alternatively you may listen to numbers called out by your teacher or lecturer, in which case the "input device" will be your ears. As you read (input) each number add it to the total so far ie. keep a running total. When you read the number 999 don't add that to the total. Instead, you should write down (output) the total. By the way, there is nothing special about 999, it just happens to be the number chosen for this example. In the following paragraphs the instructions will be repeated in a way which is closer to the way instructions are given to computers.

PREPARING THE COMPUTER
11.9 a. The problem is "How to add up a set of numbers and produce a total."
   b. The solution to this problem will be a set of instructions in the computer's own language (English in the case of a "human computer"). This set of instructions is called a **program** (Note the spelling program **not** programme). Program instructions are obeyed slavishly by real computers, which are only machines, so every effort must be made by the programmer to get the program right.
   c. The program must be fed into the computer and stored in main memory (memorised). Remember *you* are playing the part of the computer.
   d. Once the program is "loaded" into main memory the computer can carry out the instructions in sequence when commanded to do so. Suppose that in this case the command is "RUN". (ie. when you read the word "RUN" carry out the program instructions which you have memorised).

THE PROGRAM
11.10 Here is a program to add up a set of numbers (fig 11.5). Pretend you are the computer and "LOAD" it into main memory (ie read and memorise it). The number 999 is used in a special way, as indicated earlier, and is **sentinel value** or **rogue value.**
Note: In the following program "**input**" means read and "**print**" means write.

PROGRAM: To add up a set of numbers and produce a total.	
INSTRUCTION NUMBER	INSTRUCTION
1	Start with total of zero
2	Sentinal value is 999.
3	Repeat the sequence of insruction from 4 to 6 inclusive
4	Input a number
5	If the number just input is the sentinel value then discontinue the sequence of instructions to be repeated and proceed with instruction 7
6	Add the number to the total NB. End of repeated instruction sequence
7	Print the total
8	Stop

Figure 11.5. A "Program" for a Person Pretending to be a Computer

PROGRAM EXECUTION
11.11 a. Here is the data to be input by the program:
5, 4, 7, 1, 999.
The numbers to be added are 5, 4, 7 and 1. The number 999 is a "sentinel value", it comes at the end of the numbers to be added to indicate the end of the data. It does not belong to the set of numbers to be added and is therefore called a "rogue value". You will see how this works when you execute the program.

b. By now you should have memorised the program and have your data ready, so that you are ready to carry out the program instructions (execute the program). When you next read the word "RUN" (or when your lecturer/Teacher says it) execute the program. **RUN.**

c. Your "output" should have been 17 (The total of 5, 4, 7 and 1). If it was not try again after you have read the next paragraph.

11.12 Program Trace. The following table is called a "trace table". It traces the sequence in which program instructions were performed and the data values at each stage. Follow the program and tick table values as you go.

Sequence of program instruction by numbers given in fig 11.4	The value of the total as the program progresses	The value of the number Input as the program progresses
1	0	–
2	0	–
3	0	–
4	0	5
* 5	0	5
6	5	5
4	5	4
* 5	5	4
6	9	4
4	9	7
* 5	9	7
6	16	7
4	16	1
* 5	16	1
6	17	1
4	17	999
* 5	17 This	999
7	17 value	999
8	17 is output	999

* repeated instruction sequence.

Figure 11. 6. A Program Trace

Producing a "trace table" in the manner is known as giving a program a "dry run". It is one way for the programmer to check that the program is correct before using it on the computer.

11.13 The program instructions in fig 11.5 were rather long winded compared with a real computer program. Figure 11.7 shows what the program might look like if re-written in computer programming language. There is no need for you to study the details of this program.

```
Program  Addup
     Constants
          sentinel = 999
     Variables
          total: Numeric
Begin
     total := 0
     Loop
          Input number
          if
               number = sentinel
          then
               exitloop
          else
               (*add number to total*)
               total := total + number
          endif
     endloop
     print total
end.
```

Figure 11.7. A Computer Program

A COMMON EXAMPLE OF THE HARDWARE ELEMENTS

Having gone into some detail about what the elements of a computer are and how they work it may help to relate the elements of the computer to a common example. Since most students make use of Personal Computers (PCs) of one kind or another a PC is used to illustrate the terminology used to describe the elements of the computer. Please refer to figure 11.8.

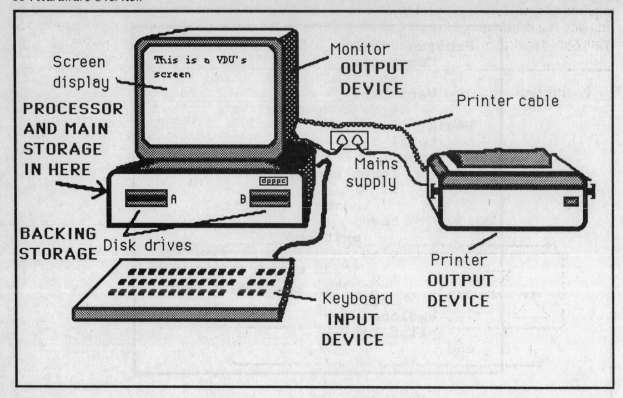

Figure 11.8. A Personal Computer with the elements of a computer system labelled

INPUT

11.14 Input to the very early computers was a slow and tedious process, often requiring an operator engineer to enter data or instructions directly into the computer's main storage by means of switches on a control panel. The method is sometimes used today as part of engineering test procedures.

11.15 Today, the input of data is much simpler than it was in the past. Most people are able to use computer keyboards to enter small amounts of data, even if they are not trained in typing. For larger volumes of data properly trained staff can be used to type in the data or it may be possible to use alternatives to the keyboard, but more of that later.

11.16 At one time, however, the standard ways of entering data were less direct than the methods commonly used today and involved the use of special media. Two very popular media were **punched cards** and **punched paper tape.** These media are now obsolete but will be described briefly in a later chapter on the origins of computers. Some modern methods of entering data into a large computer are indirect. For example, data may first be input to a small computer and stored on a floppy disks and then the floppy disks may be used as input media to the larger computer.

11.17 Sometimes data typed in on a keyboard is copied from the documents on which it was first recorded called **source documents.** This copying process is called **transcription.** To avoid **transcription errors,** ie. mistakes in copying, the person doing the typing may be required to type data in *twice*. The data typed in the second time is compared with that typed in first and if a difference is detected an error has occurred and has to be corrected perhaps by re-typing yet again. The process of checking for correct transcription is called **verification.**

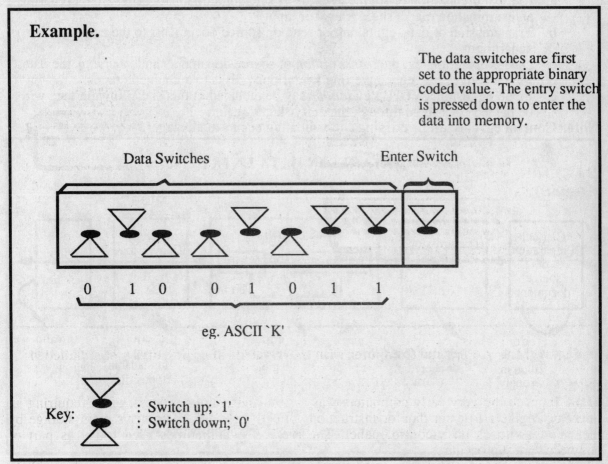

Example.

The data switches are first set to the appropriate binary coded value. The entry switch is pressed down to enter the data into memory.

Data Switches   Enter Switch

0   1   0   0   1   0   1   1

eg. ASCII `K'

Key: : Switch up; `1'
          : Switch down; `0'

Figure 11.11

11.18 Validation. *After* data has been input it is usually checked by the computer to see that it obeys the rules which apply to it. For example checking that the data is of the correct type eg. detecting letters where numbers should be. If such an error occurs the computer will produce an error message and the data will be checked at source, prepared and input again. Careful checking of source documents in the first place reduces this problem.

11.19 Media Conversion. In paragraph 11.6 it was mentioned that data might first be input onto floppy disks using a small computer. Since data can only be read from floppy disks relatively slowly and each disk has a limited capacity the data might be transferred onto a faster medium such as magnetic tape which can hold far more data and can be read very many times faster. This transfer of data from one medium to another is called **media conversion.**

STAGES IN DATA ENTRY

11.20 It should have become clear from the examples just given that there are several stages in entering data into the computer. Here are the stages in data entry:-

    a. Clerical preparation of source documents (including manual checks). eg. Preparing an examination marks sheet ready for input.

    b. Transmission of data. eg. taking or sending source documents to the computer department.

    c. Data preparation. eg. the *transcription* of source documents and *verifying* the data.

    d. Media conversion. eg. converting from floppy disks to a magnetic tape.

    e. Input. eg. using a VDU. *Validation* may be included in this stage. Invalid data will be passed back to go through the entry stages again.

Note. Control eg. checking, verifying and validating occurs at all stages.

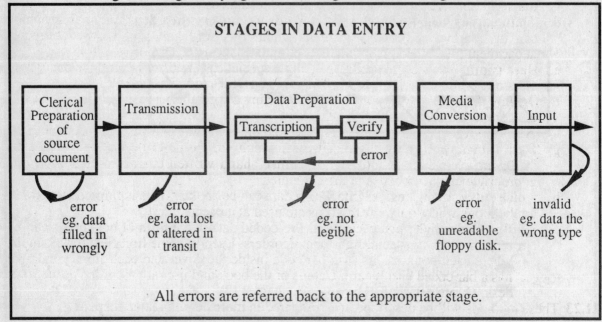

Figure 11.10.

SOLVING THE PROBLEMS OF DATA ENTRY

11.21 Some of the main problems resulting from the traditional stages in data entry are:-

    a. The preparation of source documents is slow, laborious and error prone.

    b. The **"keyboard bottleneck"** ie. typing speeds are very slow compared with computer input speeds.

    c. The waste of non-reusable media eg. source documents may be used once and then discarded.

    d. Transcription errors.

    e. Transmission delays or losses.

    f. The general problem of slow speeds, high costs and inefficiency.

11.22 Approaches to solving these problems (**NB.** Some of these approaches tackle *all* the problems to some extent. Other approaches tackle specific problems)

a. Preparing data *directly* onto a backing storage medium. This is done by using a small computer such as a PC to take data from the keyboard, verify it (and maybe validate it too) and then to transfer it onto backing storage. The backing storage medium is then transferred to the computer on which it is to be processed. Before PCs were so widely available this work was done on special purpose systems called **key-to-tape** or **key-to-disk** systems.

b. On-line data entry. eg. entering data directly onto the computer by using a VDU. Connecting many VDU's to one computer at the same time may also reduce the "keyboard bottleneck".

c. Preparing the source document so that data can be read directly from it by an input device. Details of such devices will be given in the next chapter. This method looks very attractive because it eliminates the keyboard altogether, automates transcription, increases speeds and reduces media costs.

d. **Data capture** eg. attaching special cards to garments in a department store which can be removed from the garment when it is sold and sent to the computer department for immediate input. This eliminates most stages of data entry.

e. **Data capture as a by-product** eg. using a special cash register to produce details of sales on an input medium such as magnetic cassettes (details later).

f. **On-line data capture at source** eg. connecting a special cash register directly on to the computer.
   (NB. The *examples* in d, e and f are all examples of **Point of Sale (PoS)** data entry).

g. **Data tablets and pads.** These devices, which will be described more fully in the following chapters, are able to "recognise" hand written characters and input the appropriate character codes to the computer.

h. **Voice entry.** Using devices into which data can be spoken. This is limited to a few applications where only a few words are used at present.

i. **Bar Codes/light-pen recorders.** Pre-coded data in the form of bar stripes can be read directly by special light-pen recorders. Used in some libraries, for example, where each book has its own bar code inside the cover and each library member has a bar coded user's card. Details of the book and user are recorded at the issue desk. (More details will be given in chapter 13).

11.23 These methods will be described and compared in more detail in later chapters.

OUTPUT

11.24 The development of output devices has been largely concerned with trying to find ways of improving the speeds, costs and reliability of output devices such as printers. Print quality and quietness have been other aims for some applications.

11.25 Character Printers. In the lower speed ranges printed devices mimic the typewriter by printing *one character at a time*. These devices are called *character printers*. Most of the printers which produce high quality print are character printers.

11.26 Line Printers. The majority of high speed printers *print whole lines at a time* (or appear to) and are consequently called *line printers*.

11.27 Page Printers. Some rather special printing devices are able to print "pictures" one page at a time. The "picture" may be a "picture of printed lines." Two examples are the Laser Printer and the facsimile printer which is now being used for a special type of data transmission called **teletex** (**not teletext** - see later).

The IBM System/23 incorporates a separate display that can be tilted, rotated, and easily adjusted up and down, a separate height adjustable keyboard (with palm rest), and a processor. Picture courtesy of IBM.

11.28 Other alternative forms of output which have been developed extensively in recent years are:-

a. Video output eg. on special purpose VDU's perhaps using colour or animation. Many of these special purposes are concerned with information retrieval. For example **viewdata** is a computer based information system which is available to users with special VDU like terminals connected to a telephone. In Britain British Telecom run a viewdata service called **Prestel.**

b. Graphic output. eg. Devices able to produce draughtsman's pictures or drawings on paper or on a video screen.

c. Speech or music output. These are still under development although a number of small scale applications are well established.

d. **COM. COM** stands for **Computer Output on Microfilm.** The equivalent of many pages of computer output are photographically reduced in size to fit on a very small area of film. The data on the microfilm can be seen by the user of a special enlarging viewer.

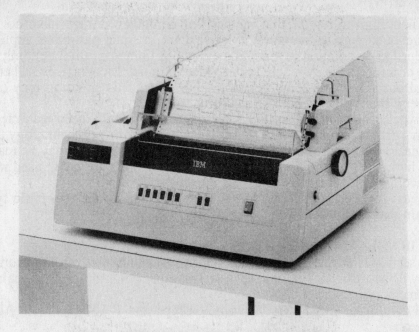

An IBM 3287 Printer. Picture courtesy of IBM.

The beltbed pen plotter is a unique CalComp design in which the drafting medium, in this case any size up to A00, is taped to a continuous belt of stable polyester film which moves up and down in the x axis while the pen moves back and forth along the y. Photograph with caption courtesy of CalComp Ltd.

STORAGE

11.29 It is important to realise that methods of computer storage have not replaced manual methods of data storage to any great extent except in some particular applications, but have been developed as an addition to manual methods. A library is still a building full of books, not a collection of information available at our video terminal. Most offices still contain more filing cabinets and box files than computer storage devices. This situation may change before too long however if many current predictions come true.

11.30 The types of data stored on computers have traditionally been restricted to numbers and text, and have excluded pictures and sounds. The newer forms of technology used in computers are able to deal with pictures and sound very effectively and there may be many developments on the way in the next few years. Already digital computers are being used in the recording of music by record manufacturers.

11.31 The next few sections deal with the developments in the two basic types of computer storage; **main storage** and **backing storage.**

MAIN STORAGE (MAIN MEMORY)

11.32 This section is primarily concerned with physical features of main storage rather than its use which will be discussed in chapter 14. The most common type of main storage is **semi conductor** memory.

11.33 Semi conductor memory. The common type, the **RAM** (Random Access Memory) is described here.

    a. Each bit in semiconductor memory is represented by a single cell which may be regarded as a microscopic electronic circuit with two distinguishable states used to represent "O" and "1". Cells arranged into rows and columns are built onto a single "chip" of silicon some 3mm x 3mm, in what is clearly a most advanced manufacturing process, since 2,048,000 cells may be formed on a single chip, and thousands times more on larger chips! (see Figure 11.11).

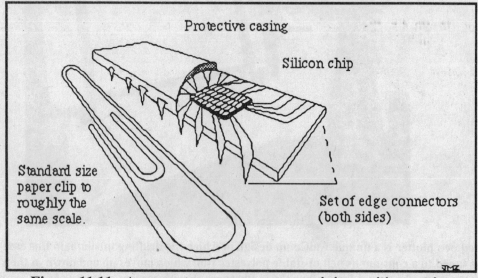

Figure 11.11   A computer component containing a silicon chip.

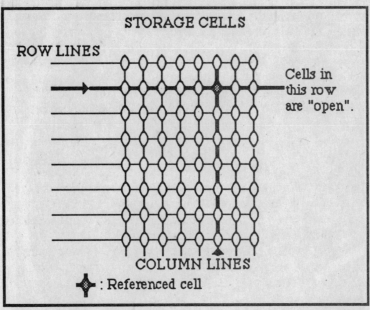

Figure 11.12   Access to a storage cell in a silicon chip.

b.   Each cell can be *electrically charged* **or** *not electrically charged* representing "1" and "0" respectively. If a row line is made electrically active it causes all cells in that row to switch open so that they can be charged or discharged through a column line. A column line for one cell in the row may then be switched on, **either** to pass charge into the cell (State "1") or to allow the cell to discharge (State "0"). Since charge can only flow from a charged cell, an observable discharge reveals the state of a cell and provides the means of reading from memory. A cell discharged by reading from it must be recharged to preserve its state.

c.   Charge slowly leaks from the cells and has to be topped up constantly. This is called "refreshing". Strictly speaking this is a feature of one type of RAM called **dynamic RAM.** Refreshing is not required in the other type of RAM which is called **Static RAM.** In static RAM THE "cells" stay "latched" in a "1" state or "0" state by the provision of a constant power supply. This dependence on a constant power supply by static and dynamic **RAM** means **RAM** memory is *volatile.* (ie. data is lost when the power supply is removed.

d.   Semiconductor memory is faster to access, more compact and cheaper to produce than a technology used until the 1970s known as core-storagewhich is now obsolete.

11.34 ROM. A non volatile semiconductor alternative to RAM is ROM (**R**ead **O**nly **M**emory) in which all cells are set permanently during manufacture. ROM has a number of uses eg. to store data or instructions which the computer needs all the time form the moment it is switched on.

11.35 Further details of main storage will be described in chapter 14.

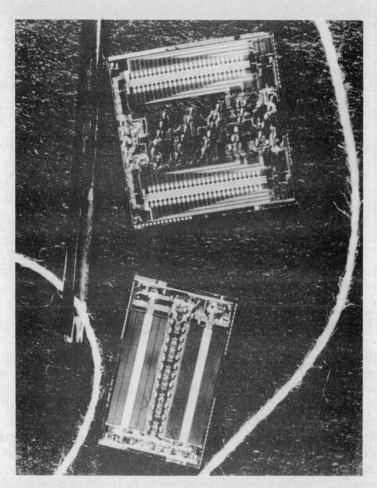

An IBM 64,000 Bit Dynamic RAM chip, older model and newer model (40% smaller) compared with a needle and thread. Picture courtesy of IBM.

BACKING STORAGE

11.36 Backing storage devices are required to hold large volumes of data which can be input to main memory quickly when required. Strictly speaking it is the medium attached to the device which holds the data not the device itself eg. reels of tape on a magnetic tape unit. (see figure 11.8)

11.37 On-line storage and off-line storage. This is best explained by example. Data on a reel of magnetic-tape is **on-line** when the tape is attached to a magnetic tape unit which is connected to, and under the control of a computer, but **off-line** when the tape is removed from the device, but held ready for use.

11.38 Magnetic Tape Unit and Magnetic Tape. Magnetic tape units have been developed and improved over many years so that they are now one of the most robust and reliable types of backing storage devices. Magnetic tapes are relatively cheap, hold vast quantities of data and can be used for on-line and off-line storage. Magnetic tape is also an important input medium because data on other input media are often converted onto magnetic tape prior to input (see paragraph 11.20d). Magnetic tape is also important in input by key-to-tape (see paragraph 11.22a). One other important factor concerning magnetic tape is that **industrial standards** apply to the methods of recording data on magnetic tape so that it is relatively easy to transfer large volumes of data from one computer to another by using magnetic tape. The industrial standards are rules about how things should be done to ensure that when one computer records data on magnetic tape another computer can read it.

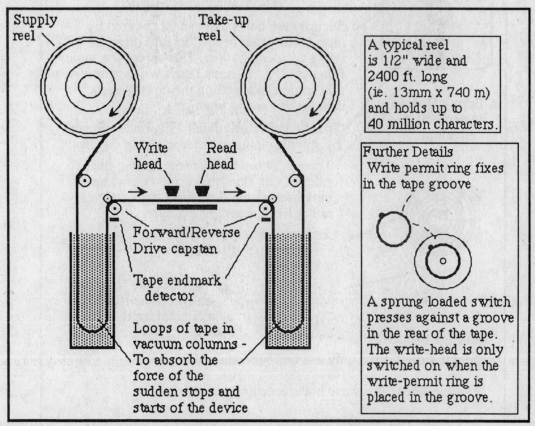

Figure 11.13 Main features of a magnetic tape unit.

11.39 The major deficiency of magnetic tape is that data can only be recorded and read from it in a **serial** fashion ie. the items of data are recorded along the tape one after another and when an item of data is to be read from the tape **all** the data that is recorded along the tape in front of it must be read through until the required data item is found. This matter will be discussed further in chapter 13.

11.40 Magnetic Disk Unit and Magnetic Disks. There are a wide variety of magnetic disk units available today. What they all have in common is a flat rotating circular plate coated with magnetic material on both sides. (ie. a disk). Some magnetic disks are rigid and called **hard disks** others are **flexible** and are called **floppy disks** and **diskettes.** Floppy disks gain rigidity when rotated at speed and therefore mimic hard disks very closely. Further variations and details of features will be discussed in chapter 13 but a variant on the floppy disk, the microfloppy was introduced in chapter 1.

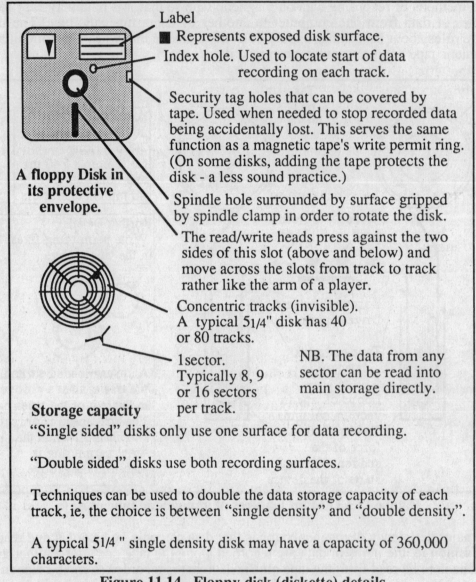

A floppy Disk in its protective envelope.

Label
■ Represents exposed disk surface.

Index hole. Used to locate start of data recording on each track.

Security tag holes that can be covered by tape. Used when needed to stop recorded data being accidentally lost. This serves the same function as a magnetic tape's write permit ring. (On some disks, adding the tape protects the disk - a less sound practice.)

Spindle hole surrounded by surface gripped by spindle clamp in order to rotate the disk.

The read/write heads press against the two sides of this slot (above and below) and move across the slots from track to track rather like the arm of a player.

Concentric tracks (invisible). A typical 5¼" disk has 40 or 80 tracks.

1 sector. Typically 8, 9 or 16 sectors per track.

NB. The data from any sector can be read into main storage directly.

Storage capacity

"Single sided" disks only use one surface for data recording.

"Double sided" disks use both recording surfaces.

Techniques can be used to double the data storage capacity of each track, ie, the choice is between "single density" and "double density".

A typical 5¼ " single density disk may have a capacity of 360,000 characters.

Figure 11.14   Floppy disk (diskette) details.

11.41 Direct Access. The most important feature of magnetic disks compared with magnetic tapes is their ability to provide **direct access** to data in addition to the **serial access** provided by magnetic tape. What this means is that it is possible to locate and read data recorded on the disk surface without the need to read through all preceding data. This is illustrated in figure 11.14

by using a floppy disk as an example.

11.42 Solid State Backing Storage. Magnetic tape units and magnetic disk units have many moving parts which carry with them the risks of mechanical failure of faulty operation caused by wear and tear. Wholly electronic backing storage eg. comprised of suitable semiconductor material, would have an advantage over magnetic tapes and disks in that such "solid state" devices have no moving parts. Two types of semi-conductor memory have had some measure of success in attempting to provide large capacity solid state memory devices. These are:-

    a. **Magnetic bubble memory.**
    b. **Charge Coupled Devices (CCD's)**

    These devices can compete with magnetic tapes and disk in terms of the speed with which data can be read, but not in terms of storage capacity. Both types of device use what is essentially serial access. Magnetic bubble memory is non volatile. CCD's have volatile memories and may therefore be regarded as devices half way between RAM and disks in terms of the volatility, speeds and capacities.

ARITHMETIC LOGIC AND CONTROL

11.43 The development of the hardware for purposes of arithmetic logic and control follows the development of semi conductor technology very closely. The move has been from transistors to integrated circuits (IC's) to LSI (Large Scale Integration) and now VLSI (Very large scale integration)

11.44 The whole of the arithmetic logic and control units of a small computer can be formed on a single silicon chip to form a **micro-processor unit** (MPU). Some special purpose MPU's are used in items such as digital watches and clock, cameras, pocket calculators, cash registers and electronic games. The RAM and ROM memories used with these MPU's are constructed in a similar way.

11.45 The MPU's are associated RAM's and ROM's are usually made by one semiconductor fabrication technology called **MOS technology** (Metal-Oxide-Semiconductor). There are numerous variants eg. PMOS, NMOS, CMOS, SOS, VMOS, HMOS etc.

11.46 An alternative fabrication technology BIPOLAR technology is used to produce the components of processors and memories in larger computers such as minicomputers and mainframes. Variations in this technology are Schottky bipolar and I^2L (Integrated Injection Logic).

11.47 The details of technology names need not concern us greatly, except in so far as they are the technological basis for some significant differences in construction and performance between microcomputer based systems on the one hand, and minicomputer and mainframe computer systems on the other. Both technologies continue to improve.

EVALUATING HARDWARE

11.48 The developments which have taken place in computer hardware and which continue to take place can be judged favourably in terms of improvements in speeds, capacities, size, reliability and costs. These improvements have extended the range of activities in which computer technology is practicable. This trend can be expected to continue but we are still a long way from the ideal computer. In the case of any one particular application of computers the hardware must be considered not only in terms of speed, capacity, size, reliability and cost but also in terms of such things as ease of use, consistency, accuracy and robustness. The next few chapters provide further details of computer hardware and the problems of choosing the appropriate methods and media for a given application.

SUMMARY
11.40 a. The developments of computer hardware were covered under these headings:-
  i.   Input
  ii. Output
  iii. Storage - Main Storage and Backing Storage.
  iv. Arithmetic, Logic and Control
  b. The stages of data entry were introduced:-
  i.   Clerically prepared source document.
  ii. Transmission of data.
  iii. Data preparation eg. **transcription** and **verification.**
  iv. Possible conversion from one medium (eg. floppy disk)
  to another (tape).
  v.   Input of data to the computer for **validation.**
  Control takes place at all stages.
  c. Common problems of data entry were outlined:-
  i.   Slow, laborious and error prone source document preparation.
  ii. The "Keyboard bottleneck".
  iii. The waste of non-reusable media.
  iv. Transcription errors.
  v.   Transmission delays or losses.
  vi. General problems of slow speeds, costs and inefficiency.
  d.   Approaches to solving the problems were introduced and will be discussed further in the next chapter.
  e.   The developments of output devices were described and some common methods were introduced ready for detailed discussion in the following chapters.
  f.   Developments in storage technology were introduced including core store, RAM and ROM semiconductor memory, magnetic tape units, magnetic disk units and solid state backing storage.
  g.   Factors on which to judge computer technology were outlined eg:-
  i.   Speed
  ii.   Capacity
  iii. Size
  iv.   Reliability
  v.   Robustness
  vi.   Ease of use
  vii. Consistency
  viii. Accuracy.

POINTS TO NOTE
11.41 a. Just because computer technology looks impressive does not mean we should always use it whenever we get the chance. We should start by looking at problems which need to be solved, and if after analysing the problems and taking all relevant factors into consideration we find that a computer system is the solution, then we should use

QUESTIONS A *(With answers)*

1. An **acronym** *is a word made from the initial letters of other words. What do the following acronyms stand for?*
   a. RAM
   b. LSI
   c. MPU
   d. COM
   e. ROM
   f. PoS
   g. CCD
   h. VLSI
   i. ALU
   j. CPU

12. *What are the functional elements of a computer?*

3. *Define the following terms:-*
   a. Media conversion
   b. Verification
   c.Validation
   d. Transcription error.

4. *Distinguish between on-line storage and off-line storage. Give one example of each type.*

5. *What is meant when it is said that a data storage media is volatile? Which of the following types of memory are volatile?*
   a. Magnetic tape
   b. RAM
   c. Magnetic Disk
   d. ROM
   e. Changed Coupled Devices.
   f. Magnetic bubble memory.

QUESTIONS B *(without answers)*

1. *List the stages in data entry and explain what is meant by "control" in the data entry process.*

2. *List the problems commonly associated with using keyboards for data entry. Describe some alternative methods used to overcome this problem.*

3. *With reference to magnetic tape and floppy disks distinguish between direct access and serial access.*

**A magnetic tape (reverse side) with a write permit ring visible and
removed from the back of the tape
The pen tip is pointing to the "Load point marker" at the start of the tape.**

A pad and puck used as an attachment to a VDU for non-keyboard data entry

**Feedback model 490 Multi-Function Industrial Terminal with Slot Bar
Code Reader and Feedback 479 Wand attachment
(Picture courtesy Feedback Data Ltd).**

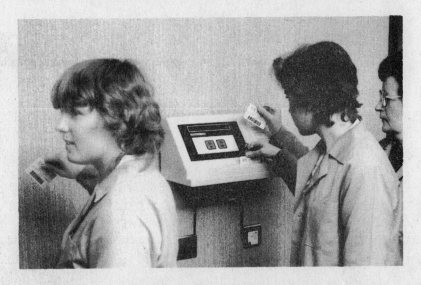

**Feedback 496 Time/Event Reporting and Enquiry Terminal
(Picture courtesy Feedback Data Ltd)**

An Apple Macintosh SE with Apple Laserwriter II laser printer
Courtesy of Apple Computers UK Ltd.

12 Interactive devices and their uses

INTRODUCTION

12.1 This chapter describes the features and uses of interactive devices. Such devices are used for "interactive on-line computing" that is to say there is a direct two way connection between the device and the computer which enables the user to have a "dialogue" with the computer.

12.2 The subject matter is covered under the following headings.

a. The Visual Display Unit (VDU)
b. Graphics for the VDU
c. Terminal Typewriters
d. Personal Computers as terminals
e. Workstations
f. Windowing Systems.

Note that the a "**terminal**" is any device capable of both input and output. A terminal may be used to communicate with the computer possibly from some remote site via a suitable link eg. telephone.

THE VISUAL DISPLAY UNIT (VDU)

12.3 Most of the basic feature of VDUs were covered in earlier chapters starting with chapter 1 but there are a few more features and variations which deserve a mention.

a. It is a **dual-purpose** device with a keyboard for data input and a cathode ray tube for output. The latter is similar to a TV screen.
b. **The keyboard** resembles the QWERTY typewriter keyboard, but usually has several additional keys, which are used to control and edit the display.
c. **Characters** are displayed on the screen in a manner that resembles printed text. A typical full screen display is 24 rows by 80 columns (ie, 1920 characters).
d. The display can normally be generated in two different modes:
   i. **Scrolling mode** in which lines appear at the bottom of the screen and move upwards rather like credits on a movie film.
   ii. **Paging Mode** in which one complete screen full is replaced by another, rather like a slide projector display.
e. Most VDUs have features which allow particular parts of the display to be highlighted or contrasted. For example.
   i. **Inverse (Reverse) video** ie. black or white instead of white on black.
   ii. **Blinking** displays
   iii. **Two levels of brightness**
   iv. **Colour** – on the more expensive models.
f. **Cursor controls**. A cursor is a small character-size symbol displayed on the screen, which can be moved about the screen both vertically and horizontally by means of special keys on the keyboard. During data input, the display may resemble a blank form. In this case data may be entered by first moving the cursor to a space on the "form" and then typing in the data. Further keys may allow the data to be edited or corrected.
g. **Mice & Joysticks.** These devices have a variety of uses as alternatives to the keyboard. In simple cases they can be used to move the cursor about the screen. As the mouse is moved about the desktop the cursor moves about the screen. A button on top of the mouse can be pressed when the desired position is reached. The

motion of the mouse is sensed by a rolling ball which is mounted in the underside of the mouse and in contact with the desktop. The joystick can be moved left, right, up or down to move the cursor and also has a button used like that on the mouse.

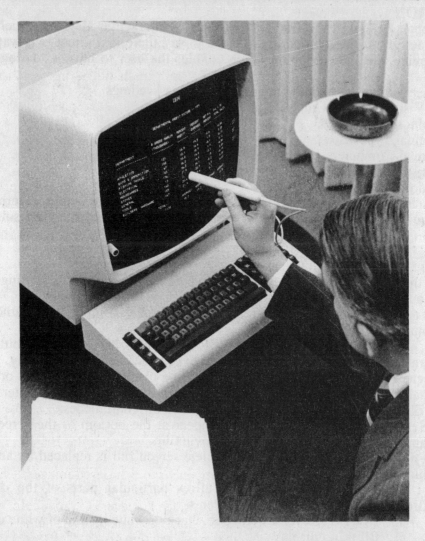

An IBM 3277 model 2 Information Display Station and Light Pen. Picture courtesy of IBM.

h. **Graphics Versions.** Some VDUs have high quality displays which can be used for line drawings, draftsmens drawings etc. The more advanced models have what are called **"bit-mapped displays"**, which means that the whole screen is organised into rows and columns of dots which are a copy or "mapping" of a corresponding representation held in memory.

i. **Light Pens.** A special pen used in conjunction with a graphics VDU. The VDU can detect the location of light shining on the screen by means of special hardware and software. This is a design aid which simplifies input of details of positions on the screen.

j. **Touch Terminals.** An alternative to the light-pen. The VDU can detect when a point on the screen is touched.

k. **Voice Data Entry (VDE).** Additional circuitry plus a microphone is added to the VDU. The unit can be switched to "learn" a number of words, typically less than 200, which it achieves by recording a "sound pattern" for each word typed in. When the unit is switched to input it displays and inputs any word which it recognises. These units are particularly suitable for people wishing to use a few words again and again in situations where their hands are not free to use a keyboard eg. people in laboratories, invalids or "Quality Controllers" ie. people who inspect the quality of goods during manufacture and who take corrective action if the quality drops.

l. **Inbuilt microprocessors.** The numerous internal functions of almost all modern VDUS are controlled by inbuilt microprocessors. The more expensive models are often called **intelligent terminals.** These devices are sometimes capable of limited amounts of processing, and with further enhancements these devices can often be turned into small microcomputer systems in their own right. An advanced VDU or a Personal Computer able to not only act as a terminal but also able to do some processing itself is sometimes called a **workstation.** A more precise definition of a work station will be given later.

GRAPHICS FOR THE VDU

12.4 The **VDU** can be used to display a variety of pictures, diagrams, graphs, line drawings animated cartoons etc. The general term for all such forms of output is **computer graphics.**

12.5 The two basic methods of producing graphical images are:
   a. Block based images
   b. Pixel based images.

12.6 **Block based images** are simple and effective. The basic building *blocks* are **graphics characters** which the device can display or print in addition to the ordinary alphabetic and numeric characters (see Fig. 12.1). The graphics characters available vary from device to device. One standard form of block based image is that used on the British TV ceefax and oracle services.

12.7 **Pixel based images** are of a higher quality than block based images. The principle is basically the same as that used for simple dot matrix character printing (Fig. 12.1) ie. the image is built up from an appropriate combination of dots. To achieve this the whole VDU screen is organised into rows and columns of individual "dot" positions called pixels. On a black and white screen each pixel can simply either be on (black) or off (white) (see Fig 12.1). On a colour screen each pixel may comprise a cluster of red, green and blue primary coloured dots which can be on and off in different combinations.

12.8 The more pixels there are, the more detail can be represented, ie. the higher the **resolution.** A screen with more than 30,000 pixels will normally be classified as a **high resolution graphics (HRG)** screen and will be capable of representing reasonably smooth curves and accurate drawings. Therefore, it will be sutable for specialist graphics applications.

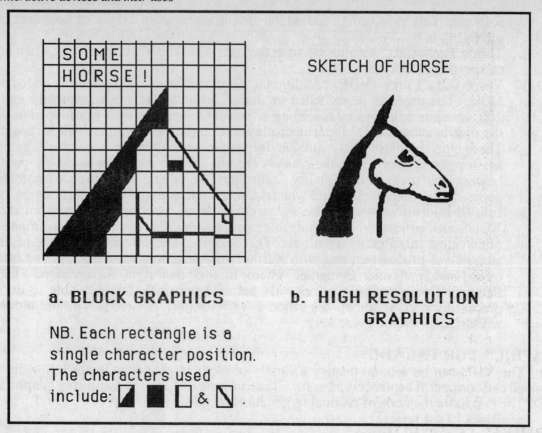

Figure 12.1. Computer Graphics.

12.9 Many graphics workstations provide software which allows pictures to be created by the use of devices such as **mice** (12.3g). For example, by holding down the button on the mouse while moving the mouse across the desk top a line may be drawn across the screen. The graphics facilities can also be used to allow the user of the device to operate it in simpler and more visually interesting ways. For example, alternative operations available to the user may be represented by simple graphical images called **icons** which the user can select by means of a mouse. A pointer on the screen is moved by using the mouse so that the pointer is above the required icon. The mouse button is then clicked to select the operation represented by the icon (see Fig. 12.2).

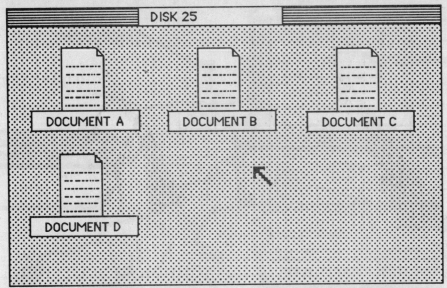

The figure shows a simple screen display of the contents of a diskette. Four documents, A, B, C and D are available for inspection. A particular document can be selected by moving the arrow over it by means of the mouse and then clicking the mouse's button. Each document is represented by its own named icon.

Figure 12.2. A Graphical Display Using Icons and a Mouse.

TERMINAL TYPEWRITERS

12.10 Terminal typewriters provide input via a keyboard and output via a character printer. So the terminal typewriter provides **hard copy** ie. output on printed paper. They have become far less popular in recent years because they lack the features of VDUs and hard copy can be obtained by other means.

12.11 Consoles. When a terminal is being used to control or monitor the computer, rather than for data or program input or output, it is said to be acting as a console. Some terminals on large systems may be permanently used as consoles and operated by trained staff called **Operators.** Other terminals may be used as consoles from time to time.

PERSONAL COMPUTERS USED AS TERMINALS

12.12 There are many situations in which people who use terminals connected to minicomputers or mainframes also use Personal Computers (PCs). To save on the cost of hardware, and on desktop space, they may use their PC as a terminal instead of having a separate terminal. For this to be possible the PC must be fitted with the correct hardware and use **terminal emulation** software (details follow).

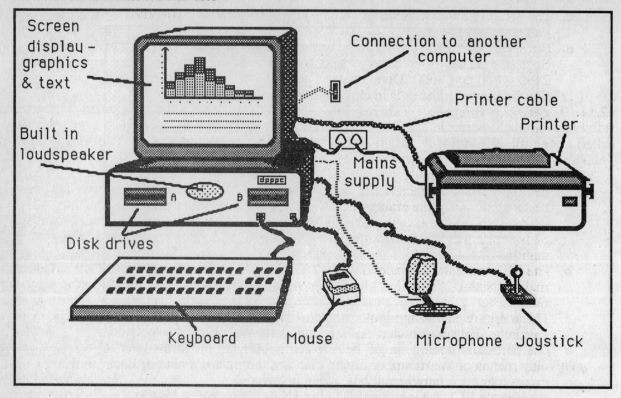

Figure 11.10. Personal Computer with a Selection of Input and Output Devices.

12.13   PC features. As was just indicated, the PC's hardware must have suitable features that may require the fitting of some extras. There must be a suitable socket on the outside of the PC to which a terminal lead can be connected. Although this sounds a simple requirement there are a number of things that have to be set up correctly for such an arrangement to work. Usually, small computers such as PCs have a number of sockets fitted to them each of which has been designed to be connected to a particular type of peripheral device. These external points of connection are called   **ports** . A "**communications port**" normally has the properties needed for connecting the PC to a terminal lead. It is helpful to be familiar with some of the issues involved.

a.   **Interfaces** A special piece of circuitry is fitted inside the computer and sits between the computer and the port. Its purpose is to provide a compatible connection between the two. Such a device is called an   **interface**.

b.   Interfaces are either **serial** or **parallel**. A serial interface sends or receives the bits comprising each character code one at a time, whereas a parallel interface sends the set of bits all at once. As a consequence, more socket pins are used in parallel ports. A very common standard serial interface is the   **RS232C**.

c.   Most ports are **bidirectional**, ie, they can send and receive data. Some printer ports can only send data and can therefore not be used with a terminal connection.

170

d. The sending and receiving of signals at a port is usually governed by a set of rules known as **protocols**.

e. The speed with which data can be transmitted through the port can usually be varied. Such speeds are often expressed as **baud rates**. Common settings are 330, 1200, 2400, 4800 and 9600. Divide these figures by 10 to get a *rough* approximation of the corresponding speeds in characters per second.

12.14 Terminal emulation. By themselves the hardware connections are useless without a suitable program running in the PC to make the PC behave like a VDU. Such a program is called a **terminal emulator**. Many different terminal emulators are on sale as standard "packages". A typical terminal emulator has the following features:

a. The emulator normally provides a set-up facility, which enables the user to choose the appropriate characteristics and settings needed. For example, the baud rate may be selected. Also, the emulator may present the user with a choice of standard VDU types. Very common options are VT100 and VT220, which are the model numbers of two popular VDUs manufactured by Digital and since copied by various other manufacturers.

b. The PC's keyboard is made to behave just like a VDU keyboard even to the extent of making special "**function keys**" behave in the same way if the emulation is a good one.

c. The screen behaves and looks just like the VDU screen. In a good emulation even special graphics symbols will display the same way.

d. In addition to making the PC behave like a VDU many terminal emulation packages also provide a **file-transfer** facility, ie, a means by which data and programs may be copied directly between a disk in the PC and the disks on the main computer to which the PC is connected as a terminal. This can aid data entry to the main computer.

 Note. Although this discussion has been about the use of PCs as terminals it is possible to use some home computers as terminals too and in much the same way as PCs.

WORKSTATIONS

12.15 A typical workstation looks similar to a PC because it is a desktop computer with screen and keyboard attached. However, it is different in a number of respects as will be seen from the following list of features.

a. It is larger and more powerful than a typical PC. For example, many popular workstations use 32-bit microprocessors whereas PCs are typically 16-bit microcomputers.

b. It is fully connected into a computer network as another computer on the network in its own right and not just running a terminal emulator.

c. It has high-resolution graphics on bit-mapped screens as a standard feature.

d. It has more sophisticated software than a PC which enables it to carry out several different tasks at the same time.

Consequently, workstations are normally used by professionals for particular kinds of work such as Finance (dealer rooms), Science and Research, and Computer Aided Design.

Examples of workstations are the Digital VAXSTATION 3500 and the SUN SPARCstations.

Note. It is possible to use some PCs as low-performance workstations.

The Sun SPARCstation 1
Photograph courtesy of Sun Microsystem Ltd

WINDOWING SYSTEMS

12.16 A **window** is a rectangular area on a display screen in which text or graphical images may be displayed. Several windows may be displayed on a screen at the same time. Most workstations and some PCs use software that handles all screen displays by means of windows. These **windowing systems** normally have a number of common features:

a. **Windows** are displayed on the screen, normally using bit-mapped graphics, in a manner resembling rectangular pieces of paper placed on a desktop. Indeed, one large window, "beneath" all the others, is normally called the "**desktop window**". A window designated as being "on-top" obscures the view of any part of any window beneath it.

b. **Mice** may be used in conjunction with windows to provide additional means for the user to interact with the system.

c. **Icons** may be displayed in windows on the screen and used in conjunction with a mouse in the manner described earlier. A user may move the mouse so that the pointer is over an icon representing a document and then double click the mouse button to "*open*" the document. The document opens with the creation of a new window on the screen in which the document's contents may be seen.

d. **Pull-down menus** are special-purpose windows associated with text headings displayed at the top of windows, especially the desktop's. For example, when looking at a document in a window, there may be a heading at the screen top called "EDIT". If the mouse is moved above the word "EDIT" and then pressed a small window appears beneath it, *while the mouse key is held down..* This **pull-down**

menu will list a set of options available to the user (eg, FIND or CHANGE). If the user moves the mouse over an option and then lets go of the mouse button then the computer will carry out the selected action, in much the same way as it would if it was receiving typed commands.

This combination of features is sometimes known as a **WIMP interface (Windows Icons Mice and Pull-down menus).** This kind of windowing was promoted very successfully in the early 1980s by Apple Computers on their Macintosh computer. Since then a number of similar interfaces have been introduced on other computers.

12.17 A number of windowing systems are in common use today and the reader is strongly urged to get first-hand experience of using one. Two common alternatives are the system used on the Apple Macintosh or the Microsoft Windows package, which is available on IBM PCs and compatibles. The **X-windows system,** which is used on many workstations, may also be available to some readers

SUMMARY

12.18 The subject matter was covered under the following headings:
  a. The Visual Display Unit (VDU)
  b. Graphics for the VDU
  c. Terminal Typewriters
  d. Personal Computers as terminals
  e. Workstations
  f. Windowing Systems.

POINTS TO NOTE

11.41 a. A **desktop computer** is, as the name suggests, any computer that can be used on a desk or table. The three common types of desktop computers are Home Computers, Personal Computers and Workstations.
  b. A general name for an interactive system exploiting graphics capablities to provide windowing systems supporting a combination of text and images is **Grapical User Interface (GUI** pronounced "gooey").

QUESTIONS A *(With answers)*

1. a. *What is a workstation?*

  b. *What is a personal computer and how can a personal computer act as a workstation?*

QUESTIONS B *(Without answers)*

1. *Explain the meaning of the term WIMP.*

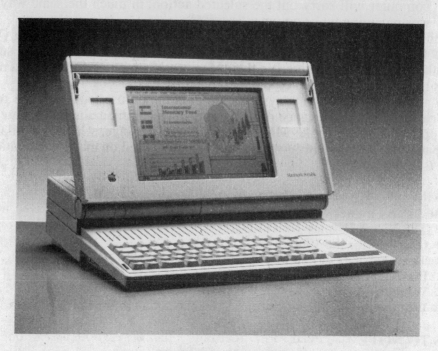

The Macintosh portable
Courtesy of Apple Computers UK Ltd

13 Input & output devices, media and uses

INTRODUCTION

13.1 This chapter describes the features and uses of a variety of input devices, output devices and their media. It also describes the methods associated with using the devices and media. The chapter attempts to give a balanced view of traditional methods and many newer alternatives. Input devices are covered first, followed by output devices.

MAGNETIC TAPE UNIT AND MAGNETIC TAPE

13.2 Magnetic tape, which we may think of as being primarily a storage medium, can also be an important input and output medium. Its use as an output medium is normally for the purpose of input at some future time. The output tape may contain data to be transferred to another computer. Alternatively, it may contain data to be kept for later input to the same computer. Tapes used in that way are an example of what is called **off-line storage.**

13.3 Magnetic tape units are dual purpose devices with read heads used in input and write heads used in output. The device is only able to write encoded data onto a tape when the tape has been fitted with a "write-permit" ring (Figure 11.13). This is a security precaution to prevent data loss since rewriting on a magnetic tape destroys any data which has previously been recorded on the tape.

13.4 **Features of the Tape Unit.** (See Figure 11.13)

    a. It holds the magnetic tape reel and also a second reel for "taking up" the tape (similar in concept to a tape recorder).

    b. It has a "read head" for "reading" the information stored on the tape, ie. for transferring data   from the tape into main storage.

    c. The tape moves past he read head at up to 200 inches per second.

    d. Data is recorded (written) in blocks as the tape moves past the "write" head at a *constant* rate. After a block has been written, the tape slows down and stops. On being instructed to write again, the tape accelerates up to the speed required for writing and another block is written onto the tape. No writing takes place during the acceleration and deceleration time and this therefore leaves a gap between each block of data on the tape. This INTER RECORD GAP measures some 3/4".

13.5 **Features of the Magnetic Tape**

    a. It is 1/2" wide and 2400 ft. long (typically.)

    b. It has a plastic base, coated with magnetisable material on *one* side.

    c. Data is stored in tracks. There are 7 or 9 tracks (depending upon the tape unit) which run the length of the tape. The data is coded so that one CHARACTER is recorded across the 7 or 9 tracks .

    d. An aluminium strip, called a "load point marker", marks the physical beginning of the tape for recording purposes; (the first 20ft or so is not used, apart from threading into the unit). Similarly, the physical end of the tape is marked by an "end of reel marker" (the *last* 20 ft or so is not used for recording).

    e. The *density* of recording can vary between 200–6,250 characters to the inch, but is most commonly 800 or 1600.

    f. The tape is re-usable ie. can be overwritten (as can tape used with tape recorders) - 20,000–50,000 passes are possible.

    g. It has a practical storage capacity of 40 million characters (approx.) per reel.

13.6 Unlike a domestic tape recorder, the tape on a magnetic tape unit stops and starts between "blocks"of recorded data. A **block** is a group of records treated as a single unit during transfers of data to or from the magnetic tape.

Reading takes place when the tape is moving at a high *constant* speed past the read head. Reading automatically ceases when the inter record gap is sensed by the read head. The tape decelerates to a stop on termination of one "read"and accelerates up to its reading speed at the commencement of the next "read".

13.7 Physical Records and Logical Records. A block as described in paragraph 13.6 is sometimes called a **physical record.** The data records from which the block is made are then called **Logical Records** in order to distinguish between the two. This should become clearer after you have seen the example in the next section.

BLOCKING OF RECORDS

13.8 The gaps created between each record on tape represent wasted space but more importantly they represent unproductive *time* spent by the tape unit in slowing down and accelerating in between each write and read operation. In order to reduce the number of IRGs and thus speed up the *total* time taken to process a tape file the technique of blocking records is adopted. Thus a single "read"or "write" instruction will cause a number of records to be read or written (see Figure 13.1).

13.9 Head labels and Trailer labels.

    a.   The first block recorded on a tape file is called the **header-label** or **header-block.** It holds details of the name and number of the file so that it can be identified, and also holds a file description eg. details of the blocking factor (ie. the number of records per block).

    b.   The last block recorded in a tape file is called the **trailer-label.** It is "recognised" by the computer as a mark indicating the end of the file. It may repeat details given in the header label and may also provide extra information eg. it may indicate that the file is continued on another tape.

DOCUMENT READERS

13.10 A number of methods have been successfully developed to enable data to be read directly from source documents. This provides a number of advantages. The devices fall into two main categories:-

    a.   Mark Readers

    b.   Character Readers.

13.11 Mark Reading. The older type of mark readers detected pencil marks on paper by using electrical contacts which "brushed" the paper surface. A pencil mark coming between the contacts will conduct electricity thereby completing an electric circuit and being detected. This method is known as **mark sensing.** The newer methods involve directing thin beams of light onto the paper surface which are reflected into a light detector, unless the beam is absorbed by a dark pencil mark, ie. a mark is recognised by the reduction in reflected light. This is known as **OMR** (Optical Mark Recognition).

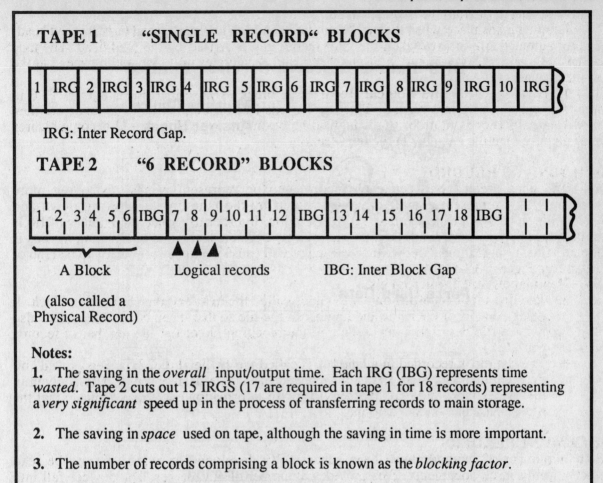

TAPE 1   "SINGLE RECORD" BLOCKS

| 1 | IRG | 2 | IRG | 3 | IRG | 4 | IRG | 5 | IRG | 6 | IRG | 7 | IRG | 8 | IRG | 9 | IRG | 10 | IRG |

IRG: Inter Record Gap.

TAPE 2   "6 RECORD" BLOCKS

| 1 2 3 4 5 6 | IBG | 7 8 9 10 11 12 | IBG | 13 14 15 16 17 18 | IBG | |

A Block   Logical records   IBG: Inter Block Gap

(also called a
Physical Record)

Notes:

1.   The saving in the *overall* input/output time. Each IRG (IBG) represents time *wasted*. Tape 2 cuts out 15 IRGS (17 are required in tape 1 for 18 records) representing a *very significant* speed up in the process of transferring records to main storage.

2.   The saving in *space* used on tape, although the saving in time is more important.

3.   The number of records comprising a block is known as the *blocking factor*.

4.   The block is the *physical* unit of transfer between the tape and internal storage and the IRG is now referred to as the IBG.

5.   The individual records making up the block are known as the *logical records*.

6.   The size of each block will depend on:-

   a.   The size of the logical records.

   b.   The size of internal storage available for input/output purposes.

Figure 13.1. The blocking of records.

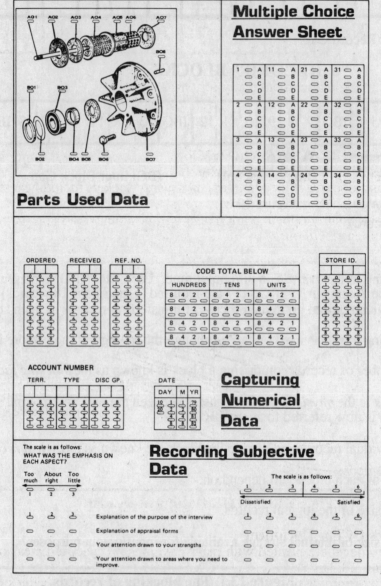

A Specimen OMR document courtesy of DRS Ltd. of Milton Keynes.

Number to be coded

		0	1	2	3	4	5	6	7	8	9
3		0	1	2	3	4	5	6	7	8	9
5		0	1	2	3	4	5	6	7	8	9
1		0	1	2	3	4	5	6	7	8	9

A marked document ready for OMR.

Figure 13.6.

OPTICAL MARK READERS AND OMR
13.12 Features of an Optical Mark Reader.
    a. It has a document feed hopper and several stackers including a stacker for "rejected" documents. (See Figure 13.3).

    b. A good quality optical mark reader will be able to read approximately 10,000 A4 documents per hour.

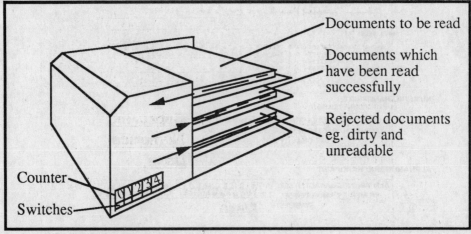

Documents to be read

Documents which have been read successfully

Rejected documents eg. dirty and unreadable

Counter

Switches

Figure 13.3. OMR Document Reader.

13.13 Features Of The Document
    a. Documents are printed with mark positions on specified areas on the document (see Figure 13.3).

    b. Predetermined positions on the document are given values. A mark made in a position using a pencil is read by the reader.

    c. Good quality printing and paper are vital.

    d. Documents require to be undamaged for accurate reading.

    e. Sizes of documents, and scanning area, may be limited.

Listed below are some of the more common fonts that
are readable by the Scan-Data OCR systems.

ALPHANUMERIC

OCR-A

```
ALPHA CHARACTER SET:
       UPPER CASE: A B C D E F G H I J K L M N O P Q R S T U V W X Y Z
       LOWER CASE: a b c d e f g h i j k l m n o p q r s t u v w x y z
NUMERIC CHARACTER SET: 0 1 2 3 4 5 6 7 8 9
      PUNCTUATION: \ ' , . : ? "
          SYMBOLS: - = / Y H J $ % & * + ( ) |
                   ▉ Λ ⌐ ↑ ↓ ↦ ↙ Δ °
```

OCR-B, ECMA-11 STANDARD

```
ALPHA CHARACTER SET:
       UPPER CASE: A B C D E F G H I J K L M N O P Q R S T U V W X Y Z
       LOWER CASE: a b c d e f g h i j k l m n o p q r s t u v w x y z
NUMERIC CHARACTER SET: 0 1 2 3 4 5 6 7 8 9
      PUNCTUATION: ; ' , . : ? !
          SYMBOLS: - = / + ä $ * ( ) - ▉ |
```

PICA 72

```
ALPHA CHARACTER SET:
       UPPER CASE: A B C D E F G H I J K L M N O P Q R S T U V W X Y Z
       LOWER CASE: a b c d e f g h i j k l m n o p q r s t u v w x y z
NUMERIC CHARACTER SET: 0 1 2 3 4 5 6 7 8 9
      PUNCTUATION: ? ; : , . '
          SYMBOLS: $ & + ( ) * % # = / - @
```

1403 SELECTRIC

```
ALPHA CHARACTER SET: A B C D E F G H I J K L M N O P Q R S T U V W X Y Z
NUMERIC CHARACTER SET: 0 1 2 3 4 5 6 7 8 9
      PUNCTUATION: ; ' , . :
          SYMBOLS: / - ¤ # $ % £ = + *
```

NUMERIC HANDPRINT

```
NUMERIC CHARACTER SET: 1 2 3 4 5 6 7 8 9 0
  ALPHA CHARACTER SET: A C T X
             OPTIONAL: + /
```

ALPHANUMERIC HANDPRINT

```
ALPHABETIC CHARACTER SET: A B C D E F G H I J K L M N O P Q R S T U V W X Y Z
   NUMERIC CHARACTER SET: 1 2 3 4 5 6 7 8 9 0
              SYMBOLS: + / * < >
```

Figure 13.8. Courtesy OCR Scan-Data.

Note. There are various organisations which lay down standards for optical character design.
For example the International Standards Organisation standards for OCR include OCR-A and
OCR-B shown above. ECMA-II is a standard laid down by the European Computer
Manufacturers Association, and so on.

13.14 Applications. OMR has a wide variety of uses. A typical sample is the multiple choice examination answer sheet.

OPTICAL CHARACTER READERS AND OCR
13.15 Features of an optical character reader.
   a. The basic document reader has an input stacker and a number of output stackers.
   b. Additional features to be found in a complete OCR system are magnetic tape units for media conversion, and VDU and other keyboard devices for the correction of misread data or entry of additional data.

13.16 Features of the document.
   a. Alphabetic and numeric characters are created in a particular type style on good quality paper. The characters look so nearly like "normal" print that they can *also* be read by humans.
   b. Characters are created by a variety of machines (eg. line printers, typewriters, cash registers) fitted with the special type-face. More recently it has been possible to complete documents in *very neat* handwritten print (See Figure 13.4)

13.17 Applications. OCR is used extensively in connection with billing, eg. gas and electricity bills and insurance premium renewals. In these applications the bills are prepared in OC by the computer, then sent out to the customers who return them with payment cheques. The documents re-enter the computer system (via. the OC reader) as evidence of payment. This is an example of the "turnaround" technique. Notice that no transcription is required. **Giro-forms** also use OCR.

The use of OCR Is likely to become more and more widespread as this technology continues to improve.

MAGNETIC INK CHARACTER READERS AND MICR
13.18 Features of Magnetic Ink Reader.
   a. Documents are passed through a strong magnetic field causing the iron oxide, in the ink encoded characters, to become magnetised. Documents are then passed under a read head when a current flows, at a strength according to the size of the magnetised area (ie. characters are recognised by a magnetic pattern). These characters appear on most cheques.
   b. Documents can be read at up to 2,400 per minute.

13.19 Features of documents.
   a. The quality of printing needs to be very high.
   b. the characters are printed in a highly distinctive type style using ink containing particles of iron oxide which gives the required magnetic property.

13.20 Application. One major application is in Banking (see Figure 13.5) although some local authorities use it for payment of rates by instalments. Cheques are encoded at the bottom with account number, branch code and cheque number *before* being given to the customer (ie pre-encoded). When the cheques are received *from* the customers the bottom line is completed by encoding the *amount* of the cheque (ie. post-encoded). Thus all the details necessary for processing are now encoded in MIC and the cheque enters the computer system via a magnetic ink character reader to be processed.

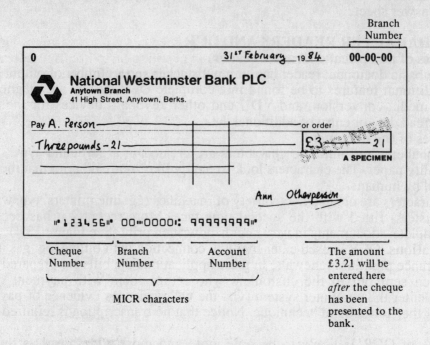

Branch Number

National Westminster Bank PLC
Anytown Branch
41 High Street, Anytown, Berks.

0

31ˢᵀ February 19 84

00-00-00

Pay A. Person _____ or order

Three pounds — 21 _____

£3 — 21

A SPECIMEN

Ann Otherperson

⑈123456⑈ 00⑈0000: 99999999⑈

Cheque Number

Branch Number

Account Number

MICR characters

The amount £3.21 will be entered here *after* the cheque has been presented to the bank.

Figure 13.9. Courtesy National Westminster Bank.

An IBM 3890 Document Processor being used for MICR cheques. Picture by courtesy of National Westminster Bank.

PADS AND TABLETS

13.21 These devices are able to recognise neat hand writing by means of a sensitive pad on

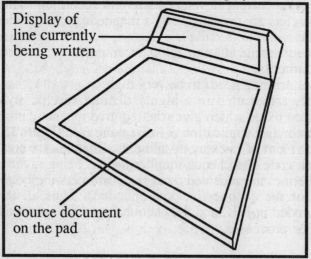

Display of line currently being written

Source document on the pad

which the source document can be filled in by hand using ball pen or pencil. They may appeal to the non typist but require neat hand printing.

DATA CAPTURE AT POINT OF SALE (PoS)

13.22 The retail industry is well advanced in many aspects of computer input. The larger stores and supermarkets rely on up to date information concerning their sales and goods left in stock. the methods used are too numerous to mention in detail so the following sections deal with a few of the more common methods.

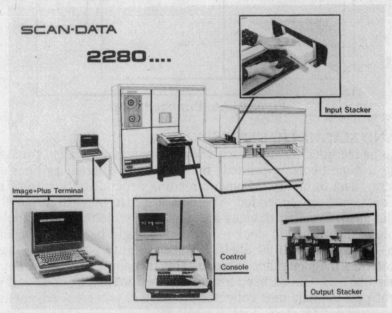

The 2280 Highspeed OCR System from OCR Scandata. Picture courtesy of OCR Scandata Ltd.

PUNCHED TAGS (OF WHICH THE KIMBALL TAG IS PROBABLY MOST COMMON)

13.23 The use of tags as a data collection technique is usually associated with clothing retailing applications although they are also used to some extent in other applications.

    a. Small cardboard tags are used as miniature punched cards.

    b. Using a special code, data such as price of garment, type and size, and branch/dept are *punched* into the tag, by a machine. Certain of the data is also *printed* on the tag (See Fig. 13.6).

    c. Tags are affixed to the garment before sale and are *removed* at the point of sale. At the end of a day's trading each store will send its tags (representing the day's sales) in a container to the Data Processing Centre.

    d. At the centre the tags are *converted* to more conventional media for input to the computer system.

    e. Note that *data is "captured"* at the source **(point of sale)** in a machine-sensible form and thus needs no transcription and can be processed straight-away by a machine.

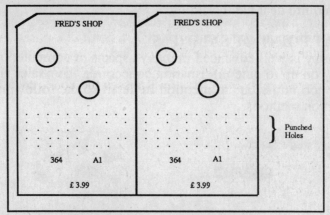

Figure 13.6. Punched Tags.

BAR-CODED AND MAGNETIC STRIPS

13.24 a. Data can be recorded on small strips which are read optically or magnetically. Optical reading is done by using printed "bar-codes'; ie. alternating lines and spaces which represent data in binary. Magnetic reading depends on a strip of magnetic tape on which data has been encoded. The data are read by a "light-pen" which is passed over the strip. Portable devices are available which also include a key-board. An example of their use is in stock recording; the light-pen is used to read the stock code from a strip attached to the shelf, and the quantity is keyed manually. The data are recorded on a magnetic tape cassette. This technique is also used at check-out points in super-markets. Goods have a strip attached and stock code and price are read by the light-pen. the data thus collected are used to prepare a receipt automatically, and are also recorded for stock control purposes.

a. 11-Digit Symbol

b. 7-Digit Symbol

Courtesy IBM

One particular type of Bar-Coding used on packets of consumable products such as foods. The numbers are coded in bar-coded strips and printed on OCR characters. The code is called a **UPC** (Universal Product Code) in the USA and a **EAN** (European Article Number) in Europe. The left hand digit "O" in "a" above represents the country of origin eg. "0" is the USA "5" is the UK. The next four digits are the manufacturers code and the last five are the product number.
Such details would not be asked for in an examination but serve as a good illustration of a specialised coding system.

Figure 13.7

b. Laser scanners attached to cash registers have been developed to read EAN's passed over them and input the product details. A small computer within the cash register, or to which the cash register is attached, is able to determine the correct price from the EAN code and an itemised receipt is produced automatically by the cash register. The cash register "operator" passes the codes over the scanner instead of typing in prices.

The IBM 3660 Supermarket System incorporates a high speed optical scanner.
As an item is pulled across the scanner's window a laser beam reads the European Article Number (or Universal Product Code in the US) bar code printed on the side of the package and the system automatically decodes the registers the information on the symbol.
The item can be of any shape or size and the bar code can be passed over the window in any direction.
Picture courtesy of IBM.

BY-PRODUCT
13.25 Data can sometimes be captured as a by-product of some other operation. For example some cash register and accounting machines produce magnetic cassette tapes of the data being entered into them as they are being operated. The data can be input to the computer at the end

of the day.

ON-LINE SYSTEMS

13.26 The ultimate in data collection is to have the computer linked *directly* to the source of the data. If this is *not* feasible then the next best thing is to "capture" the data as near as possible to its source and feed it to the computer with little delay.

13.27 Such methods involve the use of data transmission equipment. The computer is linked to the terminal point (the source of data or near) by a telephone line and data is transmitted over the line to the computer system.

13.28 Data enters the terminal either by keying in via a keyboard or is transmitted using a paper tape attachment or some other medium (data having been transcribed from the source document previously).

13.29 On-line methods obviate the need for physical transportation of source documents to the processing point. There is also less delay in producing processed information especially if the data link provides for two-way transmission of data (ie. from terminal to computer and computer to terminal).

13.30 Such systems can involve large capital outlay on the necessary equipment which is usually justified in terms of speed of access to computer files and quicker feed-back of information. Such costs cannot be justified in many cases and then other forms of data capture may be satisfactory alternatives.

13.31 On-line systems are the only practical choice for some applications. One example is the computer which controls a machine or factory process. It must receive input directly from source in order to be able to respond at a moment's notice. (Figure 13.7).

DATA TRANSMISSION

13.32 The importance of data transmission as a stage in data entry has been highlighted by several examples in this and the previous chapter.

13.33 Data transmission refers to any movement of data from one location to another but in this text data transmission by "telecommunications" equipment will be considered. The subject will be discussed in detail in chapter 16.

PRINTERS

13.34 As was indicated in (11.25 –11.27) a basic classification of printers is:
  a. **Character printers** which print one character at a time.
  b. **Line printers** which print one line at a time.
  c. **Page printers** which print whole pages at a time.
13.35 Other classifications are:
  a. **Impact** or **Non-Impact.** Impact printers **hit** inked ribbons against paper whereas non impact use other means of forming a character image in the paper eg. Thermal, electrostatic or light.
  b. **Shaped or dot matrix.** The difference is explained in Figure 13.9
  c. **By Technological features** - there are so many, so they will only be mentioned later in the text where appropriate.

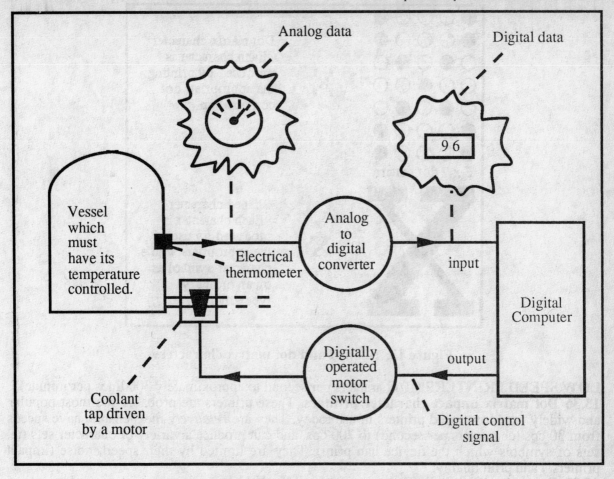

Figure 13.8. On-Line Control of a Process.

   d. **By application.** eg.
       i.   General purpose.
      ii. Small business use, etc.
   e. **By Speed.** This classification will be followed shortly under the headings:-
       i.   Low speed
      ii. Medium to high speed
   f. **By the quality of the output.**

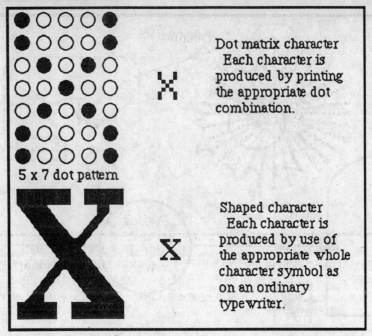

5 x 7 dot pattern

Dot matrix character
Each character is
produced by printing
the appropriate dot
combination.

Shaped character
Each character is
produced by use of
the appropriate whole
character symbol as
on an ordinary
typewriter.

Figure 13. Shaped and dot matrix characters

LOW SPEED PRINTERS (10 characters per second to approximately 300 lines per minute).
13.36 Dot matrix impact character printers. These printers are probably the most popular and widely used low speed printers in use today. They are *relatively* inexpensive, have speeds from 30 cps (characters per second) to 200 cps, and can produce a variety of character sets (ie. sets of symbols which the device can print). They are limited by their speed, noise (impact printers!) and print quality.
13.37 Daisywheel Printers. These are impact shaped character printers with typical speeds of about 40 cps. They give very high quality print. They have exchangeable print heads which look like 60 mm diameter spoked rimless wheels with individual characters located sideways on the end of each spoke. To print each character the wheel is rotated and the appropriate spoke is struck against an inked ribbon.
13.38 Daisywheel printers are used in applications where print quality must be high even at the cost of slow speed. For example the user of the printer may want letters to be produced which look as if they are personally typed. They are slow, noisy and *relatively* expensive.
13.39 Other low speed printers. There are many other low speed printers too numerous to mention. Two others worth a mention are:-
   a. **Thermal Printers.** These are non-impact character matrix printers which print onto special paper using a heated print head. They are very quiet and this gives them a big advantage for some applications, eg. in hospitals.
   b. **Inkjet Printers.** These are non impact character matrix printers which fire ink droplets onto the paper by using an "electrostatic field". They too are very quiet but are not so widely used at present although they are growing in popularity.

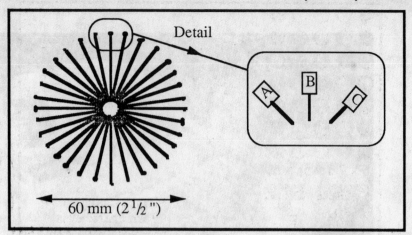

a. **The whole
Daisy wheel**

b. **Detail of the
daisywheel spokes**

Figure 13.10.

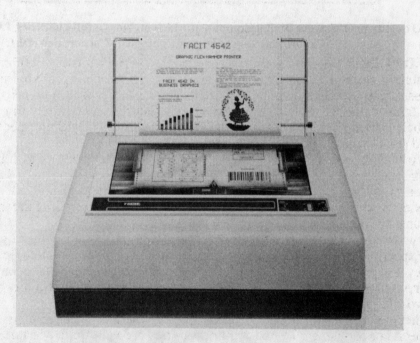

**The Facit 4542 "Flex-Hammer" Printer, Quality Dot Matrix Printers like this one can compete favourably
with daisywheel printers in terms of price and performance.
Picture courtesy of Facit Data Products Division.**

**The LQPO3 quality printer from Digital Equipment which includes a full-character 130-petal daisy wheel
(Picture courtesy of Digital Equipment Corporation (DEC))**

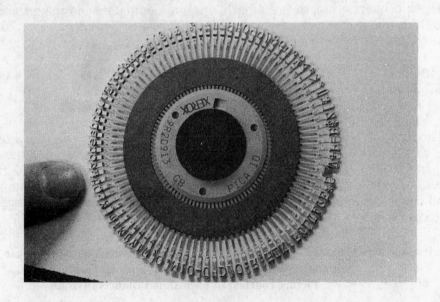

A daisy wheel

The LN03 desk-top laser printer from Digital Equipment Corporation
(Picture courtesy of Digital Equipment Corporation (DEC))

MEDIUM TO HIGH SPEED PRINTERS (Typically 300-3000 lines per minute)
13.40 These printers are used principally on mini computers and main frame computers. Just stop and think about these speeds for a moment. Many line printers print 120 or 132 characters on a line (ie. the lines are wide) and now imagine up to 50 such lines being printed in just one second.
13.41 Line Printers. These are impact shaped-character printers. The main types are:
   a. Drum printers
   b. Chain printers   See Figure 13.11
   c. Band printers
   The drums, chains or bands rotate at constant speed and are struck by hammers as the required characters pass the print positions. Characters do not get printed one at a time from left to right. Instead they are printed in the order in which they pass under the hammer. By using continuous stationary with interleaved carbon up to 7 copies may be obtained at a time. The band and chain printers are similar in principle but the bands which are made of steel may be exchanged quite easily to provide a variety of character sets.

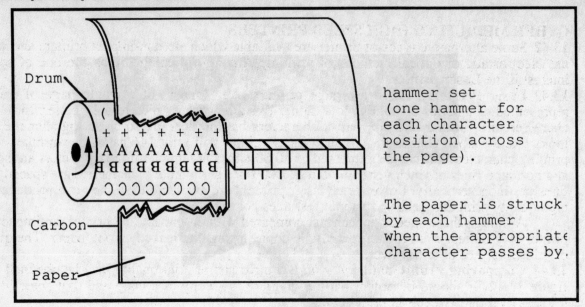

hammer set (one hammer for each character position across the page).

The paper is struck by each hammer when the appropriate character passes by.

a. A Drum Printer

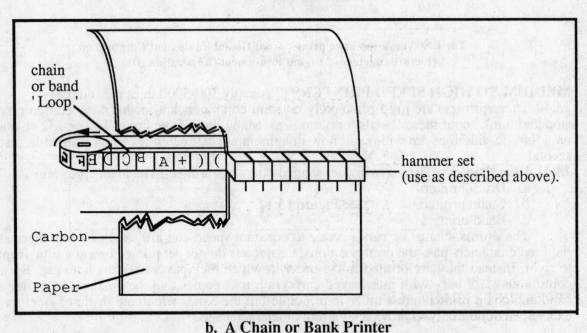

hammer set (use as described above).

b. A Chain or Bank Printer

Common speeds for impact line printers are 300, 600 and 1200 Lpm (Lines per minute).

Figure 13.11. Impact Line Printers - Main Features of Operation

OTHER MEDIUM TO HIGH SPEED PRINTERS

13.42 Some alternative types of printer are available which are non-impact printers and which use electrostatic or optical methods of printing. Among **optical printers** the one of special interest is the **Laser printer.**

13.43 Laser Printers. These are page printers. An "image" of a whole page of print is represented as a series of minute dots, rather like a newspaper picture only better. Individual characters are formed like dot matrix characters but the dots are so close together the print looks like a shaped character. A typical Laser printer will print 146 pages per minute! When printing characters this can be expressed as 10,500 lines per minute if the characters are spaced at a normal 6 lines per inch vertically but 21,000 lines per minute if characters are spaced at 12 lines per inch vertically. Lower price laster printers are available too. They can produce very high quality print at speeds up to about 500 lines per minute.

Although these speeds appear fast compared with an impact line printer, an impact line printer may be faster at producing multiple copies using interleaved carbon paper. The quality of print would be poor however.

13.44 Comparing Print Quality. A *rough* comparison of print quality may be obtained from figure 13.12. It should be noted that the diagram is a copy of a copy and that *some* matrix printers rival daisywheels in print quality.

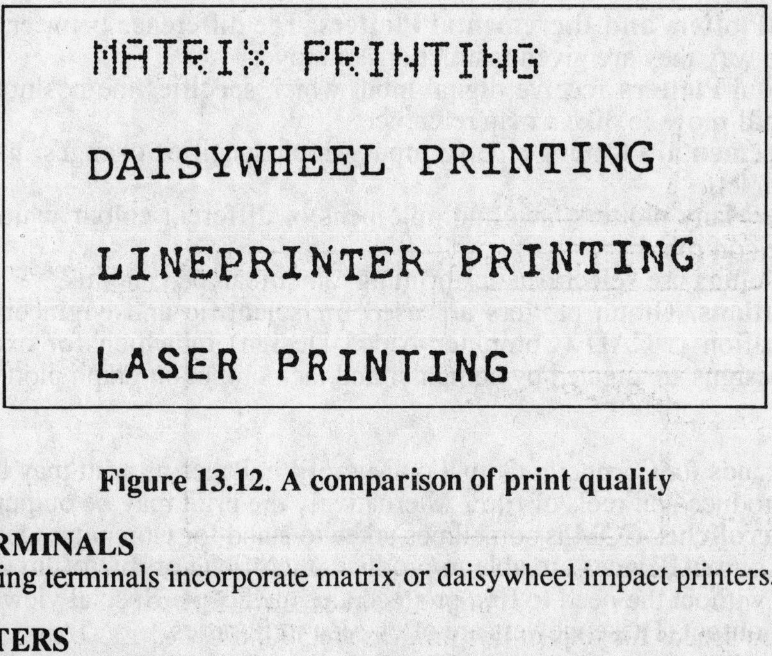

```
MATRIX PRINTING

DAISYWHEEL PRINTING

LINEPRINTER PRINTING

LASER PRINTING
```

Figure 13.12. A comparison of print quality

PRINTING TERMINALS

13.45 Most printing terminals incorporate matrix or daisywheel impact printers.

GRAPH PLOTTERS

13.46 These devices provide a completely different form of output and have a variety of applications. Two basic types are:-

    a. **Flat bed type.** The pen moves up, down, across or side to side.

    b. **Drum type.** The pen moves up, down and across. The paper provides sideways movement.

NB. The up/down movements allow the pen to move from point to point with or without making a line.

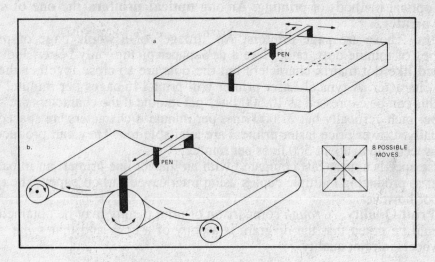

Figure 13.13. Types of plotter.

13.47 Digital Plotters and Incremental Plotters. The difference between these two types of plotter is in the way they are given instructions to move:-

    a. **Digital Plotters** receive digital input which specifies the position to which the pen should move ie. like a map reference.

    b. **Incremental Plotters** receive input which specifies changes in position eg. move 2mm left.

13.48 Colour. Many plotters have multiple pens of different colour which may be changed under machine control.

13.49 Some plotters use "electrostatic" printing rather than pen and ink.

13.50 Applications. Graph plotters are used for scientific and engineering purposes. One special application is CAD (Computer Aided Design) in which for example machine or architectural designs are created by computer and then output on graph plotters.

COM

13.51 COM stands for Computer Output on Microfilm. Pages of print may be photographically reduced and produced on reels of film. Alternatively the print may be output on small sheets of film called **microfiche.** COM is sometimes taken to stand for Computer Output on microfiche.

13.52 Special output devices are able to produce microfiche or microfilm output from data on magnetic tape without the need to first produce a printed copy. Special viewers must be used to read the COM output. These viewers are often seen in libraries.

CAPACITY AND SPEEDS

13.53 a. A typical 16 mm roll of film will hold the equivalent of 3,000 A4 pages. *One* typical microfiche measuring 105 mm x 148 mm will hold the equivalent of about 98 pages

a. A desk to A3 flatbed 8-pen plotter from CalComp designed for plotting business and scientific graphs and charts on paper or on clear acetate for projection.
Photograph with caption by courtesy of CalComp Ltd.

b.   A high speed desk top drum plotter from CalComp which uses A4 size continuous fan folded paper or clear film. Photograph with caption by courtesy of CalComp Ltd.

of A4 reduced in size about 24 times.

b. COM output devices can work at speeds of up to 120,000 characters per second.

13.54 Applications. COM is good for reference purposes when the data on it does not become out of date too quickly and where storage space is a problem. Library catalogues are often held on Microfiche or microfilm.

SPEECH OUTPUT

13.55 There are a few specialist applications using computer speech output. At present the sounds produced sound rather unnatural. One application is a book reading machine for the blind. The machine does an OCR type scan on each page of a book and produces "spoken" output.

SUMMARY

13.56 A number of devices and media have been covered. They are:

- a. Magnetic tape unit - Magnetic tape (prepared in various ways).
- b. Document readers - eg. for MICR, OMR or OCR
- c. Voice Data Entry - sound/speech.
- d. Data pads or tablets - Hand written document.
- e. Data Capture Devices eg. Tag readers, Bar-code readers and Laser scanners.
- f. By product devices - eg. Cash registers.
- g. On-line devices - eg. Terminals (f above) or special instruments.
- i. Printers
- j. Printing terminals.
- k. Graph plotters.
- l. Computer Output on Microfilm (COM)
- m. Speech output.

13.57 Printers were considered with reference to various classifications.

- a. Character - Line - Page
- b. Impact - Non impact
- c. Shaped - Dot matrix
- d. Technological features
- e. Purpose
- f. Speed - low, medium, high.
- g. Print quality.

13.58 Printers considered were:-

- a. Dot matrix impact character printer - General Purpose. (low speed)
- b. Daisywheel printers - Quality Print. (low speed)
- c. Thermal and Inkjet printers - Quiet (low speed)
- d. Line printers (Medium to high speed impact printers)
  - eg. i. Drum type
  - ii. Chain type
  - iii Band type
- e. Laser Printers - High speed page printers

POINTS TO NOTE

13.59 a. Common abbreviations are:-
      i. MICR (Magnetic Ink Character Recognition).
      ii. OCR (Optical Character Recognition)
      iii. OMR (Optical Mark Recognition)
      iv. PoS (Point of Sale)
      v. EAN (European Article Number).
      vi. PASS (Packet Switching System).
      vii. PABX (Private Automatic Branch Exchange)

    b. A major manufacturer of punched tags is KIMBALL and thus you may find them referred to as KIMBALL TAGS.

    c. Note how *on-line* systems speed up response times but the costs of on-line systems are such as to make many data capture methods more attractive than on-line methods.

QUESTIONS A *(With answers)*

1.   What is a "block" of data on a magnetic tape? Why are blocks used?

2.   A computer program requires the user to type in a date in the form of yymmdd where yy is the year number mm is the month number and dd is the day number. For example, 15th July 1987 is entered as 870715. Use this example to explain the difference between verification and validation.

3.   What are the functions of the "header-label" and "trailer-label" on a magnetic tape. What information do they contain.

4.   Distinguish between mark sensing and optical mark recognition.

5.   What is meant by "data transmission"?

6.   Describe the use of a "write-permit" ring on a reel of magnetic tape.

7.   Why is it sometimes useful to have computer output on microfilm?

8.   Distinguish between the following:
    a.   Pixel
    b.   Icon
    c.   HRG
    d.   Mouse

9.   Suggest suitable devices or media for the following:
    a.   High quality print
    b.   A high quality line drawing
    c.   Quiet printing

    d.   Fast production of large volumes of output with multiple copies

    e.   Economical printing of small quantities of data

QUESTIONS B *(Without answers)*

1. Distinguish between a physical record and a logical record.

2. Compare the methods of input and verification used in key-to-disk and key-to-floppy disk with the methods used for punched cards, paper tape and key-to-tape.

3. Refer back to chapter 11 and the problems involved in data entry. Which problems are overcome by OCR and MICR?

4. What effect might "Electronic Mail" have on a postman and on ordinary members of the public?

5. Write brief notes on each of the following types of printer. Make clear the differences between them in terms of speed, cost and method of operation, and suggest suitable applications.
    a. Daisy wheel printer
    b. Chain or band printer
    c. Dot matrix printer
    d. Laser printer

6   Consider the following line of text. "THE PUNCHED CARD IS A DP DINOSAUR". Compare the sequence in which characters would be printed on
     a. a character printer
and b. a drum printer

7.   Imagine that your college administration is to install a small computer system for student records and word processing. It is required that some output is to be of high print quality while the bulk of output will not have this restriction. It is decided to buy two printers. Which would you recommend and why?

14 Storage Devices, Media and Uses

INTRODUCTION
14.1 This chapter deals with storage devices, methods, media and uses in two stages. Main storage is considered first, and the emphasis is on operational features since many physical features have already been covered in chapter 11. The second stage in the chapter deals with backing storage, and in order to aid understanding many aspects of the use of backing storage for file handling are included.

MAIN STORAGE (MAIN MEMORY)
14.2 Features of main storage. Some basic physical features of main storage were introduced in chapter 11. Here we take a broader view of the features of main storage which are:-

    a. Its operation is wholly electronic, and consequently very fast and reliable. In the most modern computers the electronic memory circuits are also highly miniaturised.

    b. Data is almost instantly accessible from main memory because of its electronic operation and close proximity to the processor. For example, an item of data may be retrieved from main storage in less than one millionth of one second. For this reason main storage has yet another name, **immediate access storage. (IAS).**

    c. Data *must* be transferred to main storage before it can be processed by the processor. High access speeds then contribute to fast processing.

14.3 Uses of Main Storage. Ideally, Main Storage would be used to store all data requiring processing, in order to achieve maximum processing speeds. Main storage is expensive, however, and the practical solution is to limit the size of main storage and supplement it with less expensive backing storage. Thus limited capacity, coupled with the need to hold data in main storage for processing, results in main storage being *used* as a short term memory.

    It stores
    a. Instructions waiting to be obeyed
    b. Instructions currently being obeyed
    c. Data awaiting processing.
    d. Data currently being processed
    e. Data awaiting output

14.4 An area of main storage being used for data currently being processed is called a **working storage** area and an area being used for data awaiting processing or output is called a **buffer area** (figure 14.1).

    Working storage is also called "scratch pad storage".

THE OPERATIONAL FEATURES OF MAIN STORAGE (IAS)
14.5 To understand the principles of how data is placed into main storage we will imagine it to be arranged like a set of boxes, and relate this to physical details later. The boxes are numbered from zero upwards so that each box can be identified and located. What is usually called a **"Location in main storage"** corresponds to one of our boxes, and the **"location address"** corresponds to the number of the box.

    eg.

0	1	2	3	4	5

    etc.

Once data is stored in a location in main storage it remains there until it is replaced by other data. Data placed into the same location will destroy what was there previously (rather like the latest recording you make on a tape recorder will destroy the previous one). Accessing and fetching data from main storage is really a copying action which does not result in the data being deleted from main storage (just as playing a tape recorder does not erase the tape).

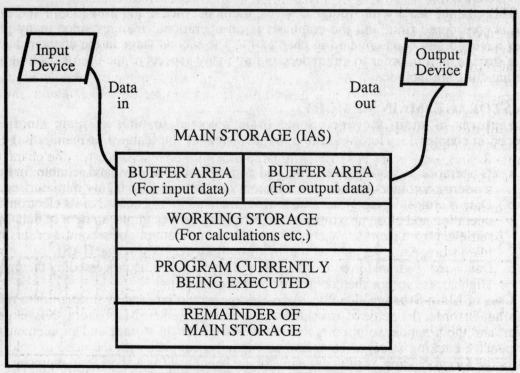

Figure 14.1. A simplified View of Main Storage in Use.

14.6   Random Access. It is possible to fetch data from the locations in main storage in any order, and the time taken does not depend on the position of the locations. We summarise that by saying we have **random access** to data in main storage. This is also known as **direct access**.
14.7   The term **"immediate access storage (IAS)"** was mentioned in paragraph 2. It is another *name* for main storage. Random access is a *feature* of main storage. RAM (Random Access Memory) is a *type* of memory (11.25) so take care over your choice of words!
14.8   Details of a single location. Each location in main storage consists of a set of tiny devices each of which can be in one of two states at any one time (eg. On or Off). The two states of each device are used to represent binary O(Off) and 1 (On), and hence the complete set of two-state devices in each location provides a method of coding data, rather like that used with input media such as paper tape. We may thus talk of a location in main storage as being so many bits long. For a given computer the number of bits in each location will be the same fixed number for all locations eg. *each* location could contain 16 bits, and *each* location would be addressable.

BYTES AND WORDS

14.9 Each location in main storage is usually said to hold a unit of data called a **word**. Words can often be subdivided into smaller units called **bytes**. The real situation is much more complicated than this because of the many different approaches to computer design.

The next few paragraphs illustrate some common ways of designing storage. First here are some further details about bytes.

14.10 Bytes and characters. A **byte** is commonly taken to be 8 bits. Characters may be represented by binary codes eg. ASCII code. Since character codes are normally no more than 8 bits in length, there is a tendency to substitute "byte" for "character" and "character" for "byte" rather indiscriminately when describing storage capacities. The reader should be prepared to meet this in practical situations.

14.11 8-bit microcomputers. Most of the popular microcomputer based systems used in schools and colleges are "8-bit micros". In these "machines" each **word** in memory is **1 byte in length** (ie 8-bits). Each word is sufficiently large to hold the binary code for one character but program instructions are normally too long to fit into single words and are therefore spread over two or three words in sequence.

14.12 Examples of data storage.

Location Number	eg. 201	eg. 202	eg. 203
Contents	1 1 0 0 0 0 1 1	0 1 0 0 0 0 0 1	1 1 0 1 0 1 0 0
Comments (see codes in Appendix IV.3)	ASCII Code for `C'	ASCII Code for `A'	ASCII Code for `T'

14.13 16-Bit Machine. Some of the more modern microcomputers are "16-bit micros". Many mini computers are also "16 bit machines". Each word is two bytes (16-bits) in length, ie. the **"word length"** is 16-bits.

Location Number	eg. 53	
Contents	1 1 0 0 0 0 1 1	0 1 0 0 0 0 0 1
Comments (see codes in 4.13 Appendix IV.3)	ASCII Code for `C'	ASCII Code for `A'

Location Number	eg. 54	
Contents	1 1 0 1 0 1 0 0	0 0 0 0 0 0 0 0
Comments (see codes in Appendix IV.3)	ASCII Code for `T'	ASCII Code for `NULL'

14.14 Larger minicomputers and mainframe computers have even longer word lengths eg. 24, 32, 36 or 48 bits.

14.15 In *all* machines locations may be used to store data or instructions, and the stored codes are indistinguishable. In principle there is nothing to prevent a stored instruction from being used as data or vice versa! In practice storage must be used carefully to avoid such an error.

14.16 Generally speaking computers with longer word lengths operate faster than computers with shorter word lengths because data and instructions can be moved in and out of memory in bigger units. You may compare this with transferring water with a bucket rather than a spoon!

PHYSICAL DETAILS

14.17 The physical details of main storage were described in 11.23 to 11.26. According to the technology used individual bits in memory are represented by cores or storage cells etc. RAM and ROM were mentioned in chapter 10 as examples of semi conductor memory. Some other variation of the ROM deserve a mention.

14.18 ROMS, PROMS and **EPROMS.** Data or program instruction stored in ROM (Read Only Memory) is written permanently during manufacture. PROMS (Programmable ROMS) are able to have data and program written in them after manufacture (eg. by the customer) but once written become permanently fixed. EPROMs (Erasable PROMs) are PROMS which may be erased by a special process (eg. removal from the computer and exposure to ultra violet light) and then written again as for a new PROM. The uses of these various kinds of semi-conductor memory will be discussed in due course.

STORAGE CAPACITY

14.19 Storage sizes are sometimes expressed in terms of "K" ($K = 2^{10} = 1024$). This can easily be confused with "k" short for kilo or one thousand as in kg.

Examples

14.20 a. A typical 8 bit- microcomputer may have a main storage capacity of 32K words (since 1 word = 1 byte in this case this is 32K bytes too). 32K bytes is 32 x 1024 bytes ie. 32,768 bytes.

b. A 32 bit minicomputer with 256K words of main memory will have 4 bytes in each word and a capacity of 4 x 256 x 1024 bytes ie. 1 048 576 bytes.

14.21 Another common prefix is M (or Mega for million times), so 12Mbyte means 12 million bytes.

BACKING STORAGE

14.22 Ideally, all data for processing should be stored in main storage so that internal operations can be carried out at maximum speed. As it is, main storage is rather more expensive than backing storage and is therefore only used for storing the instructions and the data currently being operated on. Backing storage is provided for the mass storage of programs and files, ie. those programs and files not currently being operated on but which will be transferred to the main storage when required.

14.23 Magnetic Tapes and Disks were introduced in 11.38 to 11.40 and further details will follow shortly. First there follows a summary of backing storage devices and media.

14.24 Backing storage devices and media.
   a. **Magnetic tape unit - magnetic tape (Figure 11.13).**
      Alternative types:-
         i.   Cassette tape units - tape cassettes (similar to domestic audio cassettes).
   b. **Magnetic disk unit - magnetic disk**
      Alternative types:-
         i.   **Floppy disk unit** - floppy disks.
              A. 8" floppy (original size - now less common)
              B. 5 1/4" floppy
              C. 3 1/2" micro-floppy disk
         ii. **Hard disk units** - hard disks
              Types:-
              A. Fixed disks - ie. disks not removable from disk drive.
              B. Fixed head disks - ie. a Fixed disk which has one read/write head for every track.
              C. Exchangeable disks - ie. the disks may be removed from the disk unit (A **disk pack** is a set of exchangeable disks on one spindle).
              D. **Winchester disks** - ie. Fixed disks in hermetically sealed disk units and with some robust mechanical features.(Intended for use in adverse environments eg. ones that are "dusty" or "humid".)
   c. Optical disk unit - optical disk
   d. Other auxiliary storage devices and media.

MAGNETIC TAPE UNIT AND MAGNETIC TAPE
14.25 Physical Features. The physical features of magnetic tape were described in 10.29 and 11.4.
Data Storage
14.26 The **serial** nature of file storage on tape was mentioned in 11.4 and the concept of a **sequential** file was introduced in 8.30. The following example brings these ideas together and illustrates how magnetic tapes are normally used.

AN EXAMPLE OF USING MAGNETIC TAPE FILES
14.27 This example is about the use of very simple records of students' progress. Suppose that for just one subject the following details are kept on a record for each student. (This example is restricted to just one subject to keep it as simple as possible).

A Student's Record

Student Number	Student Name	Total of All Homework Marks	Number of Homework Marks Marking the Total
1201	John Smith	35	7

14.28 The set of these records would be a **students' file,** and this file could be arranged into the sequence of student number to form a *sequential students' file* (8.30). The student number is the *key field* (8.20) and the sequential order of the file could be by *ascending key values* (ie. 1201, 1202, 1203...) or by *descending key values* (ie. 1201, 1200, 1199, 1198....).

14.29 Storage on magnetic tape.

a. When storing data it is necessary to decide whether to allocate a fixed space for the data, which the data may or may not fill, or to allow the data to occupy only the space which it needs. A record designed as the former will be a **fixed length record** and a record designed as the latter will be **variable length record**. See figure 14.2.

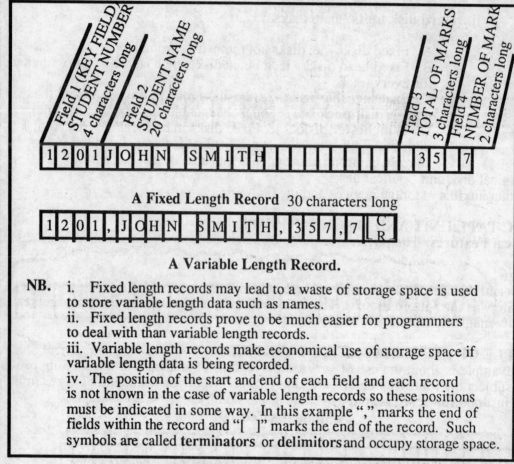

A Fixed Length Record 30 characters long

A Variable Length Record.

NB. i. Fixed length records may lead to a waste of storage space is used to store variable length data such as names.

ii. Fixed length records prove to be much easier for programmers to deal with than variable length records.

iii. Variable length records make economical use of storage space if variable length data is being recorded.

iv. The position of the start and end of each field and each record is not known in the case of variable length records so these positions must be indicated in some way. In this example "," marks the end of fields within the record and "[ ]" marks the end of the record. Such symbols are called **terminators** or **delimitors** and occupy storage space.

Figure 14.2.

NB. **Blocking** (11.7). Records are grouped into blocks on magnetic tape. Assume for simplicity that the students' records are to be stored as fixed length records in blocks of 4 records. The **student file** will be **organised** on the magnetic tape is shown in Figure 14.3.

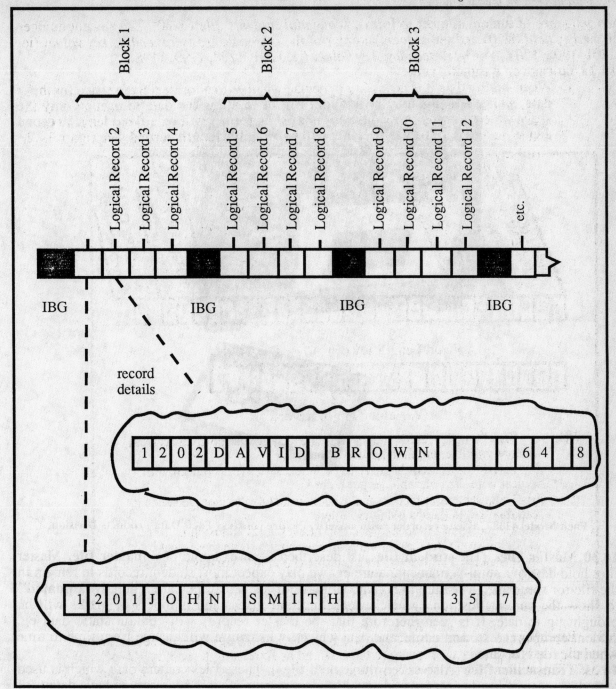

Figure 14.3. A Sequential File Organisation on Magnetic Tape.

Facit Model 4208 Cassette recorder with cassette. Picture courtesy Facit Data products Division.

14.30 Master Files. The **student file** just described is an example of a **master file.** Master files hold data of a semi-permanent nature eg. we may expect most student records to remain in the file for sometime. A feature to note about master files is that they are regularly "**updated**" to show the current position eg. each week the total marks and numbers of marks will be brought up to date. It is seen therefore that the master records will contain static data eg. student number and student name, and data which by its nature will change from time to time when the file is updated.

14.31 Transaction files (Also called **movement files**). These files contain data which is used to update master files. In order to update the student master file it is necessary to have details of the marks to be added for each student. A suitable "**student's transaction record**" might look like the one shown in Figure 14.4

STUDENT TRANSACTION RECORD	
STUDENT NUMBER	MARK
1201	9

Figure 14.4.

The key field value (1201 in this case) can be used to match the master records and transaction records when updating (See Figure 14.5).

14.32 Sorted and Unsorted Transaction files. Transaction records are often input and transferred onto magnetic tape as they are received (ie. in no particular sequence). The transaction file of student transaction records might be recorded on magnetic tape as shown in Figure 14.6.

14.33 Since the transaction file records must be matched with master file records in order to update the master file it is normal practice to "sort" the transaction records into the same key sequence as the master. When the update takes place both files can be read through once together in sequence matching records along the way and updating. Without this initial sort the update would involve moving to and fro along the files rereading records to find matches! The sorted student transaction file might be as shown in Figure 14.7. Sorting the transaction file is likely to be a lengthy process involving several intermediate steps and files. Details will be given at a later stage.

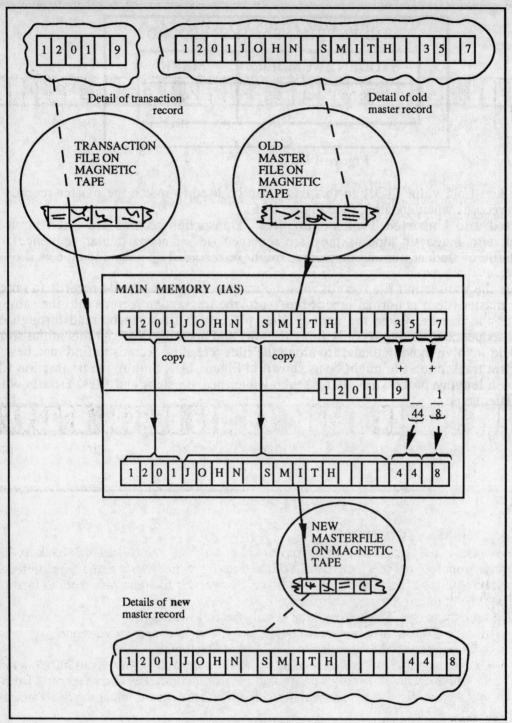

Figure 14.5.

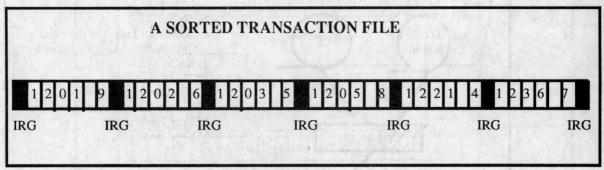

AN UNSORTED TRANSACTION FILE

| 1 2 0 5 | 8 | 1 2 0 3 | 5 | 1 2 0 1 | 9 | 1 2 3 6 | 7 | 1 2 0 2 | 6 | 1 2 2 1 | 4 |

IRG   IRG   IRG   IRG   IRG   IRG   IRG

NB.   a. This is a ``serial file'' ie. the records are in order one
after the other along the tape, but this is **not** a sequential
file because the record keys to not run in sequence.

b. The records in this unsorted transaction file are not
blocked. Such non-blocking is quite common practice for
unsorted transaction files.

Figure 14.6.

A SORTED TRANSACTION FILE

| 1 2 0 1 | 9 | 1 2 0 2 | 6 | 1 2 0 3 | 5 | 1 2 0 5 | 8 | 1 2 2 1 | 4 | 1 2 3 6 | 7 |

IRG   IRG   IRG   IRG   IRG   IRG   IRG

Figure 14.7.

UPDATING THE MASTER FILE

14.34 a. Because of the design of the tape unit it is not possible to write records back to the
same position on the tape from which they have just been read. The method of
updating a tape file therefore is to form a *new* master file on a *new* reel of tape each
time the updating process is carried out.

b. Updating a master file held on tape entails the following:-

     i. Transaction file and master file must be in the same sequence.

     ii. A transaction record is read into main storage

     iii. A master record is read into main storage and written straight out again
on a new reel if it does not match the transaction. Successive records from
the master file are read (and written) until the record matching the transaction
is located.

     iv. The master record is then updated in storage and written out in sequence

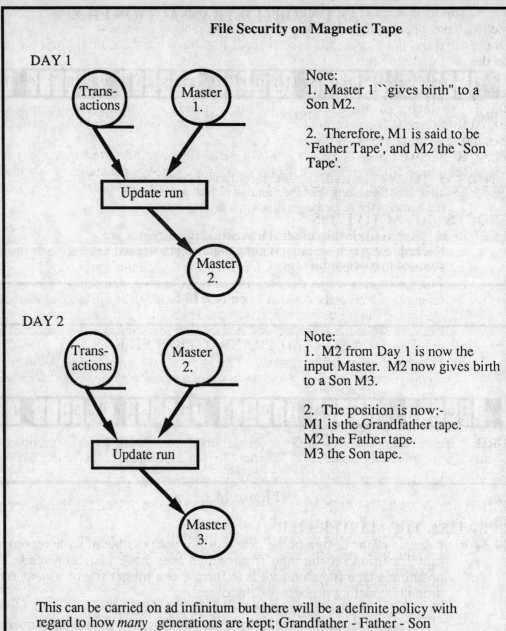

File Security on Magnetic Tape

DAY 1

Note:
1. Master 1 ``gives birth'' to a Son M2.

2. Therefore, M1 is said to be `Father Tape', and M2 the `Son Tape'.

DAY 2

Note:
1. M2 from Day 1 is now the input Master. M2 now gives birth to a Son M3.

2. The position is now:-
M1 is the Grandfather tape.
M2 the Father tape.
M3 the Son tape.

This can be carried on ad infinitum but there will be a definite policy with regard to how *many* generations are kept; Grandfather - Father - Son should be adequate. If an accident should befall M3 on Day 3's Update run then no matter, we can recreate it by doing Day 2's Run again. The keeping of the Master and appropriate Transaction files ensure security of the system's files. Notice as new `generations' are born the oldest tapes are re-used. The old information they contain is overwritten.

Figure 14.8.

on the new reel.

The four steps are repeated until all the master records for which there is a transaction record have been updated. The result is the creation of a *new* reel of tape containing the records that did not change plus the records that have been updated. The new reel will be used on the next updating run.

This method also gives **"file security"**. If for any reason the new master file is lost or damaged it can be recreated by doing the update of the old master file again (see Figure 14.8).

14.35 The details of the procedures for such updates will be covered later in chapters 28 and 29. At this stage it is convenient to mention other types of file and processing activities before looking at other devices.

14.36 Reference Files. These are a third type of file in addition to Master files and Transaction files. Reference files normally contain data of reasonable permanency which is required for reference purposes eg. a file of students' names, addresses and dates of birth.

PROCESSING ACTIVITIES

14.37 In addition to **updating** other file processing activities are:-

a. **Referencing** ie. access is made to a particular record to obtain required information eg. obtaining details of the address from John Smith's record.

b. **File maintenance** ie. the addition of new records, deletion of unwanted records or changes to records on a master or reference file eg. adding a record for a new student, deleting a record for a student who has left or changing a students address because the student has moved house. File maintenance is sometimes combined with updating.

c. **File enquiry or interrogation.** This is similar to referencing but is broader in that it covers access to non static data in order to satisfy a query eg. "What is John Smith's total mark to date?"

ACCESS TO MAGNETIC TAPE

14.38 Reference and enquiry of files on magnetic tape is made troublesome by the serial nature of the medium. Random access is important for the provision of fast and efficient file access so we now turn to look at random access devices (Disks).

EXCHANGEABLE MAGNETIC DISK UNIT AND MAGNETIC DISK PACK

14.39 Features of an Exchange Disk Unit.

a. The disk unit is the device in which the disk pack is placed. The disk *pack* is placed into the *unit* and connects with the drive mechanism.

b. Once the pack is loaded into the unit the read/write mechanism, located inside the unit, positions itself over the first track of each surface. The mechanism consists of a number of arms at the ends of which there is a read/write head for each surface. All arms are fixed together and all move together as one when accessing a surface on the disk pack.

c. The disk when loaded is driven at a high number of revolutions (several thousand) per minute and access can only be made to its surfaces when the disk revolves (See Figure 14.9).

Figure 14.9. A Hard Disk. - SHOWN ON THE NEXT PAGE

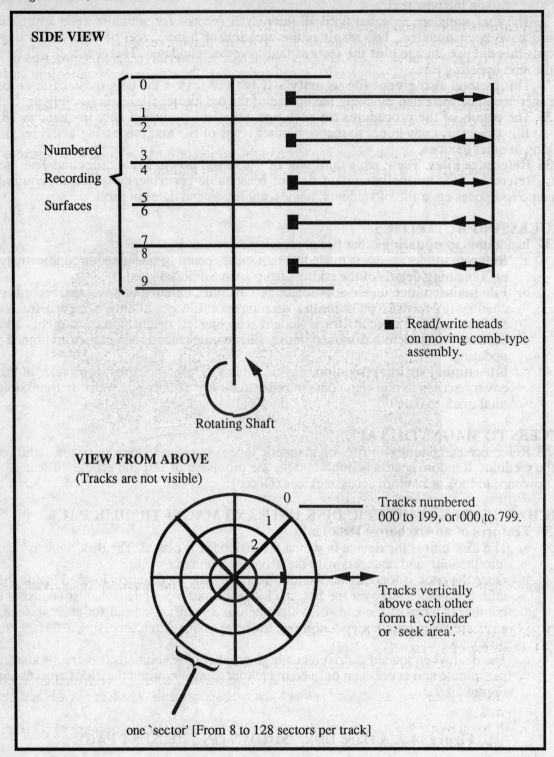

SIDE VIEW

Numbered

Recording

Surfaces

0
1
2
3
4
5
6
7
8
9

■ Read/write heads
on moving comb-type
assembly.

Rotating Shaft

VIEW FROM ABOVE
(Tracks are not visible)

Tracks numbered
000 to 199, or 000 to 799.

Tracks vertically
above each other
form a `cylinder'
or `seek area'.

one `sector' [From 8 to 128 sectors per track]

14.40 Features of an Exchangeable Disk Pack.
   a. Disks are of a size and shape similar to a long playing record.
   b. The surfaces of each disk are of a magnetisable material (except the outer-most surfaces of a pack which are purely protective). Thus there are 10 recording surfaces in a 6 disk pack and 20 in an 22 disk pack.
   c. Each surface is divided into a number of *concentric tracks* (typically 200).
   d. The disks within a *pack* are inseparable ie. the pack, of either 6 or 11 disks, is *always* used as a single unit.
   e. The two sizes of disk *pack* can store in the region of 8 and 30 million characters respectively. The latest disk packs can store 200 million characters.

An IBM System/370 Model 145 with IBM 3340 Disk Storage. (Note the removable disk pack). Picture courtesy of IBM.

FIXED MAGNETIC DISK UNIT AND MAGNETIC DISK
14.41 Features of a Fixed Disk Unit.
   a. The Unit houses a number of non-removable disks.
   b. It has read/write heads, either located on the end of "arms" (as with exchangeable disks) or serving each track (as with the magnetic drum). The latter is a Fixed head disk.
   c. It has a motor that rotates the drive at a high constant rate but because of its size, the speed will be slower than that of exchangeable disk units.

14.42 Features of a Fixed Disk.

The disks are generally *larger* than disks in an exchangeable disk pack. Otherwise they have similar features to exchangeable disks.

OTHER TYPES OF DISK

14.43 Details of *floppy disks* were given in Figure 10.9. Floppy disks have much smaller storage capacities than hard disks and are much slower to access (ie. it takes longer to read data from a floppy disk into memory than it does to read it from a hard disk).

A Kennedy Model 5380 Winchester Hard disk System with cover removed to reveal read/write head positioned over the disk. Picture courtesy of Kennedy International Inc.

14.44 One variation on the diskette which has become popular in recent years is the **microfloppy** disk. (see fig 1.3). These disks are normally 3 1/2 inches in diameter and are used on a variety of small microcomputer based systems and workstations eg. the Apple Macintosh or the IBM PS/2. They are generally regarded as an improvement over the normal 8 inch and 5 1/4 inch diskettes because of these features:

a. They have a more rugged plastic cover which keeps the whole disk surface covered and protected when not in use.
b. The cover has a slot giving the disk drive heads access to the disk which is automatically slid open while the diskette is inserted into the drive but otherwise is held closed against dust and dirt by a tiny spring.
c. The microfloppies have storage capacities comparable with those of their larger counterparts and are thus more space efficient.

14.45 Winchester disks. These have the same features as Fixed disks subject to the comments made in 14.24.

ORGANISATION AND ACCESS OF FILES AND DISK

14.46 It is beyond the scope of this book to deal with the details of this topic but general aspects will be dealt with in this section.

The cylinder concept.

Consult figure 14.9 where the disk pack is illustrated and note the following.

a. There are *ten* recording surfaces. Each surface has 200 tracks.

b. There is a read-write head for *each* surface of the disk pack.

c. *All* the read-write arms are fixed to one mechanism and are like a comb.

d. When the "access" mechanism moves, all ten read-write heads move in *unison* across the disk surfaces.

e. Whenever the access mechanism comes to rest each read/write head will be positioned on the *equivalent* track on *each* of the *ten* surfaces.

f. For *one* movement of the access mechanism access is possible to *ten* tracks of data.

g. The floppy disk is a simplified version with just one or both surfaces being used.

Use is made of the physical features already described when organising the storage of records on disk. Records are written onto the disk starting with track 1 on surface 1, then track 1 on surface 2, then track 1 on surface 3, and so on to track 1 on surface 10. One can see that conceptually the ten tracks of data can be regarded as forming a CYLINDER, also called a "seek area" see Figure 14.10.

14.47 In order to illustrate the concepts of disk file organisation and access, examples will be given based upon floppy disks which are relatively simple to describe. (See Fig. 11.14).

14.48 Example. For the purposes of this example assume a single sided floppy disk is to be used which has 40 tracks with each track divided into 8 sectors. Assume that data is written to or read from the floppy disk in complete sectors ie. assume that a sector corresponds to a block on magnetic tape ie. it is the unit for transferring data to or from the device.

14.49 Disk Address. Each sector on the disk has a unique "disk address" which in this example consists of

a. A track number 00-39

b. A sector number 0-7

14.50 Direct Access. Data on any sector can be accessed directly by using its disk address. ie.the read/write heads can be moved until they are over the specified track (without reading data on the way) and then as the specified sector passes beneath the read/write heads it is read from the disk into main memory.

The time for all this to happen is called the **access time.** The time taken by the read/write heads to get to the track is the **seek time.** There is a **rotational delay** time as the disk comes round beneath the read/write heads and there is **data transfer time** as the data is read into main memory.

ie.**Access time = seek time + rotational delay + data transfer time.**

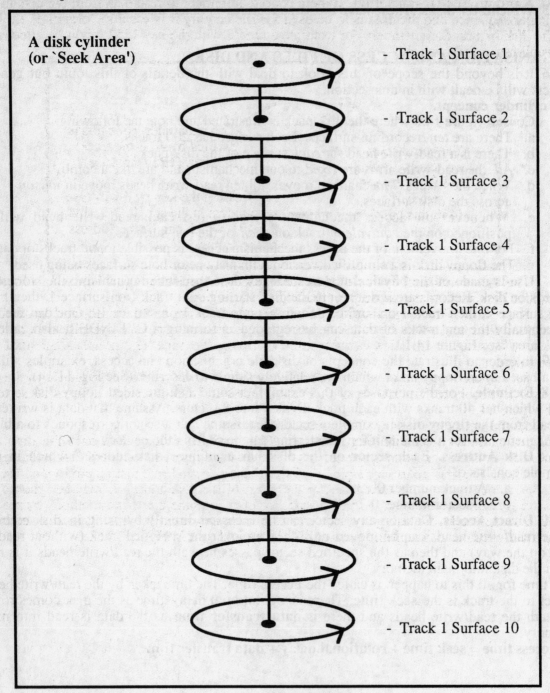

A disk cylinder (or `Seek Area')

- Track 1 Surface 1
- Track 1 Surface 2
- Track 1 Surface 3
- Track 1 Surface 4
- Track 1 Surface 5
- Track 1 Surface 6
- Track 1 Surface 7
- Track 1 Surface 8
- Track 1 Surface 9
- Track 1 Surface 10

Figure 14.10.

14.51 Random File Organisation. If there is no requirement to read data from the disk in any particular sequence and the data is to be used for file enquiry it is usual to "organise" the data on the disk in a random manner. For example a record with the key 1252 might be allocated a disk address as follows:

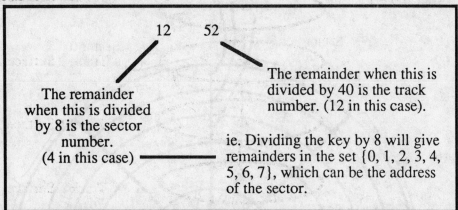

This is a simplified example of an **addressing algorithm** it can be used to locate a record for both writing and subsequent reading given the key.

14.52 Sequential File Organisation. When master files are to be stored, and updated by transaction files, and when there is little need for file enquiry, it pays to organise data onto the disk in away which mimics organisation on magnetic tape ie. to use sequential file organisation.

Sequential organisation of files on disk involves writing records in sequence to the disk in this strict sequence. Track 0 sector 0, Track 0 sector 1, Track 0 sector...... Track 39 sector 7. (See Figure 14.11).

ie. sequential organisation only allows sequential access.

14.53 Index Sequential File Organisation. This involves writing data onto the disk as a sequential file but in addition some sectors of the disk are reserved to record disk addresses of data records. The disk addresses stored on the disk may be read into main memory and used as an index to obtain the data **randomly,** or the index of the disk addresses may be ignored and the data is read **sequentially.** A third possibility is to combine these two methods by reading the file sequentially but using the index to skip over unwanted records. This is a **selective sequential** method. A simplified form of disk index is shown in Figure 14.12.

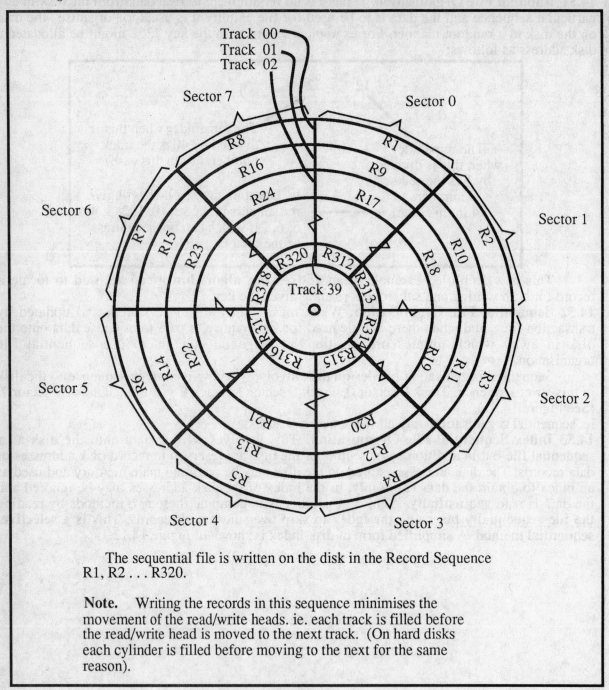

The sequential file is written on the disk in the Record Sequence
R1, R2 . . . R320.

Note. Writing the records in this sequence minimises the
movement of the read/write heads. ie. each track is filled before
the read/write head is moved to the next track. (On hard disks
each cylinder is filled before moving to the next for the same
reason).

Figure 14.11.

NB. Having written data onto the disk in this way it must be read back in the same fashion.

**Figure 14.12.
A simple Index
Sequential Disk File
on Floppy Disk.**

Index held on Track 0

HIGHEST KEY IN SECTOR	DISK ADDRESS	
1207	01	0
1236	01	1
1256	01	2
1274	01	3
1282	01	4
1290	01	5
1315	02	0
1327	02	1
1337	02	2
1349	02	3
1362	02	4
1379	02	5
1396	03	0
1408	03	1
1415	03	2
1426	03	3
1435	03	4
1446	03	5
1463	39	0
1476	39	1
1490	39	2
1499	39	3
1512	39	4
1530	39	5

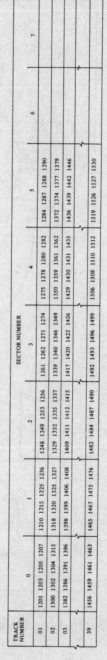

TRACK NUMBER	SECTOR NUMBER							
	0	1	2	3	4	5	6	7
01	1201 1203 1205 1207	1210 1215 1225 1236	1248 1249 1253 1256	1261 1262 1271 1274	1275 1278 1280 1282	1284 1287 1288 1290		
02	1300 1302 1304 1315	1318 1320 1325 1327	1329 1332 1335 1337	1339 1340 1346 1349	1350 1359 1361 1362	1372 1374 1377 1379		
03	1382 1386 1391 1396	1398 1399 1406 1408	1409 1411 1412 1415	1417 1420 1422 1426	1429 1430 1431 1435	1436 1439 1442 1446		
39	1456 1459 1461 1463	1465 1467 1475 1476	1482 1484 1487 1490	1492 1493 1496 1499	1506 1508 1510 1512	1519 1526 1527 1530		

NB. Whole records are stored (4 records per sector in this example) but only their keys are shown in this diagram.

219

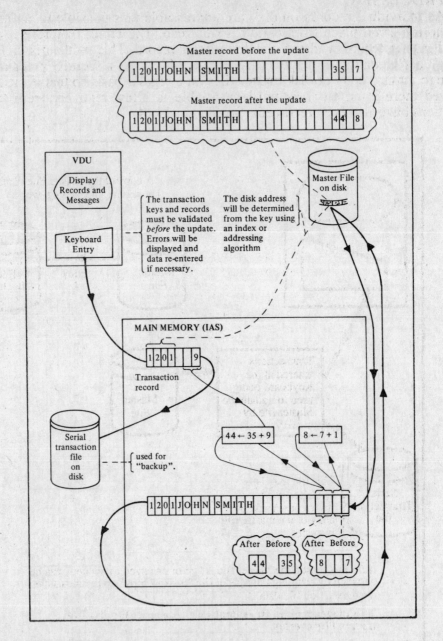

Figure 14.13. On-Line Update of a Master File on Disk using Random Access and Overlays.

Note. Sequential disk file security is provided in the same way as magnetic tape file security.

220

DISK PROCESSING

14.54 As individual records on disk are addressable it is possible to *write* back an updated record to the same place from which it was read. The effect therefore is to *over write* the original master record with the updated master record. This method is called "**Updating by overlay**" or "Updating in place". (See Figure 14.13). As a security precaution it is common practice to make a copy of disk master files on a regular basis so that if the file is damaged or destroyed there is an old master file available to allow recovery from the loss, provided transactions have also been recorded. (See Figure 14.14).

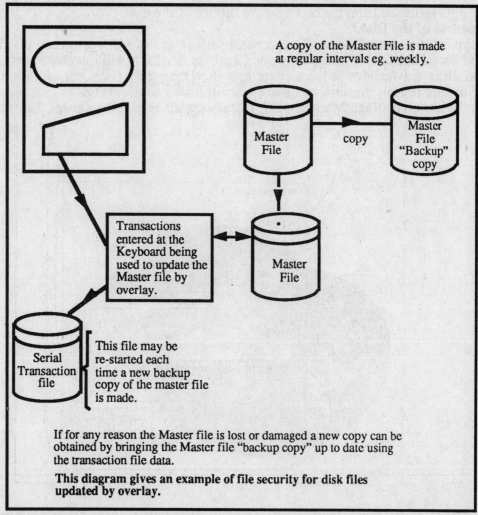

A copy of the Master File is made at regular intervals eg. weekly.

Master File

copy

Master File "Backup" copy

Transactions entered at the Keyboard being used to update the Master file by overlay.

Master File

Serial Transaction file

This file may be re-started each time a new backup copy of the master file is made.

If for any reason the Master file is lost or damaged a new copy can be obtained by bringing the Master file "backup copy" up to date using the transaction file data.

This diagram gives an example of file security for disk files updated by overlay.

Figure 14.14.   Example of file security for disk files updated by overlay.

OPTICAL DISK UNIT AND OPTICAL DISK

14.55 They work on a similar principle to that used for the domestic compact disk (CD) which has become very popular as a replacement for the LP record. Some exchangeable optical disk drives actually use disks that are physically the same as CDs. This is not so surprising since CDs record sound in digital form.

14.56 Features of the Disk Unit.

    a. The device is similar in appearance to a fixed magnetic disk unit but data is written onto the disk by burning a permanent pattern into the surface of the disk by means of a high precision laser beam.

    b. Data is read back by using the laser at lower intensity and detecting the pattern of light reflected from the beam by the surface of the disk.

14.57 Features of the Disk.

A typical disk looks like a CD and has a surface of 40,000 tracks each divided into 25 sectors and a total capacity of staggering one Gigabyte (ie. 1,000 million characters).

14.58 The disks are far less prone to data loss than magnetic disks but are non-reusable at present. For this reason the disk are sometimes referred to as "**WORM**" storage. WORM stands for "Write Once Read Many times". Access speeds tend to be slower than for magnetic disks.

CD-ROM Disks _ the size of CDs, and providing WORM optical data storage.
Picture courtesy of PHILIPS.

OTHER BACKING STORAGE DEVICES AND MEDIA.

14.59 There are many other forms of backing storage in use today, many of them aimed at specialist uses.

14.60 RAM disks (also called silicon disks) are popular on personal computers and work stations. They are not disks at all in fact. Rather, they are RAM memory being used as if it was a diskette. The advantage is fast performance but any data to be kept must be copied onto a magnetic disk before the computer is switched off because RAM disks are volatile. Thus the uses of RAM disks are limited.

A Kennedy Model 6809 Magnetic Tape Streamer used to provide fast, efficient and cost effective back up of fixed disks. Picture courtesy of Kennedy International, Inc.

14.61 Solid State Storage devices were described in sufficient detail in chapter 11. The methods of organising and accessing data are modified combinations of the methods already described in this chapter.

SUMMARY

14.62 a. Main storage is a fast, wholly electronic, random access memory which is used as a short term memory for data awaiting processing or output, or which is being processed.

   b. Data stored in main memory is identified and located by the memory location address.

c. Locations in main memory are called **words** which are often sub divided into smaller units called **bytes** (1 byte = 8 bits).
d. Physical types of memory (all of which are semiconductor memory) include:-
    i. RAM
    ii. ROM and variants eg. PROMs EPROMs etc.

14.63 a. Backing Storage (Auxiliary Storage) is used to supplement main storage. It provides larger storage capacities than main storage but slower access speeds.
b. Backing storage devices and media include:-
    i. Magnetic tape unit - magnetic tape
    ii. Magnetic disk unit - magnetic disk
    iii. Optical disk unit - optical disk
c. Magnetic disks are of major importance and have many variations:-
    i. Hard Disks A. Fixed disks
                  B. Fixed head disks
                  C. Exchangeable disks (in disk packs)
                  D. Winchester disks
    ii. Floppy Disks (Diskettes).
d. The physical nature of the storage devices will have a direct bearing on the way files are organised on it, and also on the methods of access.
e. Files may be broadly classified as master files, transaction files, and reference files.
f. Four file processing activities are: Updating, Referencing File Maintenance and File Enquiry or Interrogation.
g. Magnetic tape is a serial medium and can only be accessed serially.
h. Files on magnetic tape are:-
    i. Written onto tape, and read from tape in units called blocks (physical records) separated by IBG's (Inter Block Gaps). The blocks are comprised of logical records.
    ii. Updated by creating physically different files each time.
i. Disk is an addressable medium and therefore specific records can be accessed leaving the rest of the file undisturbed.
j. Organisation on disk is by cylinder, track and sector.
k. The overlay or "in place" method of updating can be used on disk.
l. A summary of methods of file organisation and access is given in figure 14.15.

FILE ORGANISATION METHOD	METHOD OF ACCESS	POSSIBLE MEDIUM	POSSIBLE USE
1. Serial	Serial	Magnetic Tape or Disk	Unsorted trans-action file.
2. Sequential	Serial (Sequential)	Magnetic Tape or Disk	Sorted trans-action file or Sequential Master File.
3. Index Sequential	a. Sequential b. Selective Sequential c. Random	Disk (**Not** Magnetic tape)	Master files requiring a variety of processing activities
4. Random	Random	Disk (**Not** Magnetic tape)	Master files requiring *fast* reference or enquiry.

Figure 14.15.

POINTS TO NOTE

14.64 a. As Semiconductor main memory becomes relatively cheaper there is less emphasis placed on minimising the use of main storage, and so more emphasis can be placed on making reliable and effective use of main storage.

b. Today the backing storage medium of major importance in file processing is magnetic disk. Magnetic tape continues in importance as a major medium, but more for its use in holding "backup" copies of files for security purposes and for its use in data input.

c. Where large files are just processed sequentially and at infrequent intervals magnetic tape remains a more suitable medium.

d. Once data has been written to an optical disk it cannot be erased but it can be read as many times as required. This is sometimes called **WORM** (Write Once Read Many).

QUESTIONS A *(With answers)*

1. List the uses of main storage.

2. Describe what is meant by
a. location address

b. byte
c. word
d. two-state device.
e. character

and discuss their interrelationships

3. Show how the word "DINOSAUR" would be stored in main storage, using ASCII, starting at location zero in
   a.   an 8 bit machine
   b.   a 16 bit machine
   State clearly which characters are in which address. (See Appendix IV.3).

4. What is PROM?

5. Distinguish between fixed and variable length records. Make it clear how each field is located within a record in each case. What are their relative advantages?

6. Describe the grandfather-father-son concept as used for master files. Why is this technique used?

7. List four main file processing activities and briefly explain the differences between them.

8. Describe the concept of a "disk address".

9. In disk processing, where updating by overlay is used, data can be lost through system failure or malfunction. What precautions are taken in order to aid recovery?

QUESTIONS B *(Without answers)*

1. What is IAS?

2. Place in order of data access speed from fastest to slowest:-
   a.   Fixed head disk.
   b.   Floppy disk (diskette).
   c.   Main memory
   d.   Exchangeable disk.

3. Explain the difference between a **serial file** and a **sequential file**. When are they effectively the same?

4. Explain the difference between **file updating** and file **maintenance.**

5. What physical features make a magnetic disk faster than a floppy disk for data access?

6. Refer to the student record example in this chapter. If the master file is updated using the **unsorted** transaction file given in figure 9.31, how many new copies of the master file

would have to be made before all transactions had been processed? How many if the transactions file was sorted?

7.   *A random disk file is stored on a disk for which the seek time is 10ms the rotational delay is 0.5ms and the data transfer time is 0.2ms. How long will it take to perform two reads from the disk?*

8.   *Distinguish between sequential files and index sequential files stored on disk. Which would you use for the following applications:-*
     a.   A file containing names and addresses which is used on a regular basis to produce a mailing list but which is used for no other purpose.
     b.   A customers' accounts file which is processed monthly for all customers but which is needed daily for credit checking.
     c.   A file of employee details which is used once a week to produce a weekly wages payroll.
     State any assumptions that you have made.

15 Choice of Hardware

INTRODUCTION
15.1 This chapter looks at the factors influencing the choice of methods and media for input, output and storage. Many media are multipurpose, serving an important role in input, storage and output eg. magnetic tape. Some dual purpose devices such as the VDU appear as part of a variety of input and output methods. Detailed tables of comparison have not been included in this edition because they are an "overkill" for the courses at this level.

FACTORS INFLUENCING THE CHOICE OF METHODS AND MEDIA
15.2 The choice of methods and media for a given application will be influenced by the following factors.
- a. **Appropriateness.**
- b. **Cost.**
- c. **Time.**
- d. **Accuracy.**
- e. **Volume.**
- f. **Confidence.**

15.3 All the factors just listed are to some extent related to each other. For example delays in getting required data (**time**) may **cost** money, damage **confidence** and make the method being used appear **inappropriate**.

APPROPRIATENESS
15.4 Suitable applications of particular media will be tabulated later. At this stage it should be noted that deciding what is appropriate involves:-
- a. Having a clear idea of what is ideally required by analysing the application carefully.
- b. Knowing the features of available media and the methods associated with them.
- c. Knowing the advantages and disadvantages of the available methods and media.
- d. Taking *all* factors into consideration when making the choice of methods and media.

COST
15.5 Cost is often an overriding factor. Most organisations will have a spending limit within which the best available solution to their problem must be found. In addition to this, **costs** are usually compared with the **benefits** which can be obtained ie. an organisation will make sure that the expenditure is not just possible but desirable.

15.6 The elements of cost are:-
- a. **Staff.** New staff may be needed to operate the new system. Existing staff may need training or staff may no longer be needed.
- b. **Equipment.** Equipment may need to be rented, or purchased and maintained.
- c. **Buildings.** More floor space may be needed or the "environment" (eg. air and electricity supply) may need alternation.
- d. **Media.** Printer paper are *not* re-usable and can prove very costly.

TIME
15.7 The value of information is often closely related to the *speed* with which it can be obtained. For example an air traffic control system may provide warnings which will help to avert accidents. Try selling yesterday's weather forecast! Generally speaking the quicker the response must be, the more the response will cost. It is the *slow* and cumbersome stages in data

entry for punched cards and paper which have helped to establish newer *quicker* and easier alternatives.

ACCURACY
15.8 Inaccuracies and errors can easily arise from the use of "unclean" media or because of errors in data preparation, usually caused by human error.

Machines are more consistently accurate than human if correctly used and so increasing automation can often be the answer. Accuracy and consistency have a significant effect on confidence.

VOLUME
15.9 a. Large volumes of input data can only be handled by highly automated special purpose methods. This is illustrated by the special methods which have been developed in banks, insurance and retailing eg. MICR, OCR and PoS.

    b. Large volumes of output can only be provided by high speed devices and large volumes of output can create their own storage problems. Laser printers and COM illustrate these points.

    c. The demands for large volumes of on-line data storage are highlighted by the need for backing storage to supplement main memory and are also highlighted by the wide range of backing storage devices.

CONFIDENCE
15.10 Confidence comes more readily from successful experience. This is probably the main reason why new methods take some time to catch on.

Confidence is also affected by the accuracy, reliability and robustness of methods and media.

The robustness and reliability of computer equipment depends not only on the equipment itself but on the environment in which it is used and the expertise of the people using the equipment.

COMPARING INPUT OR OUTPUT DEVICES AND MEDIA
15.11 There is no need for the reader to remember detailed facts and figures about the various devices and media on the market in order to be successful on the courses for which this text is a preparation. In any case such information becomes dated very quickly. Nevertheless, it is important to be able to recognise how the general points made earlier in this chapter apply to particular circumstances. The reader is therefore urged to read computer magazines and periodicals on a regular basis in order to keep in touch with what products are currently available and how they are being used.

A COMPARISON OF MAGNETIC TAPE AND MAGNETIC DISK
15.12 This is a suitable place to make some general points of comparison between magnetic tape and magnetic disk.

15.13 Advantages of Magnetic Tape Storage.
    a. **Cost** - reels of tape cost £25 (or less) as opposed to disk packs which cost £250 (approx.), and are therefore, much cheaper. Costs of associated drive units are not significantly different from those used with disks.

b. **Storage capacity** - potentially relatively high. Each reel has 40 million characters capacity but typically it is utilised to the same extent as with disk.

c. **File security** - physically different brought-forward and carried-forward tapes are used in processing and therefore measures of file security can be said to be built-in. (This uses the grandfather-father-son concept).

d. **High activity** - tape is suitable for "high activity" batch processing ie. where sequential files are updated and where *most records* require an update.

e. **Off-line storage** - tape reels represent a cheap form of off-line storage.

f. **File maintenance** is facilitated because it is relatively easy to insert, delete or amend records on tape.

g. **Software** - no complicated software is required to handle files on tape as can be necessary with disk.

h. **Source data** can be keyed directly on to tape using a Magnetic Tape Encoding machine. This is not possible with disk which requires use of the computer.

i. Industrial standards apply to magnetic tape so tapes are useful to bulk data transfer between different systems.

15.14 Advantages of Magnetic Disk Storage.

a. **Addressable medium** ie. DAS (Direct Access Storage), - each record can be located independently; this is not possible with magnetic tape which is essentially a serial storage medium, ie. SAS (Serial Access Storage).

b. **File organisation** - files can be arranged sequentially or in a random manner, whereas magnetic tape is confined to serial file organisation.

c. **Access** - access to records stored on disk may be sequential (using an index in case of index sequential files) or random. Time taken to locate a record is independent of the position of that record.

d. **Storage capacity** - disk packs of the removable type have a high capacity. One such pack may hold some 60 million characters or more.

e. **Data transfer speed** - this is high and much faster than all except the latest model tape devices. Current disk units have data transfer speed of about 800 k bytes per second.

f. **On-line "real time" processing** - This is only possible using disk. Disk access provides the speed in processing to affect events as they happen ("real time").

g. **Information availability** - requests for information can be answered quickly and at random.

h. **Low activity** - disk is a suitable medium for "low activity" processing. No time is wasted reading and writing redundant records as with magnetic tape.

i. **Software etc., storage** - disks are ideal for the storage of programs which are constantly needed in main memory.

15.15 From the previous two paragraphs it should be relatively easy to see why disk is now the major medium for file processing and why magnetic tape continues to be of importance for data input, backup, off-line storage and bulk data transfer.

SUMMARY

15.16 a. Factors affecting the choice of methods and media include:-
   i. Appropriateness
   ii. Cost

       iii. Time
       iv. Accuracy
       v. Volume
       vi. Confidence.
   b. The tables in this chapter are a summary in themselves.

POINTS TO NOTE

15.17 a. Technology is constantly changing. It is therefore more important to understand the factors affecting the choice of media than it is to remember details about particular devices or media.

       b. Advantages and disadvantages are relative eg. it is no good saying "Magnetic Disks are better than Magnetic tapes" because disk will be "better" for some uses and tape will be "better" for others.

QUESTIONS A *(With answers)*

1.   *List and briefly describe the factors influencing the choice of methods and media.*

2.   *Compare the relative advantages of a VDU and printer terminal for on-line computing.*

3.   *Suggest suitable media or methods for these applications.*
     a. Automating the handling of bank cheques.
     b. Handling the marking of multiple choice examination papers.
     c. Input of a limited number of words when neither hand is free.
     d. Collecting details of stock sales in a retail clothing shop.
     e. Recording stock details of items on shelves in a supermarket.
     f. Low speed printing where a number of different character sets are needed.
     *g. Very fast single copy printing where **very large** numbers of pages containing print of reasonable quality have to be printed every day.*
     h. Storing details of a library catalogue for reference purposes within a library.
     *i. **Permanent** storage of a program within a small computer.*
     j. Direct access storage of a very large file used once a week.
     k. Direct access storage on a small computer system which must be used in a slightly dusty environment.
     l. Keeping backup copies of master files.

4.   *Describe a device with WORM storage.*

QUESTIONS B *(Without answers)*

1.   *Suggest one suitable application for each of the following:-*
     a. A line printer
     b. A floppy disk unit
     c. A matrix printer.
     d. A magnetic tape unit
     e. COM
     f. OMR

    g. *MICR*
    h. *A fixed head disk*
    i. *A thermal printer*
    j. *A viewdata terminal*
    k. *OCR*
    l. *A Winchester disk.*
    m. *A VDU with light pen.*
    n. *A graph plotter*
    o. *A punched tag*
    p. *A laser printer.*
    q. *Bar coding.*
    r. *A key-to-disk system.*
    s. *A magnetic tape cassette unit*
    t. *A handwriting pad or table.*

16 Communications Systems and Uses

INTRODUCTION

16.1   In this chapter we look at the ways in which it is possible to interconnect and use various kinds of computer equipment where the equipment is at separate locations. One of the simplest cases involves data being sent to and fro between a computer and remote terminal by electronic means. The normal term for this is **point-to-point data transmission.** More elaborate systems may involve the interconnection of many computers whose users may be sharing the resources available or sending each other messages. The computers in such a system are said to be on a **computer network.**

16.2   The chapter starts with traditional forms of communication based upon the telephone system and then goes on to discuss more modern techniques including computer networks. Later it looks at the various public and private communication services available today.

TRADITIONAL METHODS OF DATA TRANSMISSION

16.3   There are two long established methods of data transmission, telephone and telex. The one which has for a long time been used for a variety of forms of data transmission is the telephone system.

16.4   It will prove useful to examine some of the basic features of the telephone system. Two key features are:-

    a.   It is **circuit switching** system, ie. when a call is placed by dialling the appropriate number the switching equipment in the exchange establishes a circuit between the caller and the answerer. The circuit is then maintained for the duration of the call.

    b.   The electrical signal transmitted takes a form which is like the form of the sound to be transmitted. It is called an **analog** signal because of its analogous form.

16.5   The simplest forms of data transmission involve the connection of terminals to a computer via a telephone line. In order to use the telephone link the *digital* signals of the terminal and computer must be converted into *analog* form in order to be transmitted along the telephone line. This can be done by a device called a **MODEM,** short for **MOD**ulator - **DEM**odulator, (see Figs 16.1 and 16.2). The modem plugs directly into the telephone wall socket in the home, office or computer room.

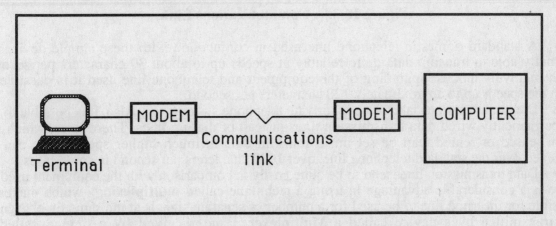

Figure 16.1. Point-to-to-Point Data Communications.

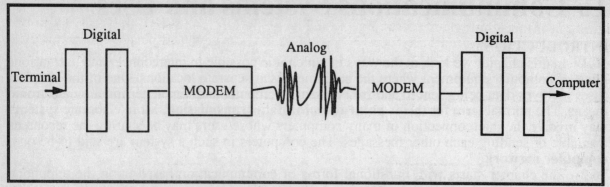

Figure 16.2 Data Transmission and the Use of MODEMS.

16.6 In the absence of a modem a portable device known as an **acoustic coupler** may be used instead (see Fig. 16.3). Modern acoustic couplers are very compact and can be very handy to use in conjunction with portable microcomputers or data collection devices. However, they tend to be slightly more error prone than modems.

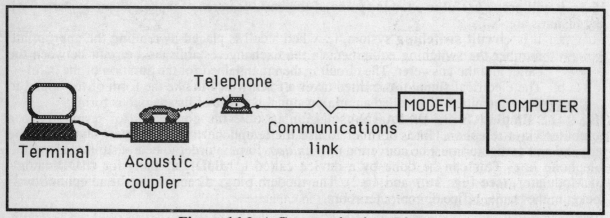

Figure 16.3. A Communications Link.

16.7 A standard domestic telephone line used in conjunction with these simple devices is normally able to transmit data quite reliably at speeds up to about 30 characters per second. With relatively modest upgrading of the equipment and telephone line used it is possible to push the speeds up to approximately 120 characters per second.

16.8 Data transmissions take place on private telephone systems too. Also, it is possible to set up permanently wired data transmission lines instead of dial-up lines. These lines, which are often leased or rented, can be set up to transmit data at much higher speeds than can be achieved over the standard telephone line, over 1000 characters per second in some cases.

16.9 Data transmission lines tend to be quite costly in comparison with the equipment used so there is a considerable advantage in using a technique called **multiplexing** which makes it possible for the same line to be used for a number of separate signals at the same time. Signals are transmitted by a device called a **Multiplexer** and received by a device called a

demultiplexer. there are many methods of multiplexing. One form of multiplexing involves a device known as a **concentrator** which is typically used to connect a number of slow terminals situated near to a single transmission line. (See Fig. 16.4) (NB. The PABX in fig. 16.4 will be discussed shortly) Data items are normally transmitted to or from the terminals' concentrator at irregular intervals and so the terminals to which they belong are recognised by identification numbers transmitted with the data items.

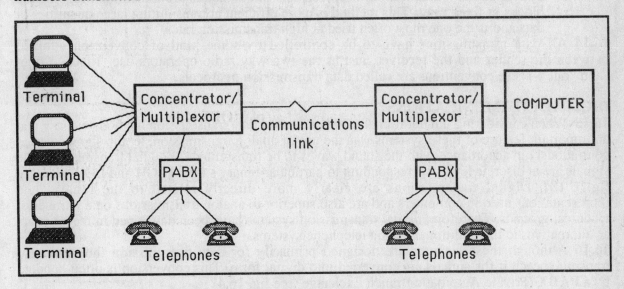

Figure 16.4 Data Communications Links.

CHARACTERISTICS OF DATA TRANSMISSION LINES

16.10 A data transmission link is normally called a **channel.** One very important characteristic of a channel is its capacity to carry data. This capacity is directly related to the range of frequencies with which it is possible to transmit **bits** (16.14) along the channel, a characteristic known as the **bandwidth** of the channel. Channels with broader bandwidth, called **broadband** or **wideband** channels, have greater transmission capacities.

16.11 The actual rate of data flow, ie. **"data transfer rate",** is often expressed in terms of the number of bits transmitted per second (bps). It normally takes between 8 and 10 bits to transmit an individual character depending upon the method of transmission. So, for example, a 300 bps line will typically carry about 30 characters per second. Maximum data transfer rates vary accordingly to the medium used. A **coaxial cable,** as used for a TV aerial, can carry up to 140 million bps which is equivalent to about 2000 telephone lines. An **optical fibre** can carry data at rates in excess of 500 million characters per second.

16.12 Transmission along a channel is possible in three modes.
  a. **Simplex:** Transmission is possible in only one direction.
  b. **Half Duplex.** Transmission is possible in both directions, but not simultaneously.
  c. **Duplex.** Transmission is possible in both directions simultaneously.

16.13 There are two alternative ways of transmitting the data:

a. **Asynchronous transmission.** The characters are transmitted singly at will at irregular   intervals in time. This method is well suited to conversational interactions and is the one most often used for transmission on standard telephone lines at low transmission rates.

b. **Synchronous transmission.** Prepared sets of characters are transmitted together as blocks at fixed rates. This method is more efficient at transmitting large quantities of data and is the one most often used at high transmission rates.

16.14 All data transmissions have to be controlled by some kind of convention adopted between the sender and the receiver, just as the two way radio operators use "roger", "over "and "out". These conventions are called data transmission **protocols.**

DIGITAL COMMUNICATIONS

16.15 When considering the traditional telephone based data transmission methods we saw that an important feature of these systems was the use of analog transmission, ie. the signals varied continuously in accordance with the sound waves to be transmitted. In digital transmissions the signals are at discrete levels corresponding to particular binary states, HIGH and LOW say (see fig.16.18). Digital transmissions are clearly more directly related to the binary data representations used in computers and are also superior to analog transmissions on a number of technical grounds. Therefore, digital transmission systems have been developed in recent years as alternatives to the traditional analog telephone systems.

16.16 Although these systems are designed primarily for data transmission they can also transmit speech if the signals are converted into digital form. This conversion is often handled by a **PABX** (Private Automatic Branch Exchange (see fig. 16.4)

16.17 There are a number of different digital transmission systems in existence. One example, is the British Telecom Kilostream service which has facilities to transfer data at rates up to 64 thousand bits per second.

MESSAGE SWITCHING AND PACKET SWITCHING

16.18 The traditional telephone circuits and modern digital circuit just described have one feature in common. They both employ fixed lines or circuit switching (16.4). In the case of circuit switching the data path has to be set up end-to-end *before* any transmission takes place and must be maintained throughout the duration of the call even if there are gaps in data transmission. Thus the system has some inherent delays and inefficiencies. Two alternatives to circuit switching which attempt to overcome its deficiencies are **message switching** and **packet switching.**

16.19 In a simple message switching circuit the transmission is done in stages with the content of the whole transmission, ie. the message, being sent along separate and successive sections of the circuit in turn. At the beginning and end of each section there is computerised unit called an **IMP** (Interface Message Processor) which is able to receive, **store and forward** the message to the destination to which it is electronically addressed. This is a form of store and forward system and has some inherent delay in it because of the need for each IMP to assemble the whole message before sending it on to the next IMP.

16.20 A rather more versatile alternative is the packet switching system. A packet consists of details of the sender, the intended destination "address", a small portion of a message and other data used for control purposes. Each packet is transmitted in the same way as a whole message in a message switching system. The packet itself enters and exits the circuit via a device called a **PAD** (Packet Assembler/Disassembler).

16.21 Packet switching does not suffer from the inherent delay of message switching and also make more flexible and efficient use of the transmission circuit because it only establishes each link for as long as is needed it to transmit each packet. The lack of delay means that packet switching systems may be used for conversational modes of transmission as well as for bulk data transmission.

16.22 The individual links, both in message switching systems and packet switching systems, tended to use digital transmission techniques.

COMPUTER NETWORKS

16.23 An interconnected set of two or more computers may be called a "**computer network**". However, if the computers in the network operate together as a single unit which to the user appears as a single computer, albeit physically dispersed, then the complete system is more accurately described as a **distributed system.** Therefore, although, *any* interconnected set of computers is often conveniently referred to as a "computer network "the use of the term often implies an interconnected set of *independent* computers and not a distributed system. However, it may be useful when considering a distributed system to be able to recognise the particular type of network on which it is based.

16.24 Networks used to interconnect computers in a single room, rooms within a building or building on one site are normally called **Local Area Networks (LANs).** LANs normally transmit data in a digital form using media such as coaxial cable or multistranded cable. In fig 16.5 there is an example of a **Local Area Network (LAN)** as may be used on a single site within an organisation. The terminals and workstations in fig 16.5 are able to connect to either one of two "host" computers at will. The network also has a **file server** and a **print server**. The former is a special computer which provides a form of auxiliary storage which can be used by any other computer on the network and the latter is a special computer which can receive data from other computers on the network and print it. There is also an **external communications server** on the LAN which enables communication between equipment on the network and system elsewhere.

16.25 LANs cannot be used over long distances. Instead **Long Haul Networks (LHNs)** are use. Long Haul Networks connect computers on separate sites, separate cities or even separate countries. They are also called **Wide Area Networks (WANs).** LHNs tend to use packet switching methods or message switching methods and exploit optical fibre media and satellite transmissions in many cases.

16.26 The feature of a typical LHN are shown in outline in fig 16.6 Computers at separate locations each have their own connection to the network. The point of connection is often called a **gateway.** When the network is used for electronic mail the gateway connection normally takes the form of some kind of **IMP (Interface Message Processor)** which has the ability to receive, store and forward messages. The communications links between IMPs can take a variety of forms such as cable, optical fibre or satellite transmission.

BASIC ADVANTAGES OF USING NETWORKS

16.27 There are many possible advantages in using networks. The basic ones are:-
    a.   The sharing of resources (eg. computers & staff) and information.
    b.   The provision of local facilities without the loss of central control.
    c.   The even distribution of work, processing loads etc.
    d.   Shared risk and mutual support.

e. Improved and more economic communication facilities in general, eg. including voice communication.

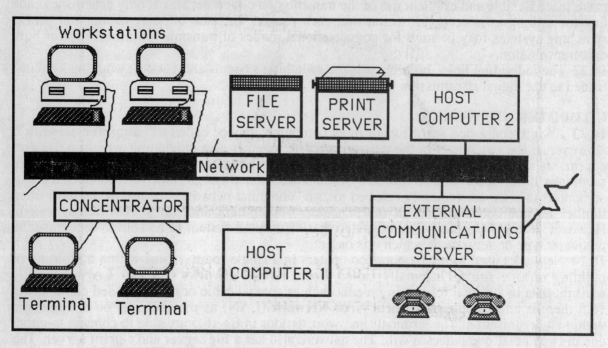

Figure 16.5. Local Area Network.

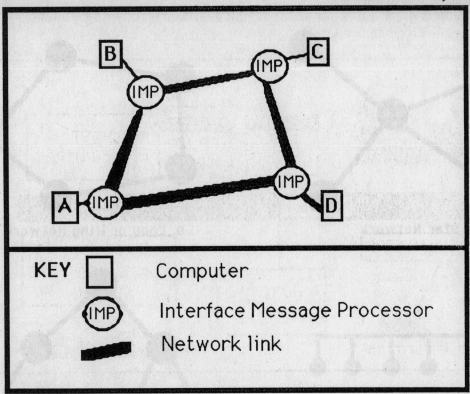

Figure 16.6. Long Haul Network.

NETWORK STRUCTURES

16.28 A number of standard network structures are shown in fig 16.7. The individual circles in fig 16.7 represent computers connected to the network in the case of LANs and represent IMPs to which computers are connected in the case of LHNs.

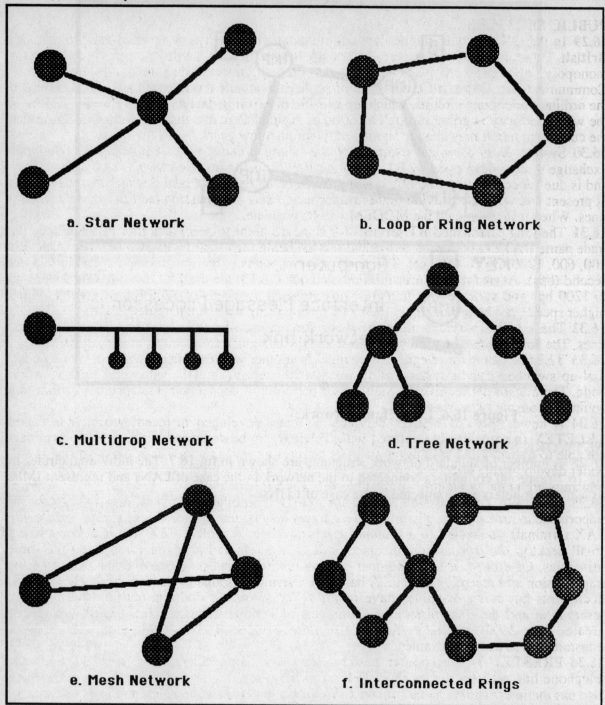

Figure 16.7. Network Structures.

PUBLIC SERVICES

16.29 In the UK the main public data communication and network services are provided by **British Telecom (BT)**. However, BT is no longer a state owned company operating a monopoly. It has been privatised and now has competition from other companies, eg. Mercury Communications. Of the different types of services available the majority are still based upon the ordinary telephone circuits, which are capable of carrying data as well as speech. However, the whole industry is going through a period of rapid change and there is every indication that the current situation may change significantly within a few years.

16.30 System X is a typical example of the changes under way. It is a digital telephone exchange system developed by BT which is currently being installed across the whole country and is due for completion in 1992. It will provide better exchange facilities than those available at present and will also provide higher performance data transmission facilities on its standard lines. When it is completed the MODEM will be obsolete.

16.31 The long established BT services for standard point-to-point data transmission have the trade name **DATEL** with each individual service being identified by its own number - DATEL 200, 600, 1200, 2400, 4800 etc. The number corresponds to the transmission speed in bits per second (bps). Asynchronous transmission methods (16.13) are used for transmission speeds up to 1200 bps and synchronous transmissions are used at speeds of 1200 bps or greater. Much higher speeds can be provided, up to 48,000 bps by using wideband circuits (16.10).

16.32 The DATEL services make provision for the use of public lines and privately leased lines. The latter tend to be used by organisations with significant amounts of data to transmit.

16.33 TELEX (short for telegraph exchange) is another well established service. It is a public dial-up switched circuit system with over 80,000 users in the UK and over a million world wide. The transmitter/receiver at each subscriber point of connection is teleprinter, similar to a computer console typewriter.

16.34 A newer form of TELEX services has been developed in recent years. It is called **TELETEX** (a name easily confused with **Teletext** - to be described later). Teletex terminals are able to transmit low resolution graphics pictures as well as text. The teletext service is still under development. There are proposals to make available a higher level teletex service which transmits high quality pictures compatible with FAX (see below).

16.35 Facsimile Transmission (FAX for short) is another service which has grown in importance in recent years. Pictures and diagrams may be transmitted from place to place using FAX terminals connected to a standard telephone line. A typical FAX terminal looks like a small desktop electrostatic photocopier. Indeed, it scans and prints pictures using the same principles. Of course, it has a number of features not found on a photocopier to enable the transmission and reception of data. A basic FAX terminal is able to transmit or receive A4 size documents but many machines have facilities for automatic dialling, multiple polling, call reservation and the transmission of documents of various standard sizes. Lines with speeds greater than 2400 bps are preferable for these devices. Then a whole document can be transmitted within a few minutes.

16.36 PRESTEL is a computer based information service available from BT over the telephone line with the aid of PRESTEL terminals. Prestel is an example of **viewdata** which also has the international name **videotex**. Viewdata systems can be either public or private. An example of public viewdata service, like PRESTEL, is shown in fig 16.8. The viewdata terminals, like those used on PRESTEL, are plugged into standard telephone sockets. In the home a telephone set may be used to display the information, provided it has been fitted with a special adaptor and keypad.

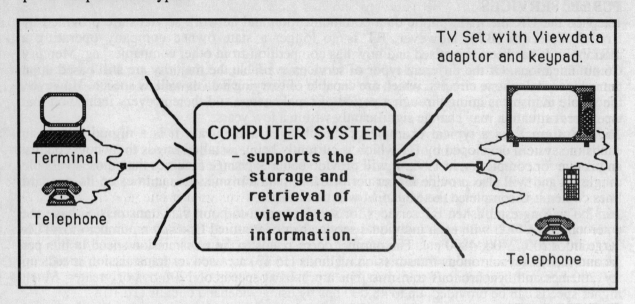

Figure 16.8. A Viewdata System.

16.37 PRESTEL has been described as an "electronic encyclopaedia for the home" but its main success has probably been in various business applications. There are currently over 60,000 PRESTEL users and over 1,200 sources of information being used to provide PRESTEL with over 300,000 "frames" of information. A "frame" is a screen sized page of information. The information which has been most successfully exploited by business is that concerning subjects such as the money markets, the stock exchange, insurance markets, agricultural markets and travel information. Users pay a standard rental plus call charges and a charge for each page viewed. Some pages may be viewed freely others may cost several pence to view for a few minutes. Organisations may purchase frame space in order to provide information to PRESTEL users. The information is fed in via a PRESTEL terminal. PRESTEL is a two-way service so a user wishing to respond to information given (eg . surveys services or advertisements) is able to do so by means of their PRESTEL terminal or keypad.

16.38 Do not confuse **viewdata** with **teletext,** which is also a computer based information system, and which has some features in common with viewdata. The important difference is that whereas viewdata is a two-way system, teletext is a receive-only system. Teletext services are provided by the BBC *(Ceefax)* and ITV *(Oracle)*. In teletext the "frames" of information are transmitted together with the TV signals using spare bandwidth. Provided the set has been fitted with a teletext adaptor it is able to decode the signals and display the frames of information on the TV screen. A hand held control pad allows individual numbered frames of information to be selected. The methods used by viewdata and teletext for displaying frames of information are compatible with one another.

16.39 PSS is a packet switching system (16.20) provided by BT and operating in a network linking major cities. The PSS network has links with other major networks including several in Europe and North America. Many companies have become major users of this service since its introduction in the early eighties and it is likely to expand even further. Each connection to the PSS network is called a PSS gateway and has an account number which is rather like a telephone number only longer.

PRIVATE SERVICES
16.40 The Public Services just described have their private equivalents. So, just as BT has introduced System X, many companies have installed private digital telephone exchanges. There are also companies running private viewdata systems. For example, several travel tour operators provide a viewdata service for travel agents.

16.41 An important trend in recent years has been the move towards integrating the various kinds of services used within the organisations. For example, if a building is to be rewired so as to provide lines from a central computer to workstations in offices it is possible to install one single digital transmission circuit containing a PABX (16.16) which is able to handle both the data communications and the telephone communications. Even greater integrations of services can be achieved if LANs are used (16.24). Devices used for viewdata or FAX can be interconnected with the main computer system, or even Personal Computers, so as to form one large information system. In such a system orders collected by a private viewdata system can be automatically processed along with those collected by more conventional means or perhaps by a member of the sales staff equipped with a portable personal computer.

ELECTRONIC MAIL
16.42 As its name suggests **Electronic Mail** has some features comparable with those of the postal service. These features are given here in outline.

- a. Each user has a "mailbox" which is accessed via a computer terminal or workstation within the system by entering an account number and password. Messages are drawn to the users attention when entering the system, for example, by displaying message headings on the screen.
- b. When a message is sent it consists of two parts:
  - i. A header which specifies the address of the sender and the address of the receiver.The address may merely be another account number in simple cases.
  - ii. The text of the message.
- c. The mailing system provides computerised ways of preparing, and editing the text of the message.
- d. The mailing system also provides computerised ways of selecting messages to be read, displaying them, saving them, deleting them, forwarding them or replying to them as required.

16.43 Electronic mail is an increasingly common facility to be found on LANs. On some LANS one computer may specialise in handling the electronic mail. Such a computer is called a "mail server", users on this LAN system always communicate with the mail server when dealing with mail. On other systems each computer takes a share of the work in processing the electronic mail.

16.44 Electronic mail on LHNs is transmitted using message switching systems or packet switching systems. There are already a number of private Electronic Mail systems which exploit public packet switching systems. The sender's computer and receiver's computer do the work of assembling the message, making the transmission and disassembling the message. BT intend to launch a public electronic mail system which will probably make use of their existing PSS system.

SUMMARY

16.45 a. The long established methods of data communication are based upon the telephone system and employ circuit switching methods and analog transmissions.

b. Digital data transmission is technically superior to analog transmissions, akin to the data representations used in computers, and is gradually replacing traditional analog methods.

c. Message switching and packet switching offer advantages over circuit switching systems.

d. Computer networks and distributed systems are becoming increasingly important because of the numerous advantages they offer over systems which are separate and autonomous.

e. Computer networks are of two basic kinds.
> i. Local Area Networks (LANs).
> ii. Long Haul Networks (LHNs)

The latter often exploit packet switching system methods of data transmission.

16.46 The following services have been discussed.

a. Digital telephone system such as System X.

b. The BT DATEL service.

c. TELEX and TELETEX

d. Facsimile Transmission (FAX).

e. Viewdata (videotex) and BT's PRESTEL

f. Teletext (BBC's Ceefax and ITV's Oracle).

g. The BT packet switching system (PSS)

h. Electronic Mail.

POINTS TO NOTE

16.47 a. Each of the services described is important in its own right in terms of its uses but it when these separate system are integrated into a single IT system that they can have a particularly significant effect on the way in which processing activities are carried out.

b. "Multiplexer" has the alternative spelling "multiplexor".

QUESTIONS A *(With answers in appendix 2)*

1. a. What is a MODEM and what does it do?
*   b. What is an acoustic coupler and when is it used instead of a MODEM?*

2. Explain the following terms
*   a. viewdata,*
*   b. teletext,*
*   c. telex*
*   d. teletex*

3. Explain the difference between messages switching and packet switching.

4. Explain the statement: "Coaxial cable has a smaller bandwidth than optical fibre"

5. Explain the difference between a print server and a file server.

QUESTIONS (Without answers)

1. What is a multiplexer and when is it used?

2. Explain the statement: "The channel from my VDU to the computer uses full duplex asynchronous transmission."

3. What is the difference between a LHN and a WAN?

4. What do IMPs do?

HOW THE COMPUTER WORKS

1. This part of the book deals with the detailed features of the computer itself and explains how it operates and the part played by programs in its operation.

2. The level of detail gone into will be much more than is needed by Business Studies students and those students taking introductory courses. Readers on such courses *are* advised to read through this Part of the book but to miss out the more difficult or detailed points.

3. The next five chapters are arranged as follows:

    a.   Chapter 17 looks at how the computer carries out arithmetic.

    b.   Chapter 18 looks at the logic and control operations carried out by the computer.

    c.   Chapter 19 describes the elements and operations of the computer. It concentrates on the processor, main memory and the way in which the processor performs program instructions.

    d.   Chapter 20 carries on where chapter 19 leaves off but by looking at the computer's own language and how it can be used.

    e.   Chapter 21 looks at how the whole computer system is organised and fits together, and relates the material to computers in common use today.

17 Computer Arithmetic

17.1 We saw in Chapter 6 how different data types can be represented in a computer using a binary code. Chapter 7 also introduced the principles behind conversion of one code into another. This chapter considers numeric codes in more detail and looks into how a computer can perform arithmetic operations.

17.2 The processor in a computer system can carry out a variety of arithmetic operations on binary numbers. It is important to realise that the processor on its own cannot make sense of the binary number - it merely manipulates it. Whether it is sensible to carry out arithmetic on the contents of a memory location is determined by the application program: if the memory location contains the ASCII code for a letter, for example, then clearly one would not expect arithmetic operations to be valid. The processor is not aware, however, that the memory location does contain an ASCII code.

BINARY ADDITION

17.3 The addition of binary numbers can be defined quite simply in the following four rules:

$$0 + 0 = 00,$$
$$0 + 1 = 01,$$
$$1 + 0 = 01,$$
$$1 + 1 = 10, \text{ ie } 1 \times 2 + 0 \times 1, \text{ or } 2.$$

The "1" in the left hand column of the final answer is referred to as the "carry", ie it has to be carried into the next column and added there. Notice that there are four possible combinations of bits that could occur in the addition of two binary numbers. Example. 00110 + 01101 (This is equivalent to 6 + 13 = 19)

These two numbers are added in a similar way to denary numbers, by writing the two numbers under each other and starting from the right hand end:

```
    0 0 1 1 0
    0 1 1 0 1
          1,   adding the first two bits,
        1 1,   adding the next two bits,
      0 1 1,   a carry bit is generated from the middle two bits,
    0 0 1 1,   again, a carry is generated,
  1 0 0 1 1,   which equals 19, the result expected.
```

Further examples are set out in the usual way, the carry being shown where is occurs.

```
   1 0 1         1 1 0         1 0 1 1 0 0
   0 1 1         1 0 1           1 0 0 1 0
  ------        ------        ----------
  1 0 0 0       1 0 1 1       1 1 1 1 1 0
   1 1 1         1
```

17.4 The same method can be applied when we wish to add more than two numbers together: the first two are added together giving a result called the partial sum. This is then added to the third number to give a new partial sum, and the process repeated until all numbers have been added. Example of multiple addition. 1101 + 101 + 10110 + 1011

1101,	first number
+ 101,	second number
10010,	first partial sum
+ 10110,	third number
101000,	second partial sum
+ 1011,	fourth number
110011,	final sum

17.5 The result contains six bits, whereas the largest number we had contained only five. In order to ensure that we line up the numbers correctly for the addition, we could add zeros to the left hand end of the number, which will not affect its value. We could thus ensure that all numbers contained the same number of bits (eg eight) as follows:

00001101,	first number
+ 00000101,	second number
00010010,	first partial sum
+ 00010110,	third number
00101000,	second partial sum
+ 00001011,	fourth number
00110011,	final sum

17.6 This is very similar to what happens in a computer: main memory is made up of locations which are identical in the number of bits that they store. An eight-bit computer will generally have memory locations which are capable of storing eight bits. Numeric examples from now on will be shown with leading zeros to help remind you of this fact.

HEXADECIMAL ADDITION
17.7 Chapter 6 showed how hexadecimal numbers can help as a shorthand notation for binary numbers. The number 1990 requires 11 bits when expressed as a binary number, but requires only three hexadecimal digits to represent it.

17.8 Two methods can be used to evaluate the addition of hexadecimal numbers:

a. The first method comprises three steps:
  i. convert the number to binary,
  ii. add the binary numbers as shown above,
  iii. convert back to hexadecimal.

b. An alternative method is to construct an addition table for hexadecimal numbers, along the lines as follows.

It is left as an exercise for the reader to complete the table. It should be noted that the numbers in the table are hexadecimal numbers, so that 12, for example, represents 18 (16 + 2) in denary.

+	0	1	2	3	4	5	6	7	8	9	A	B	C	D	E	F
0	0	1	2	3	4	5	6	7	8	9	A	B	C	D	E	F
1	1	2	3	4												
2	2	3	4	5												
3	3	4	5	6												
4	4	5	6													
5	5															
6	6															
7	7															
8	8															
9	9															
A	A															
B	B															
C	C															
D	D															
E	E															
F	F	10	11	12	13	14	15	16	17	18	19	1A	1B	1C	1D	1E

SUBTRACTION OF BINARY NUMBERS

17.9 In order to be able to carry out subtraction of binary numbers, we need to have a way of representing negative numbers. The operation A - B could result in a negative number if B is larger than A, so we must be able to cater for this.

17.10 If we can devise a way of representing negative values, then the operation A - B could be carried out as A + (-B), where (-B) is the representation we require. Before looking at subtraction, then, we will consider how a computer can handle negative numbers.

NEGATIVE NUMBERS

17.11 The only symbols available in the binary numbering system are "0" and "1". The familiar way of representing a negative value in denary numbers by placing a "-" in front of the number is not valid for a computer as we cannot invent a symbol of this type: we must devise a way which uses only the symbols available.

17.12 Sign & Magnitude Method

One method, known as the sign and magnitude (or explicit sign) method, uses the most significant bit of a binary number to represent the sign, the rest of the bits being used to represent the size of the number. Thus 00011011 can be thought of as 0 0011011 or +27. The number 10011011 would be interpreted as -27.

17.13 There are a number of drawbacks with using this method: zero can be represented both as 0 0000000 (+0) and as 1 0000000 (ie -0), which is meaningless. Another drawback is that arithmetic operations are inconsistent. For example, A + (-A) should result in 0, but, as can be seen by adding +27 to -27, this is not the case.

```
    00011011
  + 10011011
    10110110,
```
which would be interpreted as -54.

17.14 Complements.

A mechanical counter, similar to those found as tape counters in cassette tape recorders, shows an alternative way of representing values less than zero. If the counter is wound backwards (equivalent to subtracting values) then as it gets to 000 it next shows 999, then 998 etc. The value 999 could thus be interpreted as -1, 998 as -2 etc. It can be seen that the pair of numbers are connected: if they are added together they will give a result of 1000, which is a power of ten.

17.15 The range of values available on a three digit tape counter could thus be from 000 to 999, if interpreted solely as positive values. The actual value represented is obtained by adding a number to the first which will result in (1)000. The two numbers are said to complement each other, and are thus known as complements. For example, the number 776 actually represents - 224, as when these two numbers are added together they result in 1000 - the leftmost "1" here would disappear if we had only a three digit counter.

17.16 Using complements as a way of evaluating subtractions is not very common with denary numbers. It is used widely, however, by shopkeepers: if you pay for something costing 74 pence, for example, with one pound, the shopkeeper will give you the change by counting out the difference, rather than by subtracting 74 from 100.

17.17 Complements of binary numbers.

This principle can be applied to binary numbers: the complement of a binary number when added to the original number will result in a power of two, which is shown as 1000...etc. in the binary numbering system. **17.18** Consider, as an example, how we would form the complement of the eight bit number 00011010. We need a number which, when it is added to the first, will result in (1) 00000000 - the most significant "1" will be lost if we have only 8 bits for our number.

17.19 Remembering the rules of addition from above, if we add 0+1 or 1+0 we will get 1 as the result. The number 11100101 when added to the number above will thus result in 11111111.

$$
\begin{array}{r}
00011010 \\
+\,11100101 \\
\hline
11111111
\end{array} \qquad (a)
$$

17.20 A binary number made up solely of 1's is actually one less than a power of 2, eg 111 - 7, which is one less than 8, 11111 - 31, which is one less than 32. The above number is thus one less than the number we require, so by adding one to it we should have the complement of the first number.

$$
\begin{array}{r}
00011010 \\
+\,11100110 \\
\hline
100000000
\end{array} \qquad (b)
$$

Again, the most significant 1 will be lost if we have only 8 bits.

17.21 The number (a) above is known as the One's Complement of the binary number. It is obtained by changing all the bits in the original number (ie. 0 becomes 1 and 1 becomes 0). The number (b) above is called the Two's Complement, and is obtained by adding one to the One's Complement.

Further examples of forming complements.

Example 1

    00100111
    11011000, 1's complement (change every bit)
    11011001, 2's complement (add 1 to 1's complement).

Example 2

    01000100
    10111011, 1's complement
    10111100, 2's complement.

17.22 A computer generally uses the Two's Complement method as a way of storing negative values. This gives a consistent approach to arithmetic operations and does not result in a redundant representation of zero, which is the case with the one's complement and sign and magnitude methods.

17.23 Notice that although we did not actually set out to reserve the most significant bit as a sign bit, it does work out that the msb will be 0 for positive numbers and 1 for negative numbers when expressed as complements. For this reason the method is sometimes known as the implicit sign method.

SUBTRACTION USING COMPLEMENTS

17.24 Now that we have a way of representing negative values, we can carry out subtraction by adding the negative value, ie A - B is the same as A + (-B). This is shown in the following examples:

Example 1.

                00010110 - 00001101

17.25 The method is to form the two's complement of the number to be subtracted and then to add this to the first number.

                        00001101,
                        11110010,   1's complement
                        11110011,   2's complement

                        00010110,
                      + 11110011,
                       100001001,   ignore the leading 1.

The result is 1001 (9) which is the correct answer for 10110 (22) - 1101 (13).

Example 2

                00011011 - 00101101

Form the 2's complement of the number to be subtracted:

                        00101101
                        11010010,   1's complement
                        11010011,   2's complement.

Now add the two's complement:

                        00011011
                      + 11010011
                        11101110

As the msb of the result is 1, we interpret it as being negative - to find out the value represented we form the two's complement:

                        11101110
                        00010001,   1's complement,
                        00010010,   2's complement.

This value is 18, so the result obtained above is -18. The actual calculation in denary was for 27 - 45, which does give a result of -18.

MULTIPLICATION & DIVISION

17.26 Multiplication of numbers is really a shorthand method of carrying out multiple additions. When we write 37 x 15 we really mean add 37 to itself 15 times, but it is quicker to do this using the rules of multiplication.

17.27 A computer carries out its calculations very quickly (typically in microseconds), so repeated addition is a viable method for carrying out multiplication.

17.28 Division can likewise be thought of as repeated subtraction, and as we have seen above subtraction itself can be achieved by addition of complements.

17.29 Thus the four basic arithmetic operations can all be carried out using addition. This means that in the processor there is only a need to have addition circuits, together with other circuits which enable us to change the bits of a number (or "invert" the bits) for forming complements. The processor itself is thus made simpler and therefore cheaper and more reliable.

17.30 Multiplication and division operations make use of registers in which the pattern of bits can be shifted to the left or right. These "shift registers" have the effect of multiplying or dividing the number by two, depending on the direction of the shift.

Example.

The number   00001110 represents 14,

00011100 (ie shift to left) represents 28,

00000111 (ie shift to right) represents 7.

Further details are beyond the scope of this book, but the basic method is to shift and add for each bit of the multiplier.

RANGE OF REPRESENTATION

17.31 We saw above that there are four ways of writing down two bits, ie 00, 01, 10, 11. If we have three bits, then there would be double this arrangement, ie the four arrangements with a "0" attached and the same four arrangements with a "1". A fourth bit would double the number again, so that we would have 16 combinations.

17.32 This consideration tends to suggest some relationship between the number of bits and the number of combinations:

2 bits -   4 ways,

3 bits -   8 ways,

4 bits -   16 ways, etc.

17.33 The relationship is that the number of combinations is two raised to the power of the number of bits, as $2^2 = 4$, $2^3 = 8$, $2^4 = 16$ etc. If we had 8 bits then there would be 256 (2^8) different combinations.

If we were to write the bit patterns down in a sequence, we could interpret their values as if they represented numbers:

00000000 (= 0)

00000001 (= 1)

00000010 (= 2)

00000011 (= 3)

00000100 (= 4)

00000101 (= 5)

00000110 (= 6)

00000111 (= 7)

00001000 (= 8), etc.

Thus the 256 different combinations of 8 bits would be interpreted as positive numbers from 0 to 255 inclusive. Notice that the largest number that could be represented using 8 bits is 11111111, ie 255 or $2^8 - 1$.

17.34 The above considerations apply to any number of bits: the largest number that could be represented using 16 bits is $2^{16} - 1$, or 65535, whereas using 32 bits this would be 4,294,967,295 ($2^{32} - 1$).

17.35 Clearly, the more bits that are used, the larger the number that could be represented. This is very similar to a calculator: with a 6 digit display, the largest (denary) number that could be shown is 999,999 whereas a 10 digit display could show up to 9,999,999,999. Notice here how the display shows one less than a power of 10 - with binary numbers it is one less than a power of 2 which is the largest number.

17.36 The previous few paragraphs assumed that the binary number would be interpreted as a positive value, but we have seen that negative values also have to be catered for. Using two's complements, the most significant bit of the number represents the sign, so that for 4 bits we would have 8 values with a MSB of "0", and 8 values with a MSB of "1". These would thus be interpreted as being in the range from -8 to -1 (MSB = 1), and from 0 to +7 (MSB = 0).

17.37 We still have 16 values altogether, but in order to accommodate negative values the largest value represented is reduced. Instead of 255 for 8 bits, the largest positive value is 01111111, or +127: the bit pattern 1111111 is interpreted as -1 using two's complements (remember the tape counter), the largest negative number that can be represented is -128 which has a bit pattern of 10000000.

17.38 Applying this to 16 bits, the range of representation would be from -32,768 to +32,767 (and all whole numbers in between), and for 32 bits it would be from -2,147,483,648 to +2,147,483,647.

17.39 Binary fractions

The foregoing paragraphs assume that only integer numbers will need to be represented, but we have to cater also for real numbers, that is those numbers which contain fractional values.

17.40 It is beyond the scope of this book to examine in detail how fractional values can be represented in binary, but at this juncture it is worthwhile to point out that binary fractions can be built up in a similar way to decimal values, in that the place value to the right of the "**bicimal**" point represents decreasing powers of 2, ie 1/2, 1/4, 1/8th, 1/16th etc.

17.41 We can thus imagine a real number being made up of an integer part, ie that part to the left of the bicimal point, and a fractional part which is to the right of the bicimal point. A good analogy of this is a car milometer - generally a 6 digit counter with the LSD representing 1/10th of a mile. This approach of separating the number into two parts is known as "fixed point" representation.

17.42 As we have seen above, we can increase the range of representation for the integer part by allocating more bits: obviously we could do the same for the fractional part in order to be able to represent smaller values with greater accuracy. There is a limit to this approach, however: allocating an increasing number of bits to represent a number would obviously mean that more memory has to be set aside and also the time taken to carry out a calculation would increase.

17.43 Scientists and engineers often work with both very large and very small numbers, and have devised a way to represent such numbers in a form often referred to as "scientific" notation. The number here is made up of a fractional part (the "mantissa") which is multiplied by the "base" raised to some power (the "exponent"). A similar approach is often used with binary numbers, and this is known as "floating point" representation.

ERRORS

17.44 It is easy to think of a computer as an infallible machine. Mistakes can arise in its calculations, however, and these need to be identified. There are many types of error and most are attributable to the fact that a fixed number of bits are used to represent values: what happens when a calculation results in a value which cannot be represented?

17.45 Overflow

An overflow error occurs when the result of some calculation is too large to be represented. We have seen above, for example, that the range of numbers that can be represented using 16 bits is from -32,768 to +32,767. If we were to try to add +20,000 to +20,000, however, both numbers being within this range, the answer could not be represented. Similarly, -20,000 - 20,000 would also result in a number which is outside the range.

17.46 The processor inside a computer usually contains circuits which can detect overflow and an error condition can be indicated. The program which gave rise to the condition could incorporate routines to try to recover from the error, for example by converting the result into a floating point number, which would usually have a greater range than an integer. Generally, though, if overflow occurs it is classed as a "fatal" error, ie the program would terminate.

17.47 Underflow

This occurs when the result of some calculation is too small to be represented. This type of error occurs predominantly with multiplication and division operations, and although it is not generally treated as a fatal error (as the number would often be set equal to zero, it can nevertheless cause a build up of errors with repeat calculations.

17.48 An example of underflow with denary numbers is when we can only represent values to one decimal place - the number 0.05, for example, would then be too small to be represented.

17.49 Truncation

A finite (and consistent) number of bits have to be used in a computer to represent values: this means that low order bits of a fractional value are often ignored. The binary fraction for the denary value 0.2, for example, is 0.00110011001100110011... etc., ie. it is a recurring value. If we can only use 8 bits to represent this, it would be stored as 0.0011001, and converting this back to denary, we would obtain $1/8 + 1/16 + 1/128$ which equals 0.1953125 and not 0.2.

17.50 This is an example of a truncation error, caused by cutting off the least significant bits beyond some limit. Details of the steps that a programmer needs to take to try to minimise this problem are beyond the scope of this book, but the following example demonstrates how to overcome a common problem of this nature.

Example. Suppose we wish to carry out a calculation involving a variable X whose values will be increased in steps of 0.2, and we wish to do this 10 times with X starting off with a value of 2. The following pseudocode shows the outline of an algorithm to do this.

```
BEGIN
    X := 2.0
    REPEAT
        /* perform calculation */
        X := X + 0.2
    UNTIL X = 4.0
END
```

It would appear that this algorithm will satisfy the criteria set, in that X would take on the values 2.0, 2.2, 2.4, 2.6, 2.8, 3.0, 3.2, 3.4, 3.6, 3.8, and 4.0, whereupon the loop condition will be met.

17.51 If only 8 bits are available for storing the fractional value, however, then as we have seen above the computer would store the value 0.2 as 0.1953125. The variable X would thus take on the following values:

```
2.0
2.1953125
2.390625
2.5859375
2.78125
2.9765625
3.171875
3.3671875
3.5625
3.7578125
3.953125
4.1484375
4.34375 etc.
```

Notice how the values of X never actually equal 4.0 because of the truncation error in representing the fraction. These errors accumulate and will cause incorrect results in the calculation. The loop will never be terminated as the condition will never be met.

17.52 An improvement to the algorithm may at first seem to be to replace the terminating condition, ie.

```
UNTIL X > = 4.0
```

This will stop the endless loop, but the value X = 3.953125 will be used in the calculation when it is not required and so 11 calculations will be performed.

17.53 A better approach is to use an integer (which can be represented with complete accuracy) as a counter for the number of times the loop is executed, and to derive the value of X from this counter:

```
BEGIN
    startX := 2.0
    count := 0
    REPEAT
        X := startX + count/5
        /* perform calculation */
        count := count + 1
    UNTIL count = 10
END
```

As well as terminating the loop correctly, this algorithm also reduces the accumulation of errors, and when count =5, X = 3.0, which is much more accurate than above.

17.54 In languages which support a count controlled loop with variable increments (eg Pascal with FOR...DO, or BASIC with FOR... NEXT) it is bad practice for the above reasons to use a fractional increment.

SUMMARY
17.55 a. The methods of adding binary and hexadecimal numbers were explained.

b. The rules for finding one's and two's complements of binary numbers were explained.

c. The application of complements to the subtraction of binary numbers and representation of negative values were explained.

d. Methods of performing multiplication and division of binary numbers by computer were outlined.

e. The ranges of representation of binary numbers, positive, negative and fractional, were explained.

f. Overflow and underflow errors were introduced.

g. Truncation errors were described and methods of minimising them were outlined.

POINTS TO NOTE
17.56 a. Computers perform arithmetic in ways which are very different from the ways used by humans. In order to become more familiar with the workings of a computer, the reader must be familiar with the methods employed by computer systems and not just learn how to do binary arithmetic from a human perspective.

QUESTIONS A *(With answers)*

1. *Construct a Hex' addition table in the same form as the octal addition table of paragraph 6.*

2. *Perform the following additions.*
   a. i. $10101_2 + 11001_2$
       ii $110110_2 + 11011_2$
       iii $1110101_2 + 10101_2$
       iv. $10111_2 + 11011_2$
       v $101.1101_2 + 110.0011_2$
       vi. $110.0111_2 + 101.001_2$
   b. i. $372_8 + 104_8$ ii. $253_8 + 125_8$
       iii. $643_8 + 227_8$ iv. $316_8 + 574_8$
   c. i. $12_{16} + 3A_{16}$ ii $B2D_{16} + 431_{16}$
       iii. $DCB_{16} + EAF_{16}$ iv. $F79_{16} + AD8_{16}$

3. *Show how the following Integers could be stored in an 8 bit binary register using twos complement.*
   a. 22_{10}
   b. -30_{10}
   c. 37_{10}
   d. -52_{10}
   e. -75_{10}
   f. 881_{10}
   g. -97_{10}
   h. -125_{10}

4. *Perform these calculations in binary .*
   a. $22_{10} - 12_{10}$
   b. $35_{10} - 26_{10}$
   c. $28_{10} - 33_{10}$
   d. $28_{10} - 21_{10}$

5. *A 16 bit register holds numbers in two complement form with the leftmost bit as sign bit. (See the following illustration).*

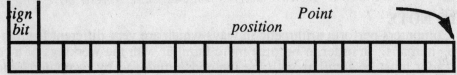

   a. *What is the largest positive number which can be stored?*
   Give your answer in binary and decimal

b.   *What is the most negative number which can be stored?*
Again give your answer in binary and decimal

6.   *Define overflow and underflow*

7.   *What is a truncation error? Explain how such an error can occur when, for example, the number 0.9_{10} is stored in a computer.*

8.   *The number 24_{10} is stored in an 8 bit register. Show the results in binary and decimal if*
a.   *the number is shifted 3 places right.*
b.   *the number is shifted 2 places left.*
State any assumptions you make in either case.

QUESTIONS B *(Without answers)*

1.   *a.*   i. $11001.10101_2 + 10111.01101_2$
         ii. $10101.11011_2 + 11011.10101_2$
     b.   i. $765_8 + 436_8$
         ii. $321_8 + 677_8$
     c.   i. $ABC_{16} + 679_{16}$
         ii. $89E_{16} + FD5_{16}$

2   *Perform these calculations in binary .*
     a. $46_{10} - 17_{10}$
     b. $19_{10} - 37_{10}$

3.   *A 12 bit register holds numbers in twos form with the leftmost bit as sign bit. (See the following illustration).*

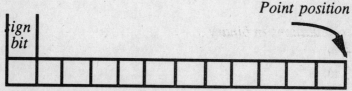

Point position

sign bit

a.   *Show how these integers would be stored*
     i. 79_{10} ii. -83_{10}
b.   i.   *What is the largest positive number which can be stored? Give your answer in decimal and binary.*
     ii. *What is the most negative number which can be stored? Give your answer in decimal and binary.*

4.   *Show how overflow could occur during the addition of two numbers held in 4 bit registers. Assume twos complement is used.*

5. The integer 27_{10} is stored in an 8 bit register. Show how the result 6_{10} might be obtained when 27_{10} was divided by 4_{10} by means of a shift operation.

18 Logic and Control

INTRODUCTION
18.1 This chapter introduces logic elements and logic networks. It explains the basic methods associated with using logic elements and networks and then goes on to give examples of applications of logic networks within the computer. In particular it deals with arithmetic adders, encoders and decoders, flipflops, and multiplexers. The difference between sequential logic and combinational logic is also explained.

SYMBOLS FOR LOGIC OPERATORS
18.2 The logic operators AND, OR and NOT were introduced in chapter 10. It proves easier to use symbols for these operators instead of writing the whole words. Unfortunately there are at least three alternative sets of symbols in common use! The three most common ones are tabulated here:-

		OPERATOR			EXAMPLES		
		AND	OR	NOT	X AND Y	X OR Y	NOT X
Three altern- ative sets of symbols	i.	$\land$	$\lor$	$\sim$	$X \land Y$	$X \lor Y$	$\sim X$
	ii.	$\cdot$	$+$	$-$	$X \cdot Y$	$X + Y$	$\overline{X}$
	iii.	$\cap$	$\cup$	$'$	$X \cap Y$	$X \cup Y$	X'

The set (ii) is in most common use in Computer Studies, and therefore that set of symbols will be used in this book. The table just given should enable the reader to convert to another set of symbols if required.

Note. Programming languages usually use AND, OR and NOT.

18.3 Here is a summary of the AND, OR and NOT operations, to remind the reader of the operations, and to familiarise the reader with the symbols.

X	Y	$X \cdot Y$	$X + Y$	$\overline{X}$
0	0	0	0	1
0	1	0	1	1
1	0	0	1	0
1	1	1	1	0

OTHER OPERATIONS

18.4   The following operations are performed so often in practical application that they have been given names.

18.5   The Exclusive OR operation (also called **Non-Equivalent** or **NEQ**).

X	Y	$(\overline{X} \cdot Y) + (X \cdot \overline{Y})$ also written as $X \neq Y$ or X NEQ Y
0	0	0
0	1	1
1	0	1
1	1	0

Note.   This operation means X or Y but *not both*

18.6   The Equivalence Operation (also called the Match operation).

X	Y	$(\overline{X} \cdot \overline{Y}) + (X \cdot Y)$ also written as $X \equiv Y$ or X EQ Y
0	0	1
0	1	0
1	0	0
1	1	1

18.7   THE NAND Operation (ie. Not AND)

X	Y	$\overline{X \cdot Y}$
0	0	1
0	1	1
1	0	1
1	1	0

18.8 The NOR Operation (ie. Not OR)

X	Y	$\overline{X + Y}$
0	0	1
0	1	0
1	0	0
1	1	0

GATES AND LOGIC ELEMENTS

18.9 Data and instructions are transmitted between the various parts of the processor or between the processor, memory and peripherals by means of **pulse trains.**   Various tasks are performed by passing pulse trains through "electronic switches" called **gates. Gates** control the flow of pulses so that logic operations are carried out. Each gate is an electronic circuit which may have provision for receiving or sending several pulses at once. Each **gate** may be regarded as a "black box" which controls the flow of pulses in a particular way.

18.10 Each gate normally performs some simple function (operation) eg. AND, OR, NOT, and for this reason gates are often called **logic elements.** It is the logic operations of gates which will concern us in this chapter, and we will *not* consider how they are made. Sufficient detail of the physical features (eg. gates may be produced as IC chips) were covered in the introductory chapters.

LOGIC DIAGRAMS

18.11 In logic diagrams **gates** are represented by *symbols* and *input* and *outputs* are represented by *arrowed lines* labelled by letters.

Example. The AND gate and its truth table.

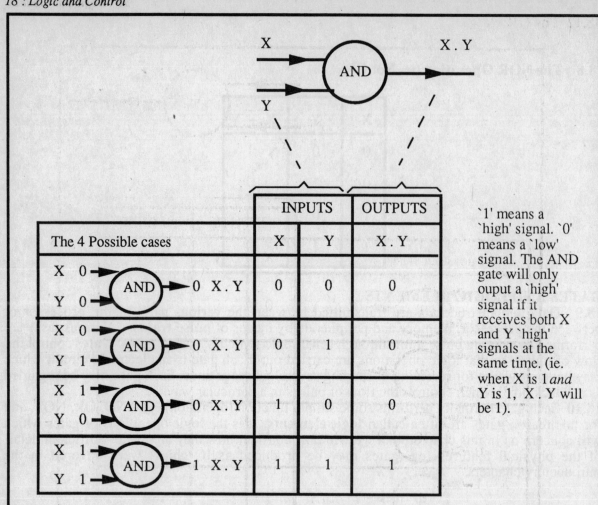

	INPUTS		OUTPUTS
The 4 Possible cases	X	Y	X . Y
	0	0	0
	0	1	0
	1	0	0
	1	1	1

`1' means a `high' signal. `0' means a `low' signal. The AND gate will only ouput a `high' signal if it receives both X and Y `high' signals at the same time. (ie. when X is 1 *and* Y is 1, X . Y will be 1).

18.12 The OR Gate.

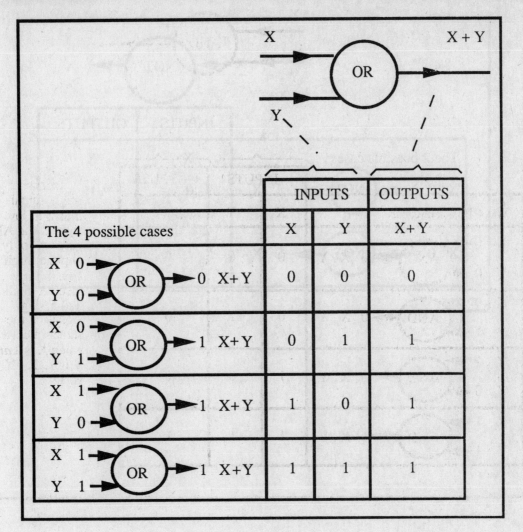

The 4 possible cases	INPUTS		OUTPUTS
	X	Y	X+ Y
X 0 → OR → 0 X+Y, Y 0 →	0	0	0
X 0 → OR → 1 X+Y, Y 1 →	0	1	1
X 1 → OR → 1 X+Y, Y 0 →	1	0	1
X 1 → OR → 1 X+Y, Y 1 →	1	1	1

18.13 The NOT Gate.

	INPUTS	OUTPUTS
The 2 possible cases	X	$\overline{X}$
	0	1
	1	0

18.14 The NAND Gate.

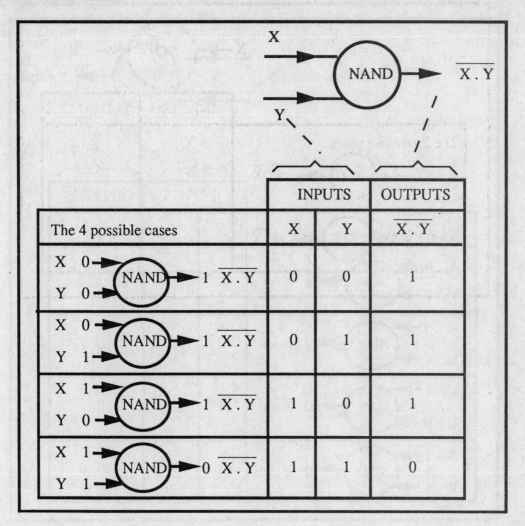

	INPUTS		OUTPUTS
The 4 possible cases	X	Y	$\overline{X \cdot Y}$
	0	0	1
	0	1	1
	1	0	1
	1	1	0

18.15 The NOR Gate.

	INPUTS		OUTPUTS
The 4 possible cases	X	Y	$\overline{X\ Y}$
X 0 → NOR → 1 $\overline{X+Y}$ Y 0 →	0	0	1
X 0 → NOR → 0 $\overline{X+Y}$ Y 1 →	0	1	0
X 1 → NOR → 0 $\overline{X+Y}$ Y 0 →	1	0	0
X 1 → NOR → 0 $\overline{X+Y}$ Y 1 →	1	1	0

18.16 The NEQ Gate (Exclusive OR Gate).

X

NEQ → X $\not\equiv$ Y

Y

Note

X $\not\equiv$ Y is $(\overline{X} . Y) + (X . \overline{Y})$

The 4 cases	INPUTS		OUTPUTS
	X	Y	X $\not\equiv$ Y
X 0→ NEQ →0 X $\not\equiv$ Y Y 0→	0	0	0
X 0→ NEQ →1 X $\not\equiv$ Y Y 1→	0	1	1
X 1→ NEQ →1 X $\not\equiv$ Y Y 0→	1	0	1
X 1→ NEQ →0 X $\not\equiv$ Y Y 1→	1	1	0

LOGIC NETWORKS (ALSO CALLED LOGIC CIRCUITS)

18.17 Gates can be connected one to another so that the outputs from some gates become the inputs to others. Such a combination of gates is called a **logic network** or **logic circuit**. Logic networks are to be found in all kinds of computer devices but there are very many logic networks within the processor. These networks perform the various arithmetic, logic and control operations which take place within the processor.

18.18 It is possible to work out what operation a logic network performs by constructing its truth table in a systematic fashion. The method is as follows:-

a. Draw up a truth table and fill in all possible INPUT combinations for the network.

b. Consider each row in the table in turn to discover the corresponding output.

c. The output for a given row in the table can be determined by working across the logic network from left to right filling in inputs and then outputs for each gate on the way. The final output at the right hand side is entered into the appropriate row of the truth table.

An example now follows:

18.19 Example. The logic network to be investigated is shown here:-

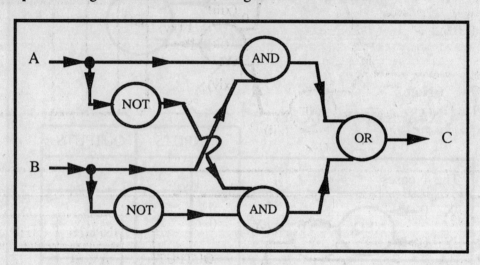

Following the steps described in paragraph 18.18.

Step a.

INPUT		OUTPUTS
A	B	C
0	0	
0	1	
1	0	
1	1	

In these diagrams the Roman numerals show a possible sequence for filling in the "0"s and "1"s.

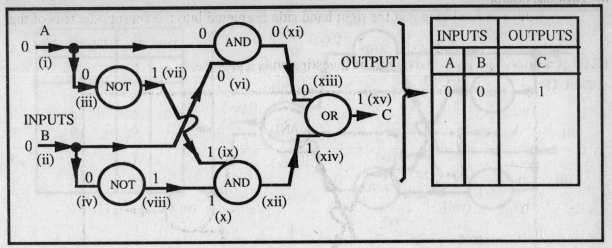

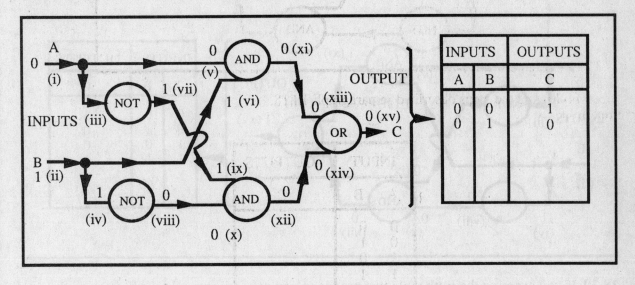

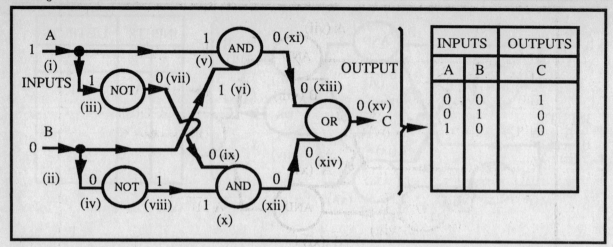

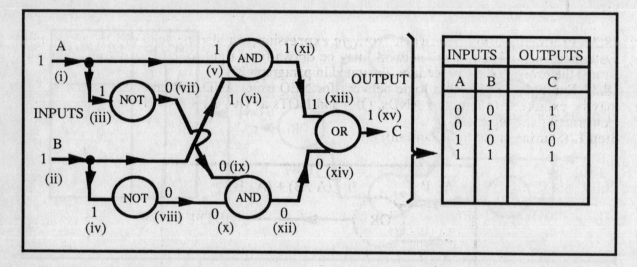

18.20 If you examine the truth table just produced you may see that it looks like the truth table in paragraph 6. We may conclude therefore that the logic network just investigated performs a match or equivalence operation.

18.21 Deriving an expression for the output of a logic network in terms of the inputs, can be achieved by filling in expressions on the network, again working from left to right. In the following diagram roman numerals are used to indicate the order in which expressions may be written in.

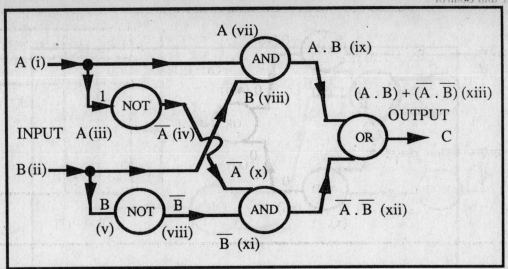

18.22 Producing a logic network from an expression can also be achieved by adopting a systematic method. The logic network may be drawn from right to left in a process which is almost the reverse of the procedure illustrated in paragraph 21.

18.23 Example. Producing a logic network for NEQ using AND, OR and NOT gates. A + B may be expressed in terms of ANDs, ORs and NOTs as (A . B) + (A . B) (see paragraph 5) Constructing the logic network.

Step 1. (Starting at the right hand side).

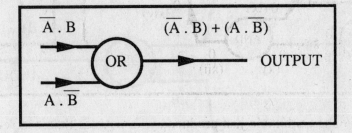

Step 2.

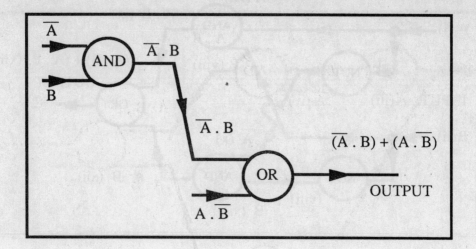

Step 3.

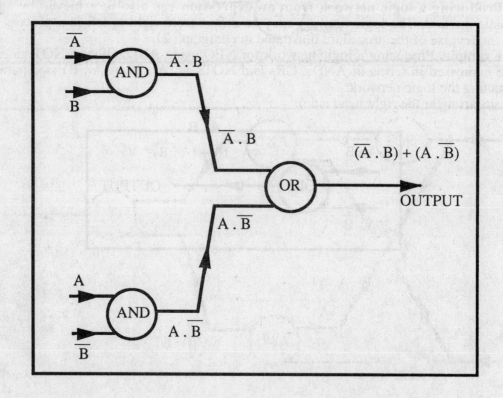

Step 4.

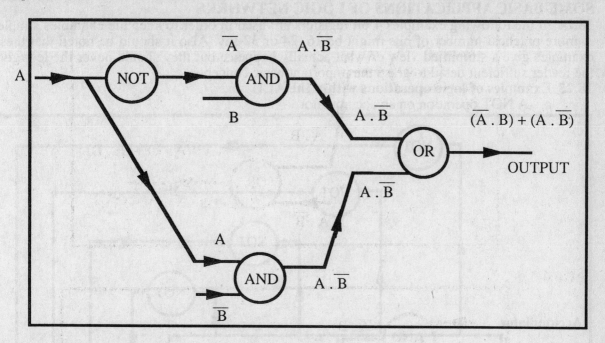

Step 5.

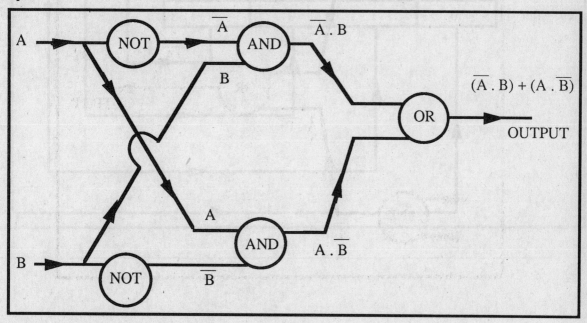

SOME BASIC APPLICATIONS OF LOGIC NETWORKS

18.24 In the following examples 4 bit registers are used in order to keep the examples simple. A more practical number of bits might be 16, 24 or 32 say. Also it should be noted that these examples give a simplified view of what actually happens, but they should never the less give the reader sufficient detail to grasp the important basic concepts.

18.25 Examples of logic operations within the ALU

    a.   A NOT operation on an accumulator.

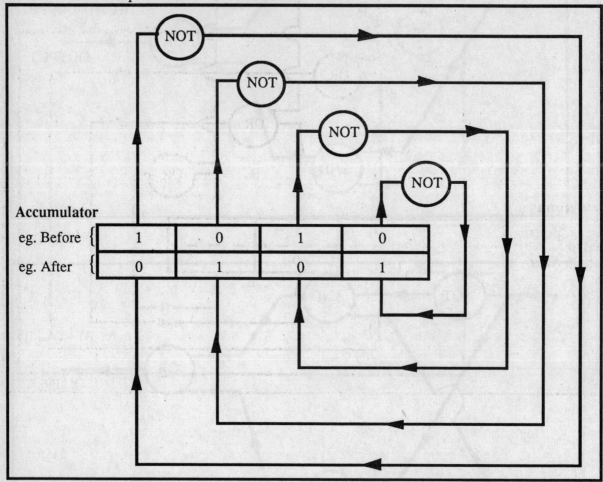

b. An OR operation between the accumulator and another register (eg. the MDR).

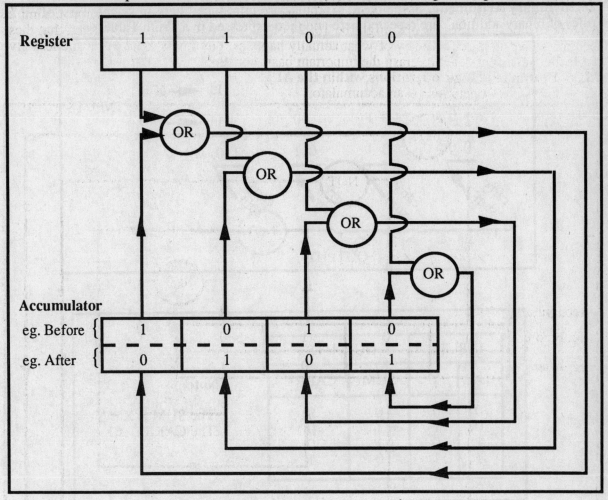

18.26 Binary Arithmetic. Some basic examples are introduced here in stages. First of all the rules of binary addition are repeated here and then expressed in a Truth Table.

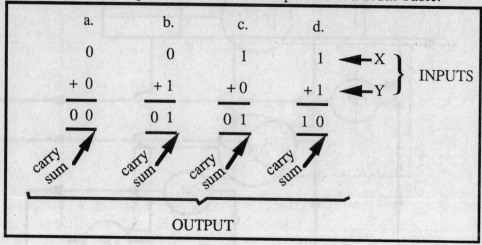

INPUTS		OUTPUTS	
X	Y	SUM	CARRY
0	0	0	0
0	1	1	0
1	0	1	0
1	1	0	1

Note

The SUM is $X \neq Y$
The CARRY is $X . Y$

276

18.27 This addition may therefore be performed by the following logic network.

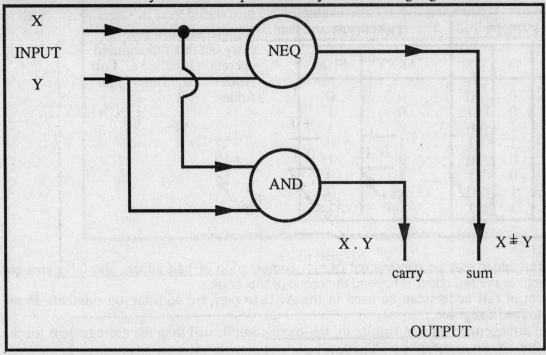

This logic network is called a **half adder.** The term *half* adder comes from the fact that the half adder does not deal with a carry from a previous sum.

18.28 Full Addition. The rules for *full* binary addition are summarised below and then expressed in a Truth table.

	a		b		c		d		e		f		g		h	
	0		0		0		0		1		1		1		1	← X
	0		0		1		1		0		0		1		1	← Y
		0		1		0		1		0		1		0		1	← Z
	00		01		01		10		01		10		10		11	

Z is previous carry

INPUT

carry sum (repeated under each column)

INPUTS			OUTPUTS	
X	Y	Z	CARRY	SUM
0	0	0	0	0
0	0	1	0	1
0	1	0	0	1
0	1	1	1	0
1	0	0	0	1
1	0	1	1	0
1	1	0	1	0
1	1	1	1	1

A logic network able to carry out this full addition operation is called a ``**Full Adder**" or ``Three Input Adder"

A full adder may be constructed from a combination of half adders and OR gates but greater detail of the full adder is beyond the scope of this book.

18.29 A set of full adders can be used in the ALU to perform addition on numbers in the accumulator and a register.

The arrangement will be similar to, but more complicated than the arrangement for the OR operation shown in paragraph 18.25b.

18.30 Other logic networks can be constructed to perform subtraction. Multiplication and Division are even more complicated operations and may either be performed by logic networks (hardware multiplication and division) or by a sequence of program instructions using SHIFT, ADD and SUBTRACT Instructions (software multiplication and division). Details are beyond the scope of this book.

ENCODING AND DECODING

18.31 Encoding involves the conversion of **one** signal from one set into a **group** of signals of another set. A device performing this task is called an **encoder.**

    a. **Example.**

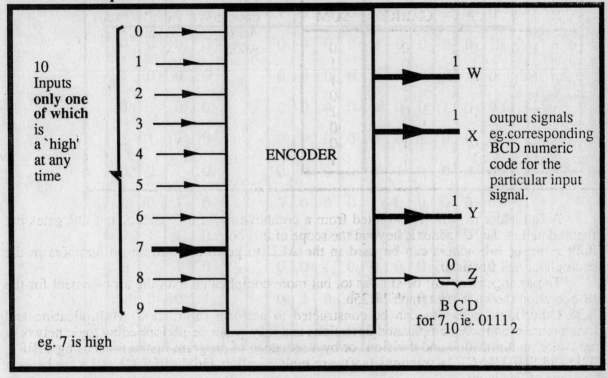

	INPUT											OUTPUT			
0	1	2	3	4	5	6	7	8	9			W	X	Y	Z
1	0	0	0	0	0	0	0	0	0			0	0	0	0
0	1	0	0	0	0	0	0	0	0			0	0	0	1
0	0	1	0	0	0	0	0	0	0			0	0	1	0
0	0	0	1	0	0	0	0	0	0			0	0	1	1
0	0	0	0	1	0	0	0	0	0			0	1	0	0
0	0	0	0	0	1	0	0	0	0			0	1	0	1
0	0	0	0	0	0	1	0	0	0			0	1	1	0
0	0	0	0	0	0	0	1	0	0			0	1	1	1
0	0	0	0	0	0	0	0	1	0			1	0	0	0
0	0	0	0	0	0	0	0	0	1			1	0	0	1

1 = high signal.   0 = low signal.

b. **Application.** An example of an **encoder** is a keyboard device eg. within a VDU where 1 of 64 lines is raised, by pressing one key and the corresponding 8 bit ASCII character is produced on 8 wires coming out of the encoder.

18.32 a. **Decoding.** This is the opposite operation to **encoding** and the device performing the task is called a **decoder.** If "n" wires are connected in, there will normally be 2n wires out, only one of which will be a logic "1" at any instant.

   b. **Example.**

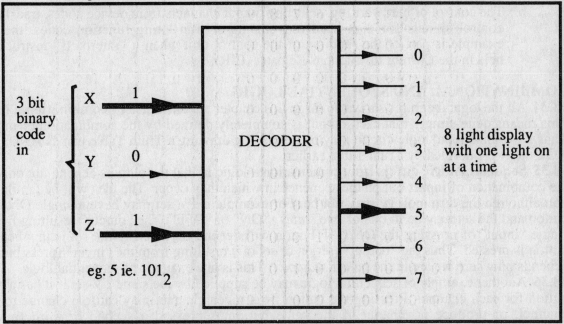

3 bit binary code in

X   1

Y   0

Z   1

eg. 5 ie. 101_2

DECODER

0
1
2
3
4
5
6
7

8 light display with one light on at a time

INPUT					OUTPUT							
X	Y	Z			0	1	2	3	4	5	6	7
0	0	0			1	0	0	0	0	0	0	0
0	0	1			0	1	0	0	0	0	0	0
0	1	0			0	0	1	0	0	0	0	0
0	1	1			0	0	0	1	0	0	0	0
1	0	0			0	0	0	0	1	0	0	0
1	0	1			0	0	0	0	0	1	0	0
1	1	0			0	0	0	0	0	0	1	0
1	1	1			0	0	0	0	0	0	0	1

18.33 Uses. Encoders and decoders are used for such things as:

    a.   Translations of **internal** binary codes to or from **external** signals for peripheral input or output actions such as printing characters, reading cards, moving pens in plotters or monitoring device status.

    b.   The control of hardware, eg. selecting output channels from device codes, translating control signals for disk head movements or translating function codes. the last example is part of the function of the control unit when it "interprets" instructions held in the Current Instructions Register (CIR).

COMBINATIONAL AND SEQUENTIAL LOGIC

18.34 All the logic diagrams shown so far in this chapter are examples of **combinational logic.** This means quite simply that each output is completely defined by the combination of inputs. Thus a combinational logic circuit may be defined by drawing a Truth Table just as AND, OR, NOT etc. were defined by Truth Table earlier.

18.35 Sequential logic differs from combinational logic in that the outputs depend not only on the combination of inputs but on the sequence in which they occur. The idea will be familiar to you although the terminology may not be. For example a TV set may have a single ON/OFF button and the set may be in one of two *states* "ON" or "OFF". The "output" resulting from a single "input" of pressing the ON/OFF button will depend on the state the set is in when the button is pressed. Thus the "output" (set on or set off) resulting from the "input" (press button) depends on where we are in the on/off *sequence.* This is one example of sequential logic.

18.36 Another example of sequential logic may be supplied by the same TV set if it has a push button for each channel. Pressing the button fro a given channel may cause a change to that channel, or produce no change if the same button is pressed a second or third time in succession. The "output" from pressing a combination of ON/OFF button and channel selector button will depend on the prior state of the set.

18.37 Sequential logic has a number of uses within the computer. For example it is used for:

    a.   Memory devices eg. RAM

and   b.   Counters eg. the SCR which is part of the ALU.

18.38 The basic logic elements from which such devices are made are devices called **Flip-Flops** or **bistable.** Flip flops have two stable operating states corresponding to binary "0" and "1" and may switch from state to state on receiving an input pulse depending upon their initial state. (Compare this with a TV with just two channel buttons).

18.39 An example of a counter.

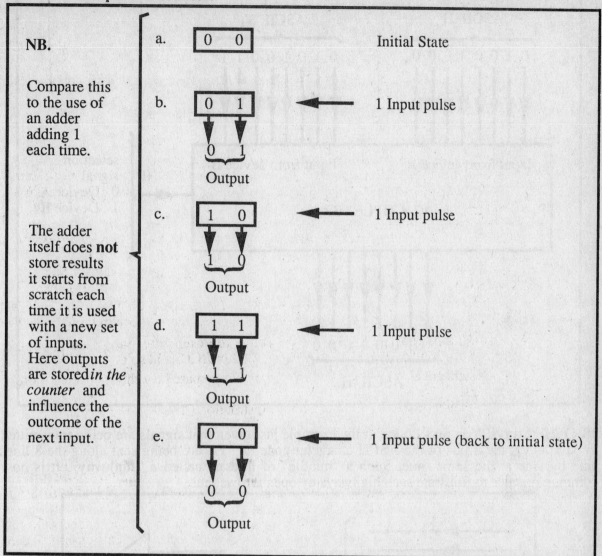

NB.

Compare this to the use of an adder adding 1 each time.

The adder itself does **not** store results it starts from scratch each time it is used with a new set of inputs. Here outputs are stored *in the counter* and influence the outcome of the next input.

a. | 0   0 | Initial State

b. | 0   1 | ← 1 Input pulse
     0   1
     Output

c. | 1   0 | ← 1 Input pulse
     1   0
     Output

d. | 1   1 | ← 1 Input pulse
     1   1
     Output

e. | 0   0 | ← 1 Input pulse (back to initial state)
     0   0
     Output

MULTIPLEXERS (MULTIPLEXORS)

18.40 Multiplexers are selection mechanisms. They have long had importance in handling multiple numbers of Input and Output devices. They have even more importance today in the way they handle the selection of data and instruction flow within modern CPU's. You may compare them with the points and signal box at a railway junction. Here is a simple example:-

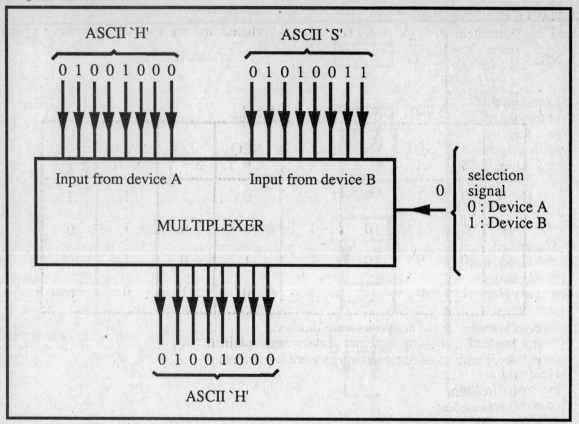

18.41 Highways. You may notice in the example just given that signals are being transmitted in parallel eg. the 8 bits of the ASCII character code for "H" are being sent along the 8 lines side by side at the same time. Such a "bundle" of lines is called a **"highway"**. It is now common practice to illustrate such highways by open arrows thus:

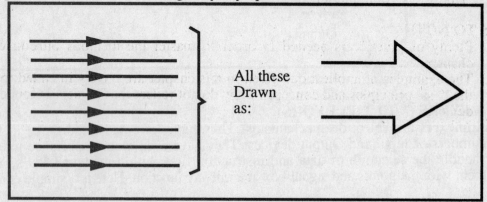

Note. The highway may contain any number of lines, not necessarily 8.

SUMMARY

18.42 a. A number of logic operators were introduced and the following operator symbols were used:
   i.   for AND
   ii. + for OR
   III. - for NOT

   b. A number of logic operators were described:-

X	Y	NOT X	AND X . Y	OR X + Y	NEQ X ≢ Y	EQ X = Y	NAND X̄.̄Ȳ	NOR X̄+̄Ȳ
0	0	1	0	0	0	1	1	1
0	1	1	0	1	1	0	1	0
1	0	0	0	1	1	0	1	0
1	1	0	1	1	0	1	0	0

   c. Gates and logic networks were defined.
   d. Methods for using logic networks were explained.
   e. Applications of logic networks were illustrated.
      eg.
      i.   Adders
      ii. Encoders
      iii. Decoders
      iv. Counters
      v.   Flip-flops
      vi. Multiplexors.
   f. The differences between sequential logic and combinational logic were explained.
   g. "Highways" were introduced.

POINTS TO NOTE

18.43 a. Plenty of practice is needed in order to master the methods introduced in this chapter.
   b. The examples of applications given in this chapter are merely intended to illustrate the basic principles and concepts. They do not reflect the full details found in actual devices.

QUESTIONS A *(With answers)*

1. *Which logic operations have the following truth tables?*
   a.

A	B	?
0	0	0
0	1	1
1	0	1
1	1	0

   b.

A	B	?
0	0	1
0	1	1
1	0	1
1	1	0

2. *Draw a truth table for the following logic network. Fill in expressions for all the lettered points in the logic network.*
   Write expressions for E, F and G in terms of A and B.

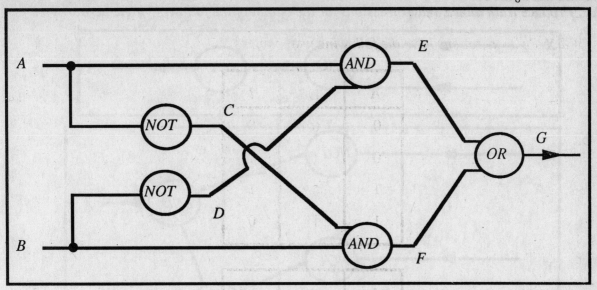

3. *Produce truth tables and expressions for the output of the following logic networks*

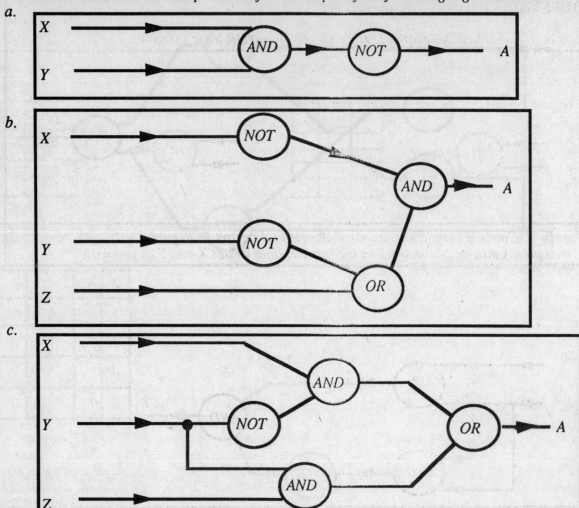

4. *Distinguish between "hardware multiplication" and "software multiplication".*

5. *Produce logic networks which correspond to the following expressions.*

a. $(X . \overline{Y}) + (Y . Z)$ *b.* $(X . \overline{Y}) + (\overline{X} . \overline{Z}) + Z$

6. *Explain the difference between an encoder and a decoder. Give one application of each.*

7. *What is a flip-flop? Give one application of flip-flops.*

8. *Define a "multiplexer" and a "highway".*

QUESTIONS B *(Without answers)*

1.   a.   *Complete the truth tables for the AND and OR logic functions.*

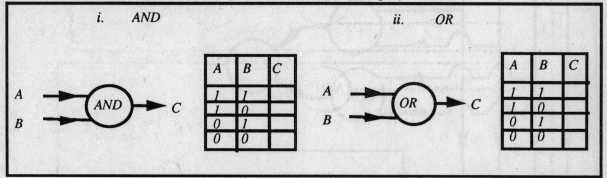

i.   AND

A	B	C
1	1	
1	0	
0	1	
0	0	

ii.   OR

A	B	C
1	1	
1	0	
0	1	
0	0	

b.   *Complete the truth table for the logic diagram in Figure 1 giving the output Z for inputs A and B. You may fill in the intermediate values X and Y as you wish*

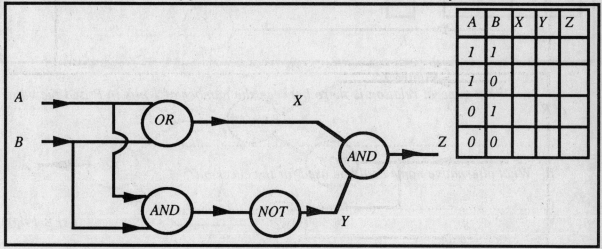

A	B	X	Y	Z
1	1			
1	0			
0	1			
0	0			

Figure 1.

c.   *The logic diagram in Figure 1 is equivalent to the Exclusive Or (EOR) logic function. EOR units are used in the logic diagram, Figure 2, which transfers the contents of register P to register Q and generates a check bit R. Find the value of R for each given value of P.*

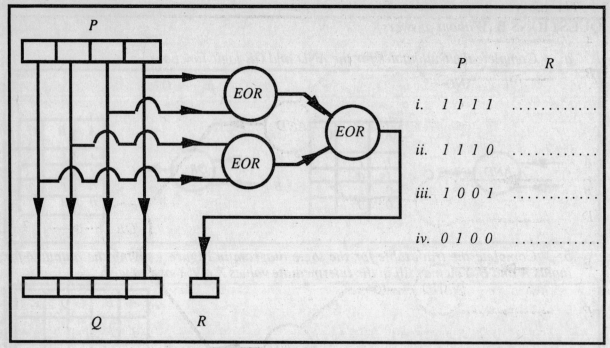

Figure 2.

d. i.   *What general relation is there between the number of 1 bits in P and the value of R?*

....

ii. *What alternative name could be used for the check bit?*

....

(AEB 1980)

2. *This diagram shows a piece of decoding logic.*

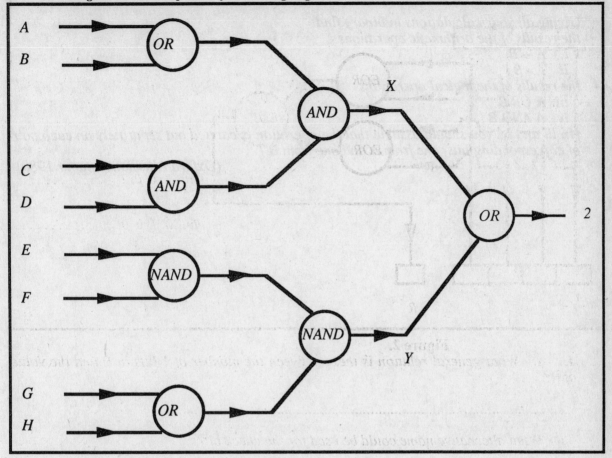

Complete the truth table for the inputs given:

A	B	C	D	E	F	G	H		X	Y	Z
1	1	1	1	1	1	1	1				
0	0	1	1	1	1	0	0				
1	1	0	0	0	0	1	1				
1	0	1	0	1	0	1	0				

(AEB 1981)

3. *Express each of the octal numbers A = 56 and B = 15 as six-bit binary numbers.*

   Giving all your calculations in binary find:
   the results of the arithmetic operations
      i. *A + B*
      ii *A - B*
   the results of the logical operations
      iii. *A OR B*
      iv *A AND B*
   [In iii and iv. you should assume that the operation is carried out separately on each pair of corresponding bits, one from A and one from B.]

   (Oxford Alternative paper 1980)

19 Elements of the Computer

INTRODUCTION

19.1 The elements of the computer were introduced in chapter 2. This chapter deals with the elements in more detail. It concentrates on the processor, main storage and the way in which the processor performs program instructions. Before you continue, re-read   11.4–11.13 and also re-read the details of main storage given in 11.32–11.35.

19.2 The processor and main storage are at the heart of the computer and both are wholly electronic. At one time it was common to refer to the processor together with main storage as the **Central Processing Unit (CPU)** but *the term CPU is best avoided* because it is sometimes used as another name for the processor which can be rather confusing!

19.3 Remember the following key points:
- a.   Main memory is used to store data *and* instruction.
- b.   The processor comprises:
  - i.   The control unit
  - ii. The arithmetic-Logic Unit (ALU).
- c.   The functions of the processor are:
  - i.   to control the sequence of instructions,
  - ii. to give commands to all parts of the computer system,
  - iii. to carry out processing

19.4 Under the control of the processor, data is received into main storage and then processed. The results of the processing are initially held in main storage but the processor may send them to output units or backing storage.

19.5 The internal organisation and operation of computers varies greatly from one computer to another. Most real computers are too complicated to describe in detail in a book at this level, and in any case most computers have their own special or unusual features which make them unsuitable as *general* examples. To overcome these difficulties a fictitious computer is described in this chapter. As you read on please remember that what you are learning about is a typical but simplified example which illustrates the basic concepts. From what you learn you should find it relatively easy to understand the operation of any computer if given sufficient time to do so.

THE BASIC PICTURE

19.6   Refer to figure 19.1. The three basic elements (control unit, ALU and main storage) are shown but not the connection between them.

The details of the connections and relation stops between the three elements will be built up in stages over the next few sections. First we look at how data is stored temporarily as it is moved around the computer.

REGISTERS

19.7 Registers are special purpose temporary storage locations which are quite separate from the locations in main storage although they can be similar in structure. There are very many registers within a computer. The ones important to an understanding of the basic operation of the processor will be introduced as they are needed.

THE ARITHMETIC AND LOGIC UNIT (ALU)

19.8 **Functions.** The ALU has two main functions:-
- a.   It carries out the arithmetic eg. add and subtract.

   b. It performs certain "logic" operations eg. AND and OR.

19.9 How it operates. The details of how the ALU operates will be built up in stages. The first detail to note is that the ALU has a set of operations which it can perform rather like the way a pocket calculator has a set of operations (+, -, x, - etc.). More expensive computers have ALUs able to perform larger sets of operations.

19.10 Accumulators. The ALU performs its operations on data which has been "loaded" into special registers within it called **accumulators,** and it also makes use of other internal registers while performing its operations. these other registers serve the same purpose as a piece of scrap paper when you or I do a calculation with paper and pencil. Our fictitious computer has one accumulator 19 bits long which matches the word length of our computer.

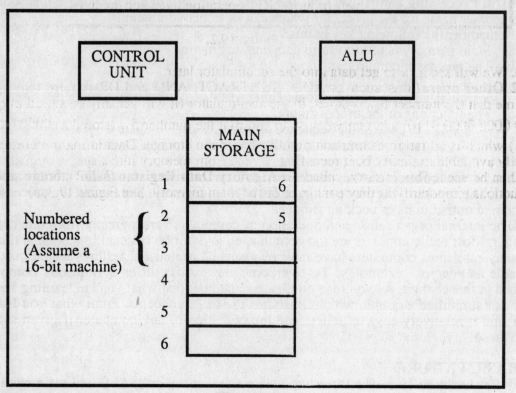

Figure 19.1.

A SIMPLE OPERATION

19.11 Consider the negation (NOT) operation   which is defined by:-

P	NOT P	COMMENT
0	1	`0' changes to `1'
1	0	`1' changes to `0'

An ALU would perform the NOT operation on data in its accumulator as shown here in

Figure 19.2.

Accumulator **Before** The ALU Peforms the NOT Operation	Accumulator **After** the ALU Performs the NOT operation
0 0 1 0 1 0 0 0 1 1 1 0 1 1 0 1	1 1 0 1 0 1 1 1 0 0 0 1 0 0 1 0

Each `0' has changed to `1'.
Each `1' has changed to `0'.

The ALU peforming a NOT operation in an accumulator.

Figure 19.2.

Note. We will see how to get data into the accumulator later

19.12 Other operations such as ADD, SUBTRACT, AND and OR require two operands. Assume that the number 6_{10} is stored in the accumulator (it will actually be stored in binary as 0000 0000 0000 0110) and that we wish to add to it the number 5_{10} (stored as 0000 0000 0000 0101) which is situation in location number 2 in main storage. Data in main memory is nore directly available to the ALU, it must first be read from memory into a special register where it can then be used. This register, called the **Memory Data Register** (MDR), holds all data and instructions temporarily as they pass in or out of main memory. See Figure 19.3.

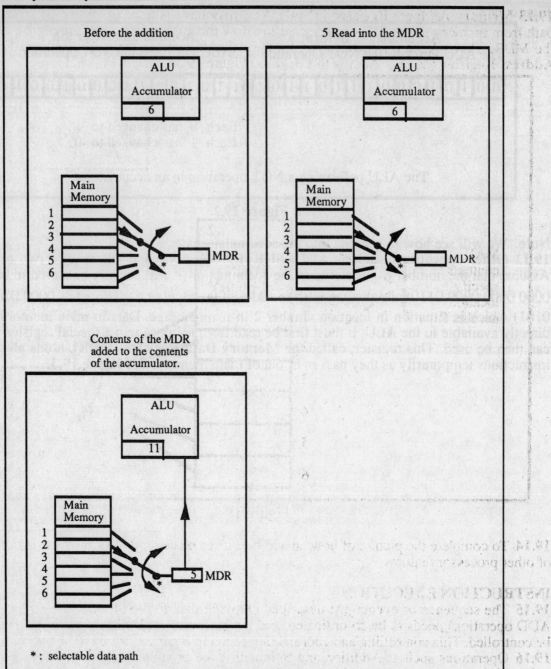

Before the addition

5 Read into the MDR

Contents of the MDR added to the contents of the accumulator.

* : selectable data path

Figure 19.3.

19.13 Memory Address Register (MAR). You may have noticed in Figure 19.3 that a data path from memory to the MDR is selected to allow the appropriate data value to be read into the MDR. This selection is determined by the value in another register called the **Memory Address Register (MAR).** Adding this detail to Figure 19.3b, we get Figure 19.4.

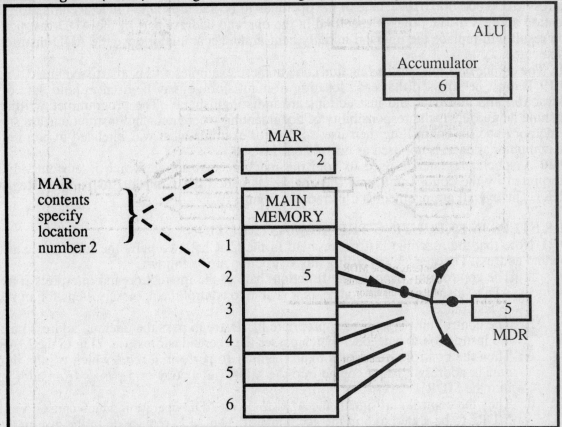

Figure 19.4.

19.14 To complete the picture of how an addition takes place requires some further knowledge of other processor features.

INSTRUCTION EXECUTION
19.15 The sequence of events just described (Moving data to the MDR followed by an ALU ADD operation) needs to be co-ordinated, and the hardware used (memory and ALU) needs to be controlled. This controlling and coordinating function is carried out by the **Control Unit.**
19.16 Operations such as Addition and Subtraction are brought about by proving the control unit with instructions in a suitable form. The control unit can then *interpret* the instructions, and causes them to be *executed* by sending command signals to the appropriate hardware.
19.17 Machine Instructions. Instructions in a form which can be used directly by the control unit are called **machine instructions** and programs, written in the form of machine instructions are said to be written in **machine language.**

19.18 A machine instruction has a number of parts. For example in our fictitious computer the first part of every instruction contains the code for the function to be carried out. The remainder of the instruction contains details of the operands. For example, the ADD instruction shown in Figure 19.5 starts with the function code for ADD (0010 2) and is followed by the "operand address" (000 000 000 0102). One of the operands to be added is held in the accumulator. The location address of the other is specified in the operand address part of the ADD instruction. The result will replace the operand initially held in the accumulator once the ADD instruction is executed.

NB. The choice of 4 bits for the function code in these examples will be discussed later.

19.19 It must be stressed that each location in main storage may be used to hold data or an instruction and that data and instructions are indistinguishable. The programmer writing in machine language has the responsibility of documenting where data and instructions are stored in memory and for controlling their use, so that for example what was intended to be used by the computer as data, is not used as instructions instead.

19.20 A special register is used to hold the machine instruction which is currently being interpreted by the control unit, and this register is called the **Current Instruction Register (CIR)**. The overall arrangement is illustrated in Figure 19.5.

THE STEPS IN EXECUTING THE ADD INSTRUCTION

19.21 Note that the machine instruction held in the CIR has two parts the **function** and the operand address. The steps in **executing** this instruction are as follows.

a. The control unit decodes the **function** part of the instruction and interprets it as an ADD instruction. The control unit is able to control the necessary steps for an ADD to take place.

b. The control unit signals to appropriate hardware to pass the operand address part of the instruction to a decoder which passes the operand address (ie. 2) in to the MAR.

c. Then the control unit signals main memory to perform a *read* which results in the data in address 2 being copied into the MDR (ie. a copy of 5 passes from address 2 into the MDR).

d. Then the control unit signals the ALU to do an ADD operation which causes 5 in the MDR to be added to 6 in the accumulator. The ALU replaces 6 in the accumulator by the total of 5 and 6. This completes the execution.

FETCHING THE NEXT INSTRUCTION

19.22 Once the control unit finishes the execution of one instruction it must **fetch** the next instruction *from* memory into the CIR (via. the MAR). The address of the *next* instruction is held in a special register called the **Sequence Control Register.** Each time the control unit fetches an instruction, it immediately increases the contents of the SCR by one, so that it is ready to be referred to when the next fetch takes place. In this way the control unit automatically deals with instructions in the order in which they occur in main storage. This overall arrangement is illustrated in Figure 19.6.

19.23 Steps in the fetch. All the following steps take place under the control of the Control Unit.

a. Copy the address of the next instruction from the SCR to the MAR (the address is 8 in the example in Figure 19.6).

b. Add one to the contents of the SCR (SCR contents become 9).

c. Read the next instruction from memory into the MDR. (ie. copy the contents of location 8 into the MDR).

d. Copy the contents of the MDR into the CIR. That completes the Fetch.

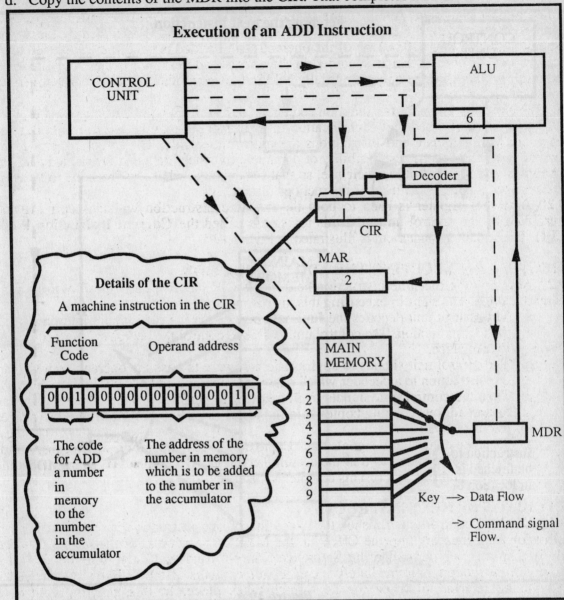

Execution of an ADD Instruction

CONTROL UNIT

ALU

6

Decoder

CIR

MAR

2

Details of the CIR

A machine instruction in the CIR

Function Code

Operand address

0 0 1 0 0 0 0 0 0 0 0 0 0 0 1 0

The code for ADD a number in memory to the number in the accumulator

The address of the number in memory which is to be added to the number in the accumulator

MAIN MEMORY

1
2
3
4
5
6
7
8
9

MDR

Key → Data Flow

-→ Command signal Flow.

Figure 19.5

We are now in a position to summarise the operational features of the control unit before continuing further.

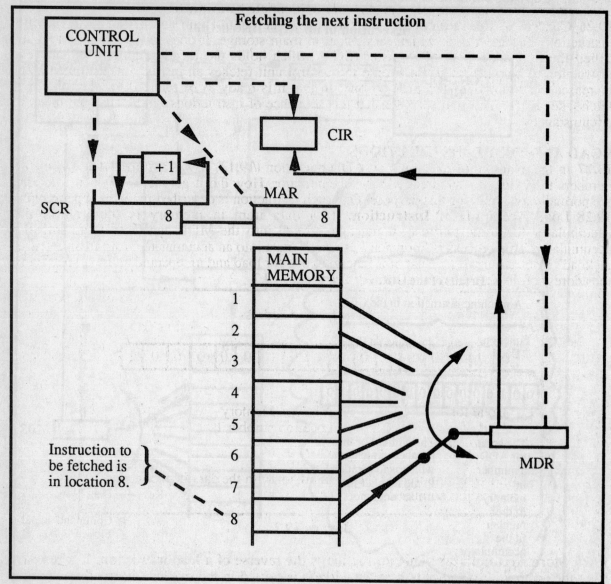

Figure 19.6

CONTROL UNIT

19.24 Function. The Control Unit is the nerve centre of the computer. It co-ordinates and controls all *hardware* operations, ie. those of the peripheral units and the CPU itself.

19.25 How it operates. It deals with each instruction in turn in a two stage operation called the Fetch-Execute Cycle:-

    a. First it *fetches* the requisite instruction from main storage via the MDR and places it in the CIR.

b. Then it *interprets* the instruction in the CIR and causes the instruction to be *executed* by sending command signals to the appropriate hardware devices.

19.26 Control of the sequence of instructions. The control unit automatically deals with instructions in the order in which they occur in main storage. It does this by using a register called the Sequence Control Register (SCR) which holds the location address of the next instruction to be performed. Each time the control unit fetches an instruction, it immediately increases the contents of the SCR by one, so that it is ready to be referred to when the next fetch takes place. You will see later that this sequence of instructions can be changed in some circumstances.

LOAD AND STORE INSTRUCTIONS

19.27 In the example of executing an ADD operation (19.12) it was assumed that one of the numbers to be added was already in the accumulator. How did it get there? Well instructions are normally available for this purpose. One such instruction is described in the next paragraph.

19.28 Load Accumulator Instruction. If a data item in memory is required in the accumulator for some purpose, it must be copied into the MDR and from there into the accumulator. This process is known as "*loading*" data into an accumulator from main storage. A "load" instruction will consist of a function code for load and an operand address specifying the address of the data item to be loaded: See Figure 19.7.

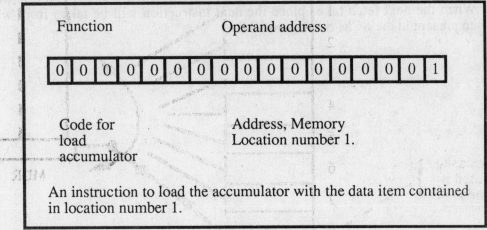

Figure 19.7.

19.29 Store Accumulator. This instruction is the reverse of a load instruction. It takes data from the accumulator and puts it in the address specified in the machine instruction operand address.

19.30 We are now in a position to describe the basic operation of the ALU.

HOW THE ARITHMETIC AND LOGIC UNIT (ALU) OPERATES

19.31 a. Data items about to be processed are taken from main storage, as directed by the control unit, and pass via the MDR into the accumulators in the ALU where they are stored. This step is referred to as "*loading*" data into an accumulator from main storage.

    b. The ALU then performs the required operation(s) on the data (eg. adding) as directed by the control unit. The ALU leaves the result in an accumulator.

    c. Results are placed in main storage, again under the direction of the control unit. This step is referred to as *"storing'"* data.

19.32 Decision Making. Some logical operations of the ALU give the computer its "decision taking ability". They do this by allowing the result of an operation to determine which instruction the control unit fetches next. This means that programs need not be just *sequences* of instructions but can be *selections* and *repetitions* of instructions too. This will be explained more fully shortly.

JUMP OR BRANCH INSTRUCTIONS

19.33 Paragraph 19.26 indicated that the control unit automatically deals with instructions in the order in which they are sequenced in main storage by increasing the value in the SCR by one each time a fetch is performed. This sequence can be altered by means of special instructions called JUMP (or BRANCH) instructions. There are two kinds of jump instructions:-

    a. Unconditional jump instructions.

    b. Conditional jump instructions.

19.34 Unconditional jump instructions. When the control unit executes an unconditional jump instruction it replaces the address in the SCR by the operand address given in the jump instruction. When the next fetch takes place the next instruction will be taken from whatever address is then present in the SCR. See figure 19.8.

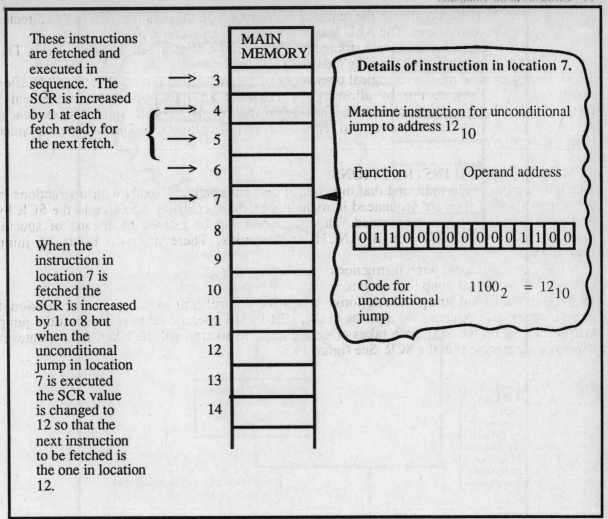

These instructions are fetched and executed in sequence. The SCR is increased by 1 at each fetch ready for the next fetch.

→ 3
→ 4
→ 5
→ 6
→ 7

8
9
10
11
12
13
14

MAIN MEMORY

When the instruction in location 7 is fetched the SCR is increased by 1 to 8 but when the unconditional jump in location 7 is executed the SCR value is changed to 12 so that the next instruction to be fetched is the one in location 12.

Details of instruction in location 7.

Machine instruction for unconditional jump to address 12_{10}

Function   Operand address

| 0 | 1 | 1 | 0 | 0 | 0 | 0 | 0 | 0 | 0 | 0 | 1 | 1 | 0 | 0 |

Code for unconditional jump

$1100_2 = 12_{10}$

Figure 19.8. An unconditional jump.

19.35 Conditional jump instructions. We have just seen how an unconditional jump instruction *always* causes the SCR to be changed (ie. the jump always takes place). A conditional jump instruction only causes the SCR to be changed if a specified condition is met. This is best illustrated by Figure 19.9.

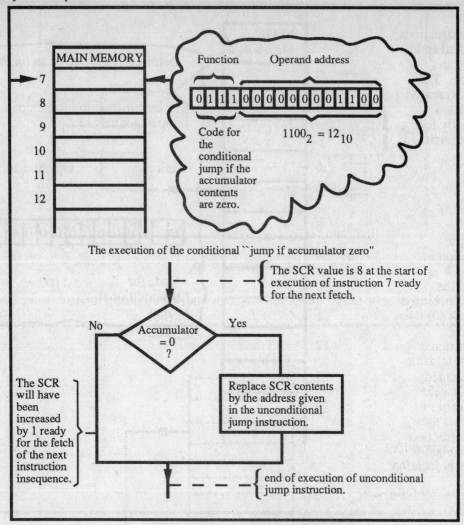

Figure 19.9. A Conditional Jump.

DECISION TAKING

19.36 The computer's ability for "decision taking" boils down to the ability to select courses of actions according to specified conditions. In programming terms this has been met in *selections* such as **IF... ELSE... ENDIF**, which as a flowchart appears as in Figure 19.10.

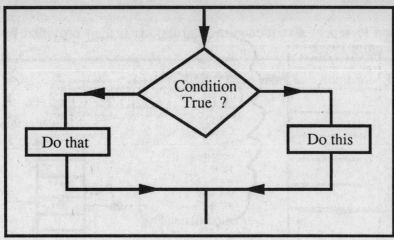

Figure 19.10.

19.37 The combined use of conditional and unconditional jump instructions provides the means of accomplishing this.

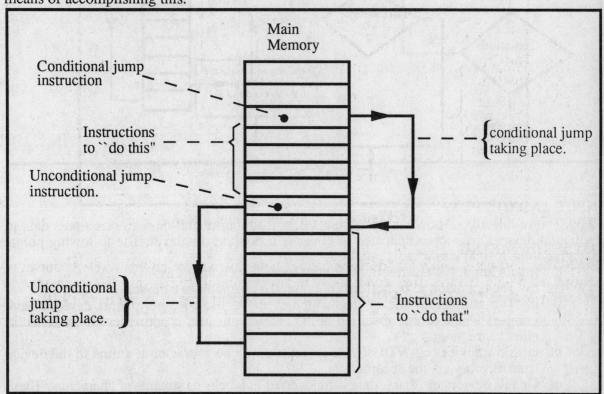

Figure 19.11.

19.38 The decision to repeat a sequence of instructions is also provided by means of jump instructions. See Figure 19.12.

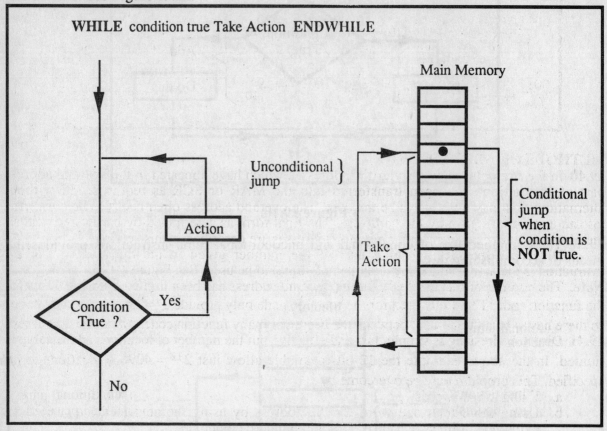

WHILE condition true Take Action ENDWHILE

Figure 19.12.

INPUT AND OUTPUT

19.39 The full details of how the CPU inputs data from peripheral devices or outputs data to peripheral devices are too complicated to cover in a book at this level. The following points may give some insight into what is involved.

    a. Input/Output (I/0) instructions usually specify such things as:-

        i. The operation to be performed eg. send a character to a device

        ii. The number of the device which is to be used ie. peripheral devices have numbers which can be specified in I/O instructions just as addresses are specified in other instructions.

    b. On slow devices eg. VDUs, data is transferred one character at a time to the device from memory via the accumulator.

    c. On fast devices eg. disks, data is transferred in blocks as streams of characters. These transfers are initiated by machine instructions but are completed automatically by hardware once under way.

    d. Numbers input as characters may be converted into pure binary as part of the input procedure. eg. 29_{10} input in ASCII as 00110010_2 (ie. "2") and 0011001 (ie. "9") will be converted as follows:-

$$0011\underbrace{\ 0010\ }0010_2 = 2_{10} \times 10_{10}\quad 10100_2 = 20_{10}$$

extract bits

$$\text{Add}\ \ 11101_2 = 29_{10}$$

$$0011\underbrace{\ 1001\ }1001_2 = 9_{10} \longrightarrow 1001_2 = 9_{10}$$

METHODS OF ADDRESSING

19.40 In the examples shown so far the addresses which have appeared in the operand address part of instructions has been transferred into the MAR or SCR as required and without alternation. this may not always be the case. The operand address often needs to be converted into an appropriate form by the hardware. The final form as determined by hardware is called the **absolute address.** Some other types of addresses are described in this section.

Direct Addressing is being used if the number given in the operand part of an instruction is the actual address of the operand (data) to be used. See Figure 19.13.

Note. The number of bits available for the operand address has been limited by using 4 bits for the function code. The 4 bits used for the function code only provide $2^4 = 16_{10}$ individual codes so there has to be a "trade-off" between the needs for many function codes and large addresses.

19.41 Direct Addressing is simple, fast and effective but the number of locations addressable is limited. In the above example the 12 bits available allow just $2^{12} = 4096_{10}$ locations to be specified. This problem may be overcome by

a. Using longer words
b. Using more than one word for the address by using the next location (called an **extended address**). This is common in micro computers.
c. Using alternative methods. Since a. and b. are frequently impractical on the one hand because longer words prove wasteful and expensive and on the other because the method is slow and complicates the fetch execute cycle.

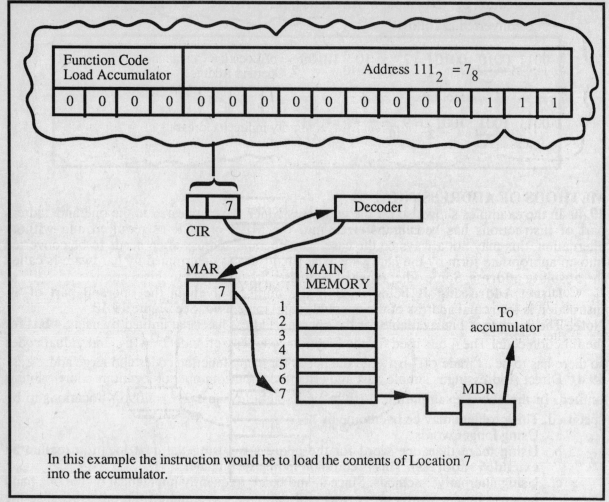

In this example the instruction would be to load the contents of Location 7 into the accumulator.

Figure 19.13. An Example of Direct Addressing.

19.42 Indirect Addressing. When **indirect addressing** is used the address given in the address part of the instruction is NOT the address of the required operand. Instead the address part is the address of the location which contains the required address. An address is **either** direct **or** indirect. This does provide a way of specifying a longer address, although the execute part of the fetch-execute cycle is longer as a consequence.

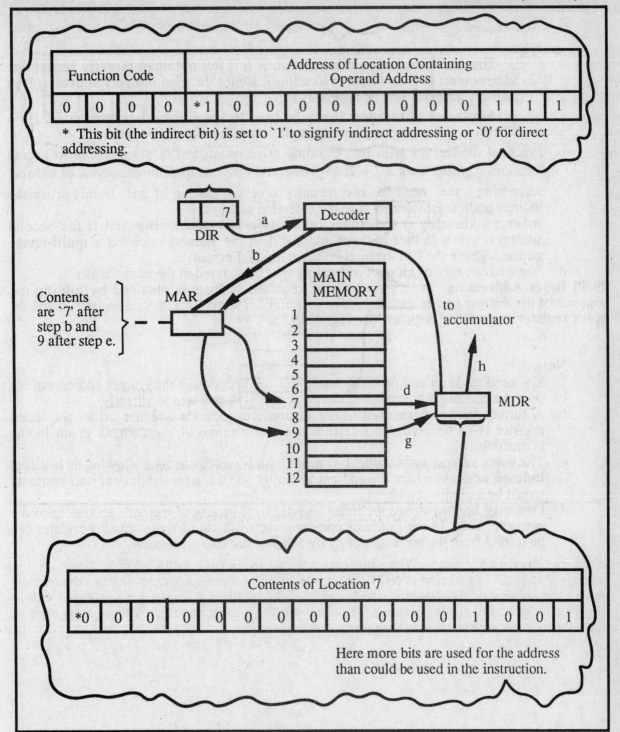

Figure 19.14. An Example of Indirect Addressing.

a. **Note.**

    i.   The data to be loaded is in location 9. It is **not obtained directly** because its address must **first** be found in location 7. Hence the term **indirect address.** (Two memory accesses will be necessary).

    ii.   Almost all of location 7 may be used to specify the data address so $2^{15} = 32768_{10}$ locations may be accessed, a considerable improvement.

b.   Practical difficulties with this example arise because it is not possible to access locations greater than $2^{11} = 2048_{10}$ directly. One unavoidable drawback of indirect addressing is the need for two memory accesses instead of one. In this sense the indirect address is no better than the extended address.

c.   Indirect addressing is sometimes called **deferred addressing** and if the second address is yet a further indirect address then the address is called a **multi-level address.** (Note the * in location 7 shown in the diagram).

d.   Some advantages of indirect addressing will be covered in the next chapter.

19.43 Index Addressing. In this method the required address is obtained by **adding** the contents of the address part of the instruction to a number stored in a special register called the **index register** or **modifier register.** See Figure 19.15.

Note.

a.   The need to do an addition may make this method slower than direct addressing but once the address is calculated it can be accessed in one step ie. directly.

b.   A further bit has been used in our example to indicate whether or not the index register is to be used. This further limits the range of the address given in the instruction.

c.   The index address and indirect bits could both be set to one thus allowing an **indirect indexed address** where the address given by address part + index register contents would be an indirect address.

d.   Data may be loaded into the index register by a variety of methods according to the computer used. In our fictitious computer we will assume that the index register can be loaded from the accumulator by means of a suitable instruction.

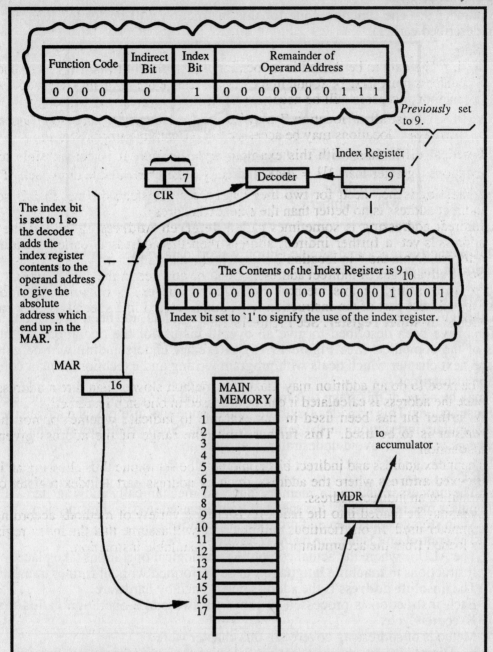

Figure 19.15. An Example of Indexed Addressing.

19.44 Immediate Addressing. In this form of addressing the data to be placed into the accumulator is provided within the instruction so it may be placed into the accumulator *immediately* ie. without the need to access memory eg. An instruction to load the accumulator

311

with the number 9. (The function code for this instruction will be for the load accumulator operation described earlier).

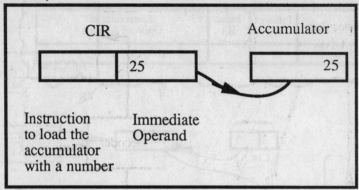

This method is quick and simple but only short data values can be handled because of the limitation of the instruction length.

THE COMPLETE PICTURE

19.45 Although a complete set of machine instructions has not been described, sufficient instructions have been described to give an overall picture of the operations of the various elements of the computer. (See Figure 19.16). A greater understanding will be gained after reading the next chapter which deals with program writing and execution using a complete set of machine instructions.

19.46 It may be noted at this stage that main storage, and many registers, may be used to store data and instructions. This provides flexibility and economy of use plus the advantage of being able to manipulate instructions in the same way as data. Such crude facilities have to be used with great care in order to avoid undesirable consequence.

SUMMARY

19.47 a. The processor and main memory have no mechanically moving parts. Electronic pulses moving at nearly the speed of light are used in data transmission.
 b. Main storage holds data and program instructions.
 c. The control unit is the *hardware* controller.
 d. The ALU is where the actual computing and logical operations take place.

19.48 a. Instructions in **machine language** can be performed without further translation.
 b. The **absolute address** is the address determined by hardware.
 c. Each instruction is processed in turn in a two stage operation called the **Fetch-Execute Cycle.**
 d. Methods of addressing covered in this chapter were
  i. Direct
  ii. Indirect
  iii. Indexed
  iv. Immediate.

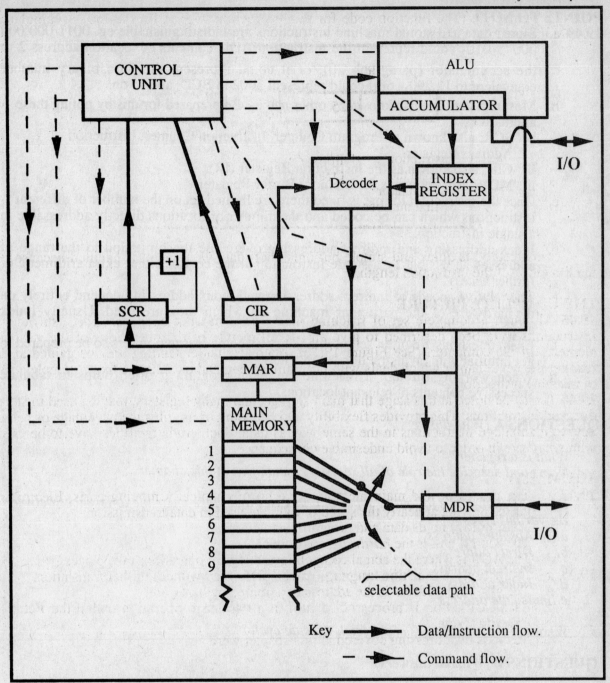

Figure 19.16. Elements of the Computer and their Operational Layout.

POINTS TO NOTE

19.49 a. Stored data and stored machine instructions are indistinguishable eg. 0011 000 000 000 010_2 could represent the instruction ADD contents of location address 2 to the accumulator (paragraph 20), or it could represent the pure binary number equivalent to $12,290_{10}$ or it could represent 3002 in BCD, and so on.

b. Most registers are also known by other names. Be prepared for this by noting these alternatives.
    i. SCR; also known as Program Counter, Instruction Counter, Instruction Address Register.
    ii. CIR; also known as the Instruction Register (IR).
    iii. MDR; also known as the Memory Buffer Register.

c. Once the instruction format is fixed there are limited set on the number of different instructions which can be coded and the number of locations directly addressable in a single instruction.

d. Index addressing and indirect addressing overcome the limitation to the range of addresses accessible by a single instruction at the cost of either extra arithmetic or further access

e. The relative speeds of indirect addressing and index addressing depend entirely on the hardware of the particular machine on which they are used. Usually Index addressing offers a greater flexibility.

f. Exam questions are often set on imaginary machine instruction sets so be prepared to get familiar with an instruction set in a hurry.

g. When working through a machine language program it often helps to tabulate successive contents of relevant locations.

QUESTIONS A *(With answers)*

1. What is a register?
Name and describe the role of all registers mentioned in this chapter.

2. Describe each of the following types of addresses and make clear the differences between the various types.
    a. Absolute address.
    b. Direct address.
    c. Indirect address.
    d. Index address
    e. Immediate address

3. What are the main stages of the fetch-execute cycle?

QUESTIONS B *(Without answers)*

1. Describe the steps involved in the processor executing the following instructions:-
    a. SUBTRACT
    b. CONDITIONAL JUMP
    c. UNCONDITIONAL JUMP

In each case clearly describe the changes in the *sequence control register*.

2. The operand address part of an instruction may be of limited length. What methods are used to overcome this limitation?

3. Stored data and instructions are indistinguishable so what determines their correct use?

20 The Computer's Own Language

INTRODUCTION
20.1 This chapter develops the ideas introduced in the previous chapter by looking at various small programs written in machine language and how they are executed. This should add to the reader's understanding of how the processor operates.

20.2 The chapter also deals with some aspects of the testing and **debugging** of programs and introduces the concepts of **assemblers** and **loaders.**

THE PLACE OF MACHINE LANGUAGE
20.3 You may remember that the processor can only directly interpret instructions if they are in machine language. Therefore, programs written in any other language have to be translated into machine language before they can be used.

20.4 The earliest computer programs were written in **machine language.** Nowadays programmers normally write programs in programming languages which are relatively easy to learn, and the programs are **translated** into **machine language** before being **"run"** on the machine. The translation is done by the computer.

20.5 The machine language programs presented in this chapter are intended to illustrate the relationship between machine language and machine operation. Since the operation of the computer is controlled by programs, an understanding of the examples should lead to a better understanding of how the computer works.

INSTRUCTION SETS
20.6 The set of machine instructions which a computer can perform is called its **instruction set.** Any operation not provided by the hardware, and therefore not in the instruction set, can only be provided by using more than one instruction.

This may be compared with the set of key functions available on a pocket calculator. Some calculators only have a minimal set of key functions (+, -, x, -) while others have large sets of key functions. On the simple calculators a task may require many keys to be pressed but on a larger calculator a single key might provide the same result eg. for x^y.

20.7 Computers with larger instructions sets cost more because more hardware is needed, but tend to operate faster and more efficiently.

INSTRUCTION FORMATS
20.8 **Instruction Format.** A machine instruction has several components. The **instruction format** is the size and arrangement of these components. Previously in 16.18 we mentioned two major components which are the **function code** which specifies the function or operation performed, and the **operand addresses,** which specifies the locations of the **operands** used.

Another example is given in Figure 20.1

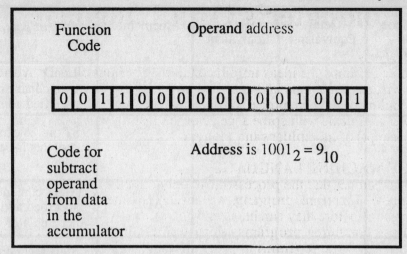

An instruction to subtract the contents of memory location number 9_{10} from the contents of the accumulator in our fictitious computer.

Figure 20.1.

20.9   Address Format. In our fictitious computer we will assume that the operand address is arranged as shown again here in figure 20.2

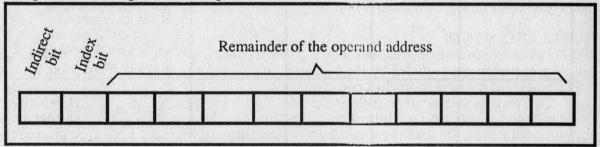

Figure 20.2. Address Format.

20.10 From the instruction format given in paragraph 20.8 it may be deduced that our fictitious computer has 16 function codes, because the 4 bits give rise to $2^4 = 16$ distinct codes:- 0000, 0001, 0010, 0011, 0100, 0101, 0110, 0111, 1000, 10001, 1010, 1011, 1100, 1101, 1110, 1111.

AIDS TO THE PROGRAMMER
20.11 Remembering which binary codes represent which functions is troublesome, so a **MNEMONIC** is associated with each code. A mnemonic is a memory aid with a sound suggesting its meaning eg. LDA might stand for **L**oa**D** Accumulator, and STA might stand for **ST**ore Accumulator, and so on. The programmer writes the program in mnemonics which can later be converted into codes.

20.12 Another programming aid is to use either Octal or Hex as a shorthand for binary. For example the instruction in figure 20.1 may be written as 3009_{16} or as 030011_8.

THE INSTRUCTION SET OF OUR FICTITIOUS COMPUTER
20.13 It is assumed for the purpose of this example that the instruction format is the one specified in paragraph 8 ie. a fixed (word) length of 16 bits of which the first 4 bits are used to represent a possible 16 function codes. The codes, their functions, and associated mnemonics are given in the following table, *and further explanation follows.*

317

Machine Code Function (Binary)	Octal Equivalent	Hex Equivalent	Mnemonic	Function
0000	00	0	LDA	LoaD Accumulator with contents of specified address.
0001	01	1	STA	STore Accumulator contents in specified address.
0010	02	2	ADD	ADD contents of the specified address to the accumulator contents.
0011	03	3	SUB	SUBtract contents of specified address from the accumulator contents.
0100	04	4	AND	Perform an AND operation on contents of accumulator and contents of specified address placing results in the accumulator.
0101	05	5	ORA	Perform an OR operation on contents of Accumulator and contents of specified address placing the results in the accumulator.
0110	06	6	JPU	JumP Unconditionally to specified address.
0111	07	7	JAZ	Jump to specified address if Accumulator contents are Zero.
1000	10	8	JAN	Jump to specified address if Accumulator contents are Not zero.
1001	11	9	JAL	Jump to specified address if Accumulator contents are Less than zero.

				Jump to specified address if **A**ccumulator contents are **G**reater than zero.
				SWAP the contents of the **A**ccumulator with the contents of the **I**ndex register.
				Perform specified operation on the accumulator using an immediate address.
				Perform a **NOT** operation on the accumulator contents.
				STOP the program ie. **HaLT** the processor.
				Perform specified Input/Output operation.

Note. In instructions where there is no memory address, eg. ACC and IOP operations, the operand address part may be used to extend the function options.

EXAMPLES OF USING THE INSTRUCTIONS

20.14 Small parts of programs are given here so as to keep the examples as simple as possible.

20.15 Example 1. Adding the contents of location address 2 to the contents of location address 3 and placing the result in location address 4.

NB. Decimal numbers are used with the instruction mnemonics because of their familiarity to the reader. In practice OCTAL or HEX would be used.

The instruction sequence is:

```
LDA  2
ADD  3
STA  4
```

(See Fig. 20.3).

Figure 20.3. FOLLOWS ON THE NEXT PAGE

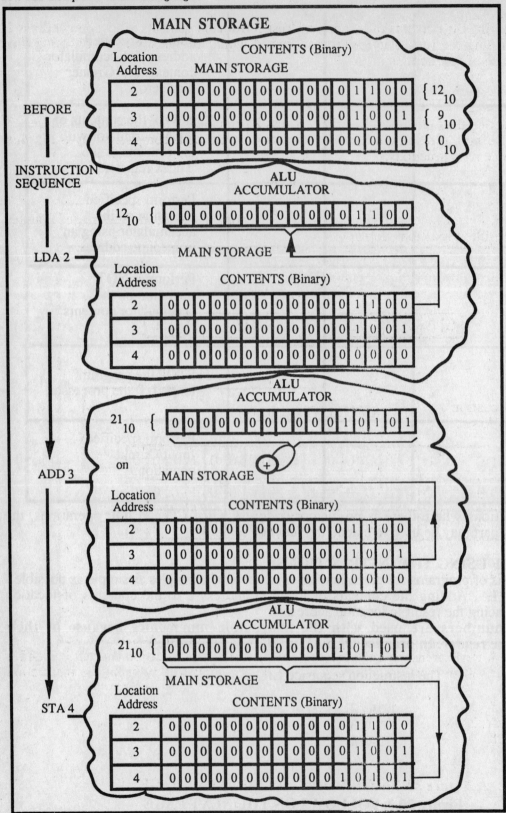

20.16 Example 2.

a. Subtracting the contents of location address 3 from the contents of location address 2 and placing the results in location address 4 would be accomplished by using this sequence of instructions:-

```
LDA   2
SUB   3
STA   4
```

b. Subtracting the contents of location address 2 from the contents of location address 3 and placing the results in location address 4 would be accomplished by using this sequence of instructions:-

```
LDA   3
SUB   2
STA   4
```

20.17 Example 3. Performing an AND operation of the contents of location addresses 2 and 3 and placing the result in location address 4.

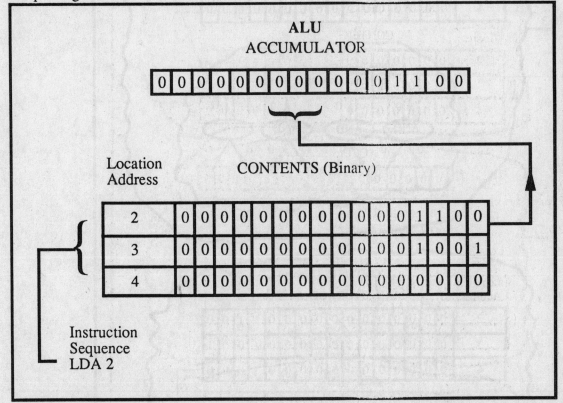

20.18 Example 4. Performing an OR operation on the contents of location addresses 2 and 3 and placing the result in location address 4 would be accomplished by using the instruction sequence:-

```
LDA   2
ORA   3
STA   4
```

Figure 20.4. - FOLLOWS ON THE NEXT PAGE

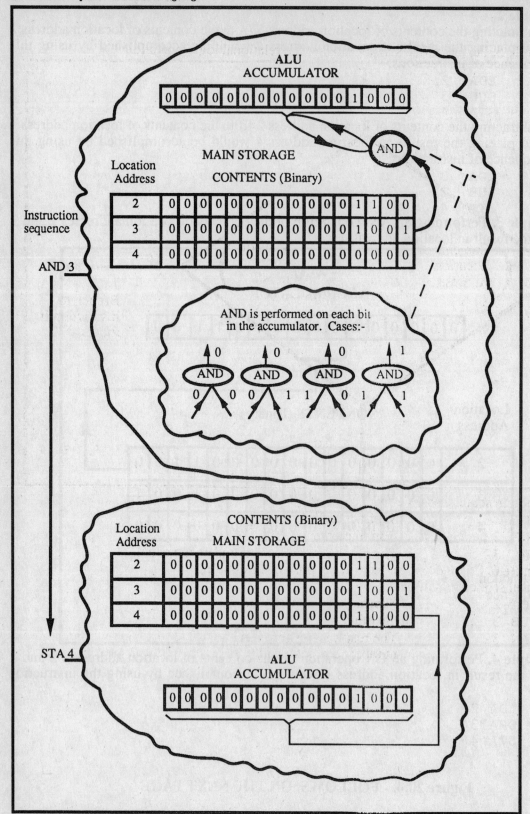

ALU
ACCUMULATOR

| 0 | 0 | 0 | 0 | 0 | 0 | 0 | 0 | 0 | 0 | 0 | 0 | 1 | 0 | 0 | 0 |

AND

MAIN STORAGE

Location Address	CONTENTS (Binary)
2	0 0 0 0 0 0 0 0 0 0 0 0 1 1 0 0
3	0 0 0 0 0 0 0 0 0 0 0 0 1 0 0 1
4	0 0 0 0 0 0 0 0 0 0 0 0 0 0 0 0

Instruction sequence

AND 3

AND is performed on each bit
in the accumulator. Cases:-

0   0   0   1
AND   AND   AND   AND
0   0   0   1   1   0   1   1

CONTENTS (Binary)
MAIN STORAGE

Location Address |
--- | ---
2 | 0 0 0 0 0 0 0 0 0 0 0 0 1 1 0 0
3 | 0 0 0 0 0 0 0 0 0 0 0 0 1 0 0 1
4 | 0 0 0 0 0 0 0 0 0 0 0 0 1 0 0 0

STA 4

ALU
ACCUMULATOR

| 0 | 0 | 0 | 0 | 0 | 0 | 0 | 0 | 0 | 0 | 0 | 0 | 1 | 0 | 0 | 0 |

322

20.19 Example 5. Performing a selection using the relational logic operation "="

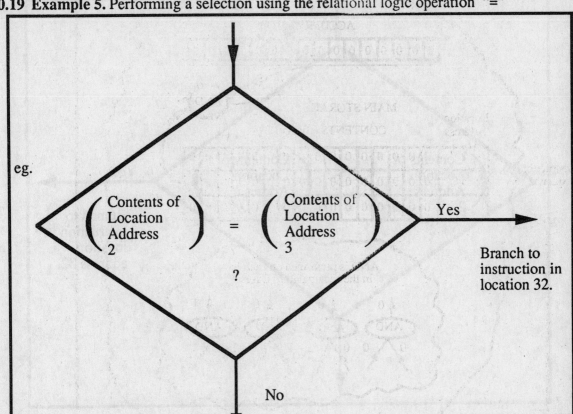

eg.

$$\left(\begin{array}{l} \text{Contents of} \\ \text{Location} \\ \text{Address} \\ 2 \end{array} \right) = \left(\begin{array}{l} \text{Contents of} \\ \text{Location} \\ \text{Address} \\ 3 \end{array} \right) \quad ?$$

Yes → Branch to instruction in location 32.

No

Instruction sequence:-

LDA	2	Subtract one number
SUB	3	from the other
JAZ	32	The result is zero if the numbers are equal.

20.20 Example 6. Change "=" to "<>" in the previous example.

The instruction sequence will be:-

LDA	2	Subtract one number from
SUB	3	the other
JAN	32	The result is not zero if the numbers are not equal.

20.21 Example 7.   Performing a selection using the relational logic operator ">".

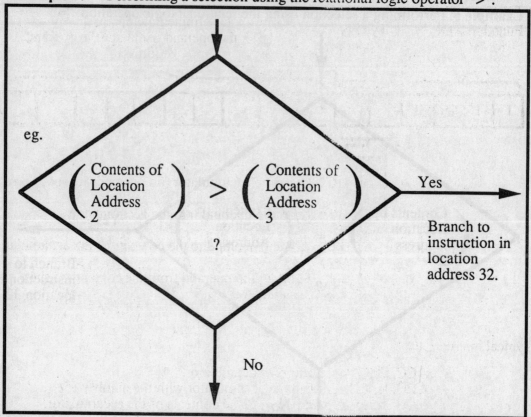

eg.

$$\left(\begin{array}{l} \text{Contents of} \\ \text{Location} \\ \text{Address} \\ 2 \end{array} \right) > \left(\begin{array}{l} \text{Contents of} \\ \text{Location} \\ \text{Address} \\ 3 \end{array} \right)$$

?

Yes

Branch to instruction in location address 32.

No

Instruction sequence:-

LDA	2	Subtract the contents of location
SUB	3	address 3 from the contents of location address 2.
JAG	32	The result is greater than zero when the contents of location address 2 are greater than the contents of location address 3.

20.22 Example 8.   Change ">" to "<" in the previous example.

The instruction sequence will be:-

LDA	2	Subtract the contents of location
SUB	3	address 3 from the contents of location address 2.
JAL	32	The result is less than zero when the contents of location address 2 are less than the contents of location address 3

INSTRUCTIONS WHICH DO NOT CONTAIN AN OPERAND ADDRESS

20.23 In some instructions there is no memory address. There are five such instruction functions listed in the table in paragraph 20.13 ie. SAI, ACC, NOT, HLT, IOP. Taking the simpler ones first, the details are as follows:-

a.   The **NOT** instruction only has one operand, the contents of the accumulator, therefore there is no need for the instruction to contain an operand address .

b.   The HLT instructions causes the processor to halt and thereby stops the program. No operand is required.

c.   The SAI instruction causes the contents of the accumulator and index register to be swapped. Neither operand is in memory so no operand address need be specified.

d. The ACC instruction will be taken to have the instruction format shown in figure 20.5.

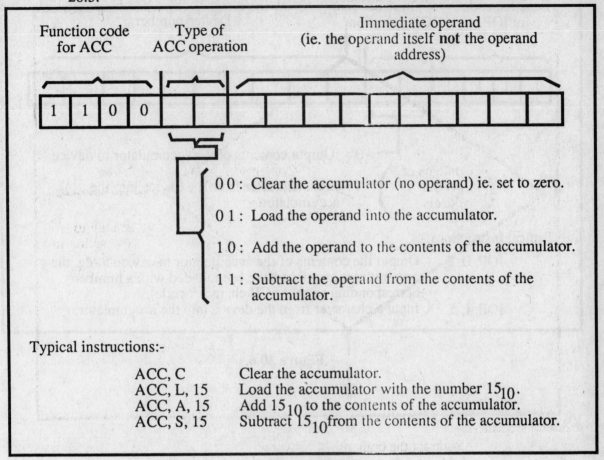

Typical instructions:-

ACC, C	Clear the accumulator.
ACC, L, 15	Load the accumulator with the number 15_{10}.
ACC, A, 15	Add 15_{10} to the contents of the accumulator.
ACC, S, 15	Subtract 15_{10} from the contents of the accumulator.

Figure 20.5.

e. The IOP instruction will not contain a memory address but will contain details such as the number of the device to be used and the type of operation (input or output) See Figure 20.6

AN EXAMPLE USING ACC AND IOP
20.24 Output of the ASCII letter "A" onto a VDU with device number 5.

ACC, L, 65	ASCII "A" is $1000001_2 = 65_{10}$
	This instruction loads "A" into the accumulator
IOP, 0, 5	This instruction output the accumulator contents to device 5.

AN EXAMPLE OF A PROGRAM SELECTION
20.25 In this example an examination mark is already held in location address 20_{10} and the pass mark is already held in location 25_{10}. If the examination mark is greater than the pass mark then the ASCII character "P", for "Pass", is to be output to device 6 otherwise the ASCII

character "F" for "Fail" is to be output to the same device. This is summarised in figure 20.7.

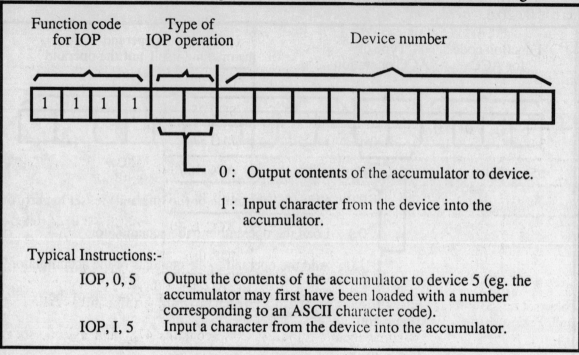

Figure 20.6.

```
IF
    (Contents of 20) > (Contents of 23)
THEN
    character :=  "P"

ELSE
    character := "F"
ENDIF
PRINT character
```

Figure 20.7.

Here is the program section

Location Address	Memory Contents (Program Instructions)	Mnemonics	Comment
32	0 0 0 0 0 0 0 0 0 0 0 1 0 1 0 0	LDA 20	} See para' 21
33	0 0 1 1 0 0 0 0 0 0 0 1 1 0 0 1	SUB 25	
34	1 0 1 0 0 0 0 0 0 0 1 0 0 1 0 1	JAG 37	
35	1 1 0 0 0 1 0 0 0 1 0 0 0 1 1 0	ACC, L, 70	ASCII ``F" is 1000110_2 = 70_{10}
36	0 1 1 0 0 0 0 0 0 0 1 0 0 1 1 0	JPU 38	
37	1 1 0 0 0 1 0 0 0 1 0 1 0 0 0 0	ACC, L, 80	ASCII ``P" is 1010000_2 = 80_{10}
38	1 1 1 1 0 0 0 0 0 0 0 0 0 1 1 0	IOP, 0, 6	

20.26 Testing the program. There are two cases to consider, ("Pass" and "Fail"). The two tables set out below are called "trace tables" and a manual program test like this is called a "dry run". Follow these two test dry runs.

    a. **"Pass" case.** Assume location address 20_{10} contains 47_{10} and assume location address 25_{10} contain 40_{10}.

This table is filled in by following the program using the test data (47 and 40).

Location Address of Insruction in the Sequence in which they are Performed	Contents of Registers at the End of Each Instruction Execution (Actual Contents are in Binary Form)			Comment
	SCR	CIR	Accumulator	
32	33	LDA, 20	47	SCR is changed by the Jump instruction.
33	34	SUB, 25	7	
34	37	JAG, 37	7	
37	38	ACC, L, 80	``P"	``P" is output to device 6.
38	39	IOP, 0, 6	``P"	

    b. **"Fail" case.** Assume location address 20_{10} contains 37_{10} and assume location address 25_{10} contains 40_{10}.

Location Address of Insruction in the Sequence in which they are Performed	Contents of Registers at the end of each Instruction Execution (Actual Contents are in Binary Form)			Comment
	SCR	CIR	Accumulator	
32	33	LDA, 20	37	
33	34	SUB, 25	- 3	SCR *not* changed by the Jump instruction.
34	35	JAG, 37	- 3	
35	36	ACC, L, 70	``F''	
36	38	JPU, 38	``F''	``P'' is output to device 6.
38	39	IOP, 0, 6	``F''	

AN EXAMPLE OF A REPETITION

20.27 A "WHILE" Loop. This program is intended to find the sum of the numbers $1 + 2 + 3 + 4 + 5 +$.... etc. up to some specified largest number. The largest number is specified beforehand. The method to be used starts with the largest number and works downwards to zero, summing on the way. When the program starts the largest number is already in location 10_{10} and when the program stops the total must be in location 11_{10}. The steps will be as shown here in figure 20.8

SUCCESSIVE CONTENTS		COMMENTS
Location Address 10_{10}	Location Address 11_{10}	
7	7	Location 11 initially holds zero.
6	13	{ $7 + 6$
5	18	{ $7 + 6 + 5$
4	22	{ $7 + 6 + 5 + 4$
3	25	{ $7 + 6 + 5 + 4 + 3$
2	27	{ $7 + 6 + 5 + 4 + 3 + 2$
1	28	{ $7 + 6 + 5 + 4 + 3 + 2 + 1$
0	28	Stop when location 10 holds zero.

Figure 20.8.

Here is an outline of the method (Fig. 20.9). The complete program is shown in Figure 20.10.

```
BEGIN
    Total := 0
WHILE
    Number <> 0
DO
    Total  := Total + Number
    Number :=  Number - 1
ENDWHILE
END
```

Figure 20.9.

Location Address	Memory Contents	Mnemonic	Comments
10	0 0 0 0 0 0 0 0 0 0 0 0 0 1 1 1		Largest Number 7_{10}
11	0 0 0 0 0 0 0 0 0 0 0 0 0 0 0 0		May be any Total value before set to zero.
12	1 1 0 0 0 0 0 0 0 0 0 0 0 0 0 0	ACC, C	Set Total to zero
13	0 0 0 1 0 0 0 0 0 0 0 0 1 0 1 1	STA 11	
14	0 0 0 0 0 0 0 0 0 0 0 0 1 0 1 0	LDA 10	Load largest Number.
15	0 1 1 1 0 0 0 0 0 0 0 1 0 1 1 0	JAZ 22	Test for end of while loop.
16	0 0 1 0 0 0 0 0 0 0 0 0 1 0 1 1	ADD 11	Add Total to Number and store as total
17	0 0 0 1 0 0 0 0 0 0 0 0 1 0 1 1	STA 11	
18	0 0 0 0 0 0 0 0 0 0 0 0 1 0 1 0	LDA 10	Subtract 1 from number
19	1 1 0 0 1 1 0 0 0 0 0 0 0 0 0 1	ACC, S, 1	Store number
20	0 0 0 1 0 0 0 0 0 0 0 0 1 0 1 0	STA 10	
21	0 1 1 0 0 0 0 0 0 0 0 0 1 1 1 1	JPU 15	Back to start of while loop
22	1 1 1 0 0 0 0 0 0 0 0 0 0 0 0 0	HLT	STOP
23	0 0 0 0 0 0 0 0 0 0 0 0 0 0 0 0		
24	0 0 0 0 0 0 0 0 0 0 0 0 0 0 0 0		

(Locations 16–17 grouped as "Add Total to Number and store as total"; locations 18–20 grouped as "Subtract 1 from number / Store number"; locations 16–21 bracketed as "While loop".)

Figure 20.10 . A program set up to perform the sum 7 + 6 + 5 + 4 + 3 + 2 + 1.

329

20.28 A "REPEAT..UNTIL" Loop. This example also illustrates the use of the Index register. A sentence is to be input one character at a time until the "." character is input. The characters, including the "." are to be stored in sequence in memory starting at location 25. For the sake of simplicity no checks on the types of characters input are included in the program ie. sentences of nonsense letters and characters can be input. Data will be input on device 7_{10}.

An outline of the method is given in figure 20.10 and the program is given in figure 20.12.

```
BEGIN
Index := 0
REPEAT
    INPUT character
    Store character in location (25 + Index)
    Index := Index + 1
UNTIL Character = "."
END
```

Figure 20.11.

Notes to figure 20.12.

  i.   STA, I, 25 is used to indicate STA using an **Index** address. The absolute address will be 25 + (Contents of Index register). On each repeat the contents of the index register will be increased by 1, so the instruction in location 13 will effectively be STA 25 then STA 26, then STA 27, then STA 28 etc.

 ii.   The Index register is acting as a **counter**. At the end of the program it will contain the number of characters input.

Location Address	Memory Contents	Mnemonic	Comments
10	1 1 0 0 0 0 0 0 0 0 0 0 0 0 0 0	ACC, C	Clear Accumulator
11	1 0 1 1 0 0 0 0 0 0 0 0 0 0 0 0	SAI	Swap to clear the index register to zero.
12	1 1 1 1 0 0 0 0 0 0 0 0 0 1 1 1	IOP, I, 7	Input a character from device 7
13	0 0 0 1 0 1 0 0 0 0 0 1 1 0 0 1	STA, I, 25	See note (i)
14	1 0 1 1 0 0 0 0 0 0 0 0 0 0 0 0	SAI	Here the Index register is increased by 1.
15	1 1 0 0 1 0 0 0 0 0 0 0 0 0 0 1	ACC, A, 1	
16	1 0 1 1 0 0 0 0 0 0 0 0 0 0 0 0	SAI	
17	1 1 0 0 1 1 0 0 0 0 1 0 1 1 1 0	ACC, S, 46	Subtract the ASCII value of ``.''
18	1 0 0 0 0 0 0 0 0 0 0 0 1 1 0 0	JAN 12	Test for repeat
19	1 1 1 0 0 0 0 0 0 0 0 0 0 0 0 0	HLT	STOP See note (ii)
20			
21			
22			
23			
24			
25			Data will be stored here.
26			
27			
28			
29			
30			

(Repeat until loop — spanning locations 12 to 18)

Figure 20.12.

331

ASSEMBLERS

20.29 The examples given so far should show the advantages of using MNEMONICS to describe machine language instructions. It seems logical to write programs in this mnemonic form and to get the machine to do the translation. A special program which can perform such a translation is called an **assembler** and the mnemonic form of machine language is called **assembly language.** One further important programming aid can be used in assembly language. It is called **symbolic addressing** and will now be described.

20.30 Symbolic Addressing. An example of an instruction using symbolic addressing is "LDA NUM" ie. load accumulator with the contents of location address NUM. "NUM" is the symbolic address.

20.31 Labels are used in assembly language to indicate the positions of symbolic addresses.

20.32 Example. Here is the program from Figure 20.10 written in assembly language.

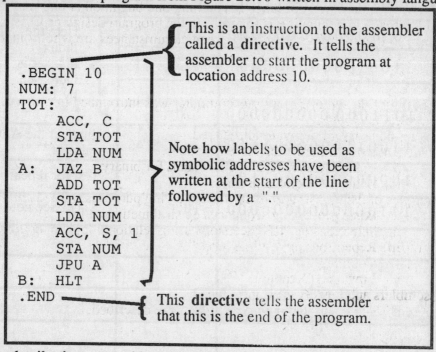

```
.BEGIN 10
NUM: 7
TOT:
      ACC, C
      STA TOT
      LDA NUM
A:    JAZ B
      ADD TOT
      STA TOT
      LDA NUM
      ACC, S, 1
      STA NUM
      JPU A
B:    HLT
.END
```

This is an instruction to the assembler called a **directive.** It tells the assembler to start the program at location address 10.

Note how labels to be used as symbolic addresses have been written at the start of the line followed by a ".".

This **directive** tells the assembler that this is the end of the program.

20.33 Further details about assemblers will be given in later chapters.

LOADERS

20.34 Before a program can be executed it must be placed into main storage. Special programs able to read programs from input or storage devices and place them into main storage are called "loaders". More details will be given in later chapters.

TESTING AND DEBUGGING

20.35 It is too easy to make mistakes when writing programs, and so programs often fail to work the first time they are tried. If a program has been well designed the faults should be easier to find and correct.

20.36 It is good practice to test a program as it is being written and before it is tried out on the computer. The method of testing shown in paragraph 26 (ie. the "trace" or "dry run") may be used to good effect.

20.37 When testing a program take care to select the test data so that it tests all cases. eg. Pick a set of data which will cover all possible selections as in paragraph 26 where the two cases "pass" and "fail" were *both* tested.

20.38 Large programs are very difficult to test completely once they are completed because of their complexity and the time needed to try all possible cases. If top-down programming is adopted it should be possible to test each program module thoroughly at each step along the way.

20.39 Despite all these testing methods programs may still be faulty when they are tried out on the computer. Well tested programs sometimes work well for a while and then suddenly produce a fault. This may happen because some combination of circumstances has occurred which the program designer has not taken into account when designing the program.

20.40 These program faults are called **"bugs"** and getting rid of these faults by making appropriate changes to the program is called **debugging**.

20.41 Debugging is often regarded as a "patching up job" In fact alterations made to programs in order to get rid of bugs are often called "patches" or "fixes"., Treating debugging in this way is rather a risky way to do things, because in patching one bug another bug may be introduced. A more sound approach to debugging is to return to the program design process, and *all* stages in programming, so that the previously unforeseen circumstances are wholly incorporated into the design.

SUMMARY

20.42 a. An **instruction set** of a fictitious computer was introduced in order to provide a set of typical examples.
 b. Aids to the programmer were introduced:-
   i. Using mnemonics for instructions,
   ii. Using Octal or Hex as shorthands for binary
   iii. Using symbolic addresses.
 c. Examples of using instructions for the following purposes were given:-
   i. Basic processing sequences eg. arithmetic and logic,
   ii. Selections eg. "IF" decisions using relational logic operators
   iii. Repetitions eg. "While loops".
   iv. Counting
   v. Input and Output
 d. Assemblers and loaders were introduced
 e. Program Testing and debugging methods were described.

POINTS TO NOTE

20.43 a. The methods introduced in this chapter need to be reinforced by plenty of practical programming exercises.
 b. Assemblers and loaders will be described more fully in later chapters.

QUESTIONS A *(With answers)*

1.   Define the terms
   a. instructions set,
   b. instruction format,
   c. address format,
   d. indirect address,
   e. index address.

2.   Define the terms "machine language" and "machine instruction".

3.   Describe the actions of the following instructions for the fictitious computer described in this chapter.

     a. *LDA*
     b. *STA*
     c. *AND*
     d. *JAZ*
     e. *SAI*
     f. *ACC*
     g. *IOP*

4.   *Work through each of the following sequences of program instructions and perform a "dry run" in which you record the contents of locations 10, 11, 12 and 13, and the contents of the accumulator at each stage.*

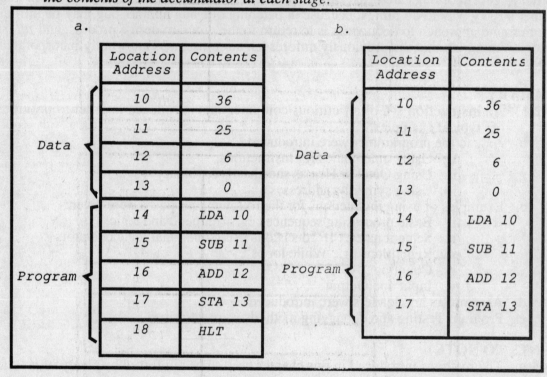

a.

Location Address	Contents
10	36
11	25
12	6
13	0
14	LDA 10
15	SUB 11
16	ADD 12
17	STA 13
18	HLT

Data: 10–13
Program: 14–18

b.

Location Address	Contents
10	36
11	25
12	6
13	0
14	LDA 10
15	SUB 11
16	ADD 12
17	STA 13

Data: 10–13
Program: 14–17

Record the contents of the accumulator in binary for parts c and d. (Remember that locations are 16 bits long in these examples).

c.

Location Address	Contents
10	36
11	25
12	6
13	0
14	LDA 10
15	ORA 11
16	STA 12
17	HLT

Data: 10–13
Program: 14–17

d.

Location Address	Contents
10	36
11	25
12	6
13	0
14	LDA 10
15	AND 12
16	STA 13
17	NOT
18	AND 11
19	STA 12
20	HLT

Data: 10–13
Program: 14–20

5.   What does the following program do? Perform a dry run in order to find out.

Location Address	Contents
10	65
11	67
12	84
13	LDA 11
14	IOP,0,3
15	LDA 10
16	IOP,0,3
17	LDA 12
18	IOP,0,3
19	ACC,L,46
20	IOP,0,3
21	HLT

Data { locations 10–13

Program { locations 14–21

NB. Data in this program should be converted to binary and used as ASCII character codes. (Use Appendix IV.3).

6. Here are 8 characters to be used as a sequence of 8 input items of test data for the following program. Perform a dry run and say what the program does.

Test data | D | O | G | . | P | I | G | | (ie. 8 ASCII characters.)

/NB. You are advised to first find the decimal value corresponding to the ASCII codes for these characters. (Use Appendix IV.3).]

Location Address	Contents
20	IOP, I, 3
21	IOP, 0, 4
22	ACC, S, 46
23	JAN 20
24	HLT

QUESTIONS B *(Without answers)*

1. *Perform 2 dry runs on the following program to determine what the program does. The first time use the ASCII character "4" as your test data the second time use the ASCII character "5". (Again use Appendix IV.3)*

Location Address	Contents
20	IOP, I, 3
21	ACC, S, 52
22	JAN 26
23	ACC, L, 63
24	IOP, 0, 4
25	JPU 28
26	ACC, L, 32
27	IOP, 0, 5
28	HLT

2.   *What output is sent to each device when the following program is executed?*

Location Address	Contents
31	67
32	79
33	87
34	72
35	69
36	78
37	LDA 31
38	IOP, 0, 2
39	LDA 34
40	IOP, 0, 3
41	LDA, 32
42	IOP, 0, 2
43	LDA, 35
44	IOP, 0, 3
45	LDA, 33
46	IOP, 0, 2
47	LDA, 36
48	IOP, 0, 3
49	ACC, L, 46
50	IOP, 0, 2
51	IOP, 0, 3
52	HLT

Data Decimal values corresponding to ASCII codes (See Appendix IV.3).

Program

3.   *Examine the example in (Figure 20.11), (Figure 20.12) and 20.28. Write a program which takes the same data from main storage and outputs it to device number 8.*

21 System Architecture

INTRODUCTION

21.1 Keeping up to date with the latest computer developments is rather like shooting at a moving target. However, most of the developments which take place from one month to the next, are only of particular importance to people buying or renting computers. New concepts, methods, ideas and principles come along at a less rapid pace, and it is these which should concern us. Even so, the reader will want to relate these concepts and methods etc. to the computers which he or she uses or sees. This chapter attempts to bridge that gap, by discussing features of modern systems, and relating them to topics covered in earlier chapters and to their applications.

21.2 The term "System Architecture" used in the title of this chapter is used in Computer Studies to mean the style of the construction and organisation of the many parts of a computer, so that the parts work together in the way intended.

21.3 Two underlying principles on which good System Architecture is based today are:-

    a. top-down design

and   b. modularity of construction

21.4 A child using LEGO bricks to make a model, is engaged in a kind of modular construction (ie. building from a set of standard components which can be joined together). The child will probably use "bottom up" design however, ie. building up parts together to form a completed model. Top-down design starts with a general concept of what is required, and progresses by developing a plan in a step by step fashion. This involves breaking the whole plan down into parts, and then filling in the details of parts towards the end. This methodology has already been illustrated by the top-down program design methods of chapter 8.

PRACTICAL FEATURES OF MODULARITY

21.5 In practical terms a "**module**" may be some physical component which carries out a specific task or series of tasks eg. a microprocessor chip or a memory chip. Alternatively a module may be some part of such a unit which has some specific function eg. the control unit, or the ALU, or an adder or a decoder and so on.

21.6 The advantages of using modules is enhanced by standardising the ways of interconnecting modules. A standard way of interconnecting the computer's modular components is by means of a "**bus**".

21.7 A bus is a single highway (18.41) which is used to interconnect the various registers and modular components within the system. Instead of each pair of components having their own interconnecting highway, which would require excessive wiring, components are all connected to the same buses and take turns at using them.

21.8 These ideas are illustrated by figure 21.1 which gives a simplified view of a 8-bit microcomputer based system. Compare this diagram with figure 19.6 and note the following points about figure 21.1. Differences between 8-bit and 16-bit computers are given too.

    a. All registers except the MAR and SCR are 8 bits long. In an 16-bit microcomputer they would be 16-bits long.

    b. The SCR may incorporate sequential logic for increasing it by 1 as part of the fetch-execute cycle.

    c. A 16 bit instruction will be spread over two successive 8-bit locations in memory and will therefore require two fetch cycles. 24 bit instructions will require 3 fetch cycles. This is an important factor causing 8-bit micros to be slower than 16 bit machines because on average a 16-bit microcomputer uses half as many fetches to get the same data.

d. The first 8 bits of an instruction may contain opcodes plus address mode details and will be fetched into the opcode register as 8 parallel bits. The remainder of the instruction (ie. the operand address) may be fetched into the MAR on a one or two cycle action according to its length. (**NB.** An opcode is a function code).

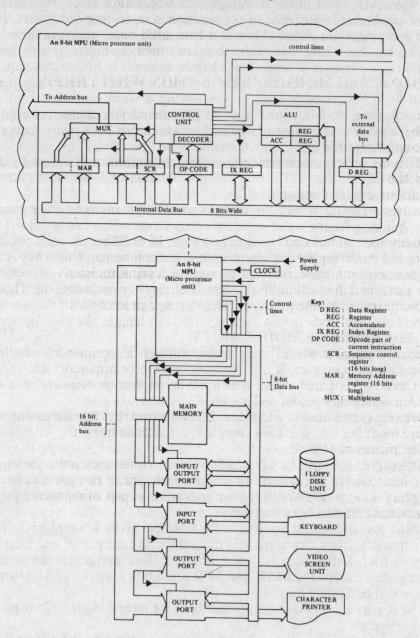

Figure 21.1. A Simplified View of a Microcomputer Based System.

340

e.   The cycles for fetches and executes take place in time with an external clock which may be operating at about 3 MHz ie. 3 million cycles (6 million pulses) per second. (One cycle has two pulses:-   )

Note. The data bus on the 8-bit machine shown in figure 21.1 is only 8-bits wide. On a 16-bit computer it would be necessary for this bus to be at least 16 bits wide to be able to obtain the contents of a single memory location in a single fetch operation. In general the size of internal buses may be some multiple of the memory location size, in order to speed up internal data transfers. So, for example, one model of processor used on a 16-bit computer might have a memory bus of 16-bits but a faster model might have a memory bus of 32 bits.

ORGANISATION OF MEMORY IN CONNECTION WITH THE PROCESSOR

21.9   A typical 8-bit microcomputer, ie one having a word length of 8 bits, will have a maximum memory size of 64k words (ie. 65536 memory locations). Each of these 64k locations will be represented by one of 64k codes which can be transmitted along the 16 bit address bus. Some of these location addresses may be "borrowed" as addresses to input and output ports. This is called **memory mapping.** A simplified diagram showing such an arrangement is shown in figure 21.2. A typical allocation of 8-bit microcomputer memory addresses for various uses is illustrated in figure 21.3.

21.10   For a 16-bit computer, ie one having a word length of 16 bits, the following features and figures are typical.

a.   Register size and bus size is typically either 16 or 32 bits.

b.   There are more registers than in an 8-bit machine eg, 8 data registers, 8 address registers, plus other special registers such as a status register.

c.   The maximum linearly addressable memory is much greater than for an 8-bit microcomputer, for example, 16 Megabytes instead of 64K!

d.   Instruction may be between 1 and 5 words in length, thereby supporting huge and complex instruction sets.

e.   External input and output is normally through a separate bus, rather than by the method of memory mapping, widely used on 8-bit computers.

f.   The clock rate is much higher than on 8-bit microcomputers and this determines the speed at which instruction and memory accesses take place.

21.11 Firmware. Programs held in ROM are called **firmware.** They are stored permanently in the ROM and are ready for use when the computer is switched on.

21.12 When the microcomputer is switched on, a control signal is sent to the microprocessor which causes it to *reset* its current instruction register to the location address of a firmware instruction eg. location 0. The processor immediately starts to execute the instruction in firmware. The *reset* control signal may either take place as part of the switching on operation, or sometimes a button, called a **boot** button has to be pressed too. This is called "booting up the system".

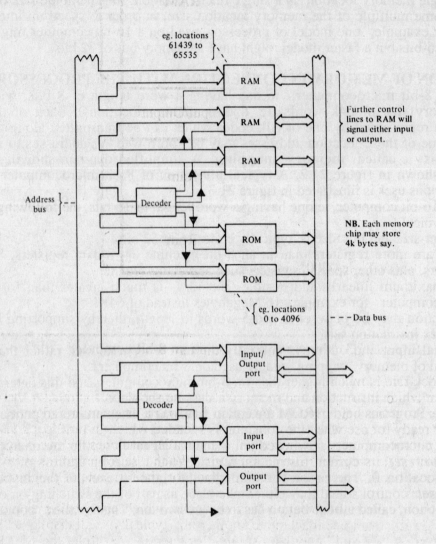

eg. locations
61439 to
65535

RAM

RAM

RAM

Further control
lines to RAM will
signal either input
or output.

Address
bus

Decoder

ROM

NB. Each memory
chip may store
4k bytes say.

ROM

eg. locations
0 to 4096

---- Data bus

Input/
Output
port

Decoder

Input
port

Output
port

**Figure 21.2. A Simplified Diagram of 8-bit Microcomputer Memory
Organisation and Allocation of Memory Addresses.**

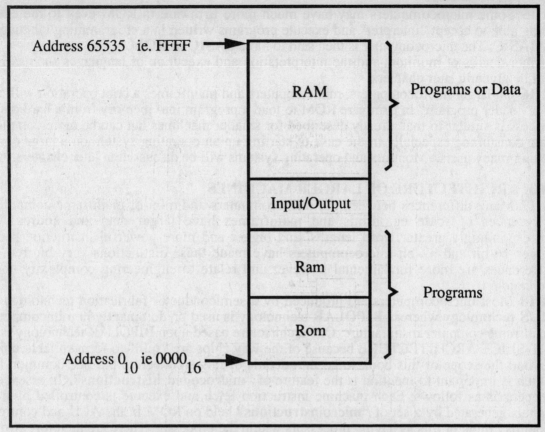

Address 65535   ie. FFFF

RAM

Programs or Data

Input/Output

Ram

Programs

Rom

Address 0_{10} ie 0000_{16}

Figure 21.3. Memory allocation on an 8-bit computer.

USE OF FIRMWARE ROM

21.13 On small microcomputer based systems like the one shown in figure 21.1 the firmware ROM normally contains a special **"loader program"** to load a program into memory from the floppy disk. Normally a special control program is loaded which in turn loads and runs a program called a **command interpreter** or **shell**. On smaller machines the two programs may be combined into a single program called a **monitor**. When a set of programs is involved in controlling the use of hardware, instead of a single monitor, the full suite of programs is called the **operating system**.

21.14 The **monitors, command interpreters** or **shells,** which start being executed after "boot up" differ greatly from one machine to another but typically will display a **"prompt"** on the video screen. A "prompt" may be a single character eg. ">" to let the user know the computer is ready for input. Alternatively, it may provide rather more information, eg "C: " might remind the user that he or she currently has access to the files on disk "C". The command interpreter may then accept interpret and obey commands typed in at the keyboard eg. "DIR", short for for "directory" may cause a list of files on disk to be displayed on the screen. On simple monitors the commands may be quite limited. On PCs the commands are typically much more extensive as in the case of Microsoft's MSDOS.

21.15 Some microcomputers may have much more firmware in ROM even to the extent of being able to accept "interpret" and execute programs written in a programming language such as BASIC. The microcomputer is then said to have **BASIC in ROM.**
Further details of monitors and the interpretation and execution of languages such as BASIC will be given in later chapters.

21.16 On larger microcomputers, minicomputers and mainframes a boot operation will cause a the "loader program" in firmware ROM to load a program into memory from a hard disk. The process is similar to that already described for smaller machines but can be more complex and time consuming especially in the case of starting up an operating system on a large computer having many users. Monitors and operating systems will be discussed in later chapters.

THE ARCHITECTURE OF LARGER MACHINES

21.17 Many differences between the microcomputers and mini or mainframe computers are differences of scale eg. minis and mainframes have larger data and address buses, correspondingly greater word lengths, and bigger and more powerful instruction sets. The newer 16-bit and 32-bit microcomputers have made these distinctions very blurred. Other differences are more fundamental however and relate to engineering complexity and chip technology.

21.18 Most microcomputers are produced by a semiconductor fabrication technology called **MOS technology** whereas **BIPOLAR** technology is used predominantly in minicomputer and mainframe computer manufacture. One architecture based upon BIPOLAR technology is called BIT-SLICE ARCHITECTURE because of the way chips are "split" to form suitable units. It's beyond the scope of this book to go into details of this architecture but one common feature which is important to mention is the feature of **"microcoded instructions"**. In essence what happens is as follows. Each machine instruction fetch and execute is controlled by a set of signals generated by a set of **"microinstructions"** held on ROM *in* the ALU and control unit. You may think of this as having processors within the processor. There are therefore two levels of instructions: Machine instructions which may be called **macro instructions** and the **microcoded instructions.**

21.19 This architecture allows the machine instruction set to be reprogrammed if required, a feature not present in the usual MOS technology microcomputer, and has the added advantage of higher speeds. Further details of microcoded instructions are beyond the scope of this book.

21.20 The larger machines also tend to have arrangements for handling input and output which are much superior to the methods used on small microcomputers. Figure 21.4 illustrates some important features of larger machine architecture. it should be noted however that there is considerable variation in the architecture of large machines depending on the manufacturer and model.

RISC AND CISC

21.21 The earlier comparisons between 8-bit and 16-bit microcomputers showed the trend towards computers having more extensive and complex sets of machine instruction so that some 16-bit microprocessors in use today have more complex instruction sets than mainframes used in the 1960s. In recent years an alternative approach to processor design has become popular in which the processor has a simple instruction set based upon a small set of instructions. The name for such machines is **Reduced Instruction Set Computers (RISC)**. The traditional alternatives are called **Complex Instruction Set Computers (CISC)**. Under some circumstances RISC machines can perform favourably compared with CISC although comparisons are difficult because it may take many RISC instructions to do what one CISC instruction would do. A RISC program will therefore be much larger than an equivalent CISC program.

NEWER ARCHITECTURAL FEATURES

21.22 Cache Memories. These are high speed RAMs which work at speeds which match the processor. They are used to hold data which has recently been accessed from other storage in anticipation of its use in the near future. Subsequent accesses if they occur will be fast. The least accessed data in cache memory is replaced by newly accessed data.

21.23 Content Addressable Storage (CAS). This storage works in the opposite way from normal storage. Suppose that each word in memory can hold 4 characters and that location 200 contains "FRED". In normal storage the address, 200, would be used to load "FRED". In content addressable memory "FRED" would be passed along a data bus and the memory would pass 200 back indicating the location of "FRED". CAS is very useful for rapid data selection or retrieval but is expensive at present.

ALTERNATIVE ARCHITECTURES

21.24 Front End Processors (FEPs). Many mainframe computer systems incorporate minicomputers which are used to handle input and output from the various devices, thus relieving the main computer of some of the tasks associated with input and output. The minicomputer being used for this purpose is called a **Front End Processor (FEP)**.

21.25 Some large computers have two or more main processors in order to handle a large load, and also to provide backup in the case of breakdown. (ie. if one processor fails the system can continue to operate). This is known as **multiprocessing.** A multiprocessing system with a FEP is shown in figure 21.5.

21.26 Distributed Systems. Over recent years there has been a steady trend towards using computer systems which have several interconnected processors placed in separate locations. Each processor tends to have its own "local" peripherals (disks, printers, terminals) in addition to any peripherals attached to some central processor. See figure 21.6.

21.27 In chapter 15 there was a detailed discussion about such systems under the heading of **computer networks.** You may remember that the term **distributed system** is used to describe interconnected computers, possibly some distance apart, which nevertheless appear to the users as a single system. For example, when the user of a distributed system uses a program he or she may not be able to tell which computer is actually doing the processing or which computer's disks are holding the data being used. In a simple network such information would probably be obvious to the user.

21.28 It is becoming increasingly popular to use distributed systems comprising many small computers rather than larger minicomputers or mainframes. Instead of one large and fast machine sharing its time between many users, several small machines each cater for their own individual users. The former is known as **shared logic** and the later is known as **distributed logic.** Both types of system are **multi-user systems.** Later in this chapter we will consider some other ways of classifying systems.

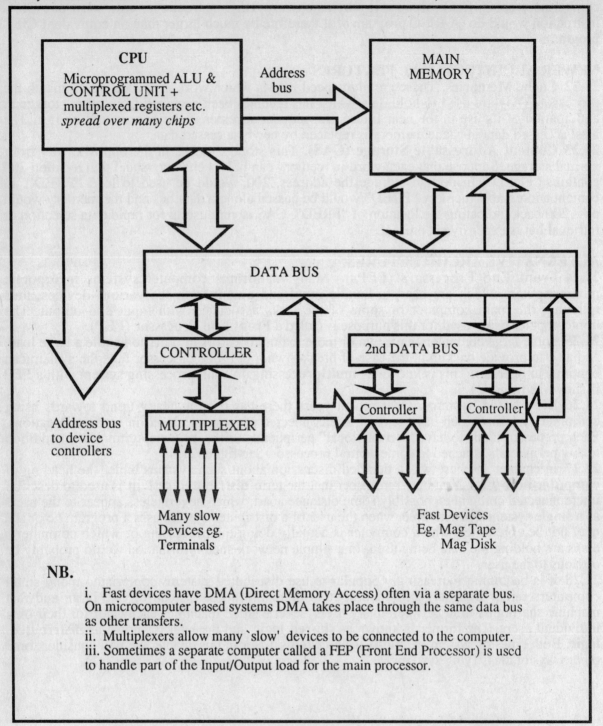

Figure 21.4. An Outline of Architecture on Larger Computers.

NB.

i. Fast devices have DMA (Direct Memory Access) often via a separate bus. On microcomputer based systems DMA takes place through the same data bus as other transfers.

ii. Multiplexers allow many `slow' devices to be connected to the computer.

iii. Sometimes a separate computer called a FEP (Front End Processor) is used to handle part of the Input/Output load for the main processor.

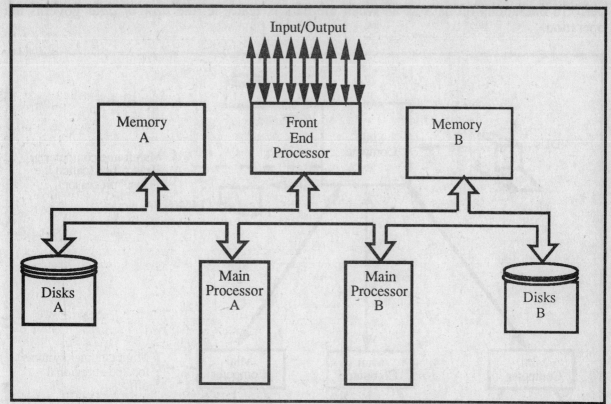

Figure 21.5. A Multiprocessing System with Front End Processor and Duplicated Disk Storage and Memory.

SUPER COMPUTERS

21.29 Although the most noticeable developments in computers over the last few years have resulted from the spread of many smaller and cheaper computers there has at the same time been a steady demand for computers with greater and greater processing power. Such computers are needed for scientific and technological research and for application in defence and weather forecasting systems for example.

21.30 The speeds of operation of these very large computers are not just measured in **MIPS** (Millions of Instructions per second) but in terms of **MFLOPS** (Millions of floating point operations per second). In the late seventies a "**Super computer**" was defined as one which could perform more than 20M flops eg. multiplying 20 million pairs of real numbers together in one second.

21.31 To achieve these super computer speeds the basic design of the computer had to be changed so that operations within the "CPU" could take place in parallel. These computes operate very differently from ordinary computers.

21.32 A notable example of such a computer is the CRAY-1 which is probably the most successful super computer in use today. There are other examples. For example ICL have a processor called a **DAP (Distributed Array Processor)**.

21.33 An even more radical change in design is to be found in **Data flow** computers which perform operations on data as an when the data is ready ie. the *flow of data* governs the operation.

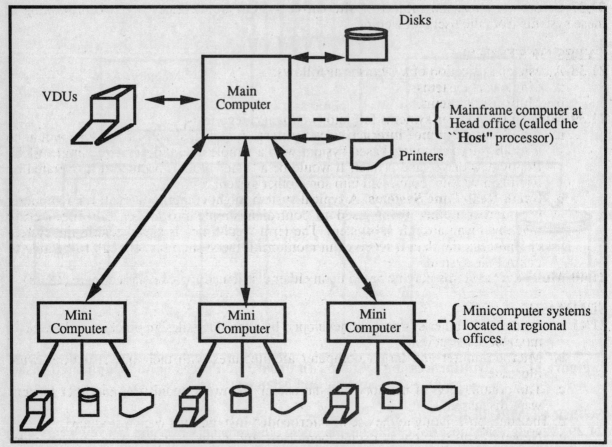

Figure 21.6. A Distributed System.

"FIFTH GENERATION" MACHINES

21.34 Massive sums of money are being spent in trying to develop the so called "Fifth Generation" computers. Japan is spending some £300 million pounds a year on such a project. There are similar projects in the USA, the European Economic Committee and in Britain, but not necessarily costing so much!

21.35 What is being aimed for is a machine which can be spoken to in simple plain language, and which is able to conduct a conversation with a human in a human-like manner. Such a machine exhibits what may be called **Artificial Intelligence (AI)**. Other features being aimed at are super computer speeds, perhaps 1000 times faster than the CRAY - 1, computer "sight", and mobility. The robots of science fiction will be science fact by the end of this century if these researchers meet their goals.

21.36 This progress *is* continuing rapidly on a number of fronts at present. For example the newer RAM chips store 1 Megabytes, and such a chip plus its casing and wires is smaller than a new penny piece.

OTHER CLASSIFICATIONS
21.37 Before we leave the subject of alternative system architectures it is worth looking at these systems from the users viewpoint.

TYPES OF SYSTEM
21.38 A basic classification of systems is as follows:-
    a. Single user systems.
    b. Multi-user systems.

21.39 Modern single user systems fall into two main categories:-
    a. **Small "stand alone" interactive computers.** A typical system of this type would be a small microcomputer based system with a simple operating system, single VDU, floppy disk drive and printer. It would be a "stand alone" machine if it operated by itself and was not connected into some other system.
    b. **Small Real-Time Systems.** A typical system might comprise a small minicomputer or microcomputer being used to control a simple process eg. an engineering machine or an aircraft subsystem. The term "real-time" is used because the system can process the data it receives in monitoring the system fast enough to be able to control the system.

21.40 Multi-user systems may be based upon either distributed logic or shared logic (18.28)

SUMMARY
21.41 a. Modern computer systems are developed by a top-down design process, and are of modular construction.
    b. Microcomputer and larger computer architectures with their bus structures were illustrated.
    c. The organisation of memory and the use of **firmware monitors,** and **boot** loaders were discussed.
    d. The concepts relating to the use of **microcoded instructions** were introduced.
    e. Newer features such as cache memories, and content addressable storage were introduced.
    f. Alternative architectures were outlined.
        i.   multiprocessing,
        ii. using front end processors,
        iii. distributed systems,
        iv. local area networks eg. rings.
    g. The super computers and aims of the "fifth generation" machine designers were discussed.

POINTS TO NOTE
21.42 a. No examination will expect candidates to have a detailed knowledge of the latest developments in computing, but it is important that the reader should be able to relate principles and methods to the computers in widespread use today.

QUESTIONS A (With answers)

1. a. Define the following terms:
      i. module
      ii. bus
   b. Why are busses useful?

2. Why are 8 bit microcomputers slower than 16 bit microcomputers?

3. What is firmware?

4. Distinguish between micro-instructions and macro-instructions.

5. Define the following terms.
   a. Cache memory
   b. Content addressable memory
   c. Front end processor.
   d. Distributed system.

6. What is meant by "MIPS" and MFLOPS"?

QUESTIONS B (Without answers)

1. If we were to construct a 128k byte memory from 8k byte chips, what would be the initial and final addresses of each chip?

2. Describe what is meant by the following expressions:-
   a. "booting up the system"
   b. "BASIC in ROM".

3. Describe, with the aid of diagrams, two alternative methods of implementing a local area network. (NB. only the basic design is required).

4. What are the features being developed for "super computers"?

SOFTWARE AND PROGRAMMING

1. This section of the book deals with detailed features of software and programming. Whenever possible the reader should combine reading these chapters with practical programming activities so that he or she can put theory into practice.

2. The detail given is intended to support the reader in practical work for examinations and coursework projects.

3. The next six chapters are arranged as follows.

    a. Chapter 22 describes the various types of computer software and provides an overview for the remaining chapters in this section of the book.

    b. Chapter 23 deals with program development and continues with ideas and methods which were introduced earlier, in chapter 8.

    c. Chapter 24 describes low level languages, explains the features and explains low level language programming.

    d. Chapter 25 explains the need for high level language and describes the features of various important high level languages.

    e. Chapter 26 introduces databases and "fourth generation languages" (4GLs).

    f. Chapter 27 introduces operating systems and describes their purpose, facilities and characteristics.

22   Software Types

INTRODUCTION

22.1   This chapter looks at the general classification of software and provides an overview for this section of the book. There is no universally accepted way of classifying software but the classification given in this chapter is consistent with most generally accepted definitions.

MAIN TYPES OF SOFTWARE

22.2   The two main classes of software are:-

a. **System Software.** The users of a computer have at their disposal a large amount of software usually provided by the manufacturer. Much of this software will be programs which contribute to the control and performance of the computer system. Such programs are given the collective name system software. Any one of these programs is a **systems program,** eg. Monitors and Assemblers are examples of systems software.

b. **Applications Software.** Applications programs do specific jobs for the user, such as solving equations or producing a payroll. Applications programs may be provided by the computer manufacturer or supplier but in many cases the users produce their own applications programs called **user programs.** A single applications program is often called a **job.** Sometimes a job may be divided into smaller units called **tasks.** A job may comprise program + data. Most applications programs can only work if used in conjunction with the appropriate systems programs.

22.3   A slightly more detailed sub-division of software into its types is as follows:

a. Operating systems and control programs.

b. Translators

c. Utilities or service programs.

d. Data Base Management Systems (DBMS)

e. User application programs

f. Applications packages

These may be further sub-divided. A brief description of each of these software types now follows.

OPERATING SYSTEMS AND CONTROL PROGRAMS

22.4   Whatever application a computer is being used for, the user of the computer will wish the computer to give efficient and reliable service without the need for continual intervention by the user. These requirements suggest that in some way the computer should monitor and control its own operation where possible. This can be achieved by the use of suitable "**control programs**", ie. a program which controls the way in which hardware is used.

22.5   The consequence of adopting this approach to controlling the way the computer is used is that under many circumstances there are at least two programs within main memory. One may be an applications program and the other will be a program which monitors, aids and controls the applications program. The latter of these two programs may be called the **monitor.**

22.6   **The monitor** program may be "resident" in main memory ie. there all the time, and will control and schedule the use of hardware by the program currently being run.

22.7   On many small microcomputer based systems, a home computer say, with keyboard and video display, the monitor will accept certain commands typed in by the user eg. a "LOAD" command to read an applications program from cassette or floppy disk and place it in main memory. The monitor carries out this function for the user. Another monitor command might be "RUN" which would cause the monitor to "pass control" to the loaded program so that its instructions were executed. When the applications program has finished its execution, or exceptionally when the applications program attempts a wrong use of hardware such as trying to divide by zero, the monitor takes over control from the applications program and displays a suitable "prompt" for the user. In the case of a premature ending to the program's execution an error message may be displayed eg. "ERROR - DIVISION BY ZERO".

22.8 On larger systems the monitor may have a comprehensive function including the following:-

    a. Handling the dialogue of prompts, commands, and error messages with the user.

    b. Managing the control of devices.

    c. Managing the allocation of memory.

    d. Allocating time to programs.

More details of these will be given in chapter 27.

22.9 On these larger systems it is common for only part of the monitor to remain resident in memory. Other parts of the monitor are brought into memory when required ie. there are "resident" and "transient" parts to the monitor.

22.10 The resident part of the monitor on a large system is often called the **Executive** or **Supervisor Program** although in other cases you may find "Monitor", "Executive" and "Supervisor Program" used as synonyms.

22.11 Operating Systems. In the example in paragraph 22.7 it was apparent that the user had to intervene at regular intervals for the loading and executing of programs, and applications programs were being executed one at a time in sequence. On larger systems the control programs are able to allow a number of programs to run on the computer concurrently and in sequence. Such control programs, which normally have many other features too, are called **operating systems.** In fact an operating system is often comprised of many control programs as you will discover when you come to the details in chapter 27.

TRANSLATORS

22.12 Any instruction presented to the computer must ultimately be expressed in machine language instructions since only machine language instructions can be directly executed by the computer.

22.13 Writing in machine language is irksome for the programmer and so the programmer uses a variety of aids one of which is the use of mnemonic codes eg. LDA and another of which is symbolic addresses.

22.14 Having written a program in this symbolic and mnemonic form ie. in an **assembly language** (17.29) it is necessary to translate this form of the program into machine code. Programs have been developed to do this translation and they are called **Assemblers.**

22.15 Assemblers are one example of a group of programs called Translators.

22.16 Other programming languages have been devised which are even easier for the programmer, more sophisticated, closer to the "language" of English and Mathematics, and these languages are called **High Level Languages** (Examples are Ada, BASIC, C, COBOL, PASCAL and FORTRAN).

22.17 Programs written in high level languages also have to be translated into machine code. There are two common strategies for dealing with this translation:-

    a. Translating the whole program completely, and then executing the machine language version.

  b. Translating and executing each instruction in turn, which means the retranslation of instructions within loops.

A translator which uses strategy (a) is called a **compiler** and a translator which uses strategy (b) is called an **interpreter.**

22.18 Just to clarify this distinction between an interpreter and a compiler more thoroughly consider this example.

22.19 Imagine that a cook who does not speak French wishes to use a French recipe. ie. the cook can only understand recipes in English, just as the computer can only "understand" programs in machine language. Suppose that another member of the kitchen staff is able to translate French into English and can act as the cook's assistant. This person is the "Translator". The cook can get the translator to translate the whole recipe into English, and write it out in full, so that in future the cook can use it again and again, without the need for any further translation. This is the case of a **compiler.** Alternatively, the cook may ask the translator to translate the recipe a sentence at a time, speaking the translated version to the cook as the cook follows the instructions. This is an example of an **interpreter.**

22.20 Using a compiler clearly makes more sense if the same program is to be used again and again, since the translation only gets done once. On the other hand if the program is only to be used once the use of an interpreter may appeal because it is more straight forward.

22.21 When using a compiler one ends up with two versions of the program. The first version, called the **"source program"** is the one written in the high level language. The compiler takes in this "source program" and produces a translated version in "machine code". The translated version is called the **"object program".** The object program has then to be loaded into memory and executed.

22.22 The procedures for using compilers and interpreters are compared in figure 22.1

22.23 You may notice that monitor commands are translated and executed just as soon as they are input. This highlights another use of interpreters ie. monitor commands are commonly handled by an interpreter.

22.24 Some compilers only translate the source program into a **"low level language"** such as assembly language instead of translating the source program into machine code. Some further translation is then necessary in order for the program to be executed. The term "low level language" is a general term which applies to languages such as assembly language which are close to machine language.

CROSS COMPILERS AND CROSS ASSEMBLERS

22.25 Cross Compilers and Cross Assemblers are translators which translate programs on one computer producing object programs which are used on a second computer. Usually the computer used for the translation is a minicomputer or mainframe and the object program is used on microcomputer.

UTILITIES AND SERVICE PROGRAMS

22.26 Utilities, also called service programs, are systems programs which provide a useful service to the user of the computer by providing facilities for performing common tasks.

22.27 Common types of utility programs are:-

  a. Peripheral transfer programs eg. file copying.
  b. Editors
  c. Sort utilities.
  d. System status utilities.

e. File maintenance utilities.
f. Debuggers.
g. Dump utilities.

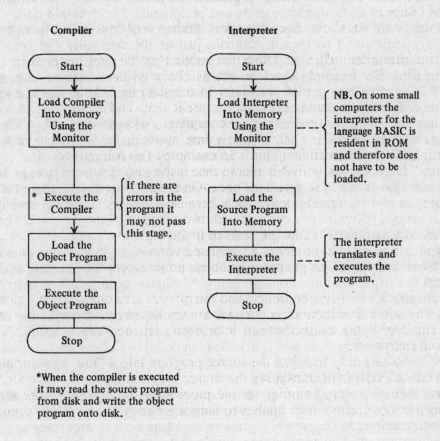

Compiler

- Start
- Load Compiler Into Memory Using the Monitor
- * Execute the Compiler
- Load the Object Program
- Execute the Object Program
- Stop

{ If there are errors in the program it may not pass this stage.

Interpreter

- Start
- Load Interpeter Into Memory Using the Monitor
- Load the Source Program Into Memory
- Execute the Interpreter
- Stop

NB. On some small computers the interpreter for the language BASIC is resident in ROM and therefore does not have to be loaded.

The interpreter translates and executes the program.

*When the compiler is executed it may read the source program from disk and write the object program onto disk.

Figure 22.1.

22.28 Peripheral transfer programs are used for such things as making a copy of a file from one storage device onto another, printing a copy of a file or reading a file from an input device onto disk.

22.29 Editors are used at a terminal and provide a series of commands which the user can use to look at a program or data and make any alterations. If for example a source program needed correction because it had failed to compile properly an editor may be used to make the necessary changes to the program.

22.30 Sort Utilities. These programs are used to rearrange file records into a specified sequence. For example an unsorted transaction file may be converted into a sorted transaction file by a utility before the file is processed.

22.31 The sorting done by a sort utility is complicated by the fact that most files are too large to be fitted into memory for sorting. This problem is overcome by tackling the sorting process in two stages. In the first stage small groups of records are read into memory, sorted into order, and then output onto backing storage in sequence. In the second stage these sequences of sorted records are merged together to form the complete sorted file.

22.32 System Status Utilities. These programs are able to provide information about the current state of use of files, memory, users and peripherals. For example it may be possible to use such a utility to see show many files are waiting in a "queue" to be output on the line printer.

22.33 File maintenance utilities. These programs may be used to perform tasks such as reorganising files. For example every so often it may be necessary to reorganise an index sequential file on disk because of changes which have occurred to the file as a result of a number of records being inserted or deleted.

22.34 Debuggers. These programs are used as an aid to removing "bugs" from programs. They provide ways of examining and changing data values and also produce printed "traces".

22.35 Dump Utilities. The term "dump" means "copy the contents of main storage onto an output device". Dumping sometimes refers to the copying of data from storage devices such as disks. This software is useful when errors have occurred during the running of a program. The program dump can be examined in order to find the hardware fault or program bug.

DATABASE MANAGEMENT SYSTEMS (DBMS)

22.36 Computer scientists have clear and precise definitions of what they consider to be true Databases. Some people selling programs which do a few clever file handling operations are far less reluctant to call their applications programs "database systems". You may remember this issue from chapter 2.

22.37 In the broadest sense, the term "database" may be used to describe the complete set of data being used for a particular application or by a particular organisation. A more precise definition will follow when this issue is discussed in detail in chapter 26.

USER APPLICATIONS PROGRAMS

22.38 User applications programs are programs written by the computer user in order to perform specific jobs for the user. Such programs are designed and tested using the stages in programming described in chapter 7. For many applications it is necessary to produce sets of programs which are used in conjunction with one another and which may also be used in conjunction with various service programs.

APPLICATIONS PACKAGES (Also see Chapters 2 – 5)

22.39 An applications package is a generalised set of programs which can be used to deal with a particular application eg. producing a payroll. In addition to the program the package also includes documentation instructing the user how to set up, use and maintain the package.

22.40 Packages tend to be available for application which are common to many users. Computer manufacturers or specialist commercial organisations called "Software Houses" produce applications packages which they can sell to a number of customers.

22.41 Advantages of packages.

    a. The user is saved the effort and expense of producing the programs. Packages are particularly attractive to small organisations with limited staff expertise who may purchase a computer plus packages and therefore need not use a programmer.

    b. The user will get well tried and tested programs provided reputable suppliers are used.

   c. Relatively quick implementations result from the use of packages.

22.42 Problems with packages.

   a. The available packages will not be tailor made to the user's requirements and may therefore cause problems of adjustment or prove unsuccessful.

   b. The organisation buying the package will have less control over the quality of work and service than it would have over work produced by its own employees.

   c. Some packages need regular updates eg. payrolls packages need to be changed with changes in government legislation. The user may be heavily reliant on the package supplier to provide the necessary updates.

22.43 When deciding whether or not to buy a package or produce its own programs an organisation has to consider the suitability of available packages, the advantages and disadvantages, and compare the costs and benefits.

TYPES OF PACKAGES

22.44 New types of application packages are appearing all the time. many are too specialised to be of general interest, so there is little to be gained in trying to produce a complete list. Nevertheless, there is some value in identifying the more common types of packages available.

22.51 The following types of packages are widely used:

   a. spreadsheets,

   b. data management packages,

   c. graphics packages,

   d. word processing packages,

   e. integrated packages,

   f. specialist packages for business,

   g. applications generators,

   h. expert systems.

22.52 Spreadsheets. These are general packages which can be used for a variety of applications. They were described in detail in chapter 2 so need no further discussion.

22.53 Data management packages. These are often called database packages but few meet the precise definition of a database given in 22.40. The **database package** described in chapter 2 is a typical example.

22.54 Graphics packages. These packages provide facilities which allow the user to do various kinds of computer graphics . Some allow the user to produce drawings or diagrams (see fig 22.2) and frequently use input devices such as mice. Some packages are aimed at particular applications areas. For example, a business graphics package might provide means of producing business charts, and graphs.

22.55 Word processing packages. As seen in chapter 4 a word processor is a special purpose computer used for the production of documents such as letters, reports and contracts. They are now widely used in business as replacements for typewriters. A word processing package can be used to enable a general purpose computer, such as a personal computer, to be used for word processing.

22.56 A typical package will provide a number of options for the user. These may be presented in the form of a menu. The options usually provided include:

   a. create a new document,

   b. edit an existing document.

    c. copy a document
    d. print one or more copies of a document,
    e. print envelopes or mailing labels.

**Figure 22.2. A Screen Display from a Product Called Macpaint
Used on the Apple Macintosh Computer.**

22.57 Integrated packages. These are really collections of packages which have been designed to be used together. For example, spreadsheet data might be easily fed into a database or displayed in diagrammatic form using a graphics package.

22.58 Specialist packages for business. There are many specialist packages available for use in business. These include packages for: company payrolls, accounts and financial planning.

22.59 Applications generators. These packages are rather different from other applications packages in that they enable the users to set up software for a specific application without writing the usual applications programs. They will be discussed further in chapter 25.

22.60 Expert systems. An Expert Systems is a specialised computer package which can perform the function of a human expert. Some of the first expert systems to gain widespread publicity were those used for medical diagnosis. A medical consultant assisted by his staff, took part in a lengthy exercise in which both the knowledge base required and the decision making procedures were transferred to the computer. Subsequently, the computer was able to ask the same questions and draw the same conclusions from the answers as the consultant so that a relatively junior doctor, aided by the computer, could be as expert as the consultant!

22.61 Expert systems normally have the following features (a medical Expert System will be used to provide examples):

a. An organised base of knowledge – often in the form of a database (eg. a set of illnesses and their symptoms).

b. A user interface able to support diagnostic or similar discussions with the user (eg. To enable the junior doctor to pose medical problems or to check an initial diagnosis).

c. A facility to hold details of the status of the current consultation. (eg. The junior doctor, in consulting the Expert System, may have to go through a lengthy question and answer session and the system has to keep track of the state of the questioning.)

d. An Inference Engine, ie. software which can use the knowledge base and current status of the consultation to either formulate further questions for the user or draw conclusions about what actions to recommend to the user. (eg. a mechanism for producing a sequence of questions for the doctor to answer so that the expert system can arrive at a diagnosis.)

e. A knowledge acquisition system, ie. a facility to update the knowledge base. It is via the knowledge acquisition system that the human expert is able to endow knowledge to the expert   system. (eg. a suitable system for entering the relevant facts about various diseases).

22.62 Although these basic components are bound to vary from one discipline to another (eg. the knowledge base for medical diagnosis is very different from the knowledge base for company law) the basic structure is the same. Therefore, an established method for developing an Expert System is to build the particular Expert System from a standard non application-specific basic system called a **shell.** It is possible to purchase a complete Expert System or merely a shell from which an Expert System can be created.

22.63 The user of the expert system sits at a terminal or work station and takes part in a question and answer session in which data about the problem is typed in. At various stages during the session, or maybe just at the end, the system makes an assessment of the problem and recommends actions to be taken.

SUMMARY

22.63
a. The main types of software were described:-
   i. System Software
   ii. Applications Software.

b. A further sub-division was also discussed:-
   i. Operating systems and control programs.
   ii. Translators.
   iii. Utilities and service programs
   iv. Data Base Management Systems (DBMS)
   v. User applications programs
   vi. Applications packages.

c. Monitors and Executives were briefly discussed.

d. Translators were introduced and classified as:-
   i. Assemblers.
   ii. Compilers

      iii. Interpreters.
e. The concepts of source programs and object programs were introduced.
f. The concepts of Low Level languages and High Level Languages were introduced.
g. Various types of utilities were discussed:-
      i. Peripheral transfer programs.
      ii. Editors.
      iii. Sort Utilities.
      iv. System Status Utilities.
      v. File maintenance utilities.
      vi. Debuggers.
      vii. Dump utilities.
h. Databases were introduced but will be discussed in more detail in chapter 26
i. The advantages and disadvantages of using applications packages were discussed.
j. Various types of packages were described.
      i. spreadsheets,
      ii. data management packages,
      iii. graphics packages,
      iv. word processing packages,
      v. integrated packages,
      vi. specialist package for business,
      vii. applications generators
      viii. expert systems.

POINTS TO NOTE

22.64 a. This chapter is intended to provide an overview of this part of the book. Many of the ideas and concepts introduced will be explained further in later chapters.

QUESTIONS A *(With answers)*

1. Distinguish between "System Software" and "Applications Software".

2. What are meant by the terms,
a. "resident in memory",   b. "transient".

3. List the functions of a monitor program.

4. Distinguish between assemblers, compilers and interpreters. Why are they useful?

5. a. List eight different types of computer package.
b. Select one package from your list and describe it in detail.

QUESTIONS B *(Without answers)*

1. Utility programs are commonly available on many computers. Describe three common utilities and justify why they should be supplied for the user.

2. A small business is considering purchasing a microcomputer. What factors must it take into account in the acquisition of software?

23 Further Programming

INTRODUCTION

23.1   This chapter discusses some further aspects of program design concerning program modularity, program structure and top down design by stepwise refinement. Modules, subprograms, procedures and functions are explained by example. The use of segmentation and overlay is explained too. The chapter also deals with the various points to be considered when preparing program documentation. That is followed by an explanation of what is meant by the term "software engineering". Finally, the chapter covers a number of techniques used for data manipulation and computer arithmetic. The main techniques considered are: sorting, searching, selecting and iteration.

FURTHER ASPECTS OF PROGRAM DESIGN

23.2   This section continues with the topic of program design which was first introduced in chapter 8. The reader may remember that in paragraph 8.9 the stages of programming were introduced, and that the early stages in programming including details of top-down design were given in the sections which followed. Later, in chapter 20, other stages in programming were illustrated, by examples of writing instructions in machine or assembly language, and by examples of program testing. Program documentation remains to be fully covered later in this chapter. First however, there are a few further points to consider regarding program features and structures.

DIVIDING PROGRAMS INTO SMALLER PARTS

23.3   The top-down design method shown in chapter 8 exploits the fact that large problems become more manageable if they can be divided into a number of smaller and simpler problems which can be tackled separately. Programs developed by this method may be expected to have a number of parts each dealing with a separate part of the problem. What is really required is that each of these parts have the properties of a "**module**". A module is *not* an arbitrary "slice" of program, it is part of a program which deals with a specific task, is largely self contained, and is carefully "coupled" to the rest of the program. An example now follows.

23.4   **Example.** Consider a program which is to take in a set of examination marks, store them in an array, sort them into order, and print out the sorted sequence of marks. For simplicity assume we are only interested in the marks and that candidates' names and other details are not included. The first stage of refinement may look like this:-

```
BEGIN
Input Marks
Sort marks
Print Marks
END
```

Figure 23.1.

23.5   There appear to be three modules in the examples in Figure 23.1:
   a.   Input Marks
   b.   Sort Marks
   c.   Print Marks
These three will only be fully modular if they are set up in the correct way.

23.6 To understand how the modules should be set up imagine that the procedure of figure 23.1 is to be carried out by **FOUR** people. One person will be responsible for doing the work of each module and a fourth person will control the other three. Thus there is one "control module". The following description should be read in conjunction with figure 23.

23.7 The person responsible for the "Control Module" will **call** on the person responsible for the "Input Marks" module to perform the input. *All* the "control module" wants back is a set of examination marks in an array, together with the number of marks in the array (ie. NUMB). It may be the case that the person responsible for "Input Marks" fails to get any marks. This can be allowed for by returning an empty array and the number of marks as zero.

23.8 The data items being *passed* between modules (ie. the array and the number of marks), are called **parameters.** In the example just given the parameter data only passed *out* of the module.

23.9 Once the "Control Module" has received the array and number of marks from the "Input Marks" module the "Sort Marks" module can be *called*. The *parameters* passed, will be the array and the number of marks. The "Sort Marks" module will pass back the array with the data sorted into sequence. Thus array data passes *in* and *out* of the "Sort Marks" module but the number of marks only needs to be passed *in,* since the control module can retain a copy of the number of marks.

23.10 Once the "Control Module" has received the sorted array back from the "Sort Marks" module it can *call* the "Print Marks" module. The same two parameters will be passed into the "Print Marks" module No data need be passed *out* from the "Print Marks" module when it has finished.

23.11 Passing Control. When the "Control" module *calls* on one of the other modules it also "passes Control" to the other module. The module which is actively being executed is the one which has control. When the "Print Marks" module has finished its task it passes control back to the "Control Module" although it does not pass back any data.

SUBPROGRAMS, ROUTINE, SUBROUTINES, PROCEDURES AND FUNCTIONS

23.12 The terms "subprogram", "routine" and "subroutine" are all used to mean a set of program instructions, forming part of a program, which carry out a specific task. In many languages subprograms are *named* and then referred to by name as was done in fig 23.2. The terms "routine" and "subroutine" seem to be more commonly used in connection with machine or assembly language programs. Aspects of subroutines particularly relevant to machine and assembly language will be covered later.

23.13 Subprograms may be divided into two types:-

    a. Procedures.

    b. Functions. (10.5)

    It must be pointed out that the two terms are often used indiscriminately as further synonyms for "sub program".

23.14 Procedures. The three modules: Input-Marks, Sort-Marks and Print-Marks in figure 23.2 are all example of subprograms, but they are also examples of procedures. Data is passed to and from procedures by means of parameters.

Figure 23.2. A Modular Program. - FOLLOWS ON THE NEXT PAGE

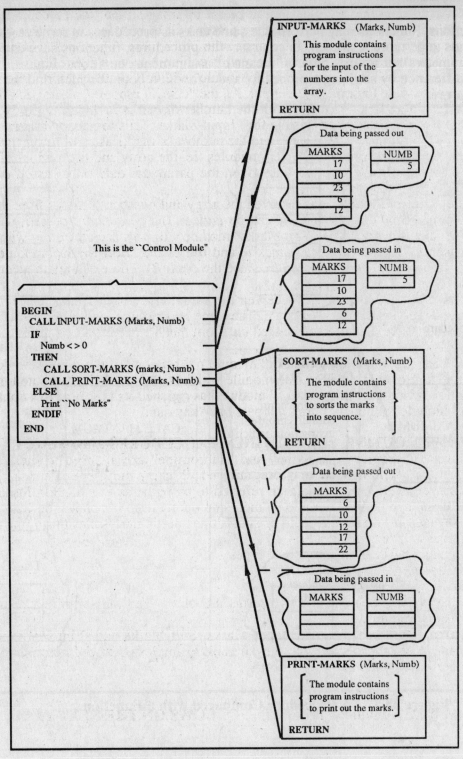

INPUT-MARKS (Marks, Numb)

This module contains program instructions for the input of the numbers into the array.

RETURN

Data being passed out

MARKS	NUMB
17	5
10	
23	
6	
12	

Data being passed in

MARKS	NUMB
17	5
10	
23	
6	
12	

This is the ``Control Module''

```
BEGIN
   CALL INPUT-MARKS (Marks, Numb)
   IF
      Numb < > 0
   THEN
      CALL SORT-MARKS (marks, Numb)
      CALL PRINT-MARKS (Marks, Numb)
   ELSE
      Print ``No Marks''
   ENDIF
END
```

SORT-MARKS (Marks, Numb)

The module contains program instructions to sorts the marks into sequence.

RETURN

Data being passed out

MARKS
6
10
12
17
22

Data being passed in

MARKS	NUMB

PRINT-MARKS (Marks, Numb)

The module contains program instructions to print out the marks.

RETURN

23.15 Functions. Functions may perform the same tasks as procedures in some cases, although their use tends to be more restricted. In contrast with procedures, functions have data passed to them by parameters but returns data by means of assignment operations. Figure 23.3 should clarify this difference by showing a procedure and a function both of which find the maximum value in an array.

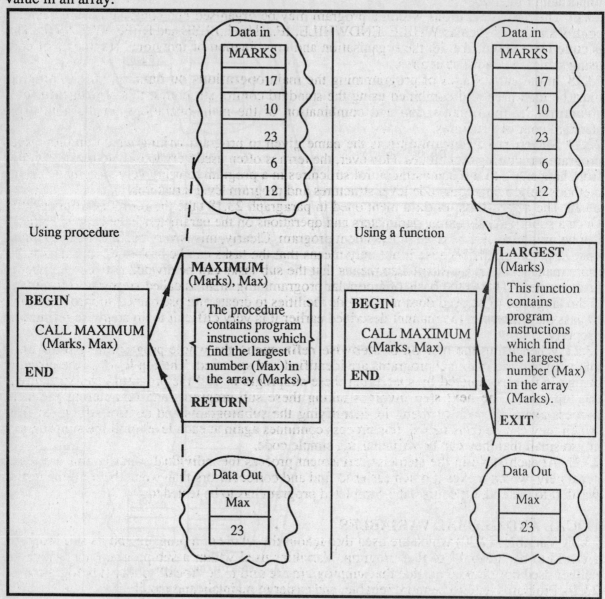

Figure 23.3.   A Procedure Compared with a Function.

PROGRAM STRUCTURE

23.16 There are two aspects to program structure.
    a. **Code level structure.**
    b. **Program level structure.**
      It is easier to examine them in that order but program level structure is the more important of the two.

23.17 The basic operations within a program may be organised and combined using standard control structures such as WHILE..ENDWHILE, IF..THEN..ELSE and REPEAT..UNTIL. This is **code level structure**, ie. the organisation and combination of individual fragments of code using standard control structures.

23.18 In the early stages of programming the main **operations on data** within the program must be identified and combined using the standard control structures. this is **program level structure,** ie. the organisation and combination of the main operations on the data using standard control structures.

23.19 Structured Programming is the name given to program writing which employs such program structuring techniques. However, the term is often used very loosely to mean anything from happening to use standard control structures in a program to using very systematic design methods employing both code level structures and program level structures.

23.20 The **operations on data** mentioned in paragraph 23.18 take the form of **subprograms**. Once a subprogram's name, parameters and operations on the parameters have been specified it can be written as if it were an independent program. Clearly, this is very useful when producing very large programs because it not only means that the tasks can be broken down into smaller more manageable sub-tasks it also means that the sub-tasks can be divided between number of programmers. This is the basis of a popular programming method called **stepwise refinement**. If the language to be used does not provide facilities to create and use named subprograms able to pass parameters in the manner described earlier it is very difficult to do stepwise refinement properly.

23.21 When using the method of **stepwise refinement** the whole programming problem is analysed and the main subprograms are identified and specified. The **top level** of the program design is then completed by specifying these subprograms and the program level structure at the top level. The next step involves taking these sub-programs and completing the same process again on each of them, ie. identifying the subprograms and control structures from which they can be constructed. this process continues again at each level until the subprograms are so small that they can be written using simple code.

23.22 At each stage in the stepwise refinement process the individual subprograms are tested separately, which makes it much easier to find and correct errors than would be if all the testing was left to the end. Of course, the completed program has to be tested too.

LOCAL AND GLOBAL VARIABLES

23.23 Variables (9.30) which are used throughout the whole of a program and its sub programs are said to be "**global**" to that program. Variables used within a sub program and which are neither used nor defined outside that subprogram are said to be "**local**" to that subprogram.

23.24 Programs tend to be more reliable, and easier to maintain and modify if
    a. the programming language in which the program is written allows both local and global variables. (Some languages eg. standard BASIC only allow global variables).

and b. global variables are only used in subprograms in which they have been introduced as parameters.

Having neither a nor b is comparable to having all the electrical goods in a house connected by the same piece of electric cable. When the fuse blows the fault will be hard to find and changing any one item may affect all the other items.

23.25 Scope. The scope of a variable is the range of program code over which the variable is defined eg. The scope of a "local variable" will probably be limited to a particular sub-program.

23.26 Nesting. Subprograms may sometimes contain further subprograms. This is an example of "nesting".

23.27 Recursion. In some languages subprograms are able to call themselves. This is an example of "recursion". Further details are beyond the scope of this book.

SEGMENTATION AND OVERLAYS

23.28 The use of subprograms carries with it the possible disadvantages of producing programs which are slightly slower to execute and which occupy more storage space. Although little can be done about loss in speed, the modularity of subroutines can be turned to advantage in dealing with problems of restricted storage space. This happens where **segmentation** is possible.

23.29 A segmented program is one which when it is executed allows some parts of the program (segments), to take turn in occupying the same area of main storage. Segments will occupy main storage when they are executed and be held on disk, say, the rest of the time. (See Figure 23.4).

23.30 Overlays. Writing programs, or parts of programs, onto the same area of main storage during execution is known as performing an overlay.

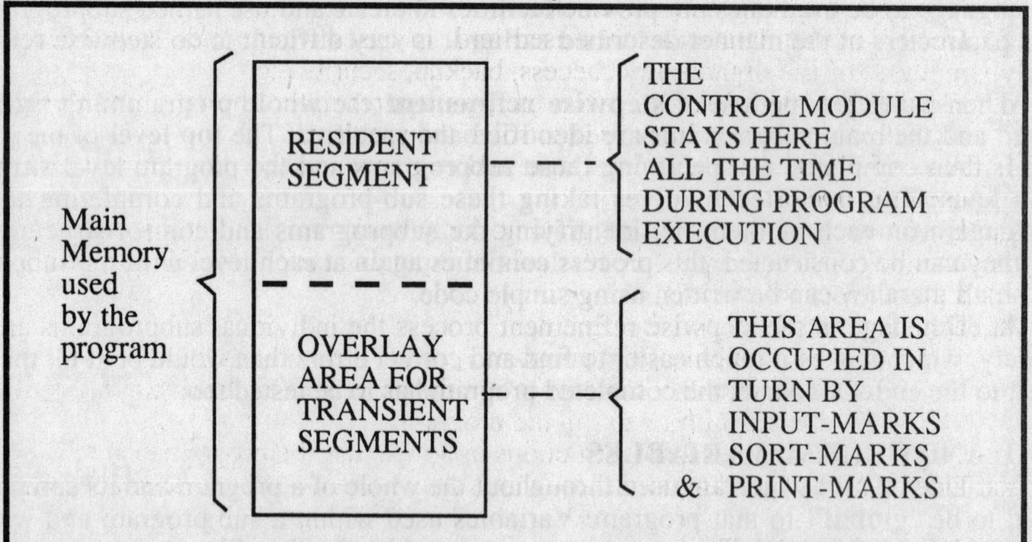

Figure 23.4 . The Program of Figure 23.2 Handled by Overlay.

PROGRAM READABILITY

23.31 Programs are easier to understand, check, correct, modify and maintain if they are written in a readable way. Producing readable programs is part of program documentation, indeed it is a form of self-documentation and is to be encouraged.

23.32 Aids to program readability are:-
a. The use of long meaningful data names.
b. Indenting of code.
c. Use of good control structures and modularity as part of the design.
d. Adding comments within the program. (Most programming languages provide some means of adding comments ie. non executable statements, within the program, eg. a REM statement in BASIC or putting comments between (* and *) as in Pascal).

PROGRAM DOCUMENTATION

23.33 There are many kinds of program documentation and some general points regarding documentation have already been made (8.16). The reader should now be ready to consider documentation in slightly more detail.

23.34 Use. Program documentation varies according to its intended use. Three main areas of use are:-
a. For the programmer's own present or future use, as an aid to all stages of programming.
b. For the present or future use of other programmers, including the programmer's supervisor, eg. for maintenance, modification or checking etc.
c. For the users of the program which may themselves vary in expertise.

23.35 Bearing these general points in mind the following items may be expected as part of the complete process of documentation.
a. Statement of the problem (**System Specification**).
b. Documents specifying the formats of inputs and outputs, including validation requirements, ranges of values etc.
c. Details of the data structures used and, in cases where files have been used, the methods of file organisation, access, backup, security etc.
d. Flowcharts, pseudocode, table etc., as appropriate, showing the design of the algorithms and procedures used to solve the problem.
f. A carefully devised set of test data and evidence to show that the test data has been used to good effect.
g. Evidence to show that the program not only works but that it has simple, effective, unambiguous and error free methods of input and output for the program's user. (ie. a good "user interface").
h. Detailed instructions to the user, eg.
    i. Limitations of the program.
    ii. Requirements in order to run the program. (eg. hardware needed).
    iii. Details of how to run the program.
    iv. Examples and instructions in how to use the program.
i. Details of the "configuration" on which the program has been developed and tested.

SOFTWARE ENGINEERING

23.36 Although almost anyone can write a simple program in a language like BASIC, just as any reasonably competent individual may be able to erect a shed in the garden, the production of larger programs to suitable standard of reliability maintainability etc. require professional methods. The shed builder is hardly a civil engineer! The adoption of systematic methods and engineering principles to the specification, design, implementation and testing of programs, including the management of such activities, has in recent years been given the name **Software Engineering.**

23.37 Although it may be argued that Software Engineering is no more than a new name for good programming principles and practices it is nevertheless a useful term to use when wishing to indicate that what is meant is professional software development to industrial standards rather than amateur code writing.

SORTING, SEARCHING AND SELECTING

23.38 Three processing activities which are often associated are sorting searching and selecting. The sorting of the elements of one dimensional array was covered by an example in 8.17, so an example will not be given here.

23.39 The advantages of sorting data into order are the faster and simpler processing methods which can be used on sorted data, as was illustrated by sequential file processing examples in earlier chapters. The same advantages are often present when processing elements in arrays.

23.40 Concordances. When key words are sorted into order the final alphabetic list is called a concordance eg. An index at the end of a book is based on a concordance.

SEARCHING AN UNSORTED ARRAY

23.41 Here is an example to illustrate a method. Assume that an array holds the candidate numbers of students who have taken a particular examination. The problem is to input a candidate number and then to search through the array to see if the candidate has taken the examination. The output will be either "FOUND" or "NOT FOUND".

23.42 Assume that

    a. the number of elements in the array is NUM.

    b. the data has already been input into the array

    c. the array is called CAND.

23.43 The method

    a. In outline the method is as follows:-

        The student number is input. Then, starting with the first element, while the student number has not been found and the end of the array has not been reached, the elements are examined in turn to see if any one of them matches the input student number.

    b. The method is given in more detail in figure 23.5 using pseudocode.

SEARCHING A SORTED ARRAY

23.44 Here the problem of the last section is repeated but now assume that the candidate numbers are in ascending sequence. The search can be conducted in the same manner **but** if at any stage the array elements being searched become **larger** than the student number the search must have failed. (See Figure 23.6).

23.45 The method of figure 23.5 can easily be modified to deal with a sorted array. (See figure 23.7)

23.46 The searches just described are called **linear searches.** There are superior methods for searching large sorted arrays but the details are beyond the scope of this book.

23.47 The method for searching an unsorted array may be adapted to search through a string to find a particular character or group of characters.

Key

```
Cand    : Array of candidate numbers
Num     : Number of elements in CAND
Posn    : Position subscript for CAND
Found   : 0 = False 1 = True

BEGIN
Input array Cand
Input Studno
Found := 0
Posn  := 1
WHILE
    (Found = 0) AND (Posn < = NUM)
DO
    IF
        Studno = Cand (Posn)
    THEN
        Found := 1
    ENDIF
    Posn := Posn + 1
ENDWHILE
IF
    Found = 1
THEN
    PRINT "FOUND"
ELSE
    PRINT "NOT FOUND"
ENDIF
END
```

NB.   A FOR .. ENDFOR loop should not be used for this search because the search may end at any state.

Figure 23.5. Searching an Array.

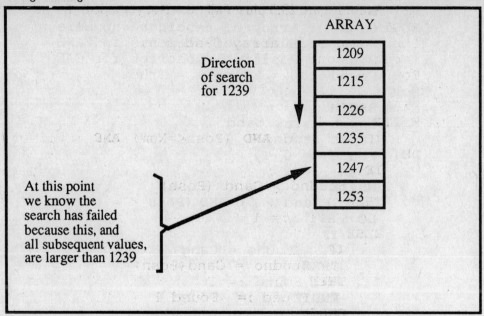

Figure 23.6. Search Example.

SELECTIONS

23.48 An example is used here to illustrate a method that may be adapted to a variety of problems. In this example a two dimensional array like the one shown in figure 23.8 is to be inspected and details of all candidates with marks greater than 40 are to be printed. The total of all such candidates is to be printed at the end.

23.49 Assuming that the array CAND has already been input and that the number of candidates is NUM, here is the method (figure 23.9).

Key As for Figure 23.5 plus Fail : 0 = Not yet failed, 1 = Search Failed.

```
BEGIN
Input and sort array Cand
Input Studno
Found := 0
Posn  := 1
Fail  := 0
WHILE
    (Found = 0) AND (Posn<=Num) AND (Fail=0)
DO
    IF
        Studno > Cand (Posn)
    THEN
        Fail  := 1
    ELSE
        IF
            Studno = Cand(Posn)
        THEN
            Found :=  Found 1
        ENDIF
        Posn  := Posn + 1
    ENDIF
ENDWHILE
IF
    Found = 1
THEN
    PRINT "FOUND"
ELSE
    PRINT  "NOT FOUND"
ENDIF
END
```

Figure 23.7. Searching a Sorted Array.

ARRAY CAND	
CANDIDATE NUMBER	CANDIDATE MARK
1209	65
1215	46
1226	52
1235	39
1247	25
1253	49

Figure 23.8. Specimen Array.

Key

Tot : Total of marks . 40
Posn : Array subscript position
Num : Number of elements in CAND

```
BEGIN
   Tot := 1
FOR Pons = 1 TO Num
   IF
       Cand(Posn,2) > 40
   THEN
       PRINT Cand(Posn,1) Cand(Posn,2)
       Tot := Tot + 1
   ENDIF
ENDFOR
PRINT Tot
END
```

Figure 23.9. A Selection Example.

ITERATION

23.50 The term **iteration** has a general and specific meaning. Iteration may merely mean simple repetition as is found in WHILE or REPEAT..UNTIL Loops, but *not* in FOR . . ENDFOR loops, which has an initialisation *followed* by a repetition.

23.51 An important specific meaning of **iteration** occurs in the case of **iterative processes** which are widely used in numerical computing.

23.52 In an iterative process for the solution of a problem, newer approximations are obtained from earlier ones by the repeated application of some formula or procedure. We say that the result has been obtained by **iteration.**

23.53 Exact Methods. Iterative methods are different from **exact methods.** If an exact **method** is used to solve an equation then the true (exact) value of the solution is obtained directly, usually by the use of a formula such as

$$x = (-b \pm \sqrt{(b^2 - 4ac)}) / 2a$$

23.54 Starting and Stopping. To start the iterative process, a first approximation is needed and sometimes more than one approximation is needed. These first approximations are called **starting values.** Starting values may be obtained by

    a. guessing
    b. prior knowledge
    c. inspection
    d. graph

An iterative process is stopped when the required accuracy is reached. Rounding of intermediate results does not affect the final accuracy.

23.55 Example. To find the cube root of 19 by an iterative method.

The root must be between 1 and 19 so we will use these as **starting values.** This method uses **two** approximations at each stage, one which is too LOW and one too HIGH. APPROX is the next approximation. The procedure is displayed in Figure 23.10.

```
Key
Low        : Low value
High       : High value
Approx     : Latest approximation

BEGIN
Low := 1
High := 19
Approx :=  (Low + High)/2
WHILE
     Approx^3 <> 19
DO
    IF
        Approx^3 > 19
    THEN
        High :=  Approx
    ELSE
        Low := Aprox
    ENDIF
    Approx := (Low + High)/2
ENDWHILE
PRINT Approx
END
```

Figure 23.10. A Simple Iterative Method.

23.56 The following table shows the first few steps using the pseudocode of figure 32.10.

LOW	HIGH	APPROX	APPROX^3	Comment
1	19	10	1000	APPROX too high, replaces HIGH
1	10	5.5	166.375	APPROX still too high, replaces HIGH
1	5.5	3.25	34.33 (2D)	APPROX still too high, replaces HIGH
1	3.25	2.125	9.596 (3D)	APPROX too low, replaces LOW
2.125	3.25	2.6875	19.41 (2D)	APPROX too high, replaces HIGH
		etc.		

The cube root of 19 is 2.66840 correct to six figures. "2D" means correct to 2 places of decimal.

23.57 Note. The process could appear to go on for ever since the cube root of 19 is irrational and therefore not expressible exactly as a decimal fraction. In practice an iterative process will reach a practical limit when the value is correct to the limits of accuracy of the computer on which it is run. This is comparable to the fact that an 8 digit pocket calculator cannot be used to give results to more than 8 figure accuracy.

USES
23.58 Iterative methods are used in the following situations.
    a. When no exact method is known
    b. When an exact method proves difficult in practice eg. by accumulating errors.
    c. When it is the most convenient method.
The repetitive nature of iteration makes the method very suitable for computer applications.

CONVERGENCE
23.59 Some general ideas are introduced here but further details are beyond the scope of this book.

If an **iterative process** gives approximations which get **nearer** and **nearer** to the **true value** then the iterative process **converges,** otherwise it **diverges.** One process is of a **higher order or convergence** than another if it converges more quickly.

The method of iteration in the example in paragraph 23.55 converged because APPROX gave better approximation to $^3\sqrt{19}$ at each stage, but it was a **low order method** since many steps were needed to get a good approximation.

SUMMARY
23.60 a. The use of modules was introduced.
    b. Subprograms, procedures and functions were explained by examples which also included the use of parameters.
    c. Local and global variables were defined.
    d. The concepts of scope, nesting and recursion were introduced.
    e. Segmentation and overlays were explained.
    f. Program structure and the method of stepwise refinement were explained.
    g. Program readability and aids to readability were discussed.
    h. Program documentation was given further consideration.
    i. Software Engineering was defined.
    j. The following techniques have been discussed:-
            i.   Sorting data items.
            ii. Selecting data items
            iii. Searching for data items
            iv. Iteration.
    k. The variations in selecting and searching resulting from data either being unsorted or being previously sorted were discussed.
    l. Iteration was defined and illustrated by an example.

POINTS TO NOTE
23.61 a. This chapter has placed stress on modules and subprograms. These must be seen as

additional features within a program design method which uses a top-down approach. Control structures such as IF.. THEN.. ELSE, WHILE etc. should be used within modules including those modules which control other modules.

b. Program documentation is part of programming, and should **not** be something which just happens after programs have been written.

c. The term "module" has a number of different meanings in programming. It is sometimes used as another name for any subprogram, but in this chapter a module was taken to be an independent subprogram which could, for example, be compiled separately and used in a number of different programs. Separately compiled program components are often called "modules" too. Such a "module" might contain several subprograms.

d. The methods introduced in this chapter should be of practical value to the reader in solving problems at this level. The reader must recognise that these are only basic methods and would not be used in solving large scale problems. The faster and more efficient alternative methods are too complicated to include in a book at this level however.

e. Being able to sort, search and select stored data at will, can be of great value in many computer applications and will become more important as manual methods of data storage are replaced by computerised systems.

QUESTIONS A *(With answers)*

1. *Define the terms,*

   a. *program module*

   b. *control module*

   c. *parameter.*

2. *Describe what is meant by "calling a module" and "passing control".*

3. *Explain the difference between a procedure and a function.*

4. *Imagine you were a programmer given the task of amending a program you had not seen before. What documentation would you expect?*

5. *What is Software Engineering?*

6. *What advantages may be obtained from sorting data into order? Give one example to support your answer.*

7. *How could the pseudocode in figure 23.7 be amended so that an array sorted into descending sequence could be searched?*

8. Perform a dry run on the pseudocode in figure 23.9 using the data in figure 23.8 as test data.

9. Produce pseudocode for a procedure which will input any positive number greater than or equal to one and then find and print out the positive square root of the number.

QUESTIONS B *(Without answers)*

1. Explain the difference between a "local" and a "global" variable.

   What is the scope of a global variable?

2. If you do practical programming as part of your course then find out about the following facilities in the language you use. Write brief notes on your findings.
   a. Facilities for subroutines/procedures and functions.
   b. Ways of allowing the use of local variables in procedures (if such facilities exist).
   c. Methods for performing overlays (if such facilities exist).

3. Sorting data into order takes time and effort, but does provide advantages in many situations. Give one example of a situation in which sorting would be essential and another example of a situation in which sorting would provide little or no benefit.

4. Produce pseudocode for a procedure which searches through a one dimensional array to find a value which may occur once, many times or not at all. The procedure should either print out the number of times the value was found or print "NOT FOUND". The values in the array are not already sorted into order.

5. Repeat question 4 assuming that the values have already been sorted into ascending order.

24 Low Level Languages

INTRODUCTION
24.1 This chapter defines what low level languages are and explains the advantages and disadvantages of using low level languages. It also explains the features of low level languages and gives examples of programming using these features. The use of Assemblers is also explained.

24.2 **Definition. Low level languages** are **machine oriented languages** in which each instruction corresponds to or resembles a machine instruction.

THE NEED FOR LOW LEVEL LANGUAGES
24.3 Low level languages were devised and developed in order to overcome the main problem associated with writing programs in machine language.

24.4 The problems associated with using machine code or language are summarised here:-
    a. All the machine's operation codes (function codes) have to be memorised.
    b. All memory addresses have to be assigned and a track kept of them (ie. we must give each variable an address and record our action).
    c. Instructions have to be written in the sequence in which they are to be executed. Thus insertions or deletions entail the **movement** of all succeeding instructions. (eg. to insert code between location 6 & 7).
    d. Subsequent revision of a completed program would be so impractical as to almost require a complete rewrite.
    e. The whole process is very time consuming and inefficient in terms of human effort.

24.5 Common Features of Low Level Languages.
    a. **MNEMONIC** codes are used in place of machine codes eg. using LDA 5 in place of 0000000000000101.
    b. **Symbolic addresses** are frequently used instead of actual machine addresses eg. using LDAN where N stands for the address which can be assigned a numerical value at a more convenient time.

24.6 The use of mnemonics helps to reduce the problems 4a and 4e. Symbolic addresses help to reduce the problems 4b, 4c. and 4d.

24.7 In 20.11 we saw the advantages of using MNEMONICS to describe machine language instructions. It seems logical to write the program in this SYMBOLIC form and to get the machine to do the translation to machine language and this is what is done with **low level languages.**

24.8 The (symbolic) low level language must be translated into machine language before use, because although easier for the programmer to work with it is not usable by the machine in symbolic/mnemonic form. This highlights the main disadvantage of low level languages compared with machine language.

 The translation is actually done by the computer by means of a special translating program called an assembler .

ASSEMBLY LANGUAGE
24.9 a. Each computer manufacturer normally devised a low level language which corresponds closely to the particular machine language used by the manufacturer. This language is called an ASSEMBLY LANGUAGE. The manufacturer provides a program called an ASSEMBLER or ASSEMBLER PROGRAM which translates the ASSEMBLY LANGUAGE into MACHINE CODE.

b. A program written in ASSEMBLY LANGUAGE is called the SOURCE PROGRAM. The translated program in MACHINE CODE is called the OBJECT PROGRAM.

(The features of ASSEMBLERS will be discussed later).

24.10 Pseudo Assembly Languages. Assembly languages differ, since the features of each assembly language depends on the particular computer on which it is used. This makes computer courses and examinations difficult to standardise. To answer this problem several low level assembly-like languages which are **machine independent** have been devised for educational purposes. They are **pseudo assembly languages** since they do not fulfil the usual task of an assembly language, but are useful educationally.

Examples are:

a. CESIL Computer Education in Schools Instruction Language
b. City and Guilds 319 Mnemonic coded.

A PSEUDO ASSEMBLY LANGUAGE

The assembly language instruction format used here is based on the instruction format used in the earlier examples in chapter 20. Here are the details.

Instruction Format

LABEL	:	FUNCTION CODE	OPERAND **OR** OPERAND ADDRESS
eg. A	:	LDA	5

(see 20.13)

Note.

a. The LABEL is **optional** and may be used either
   i. to give an instruction a symbolic address, or
   ii. to give a numerical value a symbolic address.
b. The **operand address** is used with the function codes LDA, STA, ADD, SUB, AND, ORA, JPU, JAZ, JAN, JAL and JAG (15.13) and can take these forms:
   i. a direct address or operand eg. LDA 5
   ii. a direct Index address eg. LDA, I.5
   The address will be 5 + contents of index register.
   iii. indirect, indicated by an @ eg. LDA 2 5 or LDA @ 1,5
   iv. Up to 3 letters used as a symbolic address eg. LDA NUM
c. The **operands** used with the function codes ACC and IOP are as defined in figure 20.5 and figure 20.6.
d. Operands (not operand addresses) may be positive or negative. The assembler will convert these operands into twos complement form.
e. The function codes SAI, NOT and HLT have no operands or operand addresses.

AN EXAMPLE OF USING ASSEMBLY LANGUAGE

24.11 This example deals with finding the total of a set of integer examination marks held in an array called "MARKS" In order to make the program simple to give a "dry run" to (20.26) an array with just 5 elements is considered. Assume that integers have already been read into the array.

24.12 Memory has been allocated as follows.

    a. The highest address used by the array is stored in location address 32_{10} (ie. the array occupies, locations 28_{10}, 29_{10}, 30_{10}, 31_{10} and 32_{10}).

NB.   It is common to *work down* from some highest address value when allocating memory for data.

    b. Location 33_{10} is to hold the number of elements in the array, ie. the number of marks, which in this case is 5.

    c. Location 34_{10} is to hold the total of the marks.

    d. The program is to occupy the memory locations immediately following the data. See figure 24.1

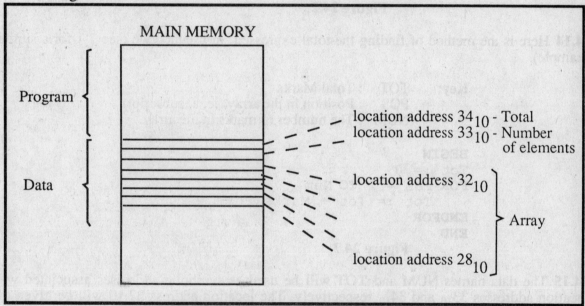

Figure 24.1. Allocation of Memory.

24.13 A specimen set of data is shown in figure 24.2

The ``Marks'' Array	
Subscript	Element Contents
1	10
2	7
3	6
4	8
5	12

The ``Marks'' Array as Stored in Main Storage		
Location Address	Contents	
	Binary	Decimal Equivalents
28	0 0 0 0 0 0 0 0 0 0 0 1 0 1 0	10
29	0 0 0 0 0 0 0 0 0 0 0 0 1 1 1	7
30	0 0 0 0 0 0 0 0 0 0 0 0 1 1 0	6
31	0 0 0 0 0 0 0 0 0 0 0 1 0 0 0	8
32	0 0 0 0 0 0 0 0 0 0 0 1 1 0 0	12

Figure 24.2.

24.14 Here is the method of finding the total expressed in pseudocode (see 7.1 for a similar example).

> **Key:**   TOT   : Total Marks
>   POS   : Position in the array (ie. a subscript)
>   NUM   : The number of marks in the array.

```
BEGIN
Tot := 0
FOR Pos = 1 TO Num
    Tot := Tot + Marks(Pos)
ENDFOR
END
```

Figure 24.3.

24.15 The data names NUM and TOT will be used as symbolic addresses associated with location addresses 33_{10} and 34_{10} respectively. The location address 32.10 will be given the symbolic address "MRK".

24.16 The assembly language program corresponding to the method of figure 24.3 is given in Figure 24.4. Examine figure 24.4 and carry out a dry run to make sure you fully understand the program. Remember that .BEGIN and .END are not assembly language instructions. They are **directives** (20.37) ie. instructions to the assembler requiring interpretation execution and not requiring translation as part of the program.

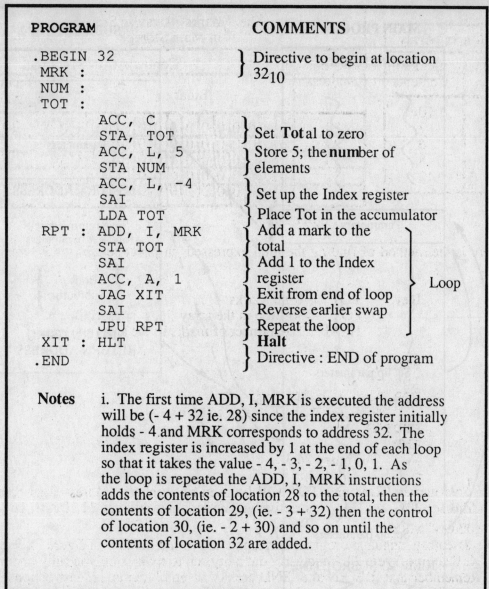

```
PROGRAM                        COMMENTS

.BEGIN 32              ⎫ Directive to begin at location
 MRK :                 ⎬ 32₁₀
 NUM :                 ⎭
 TOT :
       ACC, C          ⎫ Set Total to zero
       STA, TOT        ⎭
       ACC, L, 5       ⎫ Store 5; the number of
       STA NUM         ⎭ elements
       ACC, L, -4      ⎫ Set up the Index register
       SAI             ⎭
       LDA TOT         ⎱ Place Tot in the accumulator
 RPT : ADD, I, MRK     ⎫ Add a mark to the      �构
       STA TOT         ⎬ total                   ⎮
       SAI             ⎮ Add 1 to the Index      ⎮
       ACC, A, 1       ⎭ register          ⎬ Loop
       JAG XIT         ⎱ Exit from end of loop   ⎮
       SAI             ⎱ Reverse earlier swap    ⎮
       JPU RPT         ⎱ Repeat the loop        ⎭
 XIT : HLT             ⎱ Halt
.END                   ⎱ Directive : END of program
```

Notes   i. The first time ADD, I, MRK is executed the address will be (- 4 + 32 ie. 28) since the index register initially holds - 4 and MRK corresponds to address 32. The index register is increased by 1 at the end of each loop so that it takes the value - 4, - 3, - 2, - 1, 0, 1. As the loop is repeated the ADD, I, MRK instructions adds the contents of location 28 to the total, then the contents of location 29, (ie. - 3 + 32) then the control of location 30, (ie. - 2 + 30) and so on until the contents of location 32 are added.

Figure 24.4.

SUBROUTINES

24.17 Subroutines were introduced in (23.12). This section deals with features of subroutines particularly relevant to low level languages.

24.18 A subroutine is set of program instructions forming part of a program and used to perform a specific task. Used wisely the **same** subroutine may be used to do the same task, at different stages in the main program without the need for rewriting it each time. (See figure 24.5).

Figure 24.5. Handling Subroutines. - FOLLOWS ON THE NEXT PAGE

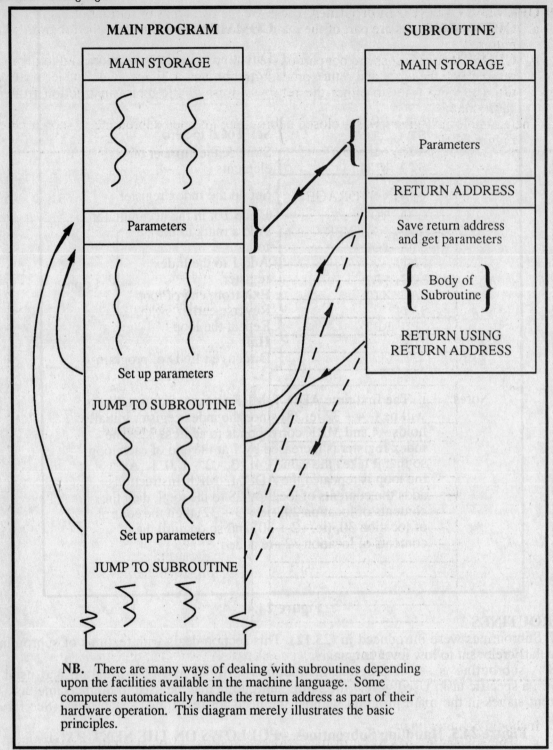

MAIN PROGRAM   **SUBROUTINE**

MAIN STORAGE   MAIN STORAGE

Parameters

RETURN ADDRESS

Save return address
and get parameters

Parameters

{ Body of
Subroutine }

Set up parameters

JUMP TO SUBROUTINE

RETURN USING
RETURN ADDRESS

Set up parameters

JUMP TO SUBROUTINE

NB. There are many ways of dealing with subroutines depending
upon the facilities available in the machine language. Some
computers automatically handle the return address as part of their
hardware operation. This diagram merely illustrates the basic
principles.

24.19 OPEN and CLOSED Subroutines. These are the two types of subroutine.

    a. **OPEN** subroutines are part of the main program and inserted into the program where required.

    b. **CLOSED** subroutines are not part of the main program. They are **linked** to the main program by the entry and return procedures outlined in figure 24.6. The term **Link** is often used to refer to either the return address or the return instruction from the subroutine.

The example just given was a closed subroutine; an open subroutine is shown here in Figure **24.6**

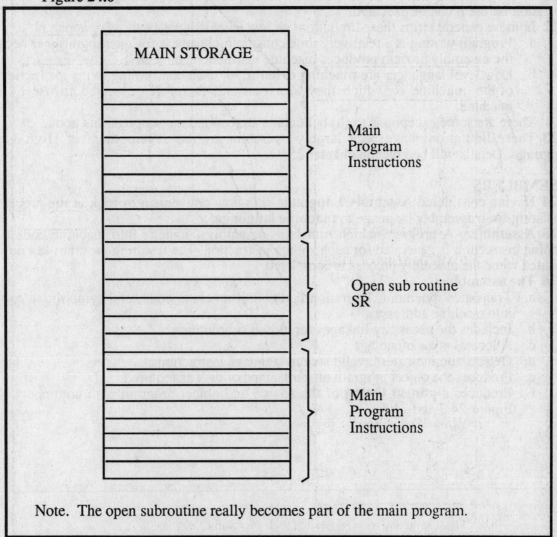

Note. The open subroutine really becomes part of the main program.

Figure 24.6. An Open Subroutine.

24.20 It should be noted that:

    a. The subroutine has to be in main storage in order to be entered. It must either be loaded along with the main program (if not already in main store) or the main program will be halted while the subroutine is loaded. In the latter case the loading is done automatically by software provided for the purpose. Most frequently the subroutines would be available on disk in such cases.

LIMITATIONS OF LOW LEVEL LANGUAGES

24.21 Despite the advantages of low level languages over machine language outlined in paragraph 3 to 8, low level languages have several significant limitations. Compared with machine language assembly language has one important disadvantage in that it requires translation before it can be executed.

24.22 In more general terms these limitations of low level languages are very apparent:-
   a. Program writing is a relatively time consuming business for the programmer because the assembly process produces machine instructions on a ONE for ONE basis.
   b. Low level languages are **machine orientated,** each conforming to the instruction set of the machine on which they are used and therefore restricted to use on that machine.

There are some exceptions to (b) but details are beyond the scope of this book.

24.23 These limitations have been largely overcome by the development of **High Level Language.** Details will be given in chapter 25.

ASSEMBLERS

24.24 Having considered **Assembly Language** it is now convenient to look at the process of translating from assembly language to **machine language.**

24.25 Assembler. A program which translates assembly language into machine code. One machine instruction is generated for such source instruction. The resulting program can only be executed when the assembly process is completed.

24.26 The assembler:-
   a. Translates mnemonic operation codes into machine code, and symbolic addresses into machine addresses.
   b. Includes the necessary linkages for closed subroutines.
   c. Allocates areas of storage.
   d. Detects and indicates invalid source language instructions.
   e. Produces the object program on cards, tape or disk as required.
   f. Produces a printed **listing** of the source and object program with comments. (See Figure 24.7 and 24.8).

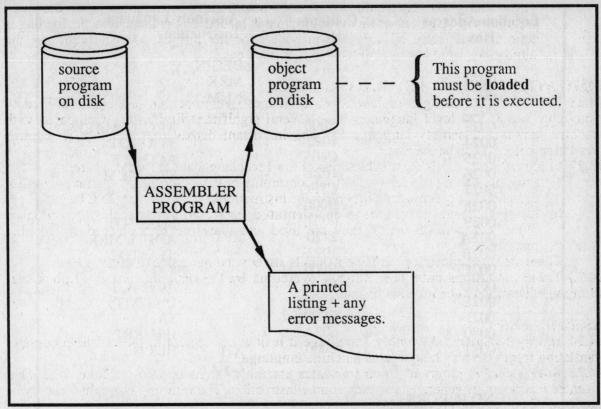

Figure 24.7. A general view of the Assembly Process.

24.27 A Directive is used to control the Assembly process, it is not assembler, but is obeyed by the Assembler when it is encountered eg. "END" indicates to the Assembler that no more source code follows. The function code of a directive eg. "END" is sometimes called a **pseudo-operation code** or **pseudo opcode.**   All pseudo opcodes in these examples can be recognised by an initial full stop.

24.28 The main stages forming the complete process are:-

a.   Input source program (in assembly language).

b.   Use the Assembler to produce an object program (in machine language). If errors are detected by the assembler the source program must be corrected and reassembled.

c.   Load object program into main memory.

d.   Execute the object program.

Location Address Hex	Contents Hex	Assembly Language Instructions	
		. BEGIN	
0020		MRK :	
0021		NUM :	
0022		TOT :	
0023	C000		ACC, C MARK
0024	1022		STA TOT
0025	C405		ACC L, 5
0026	1021		STA NUM
0027	C7FC		ACC, L, -4
0028	B000		SAI
0029	0022		LDA TOT
002A	2420	RPT :	ADD, I, MRK
002B	1022		STA TOT
002C	B000		SAI
002D	C801		ACC, A, 1
002E	A02F		JAG XIT
002F	B000		SAI
0030	602A		JPU RPT
0031	E000	XIT :	HLT
		. END	

NO ERRORS

Note. The programmer may convert the Hex codes into binary if required eg. to examine the details of a machine instruction.

Figure 24.8. An Assembly Listing.

SUMMARY

24.29 a. Low level languages were defined.

b. The advantages and disadvantages of low level languages were discussed.

c. The features of low level languages were explained. In particular the uses of **mnemonic instructions** and **symbolic** addresses were discussed.

d. Examples of the use of assembly languages were given by means of pseudo assembly language.

e. The use of **subroutines** was explained.

f. **Assemblers** were defined and their use was explained by example.

POINTS TO NOTE

24.30 a. This chapter merely serves as an introduction to low level languages and aspects concerned with programming in low level languages. This treatment of the subject should prove adequate for the reader's needs in examinations at this level, but the reader should be aware that low level languages vary greatly in their types, features and complexity because of the wide variety of machines on which they are used.

   b. Details of *how* assemblers perform the translation process are beyond the scope of this book and are not tested in examinations at this level.

QUESTIONS A *(With answers)*

1. Define the term "low level language". Why are they used.

2. Define the term "subroutine" and distinguish between open and closed subroutines. Describe the role of the return address and parameters.

NOTE

In the following problems, labels in the assembly language are used in the following ways:-

a. to give a symbolic address to an assembly instruction.

e.g XIT : HLT,

b. to give a symbolic address to a location used for data

   i. where the data value is not defined. eg. MRK:
   (Assume that when the program is loaded into main memory the location will contain whatever has been left there previously).

   ii. where the data value is defined in the assembly language program in which case the data value will be loaded into memory when the program is loaded into memory

   eg. BEGIN 30
       NUM: 7
       CHR: "A"
   Here the number 7_{10} will be loaded into location 30_{10} and the code for ASCII "A"

will be   loaded into location 31_{10}..

Use the fictitious assembly language discussed in this chapter.

3. Consider the following assembly language program.

```
BEGIN  20
NI     : 8
N2     : 3
N3     : 6
SUM : 0
       LDA NI
       ADD N2
       ADD N3
       STA SUM
       HLT
END
```

a.   In what location address is the first instruction (ie. LDA NI) stored?
b.   Write down the successive values of the accumulator contents (in decimal) as the program is executed, starting with the instruction LDA NI.
c. What does the program do?

4.   Consider the following assembly language program
```
BEGIN   10
NI      : 3
N2      : 8
SUM
DIF     :
        LDA NI
        ADD N2
        STA SUM
        LDA NI
        SUB N2
        STA DIF
        HLT
END
```

a.   What location addresses correspond to the symbolic addresses of N1, N2, SUM and DIF?
b.   Perform a dry run which shows the contents of N1, N2, SUM, DIF, the accumulator and the sequence control register when the program is executed starting with the instruction LDA N1. Show values in decimal but show the contents of the accumulator in binary and decimal.   Remember that the accumulator is 16 bits long and that negative numbers are stored in twos complement form.
c. What does the program do?

5.   What does the following program do?
(**Hint** perform a dry run and carefully examine the **binary** contents of the accumulator at each stage).
```
.BEGIN   30
NI : 3
N2 : 8
X  :
        LDA N2
        NOT
        ACC A, 1
        ADD NI
        STA X
        HLT
.END
```

6.   The following program should output the word "HELLO" to device number 3. Fill in the missing instructions.

```
.BEGIN    10
E : "E"
H : "H"
L : "L"
O : "0"
        LDA H
        IOP, 0, 3
        LDA E
        IOP, 0, 3
```

7. Devise test data values for N1 and N2 in the following program and perform a dry run to determine what the program does. (Assume N1 and N2 are both positive numbers).

```
.BEGIN 25
N1 :
N2 :
        LDA N2
        SUB N2
        JAL FST
        LDA N2
        JPU PRI
FST : LDA N1
PRI :   IOP, 0, 5
        HLT
.END
```

8. What does the following program do?

```
.BEGIN 10
        ACC, C
        ACC, S, 25
        SAI
        LDA 65
        SAI
LOP :   JAG XIT
        SAI
        IOP, 0, 5
        ACC, A, 1
        SAI
        ACC, A, 1
        JPU LOP
XIT :   HLT
.END
```

9. There is a "bug" in the following program which should output the word "DINOSAUR" to device 3. Find the bug by performing a dry run and suggest two alternative ways of correcting it.

```
        .BEGIN 20
    D   :   "D"
    I   :   "I"
    N   :   "N"
    O   :   "O"
    S   :   "S"
    A   :   "A"
    U   :   "U"
    R   :   "R"
            ACC, C
            ACC, S, 7
            SAI
    LOP:    JAZ
            SAI
            LDA, I, R
            IOP, 0, 3
            SAI
            ACC, A, I
            JPU LOP
    XIT :   HLT
    .END
```

10. *Write an assembly language program which reads in two characters from device number 2 and outputs them in alphabetic order to device number 3.*

11. *Write an assembly language program which outputs the character sequence 9, 8, 7, 6, 5, 4, 3, 2, 1, 0 to device 7*

QUESTIONS B *(Without answers)*

1. *By performing a dry run and considering the right hand four bits of the accumulator, or by any other method, find logic expressions for A, B, C and D in terms of X and Y when the following program has been executed.*

```
    .BEGIN
    D   :   12
    Y   :   10
    A   :
    B   :
    C   :
    D   :
            LDA X
            ORA Y
            NOT
            STA A
            LDA Y
            NOT
            AND X
```

```
                STA B
                LDA X
                NOT
                AND Y
                ORA B
                STA C
                LDA X
                AND Y
                NOT
                STA D
                HLT
        .END
```

2. What does the following program do?
    Hint. Use test data "O", "1", "2"

```
    . BEGIN
        A   :   "A"
        E   :   "E"
        F   :   "F"
        L   :   "L"
        O   :   "O"
        R   :   "R"
        S   :   "S"
        T   :   "T"
        U   :   "U"
        ZER :   48
                IOP, I, I
                SUB ZER
                JAZ FAL
                ACC, S, l
                JAZ TRU
                LDA E
                IOP, 0, 2
                LDA R
                IOP, 0, 2
                IOP, 0, 2
                LDA 0
                IOP, 0, 2
                LDA R
                IOP, 0, 2
                JPU XIT
    FAL     :   LDA F
                IOP, 0, 2
                LDA A
                IOP, 0, 2
                LDA L
                IOP, 0, 2
```

```
            LDA S
            IOP , 0, 2
            lDA E
            IOP, 0, 2
            JPU XIT

    TRU   : LDA T
            IOP , 0, 2
            LDA R
            IOP, 0, 2
            LDA U
            IOP, 0, 2
            LDA E
            IOP , 0, 2
    XIT :   HLT
   .END
```

3. What is a directive?

4. Explain the terms:-
   a. mnemonic code,
   b. symbolic address

5. Write a program which inputs two characters from device 2 and then outputs the one higher in the alphabet to device 4 and the one lower in the alphabet to device 3. If both characters are the same output the character "=" to both device.

6. Write a program which inputs a line of text (ie. a stream of ASCII characters) terminated by a ".". and stores the data in successive locations in memory. The program should count the number of space characters input (ie. ASCII character 32 10) and store the number in a location with symbolic address "NUM".

7. Produce an assembly listing like the one in figure 22.8 for question 7 of questions A in this chapter.

25 High Level Languages

INTRODUCTION

25.1 This chapter explains the need for high level languages and then discusses the features of high level languages. Various types of high level languages are described in outline in order to give the reader an overview of the variations which exist between high level languages. Finally the chapter discusses the use of compilers and interpreters for high level language translation.

THE NEED FOR HIGH LEVEL LANGUAGES

25.2 The development of high level languages was intended to overcome the main limitations of low level languages (mentioned earlier in 24.21) which are:-

   a. Program writing is a relatively time consuming business for the programmer because the assembly process produces machine instruction on a ONE for ONE basis.

   b. Low level languages are **machine orientated,** each conforming to the instruction set of the machine on which they are used and therefore restricted to use on that machine.

25.3 In addition to the need to overcome the limitations just mentioned, there is a need to have programs which are easy to maintain and modify, and which are easy to transfer from one computer to another.

25.4 High level languages are intended to be machine independent and are problem orientated languages (POLS) ie. they reflect the type of problem solved rather than the features of the machine. Source programs are written in statements akin to English, a great advance over mnemonics.

FEATURES OF HIGH LEVEL LANGUAGES

25.5 a. They have an extensive vocabulary of words, symbols, and sentences.

   b. Programs are written in the language and whole statements are translated into **many** (sometimes hundreds) of machine instructions. This translation is often done by a special program called a compiler which is described in the next chapter.

   c. Libraries of subroutines can be incorporated.

   d. As they are **problem oriented** the programmer is able to work at least to some extent independently of the machine.

   e. A set of rules must be obeyed when writing the source program (akin to rules of grammar in writing English). These rules which govern the structure of statements in the language constitute what is called the **syntax** of the language.

   f. Instructions in high level languages are usually called **statements.**

TYPES OF HIGH LEVEL LANGUAGES

25.6 Six main types are:-

   a. Commercial languages

   b. Scientific languages

   c. Special purpose languages

   d. Command languages for operating systems.

   e. Multipurpose languages.

   f. Applications Generators (Fourth Generation Languages)

25.7 **Commercial languages.** The most well known is COBOL (Common Business Oriented Language). It is the most widely used Commercial and Business language and the fact that something like 80% of all computer usage is of this type reflects its importance.

25.8 It was intended that any program written in COBOL would be compiled and within reason, run on any computer. This has not worked out in practice, however, and each manufacturer has his own version of the language. This applies most to most high level languages, although there are agreed standards which help to reduce the number of variations.

25.9 The main features of COBOL and other Business languages are:-
   a. Extensive file handling facilities such as the naming, movement and processing of files, records, fields, etc.
   b. close resemblance to English in terms of incorporating common English terms in sentence-like forms and avoiding mathematical notation.

25.10 Scientific Languages. The most well known
   a. ALGOL (**Alg**orithmic **O**riented **L**anguage). Used for scientific and engineering purposes and has particularly powerful mathematical facilities. (ALGOL 68 is a more recent and comprehensive version).
   b. FORTRAN (**For**mula **Tran**slation) mainly used for engineering applications but also for scientific use.

25.11 Features of these languages.
   a. Extensive arithmetic computational ability.
   b. Large library of inbuilt mathematical function.
   c. Ability to handle mathematical expressions and procedures.
   d. Array handling facilities.

25.12 Special Purpose Languages. These are languages intended to be "tailor made" for a particular type of problem, eg. Machine Control, Wages, Simulation, Control of Experiments. Examples are:
   a. **CSL** which is a Simulation Language.
   b. **Coral-66 IRTB** (Industrial Real-time Basic) and **RTL/2** which are used for real-time applications such as Process Control, ie. the direct control of physical processes, eg. Chemical plants and Power Stations.
   c. **Ada** a relatively new language developed specifically for use in the development of real-time systems by the United States Military.
   d. **Modula and Modula-2** This language is rather like an extended from of **Pascal** (see later) and is primarily especially suited to computer systems development work.
   e. **SQL** (Structured Query Language), **QUEL** (QUEry Language) and **QBE** (Query By Example) are examples of database query languages.

25.13 Command languages for operating systems. These are languages used to control the operation of the computer. The required facilities will be apparent after you have read chapter 26.

MULTIPURPOSE LANGUAGES

25.14 PL/1 was introduced by IBM as a language intended for use for business **and** scientific applications. It has been a very successful language except for the fact that its comprehensive multipurpose facilities have made it too large for use on small machines such as microcomputers and some other manufacturers have been reluctant to adopt it.

25.15 BASIC (**B**eginners **A**llpurpose **S**ymbolic **I**nstruction **C**ode). BASIC was created in 1964 by J G Kemmeny and T E Kurtz at Dartmouth College USA. The language was originally designed as a simplified version of FORTRAN for use in teaching programming. From those simple beginnings the language has grown to become a very popular multi-purpose language available on a wide variety of machines but particularly microcomputers and minicomputers. Today more commercial programs are being written in BASIC than are being written in COBOL, although BASIC is still behind COBOL in terms of the volume of commercial code already in existence.

25.16 Early versions of BASIC, and sadly many versions in use on small computers today, deserve strong criticism for having features which encourage bad programming methods. However, some newer versions such as the product "True-BASIC" devised by T.E. Kurtz and based upon the latest ANSI standard are very significantly better.

25.17 Other languages which are regarded as multi-purpose languages include **Pascal,** and **Modula** which are both languages designed by Miklaus Wirth and have features which support structured programming methods more readily than many of the older languages such as COBOL or FORTRAN. Pascal and Modula are effectively their own pseudocode. Pascal started off as a language to be used for teaching people how to program, as did BASIC, but is now widely used for general purpose programming, particularly on small computers.

25.18 One language which has gained enormously in popularity in recent years is the language called "**C**". Originally C was used as a systems programming language on the UNIX operating system. Its popularity has much to do with its availability with UNIX , its simplicity and the fact that it has proved easy to use to provide portable software.

25.19 The success of C shows how difficult it is to generalise about the suitability of languages for particular purposes. C is now being very successfully used for all kind of applications for which it was never originally intended. A new language based on C called C^{++} is also proving very popular for what is called **Object Oriented Programming.**

APPLICATIONS GENERATOR

25.20 Applications generators have been in existence for many years but in their more modern forms they are often called **Fourth Generation Languages (4GLs)** because their supporters claim, not without cause, that they offer more cost effective alternatives to the high level languages such as COBOL associated with the era of 3rd Generation Computes. They will be discussed in more detail in chapter 26.

OTHER FORMS OF HIGH LEVEL LANGUAGE

25.21 The languages described so far in this chapter may be described as **procedural languages** because they describe **how** the computational procedures are to be carried out. There are radically different approaches to programming, however, which make use of languages which are non-procedural in that they assert **what** the required result is rather than how it is done. The details of *how* are actually handled as part of the language translation process. Two basic approaches to this assertional style of programming are:

    a. **Logic Programming** for which one popular language is **Prolog.**

    b. **Functional Programming** for which there are many languages available today including **LISP, ML** and **Hope.**

FACTORS AFFECTING CHOICE OF LANGUAGE

25.22 The reader might expect that the main factor affecting the choice of programming language when solving a programming problem would be the type of language eg. COBOL for business application, ALGOL for mathematical applications etc. This is by no means always the case. Other factors often influence the choice.

25.23 Factors:
  a. Purpose of the language eg. Business, Scientific etc.
  b. Features of the languages eg. Control Structures, Data Structures, Procedures and Functions.
  c. Availability, ie. A compiler or interpreter must be available before the language can be used. This is also a factor in portability.
  d. User experience. eg. The programmer will prefer to use the languages he or she already knows.
  e. Ease of learning and use.
  f. Performance and efficiency eg. Execution speeds and memory requirements.
  g. Error checking and diagnostic facilities available eg. debuggers.
  h. Level of support eg. documentation available.

25.24 It is considered inappropriate to discuss these factors in detail in a book at this level, but the reader should at least now be aware that the choice of programming language is not a simple matter. One factor which does demand some further discussion is the features available in various languages.

LANGUAGE FEATURES

25.25 Common features upon which comparisons between languages may be made are:
  a. **Control Structures.** Pascal, C and PL/1 are languages rich in control structures eg. Pascal has WHILE, REPEAT.. UNTIL and FOR loops. IF..THEN..ELSE and CASE statements and allows the nesting of control structures. BASIC has a very limited variety of control structures.
  b. **Data Structures and Files.** Pascal, C and PL/1 provide a variety of data types and structures. Pascal allows more complex types of structures to be built from simpler one. COBOL has a variety of basic data types, provides a wide variety of file types and also has facilities for dealing with databases.
  c. **Computations.** FORTRAN, ALGOL, Pascal, C and BASIC Provide facilities for mathematical expressions and functions. Computations in COBOL may be expressed in mathematical form but are more usually expressed in an English like form eg. "ADD COST TO TOTAL COST" instead of "TOTAL-COST = TOTAL-COST + COST".
  d. **Procedures and Subprograms.** Pascal, C, FORTRAN and ALGOL have facilities for handling procedures and subprograms. Comparable features in BASIC are almost **non existent.** COBOL has facilities which gives a flexible combination of procedure calls and control structures.

25.26 There are many other features which could be discussed eg. facilities to deal with controlling the format of data being input or output but the reader should by now have some feel for the ways in which features may be compared.

LANGUAGE STANDARDS

25.27 Since High level languages are problem oriented rather than machine oriented a possible advantage of high level language is the possibility to transfer programs from one computer to another.

25.28 Unfortunately, there are a number of obstacles to portability. Perhaps the most serious obstacles are those resulting from variations which occur between different versions of each language. Each different version of the language (ie. each dialect) is usually the deliberate creation of a computer manufacturer who will try to attract new customers with a "better" product and who will then keep existing customers because their programs will no longer be portable to those of other manufacturers.

25.29 This problem has been partly overcome by the standardisation of many programming languages.

25.30 Standardisation is organised on an international basis. The international body is **ISO** (International Standards Organisation). Each country has its own standards organisation represented on ISO committees. In Britain the standards organisation is the **BSI** and in the USA the standards organisation is **ANSI** (American National Standards Institution) ANSI has produced many programming language standards which have become international standards and hence British standards. The BSI has produced some language standards too. It has already produced the standard for **Pascal** and is currently producing standards for **Modula-2** and **Prolog.**

25.31 Every few years new versions of standards appear. For example, FORTRAN 66 and FORTRAN 77 were standards produced in 1966 and 1977 respectively. COBOL 74 and BASIC 86 are other examples.

COMPILERS

25.32 Having considered high level languages it is now convenient to look at the process of translating from a high level language to machine language.

25.33 The compiler:-

- a. Translates the source program statements into machine code.
- b. Includes linkage for closed subroutines.
- c. Allocates areas of main storage.
- d. Generates the object program on cards, tape or disk as required.
- e. Produces a printed listing of the source and object programs when required.
- f. Tabulates a list of errors found during compilation eg. the use of "words" or statements not included in the language vocabulary; or violating the rules of syntax. (see Figure 25.1).

25.34 Although in outline a compiler appears to do much the same job as an assembler in fact it does far more, particularly in the translation of source statements and the linkage of subroutines.

25.35 Interpreters. High level languages may also be translated by interpreters (see 24.17). Compilers and Interpreters were compared in chapter 22 but some further points are given in the following paragraphs.

25.36 Program execution speeds are much slower when interpreters are used eg. *10 times slower* than the equivalent compiled object program.

25.37 Using interpreters simplifies the process of loading, running, changing and executing programs.

25.38 The use of an interpreter for a given language should not be regarded as a feature of the language itself. For example the language BASIC is usually translated by an interpreter but is sometimes translated using a compiler.

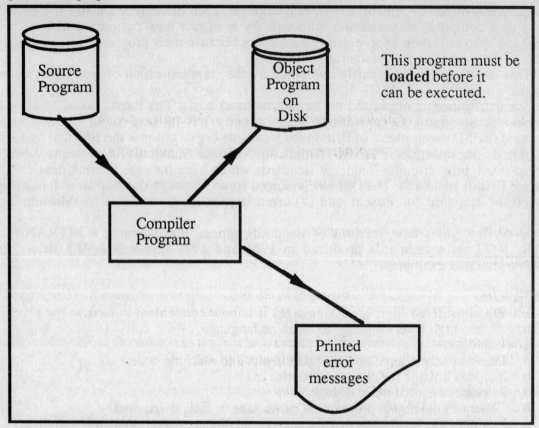

Figure 25.1. A Simplified View of the Compilation Process.

SUMMARY

25.39 a. The need for high level languages was explained.
  b. Features of high level languages were described.
  c. The various types of high level languages were discussed:-
      i. Commercial languages eg. COBOL.
      ii. Scientific languages eg. ALGOL, FORTRAN.
      iii. Special purpose languages eg. CORAL-66.
      iv. Command languages for operating systems. (details later).
      v. Multipurpose languages eg. C, PL/I, and Pascal
      vi. Applications Generators (4GLs).
  d. Factors affecting the choice of language were discussed.
  e. Language Standards were explained.
  f. Compilers were defined, explained and compared with interpreters.

POINT TO NOTE

25.40 a. A full understanding of high level languages can only be achieved by gaining practical experience in suitable high level languages. The reader should therefore try and relate the content of this chapter to practical programming in a high level language taken as part of his or her course.

QUESTIONS A *(With answers)*

1. *Distinguish between high level and low level languages. What limitations of low level languages were intended to be overcome by high level languages?*

2. *List the main types of high level languages and give examples of each.*

   In what category does the programming language which you use fall?

3. *List the factors involved in choosing a suitable programming language for a particular project.*

4. *Describe the functions of a compiler.*

QUESTIONS B *(Without answers)*

1. *What features of high level languages make them "problem orientated". Use examples to illustrate your answer.*

2. *Read paragraph 18 on language features and make a check list of the facilities mentioned there which are in the programming language for use.*

3. *What would you consider to be important language features for*
   a. *Scientific applications.*
   b. *Commercial applications.*

4. *Compare the relative advantages of using compilers or interpreters for high level language translation.*

26 Databases and 4GLs

INTRODUCTION
26.1 This chapter explains what a database is and then goes on to discuss various aspects of databases. The chapter continues an important theme introduced in chapter 3, that of information storage and retrieval. Later in the chapter there is an introduction to **Fourth Generation Languages** (4GLs) which are usually used in conjunction with databases and which have gained widespread popularity in recent years.

DATABASES.
26.2 Database Definition. A database is a single organised collection of structured data, stored with a minimum of duplication of data items so as to provide a consistent and controlled pool of data. This data is common to all users of the system but is independent of programs which use the data.

26.3 The independence of the database and programs using it means that one can be changed without changing the other.

26.4 The users of a database may find it convenient to imagine that they are just using their own data In reality the database is pooled.

26.5 Databases are normally set up in order to meet the information needs of major parts of an organisation.

26.6 It is not possible to construct a database in one single operation, it is usually built up section by section. During this process, it is possible to:-
    a. add new "files" of data.
    b. to add new fields to records already present in the base.
    c. to create relationships between the items of data.

26.7 A database requires to be stored on magnetic disk. For security purposes a copy of the database may be held on magnetic tape or disk.

26.8 Databases may be classified according to the approaches taken to database organisation. The classes are:
    a. Relational.
    b. Network.
    c. Hierarchical.
    d. File inversions.
    The last two are more basic, have a number of practical limitations and do not merit further discussion here.

26.9 Relational databases use types of tables called **relations**. The terminology is initially confusing because of the use of the name "relation" for a table and because relations are not the same as relationships. However, relational databases were developed from mathematically sound ideas, have an elegant simplicity and have become the main type in use today while still gaining in popularity.

26.10 Network databases have been around in several forms for a number of years. Much of the network approach was developed by the work of CODASYL. Network databases are based upon links that are used to express relationships between different items of data.

26.11 When new sets of data are added, it is often found that some of the required data is already stored for other purposes.

26.12 The database is maintained by a "single input". This means that just as there is little duplication of data, there is also no duplication of inputs. One transaction will cause all the necessary changes to be made to the data.

26.13 As the base is expanded, or as user requirements change, the relations in the database can be changed and new relationships can be established.

26.14 The user is unaware of the structure of the database. The Database Management System (details later) provides the user with the services needed and handles the technicalities of maintaining and using the data.

COMMUNICATING WITH THE DATABASE.

26.15 Some databases have their own computer languages associated with them which allow the user to access and retrieve data at a terminal. Other databases are only accessed via languages such as COBOL, to which extra facilities have been added for this purpose.

26.16 Data descriptions must be standardised. For this reason, a **Data Description Language (DDL)** is provided which *must* be used to specify the data in the base. Similarly, a **Data Manipulation Language (DML)** is provided which must be used to access the data. The function of these two languages may be compared to the Data and Procedure Divisions of a COBOL program, although their scope is wider and the degree of standardisation much higher. As indicated by the previous paragraph DDLs and DMLs may be either free standing or embedded in another language. The combination of the DDL and DML is often called a **Data Sub-Language (DSL)** or even a just **Query Language**. This topic will be returned to later in the chapter.

THE DATABASE MANAGEMENT SYSTEMS (DBMS).

26.17 The Database Management System is an item of *complex system software* which constructs and maintains the database in a controlled way. It also provides the interface between the user and the data in the base.

The DBMS allocates storage to data. It maintains indices so that any required data can be retrieved, and so that separate items of data in the base can be cross referenced. As mentioned above, the structure of a database is dynamic and can be changed as needed.

26.18 The DBMS maintains the data in the base by:
    a. adding new records,
    b. deleting "dead" records.
    c. amending records.

In addition to these functions (which are performed by any file maintenance program) it can expand the base by adding new sets of records or new data to existing records.

26.19 The DBMS provides an interface with user programs. These may be written in a number of different programming languages. However, the programmer need not be familiar with the physical structure of the database because the data his program requires is retrieved by the DBMS.

26.20 The DBMS provides facilities for different types of file processing. It can:-
    a. process a complete file (serially or sequentially)
    b. process required records (selective sequential or random).
    c. retrieve individual records.

It can also, as has been explained above, retrieve related records or related data within records.

26.21 The DBMS also has the function of providing security for the data in the base. The main aspects of this are:-

a. protecting data against unauthorised access.

b. safeguarding data against corruption

c. providing recovery and restart facilities after a hardware or software failure.

The DBMS keeps statistics of the use made of the data in the base. This allows redundant data to be removed. It also allows data which is frequently used to be kept in a readily accessible form so that time is saved.

26.22 Data Dictionary. The DBMS makes use of descriptions of data items provided by the DDL. This "data about data" is called a **data dictionary.**

26.23 Clearly, something so complex as a DBMS needs to be organised in a logical way and this logical organisation is achieved by having a number of distinct levels within the DBMS. At the top level, data is expressed in a form compatible with the view of individual users (as applications files, say). At the middle level the data is expressed in global terms applicable to all applications. At the bottom level the data is expressed in forms which relate to the way the data is actually stored. The DBMS transforms data as it moves it from level to level.

THE DATABASE ADMINISTRATOR (DBA)

26.24 The importance of a database is such that a special manager is often appointed, sometimes with a staff. His functions are described below.

The DBA must have a sound knowledge of the structure of the database and of the DBMS. The DBA must also be thoroughly conversant with the organisation, its systems, and the information needs of the managers.

26.25 The DBA is responsible for ensuring that:

a. the data in the database meets the information needs of the organisation.

b. that the facilities for retrieving data and for structuring reports are appropriate to the needs of the organisation.

26.26 The DBA is responsible for the following documentation:-

a. The data dictionary.

b. Manuals for users describing the facilities the database offers and how to make use of these facilities.

26.27 Another function is to supervise the addition of new data. For this purpose, the DBA will have to liaise with the managers who use the data, and the systems analysts and programmers who develop the systems.

26.28 Security of the database is also the responsibility of the DBA. The DBA may be responsible for the requirements of privacy too.

26.29 The DBA is also responsible for periodic appraisal of the data held in the base to ensure that it is complete, accurate and not duplicated.

EXAMPLES OF A DATABASE.

26.30 Organisations develop comprehensive databases over many years. An example is given here of a database used by a major computer manufacturer.

26.31 The database comprises:

a. Records of customers who have purchased or rent the manufacturer's computer equipment.

b. Records of the different items of equipment ie. processors, peripherals and other devices.

c. Records of spare parts showing the location where they are stored and the quantity held.

d.   Records of customer engineers responsible for maintenance and repairs.

26.32 The uses made of the database are too numerous to list completely, but a selection does give some idea of the facilities which a database can provide.

a. **Accounting.** Customers are billed for maintenance and rental charges. Any change in configuration automatically causes the customer charges to be amended (the "single input" principle).

b. **Spares.** The database is used to control stocks of spares. It can also be used to find the location of a spare part nearest to the installation which requires it.

c. **Modifications.** If a modification to a particular item of equipment is needed, all installations in which it is present can be quickly identified.

d. **Engineering Services.** The database shows which customers are served by which engineer (an example of the "linking" or cross-referencing of records). Engineers can be allocated to cover absence or sickness or to assist at an installation which is in trouble. The records show which types of equipment the engineers are qualified to service.

ADVANTAGES OF A DATABASE

26.33 The following are the advantages of a database:

a. Information supplied to managers is more valuable because it is based on a comprehensive collection of data instead of files which contain only the data needed for one application.

b. As well as routine reports, it is possible to obtain ad hoc reports to meet particular requirements.

c. There is an obvious economic advantage in not duplicating data. In addition, errors due to discrepancies between two files are eliminated.

d. The amount of input preparation needed is minimised by the 'single input' principle.

e. A great deal of programming time is saved because the DBMS handles the construction and processing of files and the retrieval of data.

f.   The integrated of different business systems is greatly facilitated.

FILE MANAGEMENT SYSTEMS

26.34 A number of software products have appeared on the market in recent years which appear to offer *some* of the features of databases on even the smaller computers. These products, some of which claim to be "database packages" are usually more correctly called "File Management Systems" (see chapter 3 for examples).

26.35 Typical file management systems usually have rudimentary DDLs and DMLs which allow the user to set up and maintain a few files with a minimum of programming effort or skill. Facilities are often including which allow limited but extremely useful data retrieval functions such as sorting and selecting.

26.36 A file management system may therefore be thought of rather loosely as a "computerised filing cabinet".

FOURTH GENERATION LANGUAGES (4GLs)

26.37 As indicated earlier, in recent years there has been a major increase in the use of **relational databases**. The increase has been accompanied by a number of different products which aid the development of new systems. These new products are often described as being

"**Fourth Generation Languages (4GLs)**" because they are considered to work at a higher level than normal high-level languages such as COBOL, Pascal and C; the latter often being called **3GLs.** The actual facilities provided by 4GLs vary considerably.

26.38 Most 4GLs make use of relational databases, which themselves have query languages (DDLs plus DMLs) which perform operations at a very high level. Some 4GLs are actually the combination of a database query language and other facilities.

QUERY LANGUAGE FEATURES IN MORE DETAIL

26.39 A query language normally comprises a DDL and a DML all rolled into one. The name **query language** is therefore something of a misnomer since query languages do much more than handle queries to the database.

26.40 Query languages have two basic modes of operation:

    a.   **Terminal Monitor Mode.** The user is able to use the query language at a terminal, in much the same way as a command-language interpreter is used. The idea is for the end-user to formulate ad hoc queries in order to obtain useful information from the database. The importance of such facilities is greatly overrated however, because, in practice, a great deal more control and care must be taken when accessing most databases. Nevertheless, such facilities can be of great value to those developing queries to be run in the other mode.

    b.   **Embedded Query Languages.** The query language statements are included within the code of programs written in some other programming language, eg, COBOL or C, and effectively becomes part of the program, hence the term "embedded query language".

26.41 One of the most widespread query languages is **SQL (Structured Query Language)**
SQL is an international standard for database query languages and has been adopted by many computer manufacturers and database product suppliers, eg, IBM, Digital, INGRES, ORACLE, SYBASE and INFORMIX.

QUERY LANGUAGES AND 4GLs

26.42 One feature of SQL is the way in which the statements are expressed in a form which indicated "what" result is required without specifying "how" the result
is to be obtained. For example, a simple SQL statement to get employees' names in alphabetic order might be written "SELECT name, address FROM employeetable ORDER BY name". That job is handled by the database management system. This very high level way of expressing processing requirements is one of the principal characteristics of a 4GL. For this reason SQL is itself sometimes described as a 4GL, although, as we will see, a 4GL normally has other important features too. However, some 4GLs use menu-driven user interfaces instead of a conventional "language".

26.43 4GLs may be regarded as the most modern form of "**applications generator**", a type of software which has been in existence for many years. Those who promote or sell 4GLs claim that they offer more productive and cost-effective alternatives to the high-level languages such as COBOL associated with the era of third-generation computers, hence the name "4GL". There is indeed some truth in these claims, although few current 4GLs are able to provide sufficient facilities to completely remove the need for 3GL in more than a narrow range of applications. Since there is such a variation in the features of products claiming to be 4GLs it is useful to define here those features which ought to be provided for the term 4GL to be used.

26.44 Features of a 4GL. A 4GL may be regarded as being a very high-level language which provides simple and powerful ways for the user to do such things as:

- a.   Define data.
- b.   Define what processing must be performed on the data.
- c.   Define report or screen-form layouts including the formats of printed or displayed data.
- d.   Define the processing operations to be carried out in the preparation of reports or in the user's interaction with screen-based forms.
- e.   Define input data and validation checks.
- f.   Select combinations of standard processing operations.
- g.   Handle user queries.

Depending upon the way in which the 4GL has been designed it may either be used by the end user directly or used by a computer specialist to "build" an end-user system.

Thus the 4GL **either** works by tailoring a generalised piece of software to handle a particular application **or** by using a general set of software tools to construct a particular application system

26.45 It is useful to distinguish between the following:

- a.   **A 4GL** – as described above.
- b.   **A 4GL tool.** – A 4GL tool is an item of software which *either* works in the same way as a full 4GL but which has more limited purpose *or* forms part of a full 4GL. For example, there are 4GL tools specially designed to handle the production of reports. Alternatively, SQL may be regarded as a 4GL tool.
- c.   **An applications generator**. Although a full 4GL is indeed an applications generator, the term applications generator tends to be more commonly used for simpler software products which provide flexible means of parameterising a general software package to deal with particular situations.

SUMMARY.

26.46 a.   A database is a comprehensive, consistent, controlled and coordinated collection of structured data items.

- b.   **A DataBase Management System (DBMS)** is a software system which constructs, maintains and controls a database.
- c.   Communication with the database is via the **Data Description Language (DDL)** and **Data Manipulation Language (DML)** together called a **Query Language or Data Sub-language (DSL).**
- d.   The **data dictionary** holds "data about data" in the database.
- e.   **A DataBase Administrator (DBA)** is the manager responsible for that database.
- f.   SQL is the most widespread query language.
- g.   A 4GL can be regarded as an advanced form of application generator.

POINTS TO NOTE.

26.47 a. 4GLs can be used to build **prototypes** of new systems as well as for building systems in their own right.

QUESTIONS A (With answers)

1   Explain the terms:
     a. DDL.
     b. DML.
     c. DBMS
     d. DBA
     e. Query Language

2.   Explain the term 4GL.

QUESTIONS B (Without answers)

1.   Why are databases used instead of conventional computer files?

27 Operating Systems

INTRODUCTION
27.1 The concept of an Operating System was introduced in 22.11. This chapter explains the purpose and facilities of operating systems. The characteristics of an operating system are introduced and the differences between the various common types of operating system are explained.

DEFINITION
27.2 An **operating system** is a suite of program which takes control over the operation of the computer to the extent of being able to allow a number of programs to be run on the computer without human intervention by an operator.

THE PURPOSE OF AN OPERATING SYSTEM
27.3 It can be seen from the definition of an operating system that the operating system controls the way software uses hardware. The purpose of this control is to make the computer operate in the way intended by the user, and in a systematic reliable and efficient manner. This "view" of an operating system is illustrated in Figure 27.1.

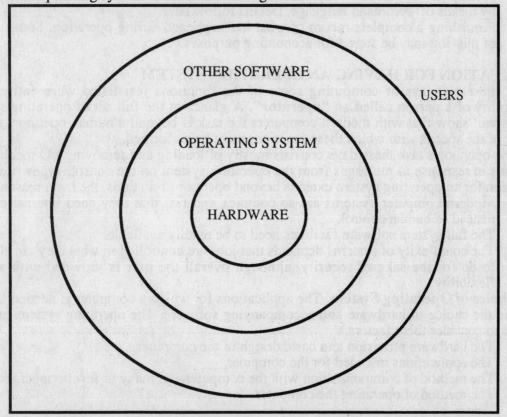

Figure 27.1. An Overview of a System Showing the Position of the Operating System.

27.4 The intended use of the computer by the user will affect the character of the required operating system. For example in the traditional commercial applications of computers, "**jobs**", comprised of user programs + data, need to be presented to the computer and processed in a way which will ensure that the maximum number of jobs get processed. At the other extreme, there are computer systems which essentially have one "job", which is to control some process, eg. controlling the action of an automated engineering machine. Here a fast response to events must be ensured. Between events the hardware may be under utilised.

27.5   In order to fulfil its purpose the operating system must carry out a number of functions. It has at its disposal, and under its control, the various system programs to accomplish this work.

THE FUNCTIONS OF AN OPERATING SYSTEM

27.6   The functions are:-

a.   The scheduling and loading of programs, or subprograms, in order to provide a continuous job processing sequence or to provide appropriate responses to events.

b.   Control over hardware resources eg. control over the selection and operation of devices used for input, output or storage.

c.   Handling errors when they occur and using corrective routines where possible.

d.   Protecting hardware, software and data from improper use.

e.   Communication with the computer user or operator by means of terminals or consoles, and through the use of monitor commands and responses. The operator (details shortly) or user may also be able to communicate with the operating system by means of command language. Details follow later.

f.   Furnishing a complete record of what has happened during operation. Some details of this log may be stored for accounting purposes.

JUSTIFICATION FOR HAVING AN OPERATION SYSTEM

27.7   In the early days of computing some of the functions just listed were entirely the responsibility of a person called an **"operator"**. A glance at the full set of operating system functions will show that with modern computers the task is beyond a human operator, simply by virtue of the speeds with which these functions must be performed.

27.8   The operator's task these days consists mostly of loading and removing I/O media from peripherals in response to messages from the operating system on the console typewriter. The justification for an operating system extends beyond operator limitations, the main reasons are:-

a.   Modern computer systems are so complex and fast that they need internal control instead of human control.

b.   The full system software facilities need to be readily available.

c.   The complexity of systems demands that jobs are controlled in what they are allowed to do for the sake of security, although overall the user is provided with greater flexibility.

27.9   **Choice of Operating System.** The applications for which a computer is needed largely determine the choice of hardware and accompanying software. The operating system supplier will need to consider these factors.

a.   The hardware provision and basic design of the computer.

b.   The applications intended for the computer.

c.   The method of communication with the computer, eg. many or few peripherals.

d.   The method of operating the computer.

METHODS OF OPERATING THE COMPUTER AND COMMUNICATION WITH IT

27.10 a. **Multiprocessing.** This is the name for the situation which occurs if two or more processors are present in a computer system and sharing some or all of the same memory. In such cases two programs may be processed at the same instant. In the remainder of this discussion assume just one processor is used unless otherwise stated.

b. **Multiprogramming.** This occurs when more than one program in main storage is being processed **apparently** at the same time. This is accomplished by the programs taking turns at short bursts of processing time. In its basic forms it merely involves low priority programs being able to exploit processor times unused by higher priority programs In its more advanced forms multiprogramming is sometimes called **multitasking** which usually implies a level of scheduling capable of supporting multiple users possibly running multiple programs.

c. **Batch processing.** The job (program + data) is not processed until fully input. The jobs are entered and stored on a disk in a "**Batch Queue**" and then run one or more at a time under the control of the operating system. A job may wait in a batch queue for minutes or hours depending on the work load. No amendments are possible during processing.
NB. The time which elapses between job submission and the return of results is known as the **turn around** time.

d. **Remote job entry** refers to batch processing where jobs are entered at a terminal remote from the computer and transmitted to the computer eg. via telecommunication links.

e. **Interactive Computing.** This occurs if the computer and terminal user may communicate with each other. (Also applies to computer communication with another device).

f. **Conversational mode.** This is Interactive computer operation where the response to the user's message is immediate.

g. **Multi-access.** This occurs if the computer allows interactive facilities to more than one user at a time.

h. **Time-sharing.** Processor time is divided into small units called **time slices** and shared in turn between users to provide multi-access.

i. **Real-time system.** A real time system is a computer system which is capable of processing data so quickly that the results are available to influence the activity currently taking place. There is often a need for multi-processing and a front end processor in these systems .

k. **Virtual memory.** This is a technique whereby programs undergoing execution but exceeding their allocation of main storage can be held in a special area on disk. From there program sections must be loaded into main storage quickly when instructions within them are about to be executed.

Different types of operating system are now described.

SINGLE USER SYSTEMS

27.11　As their name implies, these provide support for only one user at a time. They can be found on most microprocessors and on computers which are dedicated to a single function. They provide a simple command language, support for files, and I/O facilities for terminal, disk and printer. Some provide support for **multiprogramming**, ie. running more than one job concurrently, and this may be as simple as having one main job which runs in the "**foreground**" and a "**background**" job which is executed when the processor would be idle. Popular examples of this type of operating system include CP/M, MS-DOS (or PC-DOS), all of which provide interactive facilities to the user.

BATCH OPERATING SYSTEM

27.12 This is the oldest type of operating system and is characterised by a computer system which handles a batch of input which is collected over a period of time. Jobs are entered into a queue which is maintained by the operating system, and there is no provision for interaction by the user once the input has been submitted, although multi-programming may be used to optimise the use of peripherals.

MULTI-ACCESS AND TIME-SHARING SYSTEMS

27.13 A mainframe computer may support a hundred or more users simultaneously, whereas a typical minicomputer may support up to twenty or thirty. Time-sharing allows each user a time slice of less than a second, but in an interactive environment not all users will require service for each time slice: priority scheduling allows for a more rapid response. Multi-access operating systems use multiprogramming and often employ virtual memory, as described earlier. All aspects of control are more elaborate in these systems. Compare a single program system with picking up a ball throwing it into the air and catching it. Liken the ball being thrown to a program being processed, and liken the work of picking up throwing and catching to the operating system loading a program, executing it and then taking over control at the end. A multi-access time-sharing system compares with catching balls from all directions and juggling them.

REAL-TIME SYSTEMS

27.14 This type of operating system is characterised by speed of response. The system is able to respond very quickly to a change of circumstance and to initiate feedback. Examples include the control of a chemical plant, a space capsule or the monitoring of a patient's condition in hospital. In all cases, a rise of temperature would require a rapid response in order to maintain equilibrium. Reliability is very important in such systems, and hardware is often duplicated so as to be able to recover from hardware malfunction. The term "**fault-tolerant**" computer is used to describe this situation.

27.15 A real-time system which controls an engineering or manufacturing process is usually called a **Process Control System,** eg, a system to control the operation of a chemical factory plant. Response to changes must be as fast as possible and reliability is essential.

MONITORS

27.16 The simple control programs found within small computers are usually called monitors. Such monitors may be regarded as very simple single program operating systems. The term **monitor** is also used with a slightly different meaning to refer to a basic control program at the centre of the operating system together with the features of communication with the operator.

OPERATING SYSTEM FEATURES

27.17 Operating Systems should have the following features.
    a. efficiency, in terms of processor and resource utilisation, throughput of jobs, response time for multi-access systems, turn-round time etc.;

    b.   reliability, in terms of being error-free and handling all possibilities in the execution of jobs;

    c.   maintainability, in terms of enhancing facilities, modularity, correction of bugs etc.;

    d.   small size, in terms of the amount of memory and backing store required.

Clearly, some of these desirable features conflict with others.

27.18 Most operating systems are designed and written in a modular form. Many exhibit a structure which can be likened to the rings of an onion (see fig 27.1). A small central **"core"** (or **"nucleus"**, **"kernel"**, **"supervisor"**, **"executive"**) contains routines which are very time-critical, eg the interrupt handler and low-level scheduler or dispatcher. This is kept resident in memory at all times and maintains a variety of data structures to keep track of the status of other jobs running on the system.

27.19 The outer layers of the onion contain the other routines making up the operating system, and these are called into memory when necessary. A typical outer structure might be (in order of decreasing time-dependency); a memory management unit, input/output handling, file access, and scheduling and resource allocation.

27.20 The operating system interfaces directly with the hardware of the computer system. All other software makes use of the routines provided by the operating system, so there is no need for programmers to have detailed knowledge of how to control the hardware directly. These applications can be regarded as the "skin" of the onion. Later in this chapter there are further details of how operating system functions are achieved.

COMMAND LANGUAGE

27.21 A programming language used for communications with the operating system is called a command language. Most statements (commands) in the language are directives requiring immediate execution and are handled by a **command language interpreter**. These commands may also be called "**monitor commands**".

27.22 A Job Control language (JCL) is a special command language used for batch processing. It is used to identify jobs and state their requirements to the nucleus.

STORAGE MANAGEMENT

27.23 On the more basic multiprogramming systems the operating system may organise main memory into blocks of convenient size called **partitions.** (See Fig. 27.2).

27.24 In figure 27.2 the three programs in user spaces 1, 2 and 3 will each be given turns at processor time according to priorities determined by the operating system (details later). The need for reasonable performance will require all programs and system software to be held on disk so that overlays can happen quickly. With such a system it may be possible to overlay programs *or* subprograms and to make use of program segmentation.

27.25 The users' programs may be loaded into whichever partition is available, (such programs are called **relocatable programs**). On the more sophisticated systems the operating system is able to allocate, and reallocate, partitions of memory to system and user programs or subprograms and can do so continually and repeatedly in response to changes in the system. This is called dynamic allocation of main storage. As part of the **dynamic allocation** of main storage the operating system may copy programs or subprograms onto disk when it suspends their execution. Then it will overlay the main memory space with another program. Later it may copy the program or subprogram back into the same or a different part of main memory and resume its execution. This *swapping* from main memory onto disk and back in again is called **rolling out** and **rolling in.** Another term for it is **paging**.

411

27.26 Virtual Storage. The methods just described are extended on some systems so that the operating system will automatically segment programs and allocate memory to them so that the programmer may write programs with little regard for the main storage available. This is known as virtual storage since main storage can be regarded as bigger than its real size.

27.27 Storage Allocation. When dealing with the allocation of main storage space and backing storage space an operating system must keep track of how storage has been allocated. It must also protect the space allocated to one user from the accidental or deliberate interference of another user.

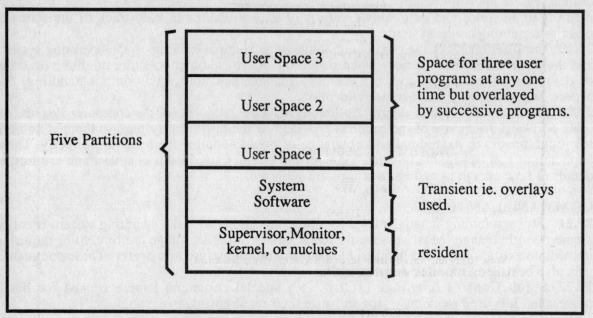

Figure 27.2. A Simple Multiprogramming System.

THE MANAGEMENT OF INPUT AND OUTPUT
27.28 The Problems of speed differences.

    a. Communications between the processor and peripherals is fraught with problems caused by the differences in speeds between the two. To put this into context the following points may be considered.

        i. A memory cycle takes less than one tenth of a microsecond i.e one ten millionth of a second.

        ii. Most instructions can be carried out well within 1 microsecond.

        iii. Some printers can only print 300 characters per second when at maximum speed, so that in the time it takes for one character to be output the computer might comfortably perform 10,000 instructions.

        iv. Even faster devices such as high speed printers make transfers of data at rates which correspond to dozens or hundreds of instructions. Compared to the processor they are slow.

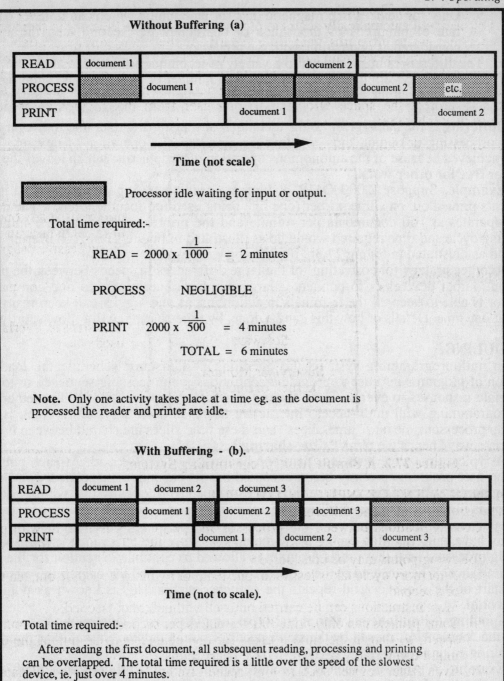

Without Buffering (a)

READ	document 1			document 2		
PROCESS	▓▓▓	document 1	▓▓▓	▓▓▓	document 2	etc. ▓▓
PRINT			document 1			document 2

Time (not scale)

▓▓▓▓▓ Processor idle waiting for input or output.

Total time required:-

$$READ = 2000 \times \frac{1}{1000} = 2 \text{ minutes}$$

$$PROCESS \qquad NEGLIGIBLE$$

$$PRINT \quad 2000 \times \frac{1}{500} = 4 \text{ minutes}$$

$$TOTAL = 6 \text{ minutes}$$

Note. Only one activity takes place at a time eg. as the document is processed the reader and printer are idle.

With Buffering - (b).

READ	document 1	document 2	document 3		
PROCESS	▓▓▓	document 1	▓ document 2	▓ document 3	▓▓▓
PRINT		document 1	document 2	document 3	

Time (not to scale).

Total time required:-

After reading the first document, all subsequent reading, processing and printing can be overlapped. The total time required is a little over the speed of the slowest device, ie. just over 4 minutes.

Figure 27.3 Buffering

413

v. Only for devices like magnetic disk or tape units, which can transfer data at the rate of hundreds of thousands of characters per second, can the speeds be considered as compatible with the processor.

b. The differences in speed lead to a variety of techniques of I/O transfer.

27.29 The operating system has an I/0 handler, ie. a number of programs and subprograms for handling input and output operations and which exploit a number of techniques. Some examples now follow.

27.30 Buffering is the name given to the technique of transferring data into temporary storage prior to processing or output, thus enabling the simultaneous operation of devices. This can only be achieved because of the autonomous operation of peripherals, which leaves the processor **free for other work.**

27.31 Example. Suppose 2,000 OMR documents need to be input and the details on the documents printed out on a line printer (one line being used for document read). The document reader operates at 100 documents per minute and the printer at 500 lines per minute. The processing cycle and time required would be as illustrated in Figure 27.3a, if buffering were not used, and as illustrated in Figure 27.3b, if buffering were used.

27.32 Another strategy for correcting for the large differences in speeds between the processor and input/output devices is to connect a large number of terminals to one computer. The processor is able to keep all the terminals in action just as one juggler can keep many balls in the air at one time. Details of how this can be done, by time-sharing, will follow shortly.

SCHEDULING

27.33 In multiprogramming systems the operating system must schedule the loading and execution of programs in order to provide a continuous job processing sequence or to provide appropriate responses to events. Time-sharing provides a popular scheduling method when multiprogramming with multi-access interactive users. In such a system a clock is used to divide up processor time into "time-slices" and these time-slices are shared between users in an appropriate way , hence the term " **time-sharing**".

27.34 A typical time-slice lasts less than one hundredth of one second. At each pulse of the clock the user program currently being executed has its execution suspended. (The user will probably not be aware of this because time slices happen so frequently that within a second its execution is likely to be resumed.) Then the operating system checks the status of each user, in strict sequence, to see whether the user requires processor time. Some may not, for example they may have paused during typing for some reason. Once the operating system finds a user requiring processor time that user's program is allowed to continue execution for the duration of the time slice. When the end of the sequence of users is reached the operating system returns to the start of the sequence and repeats the sequence again. This is known as **polling** in a **round-robin.**

27.35 Spooling (**S**imultaneous **P**eripheral **O**perating **O**n-**L**ine). This method is used to get around the "bottleneck" caused by the slow speeds of output devices in multiprogramming and time-sharing environment.

27.36 Example. A program which is to produce output for a line printer will actually direct its output to the disk. By doing so the program can complete its execution without being held up by the speed of the line printer. The program's output will join a queue to be output on the line printer when its turn comes. The queue may grow quite long at times when the computer is busy but will be reduced when the computer is less busy, this allows the line printer to spread its load over a longer time without holding up processing (See Figure 27.4).

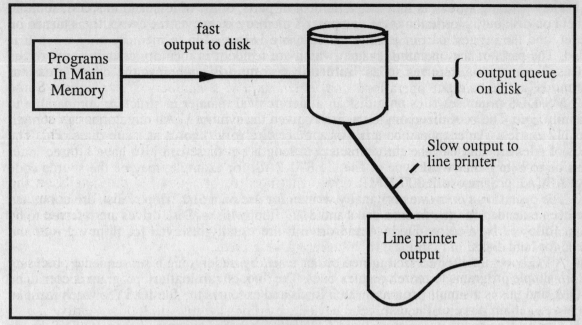

Figure 27.4. Spooling.

OPERATING SYSTEMS ON PERSONAL COMPUTERS (PCs)

27.37 There are numerous manufacturers of PCs most of whom produce machines which are designed to be so similar to IBM PCs that they can use its operating system. They actually use an operating system called MS-DOS which may be described as a "generic" operating system because it is used for a whole group or class of computers, namely those said to be "**IBM PC compatible**". The popularity of MS-DOS means that it deserves a separate description here.

27.38 MSDOS or MicroSoft disk Operating System is supplied by Microsoft Corporation for use on IBM PC compatible computers or "**clones**". IBM's own version PC-DOS can only be purchased for use on IBM PC's.

27.39 It is a single-user, single-tasking operating system which is disk based. It was first introduced in 1981 but has been enhanced many times to include extra features; the latest version is DOS-4. The large volume of IBM PCs and clones sold has helped to ensure that there is a vast amount of application software available, as well as utility programs and many programming languages.

27.40 MS-DOS provides a command line interpreter interface to the user enabling him or her to execute a program. It also handles input and output as well as managing files stored on disk. Examples of a few MS-DOS commands are given here:

FORMAT	– prepares a disk for use;
COPY	– copies a file;
DISKCOPY	– copies all files from one disk to another;
TYPE	– displays the contents of a file onto the screen;
DIR	– Lists all files on a disk;
DATE	– Reports the current date and allows user to change it;
CLS	– Clears the screen.

27.41 The operating system is split into a number of parts. Some of it is held in ROM, some of it is held on disk but is loaded into the computer's memory whenever the computer is turned on or reset, and the biggest part of it stays on disk and is loaded in to memory only when it is needed. The parts of the operating system which are resident in memory contain some of the most used commands, referred to as **"internal commands"**, whereas the other **"external commands"** reside on disk.

27.42 MS-DOS organises files on a disk in a hierarchical manner in structure comparable to the family tree. The **root directory** on a disk is given the symbol \. All directories can contain up to 112 entries. An entry can be a file or another directory (known as a sub-directory). The names of files are limited to eight characters in length but these can also have a three letter extension to help indicate the type of file: TEST1.PAS, for example, may be the source code for a PASCAL program called TEST1.

27.43 The operating system was originally written for use on a 51/2" floppy disk drive, but has since been extended to include hard disks and 31/2" floppy disks. Disk drives are referred to by a letter followed by a colon. Drive A and drive B are usually reserved for floppy drives and drive C for hard disks.

27.44 A PC boots itself when first turned on, or reset, by undergoing a set sequence building up from simple programs to more complex ones. The **"bootstrap loader"** program is contained in ROM, and this is a simple program which loads and executes the file IO.SYS which must be present at a certain place on the disk.

27.45 This in turn reads parameters from CONFIG.SYS if it exists and then IO.SYS hands control over to the system, MSDOS.SYS. This assigns memory to COMMAND.COM, the command line interpreter. Finally, if the command file AUTOEXEC.BAT exists it is executed, otherwise control is passed to the user by indicating an A prompt (or C prompt if you are using a hard disk).

27.46 MS-DOS is command driven and has been criticised by many for being unfriendly. It is possible to provide a menu as a front-end to the operating system, and this is particularly valuable for inexperienced users. A further improvement is to provide a graphical user interface, such as WIMP, whereby different functions or commands are represented by pictures or "icons" on the screen. These can be selected by moving a pointer controlled by a mouse and "clicking" on. This first became popular with the Apple Macintosh computer. Microsoft have brought out their own version for use with MS-DOS called Windows, version 3 of which became available in 1990.

27.47. As was just indicated, by reference to the Apple Macintosh, MS-DOS is not the only operating system used on PCs. Another generic operating system CP/M is used on 8-bit microcomputers although such machines are now overshadowed by 16-bit microcomputers such as IBM PC compatibles. The Apple Macintosh is probably the only main alternative machine design to the PC compatibles. Its operating system supports a very high standard user interface but is proprietary and therefore is only available on this machine.

OTHER OPERATING SYSTEMS

27.48 On larger computers full multi-user multi-tasking operating systems become available. A generic operating system which is gaining in popularity and which is available on a variety of different machines is UNIX (UNIX was developed by Bell laboratories). UNIX has a number of impressive features which have given rise to its widespread use. It is a full multi-tasking, multi-user time-sharing operating system written mostly in C, thereby making it relatively easy to port from machine to machine. It has a sophisticated and powerful command interpreter, called the **shell,** which is designed for used by computer professionals. For example, the one line command "who | sort > mylist.txt &" does the following. First shell runs the command "who" to obtain a list of who is on the system. The symbol "|" signifies that shell must use the output of "who" as the input to the "sort" command which sorts the list into alphabetic order. The mechanism for the "|" is called a "pipe". The ">" signifies that output from "sort" must be fed directly into a file called "mylist.txt" , rather than to the terminal's screen. Lastly, the "&" signifies that the command line must be carried out as a background task.

27.49 Almost all other operating systems in current use have been developed by computer manufacturers for use on particular machines, or ranges of machines, of a given make and type.

SUMMARY
27.50 a. Operating systems were defined.
    b. The purpose of an operating system was explained.
    c. The functions of an operating system were described.
    d. A number of important concepts were explained:
        i. Multiprocessing
        ii. Multiprogramming
        iii. Batch processing
        iv. Remote job entry
        v. Interactive computing and conversational mode.
        vi. Multi-access
        vii. Time-sharing
        viii.Real-time.
    e. Monitors, Executives and Supervisors were explained.
    f. The uses of command language interpreters and Job Control Languages (JCLs) were explained.
    g. The operation of various types of systems was explained.
    h. Requirements affecting operating system functions were discussed.
    i. Important operating system functions were discussed in more detail:-
        i. Storage management,
        ii. Input/Output management
        iii. Scheduling
    j. Priorities, buffering, spooling and virtual storage were discussed.
    k. Features of MS-DOS and UNIX were described.

POINTS TO NOTE
27.51 a. The operating system is usually the most complex and sophisticated software used on a computer. It is only natural therefore that this chapter only goes so far as to give an overview of operating systems even though a whole chapter is devoted to the topic.
    b. Take care not to confuse **time-sharing** with **real-time.** It is the response of a real-time system which distinguishes it from other systems. Systems controlling processes may not have multiple users but time-sharing by its nature shares time between multiple users. When many users are connected to a time-sharing system the response may be very slow and very unlike a real-time system.

QUESTIONS A (With answers)

1. Define an operating system. What is its purpose? List the functions of an operating system and which of these are provided by the operating system you use.

2. Briefly explain the following terms:-
    a. Multiprocessing.
    b. Multiprogramming.
    c. Batch processing
    d. Multi-access
    e. Time-sharing

3. What is a JCL?

4. How is the efficiency of an operating system measured?

5. What does an operating system do as part of its "storage management" function?

6. What is buffering? What problem does buffering help to overcome?

7. What is scheduling?

8. Define Time-Sharing and briefly explain how Time-Sharing works.

9. What is spooling and when might it be used?

10. Distinguish between Real-time and Time-Sharing.

11. Write brief notes on "MS-DOS" and "Unix".

QUESTIONS B (Without answers)

1. What is the purpose of a command language interpreter?

2. Briefly explain the following terms:-
    a   Partitioning
    b. Relocatable program.
    c. Dynamic allocation of memory
    d. Virtual storage.

3. What is the problem of speed difference between the processor and its peripherals. Describe two ways of trying to overcome this problem.

FURTHER APPLICATIONS

1. Earlier in this text, in chapters two to five, we examined a number of computer applications. The examples used only a minimal knowledge of Computers Studies because they were intended to be introductory in nature. In this Part of the text the examples will again be simple but this time they will try to show you how material covered earlier in the text may be applied.

2. Chapter 28 deals with a commercial application of computers of a fairly traditional kind. The examples given in the chapter are based upon a fictitious shoe shop. It concludes with a number of general observations about batch processing.

3. Chapter 29 extends the example of chapter 28 even further in order to deal with features of interactive systems. The chapter also deals with varied examples of interactive systems including transactions processing systems. It concludes with some more general observations about interactive systems.

4. Chapter 30 takes two examples to illustrate the uses of computers in control and manufacturer. The chapter therefore has an industrial bias in contrast with the business bias of chapters 28 and 29. The first example involves a simplified domestic appliance controlled by computer and the second is based upon a factory production line. Again, some general points are drawn from the examples given.

5. lastly, chapter 31 looks at the methods associated with developing applications.

28 Batch Processing

INTRODUCTION
28.1 In this chapter a *simplified* stock control system is used to illustrate the main features of batch processing. Both stock control and batch processing can be very complicated in real situations, so the reader should not assume to have gained specialist knowledge by the end of this chapter.

THE SYSTEM
28.2 The example used in this chapter concerns a shoe shop which is one branch in a chain of shoe shops. The stock control system described is used by the manager of the branch to aid his work, and therefore does not cover all the aspects of stock control dealt with by the head office.

28.3 The various items of footwear held at the shoe shop are its **stock.** This stock is a valuable resource which has to be properly managed if the shop is to achieve its primary aims of making a profit from the sale of footwear.

28.4 Failure to replace stock items which have been sold can result in lost profit through lost sales eg. if more customers wish to buy the same items. Holding stock which does not sell is a poor investment.

28.5 The aim of a **stock control** system is to aid the management of stock so as to make maximum use of stock in achieving the goals of the organisation. In this case the primary goal is to make profit. There are other goals however eg. providing a good service to customers etc.

28.6 In order to manage the stock the manager needs to hold data about the stock. This data will aid the stock control process. Therefore the data is itself a valuable resource, because of the benefits it provides in aiding stock control.

28.7 Goods enter stock when footwear is delivered to the shop from head office, goods leave stock when they are sold to customers. It is possible to keep track of stock by recording such **transactions** ie. goods-in and goods-out.

THE STOCK MASTER FILE
28.8 You may remember that master files hold data of a semi-permanent nature. In this example the stock master file holds data about all items of footwear in the shop. In a manual filing system each stock record might be like the one shown in figure 28.1. There are two particular features to note about figure 28.1:-

    a.   The use of coding, eg. colour, are abbreviated to two characters.

    b.   Plenty of space is left for data items, such as QUANTITY IN STOCK, which have to be regularly altered in order to keep them up to date.

28.9 Examine figure 28.1 further. The record gives details of a standard black boy shoe; size 5 1/2 width C in a style called "WIZARD" which costs £17.95 and is made by a manufacturers whose code is "D". This record makes provision for some data items to be changed or updated, namely, RETAIL PRICE, QUANTITY IN STOCK, and the REORDER DETAILS. The remaining data items are permanent for a given master record and the *unique* combination of such details on each stock record has its own *unique key* , the STOCK NUMBER.

28.10 Look at the QUANTITY IN STOCK on figure 28.1. It started at 20 and was reduced as shoes were sold, to 18, 17, 12 and so on. When the QUANTITY IN STOCK reached 3 it fell below the REORDER LEVEL "5" and so 10 were ordered. An "R" was placed in the INDICATOR so that the person filling in the record would know an order has been made, and therefore not reorder again, as they might otherwise have done when the QUANTITY IN STOCK fell to 2. The order of 10 arrived putting the QUANTITY IN STOCK up to 12 and "R" was crossed through. THE QUANTITY IN STOCK then fell to 11 its current value.

28.11 Other details of the master file will be returned to shortly.

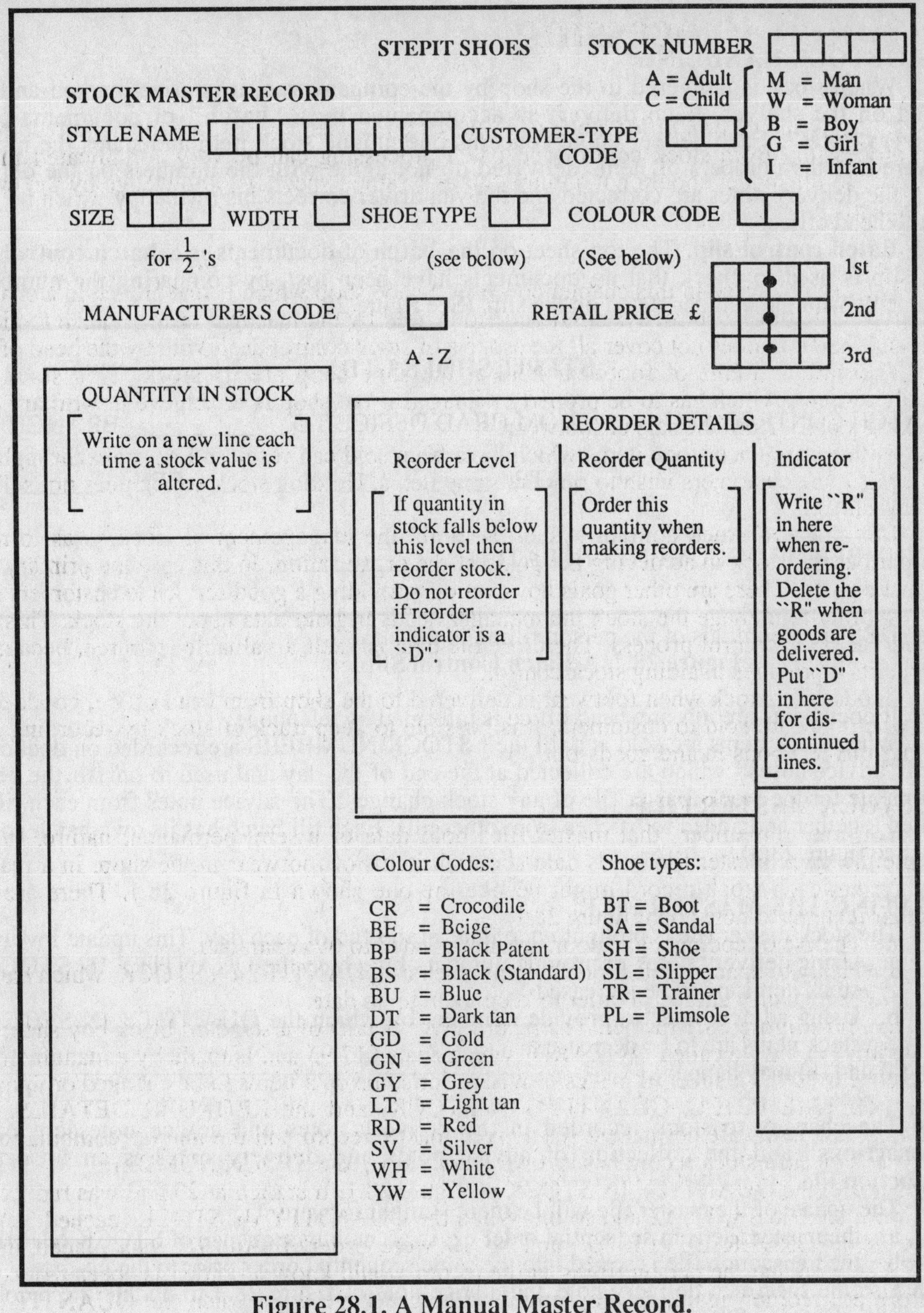

STEPIT SHOES STOCK NUMBER ☐☐☐☐☐

STOCK MASTER RECORD

STYLE NAME ☐☐☐☐☐☐☐☐☐ CUSTOMER-TYPE CODE ☐☐

A = Adult
C = Child

M = Man
W = Woman
B = Boy
G = Girl
I = Infant

SIZE ☐☐☐ WIDTH ☐ SHOE TYPE ☐☐ COLOUR CODE ☐☐

for ½'s   (see below)   (See below)

MANUFACTURERS CODE ☐   RETAIL PRICE £

A - Z

1st
2nd
3rd

QUANTITY IN STOCK

Write on a new line each time a stock value is altered.

REORDER DETAILS

Reorder Level

If quantity in stock falls below this level then reorder stock. Do not reorder if reorder indicator is a ``D".

Reorder Quantity

Order this quantity when making reorders.

Indicator

Write ``R" in here when re-ordering. Delete the ``R" when goods are delivered. Put ``D" in here for dis-continued lines.

Colour Codes:

CR = Crocodile
BE = Beige
BP = Black Patent
BS = Black (Standard)
BU = Blue
DT = Dark tan
GD = Gold
GN = Green
GY = Grey
LT = Light tan
RD = Red
SV = Silver
WH = White
YW = Yellow

Shoe types:

BT = Boot
SA = Sandal
SH = Shoe
SL = Slipper
TR = Trainer
PL = Plimsole

Figure 28.1. A Manual Master Record.

BASIC STOCK HANDLING

28.12 When stock is delivered to the shop by the company van, it is price marked and then placed on the shelves. Each delivery is accompanied by a **"batch"** of documents called **"delivery notes"**. Each delivery note concerns one unique stock item and states the number delivered. If the numbers of items delivered do not agree with the numbers on the delivery notes, the delivery notes are corrected and the van driver corrects his own copy which he takes back to head office.

28.13 Batch control slip. The top sheet on the **batch** of documents is a **batch control slip.** This slip is used to check that no documents have been lost, by comparing the number of documents with the number stated on the slip. (See figure 28.2).

```
┌─────────────────────────────────────────────────────────────────────┐
│                        STEPIT SHOES LTD.                              │
│                                                                       │
│   BATCH CONTROL SLIP     FROM HEAD OFFICE TO _____ BRANCH         │
│                                                                       │
│                          DATE __ __ / __ __ / __ __     REF  _____     │
│                                                                       │
│   NUMBER OF DOCUMENTS IN BATCH  _____                             │
│                                                                       │
└─────────────────────────────────────────────────────────────────────┘
```

Note. DBS are the initials of the person filling in the slip.

Figure 28.2. A Batch Control Slip.

If documents are missing head office is informed by telephone.

28.14 When stock items are sold at a till their STOCK NUMBERS are recorded on documents called **"advice notes"** which are collected at the end of the day and used to *advise* the person responsible for the stock master file of any stock changes. The advice notes from each till are batched together and added to batches from other tills. Each till batch has its own batch control slip (See figure 28.3).

UPDATING THE MASTER FILE

28.15 The stock master file is brought *up to date* at the end of each day. This update involves:
  a. Using delivery notes to provide numbers by which the QUANTITY IN STOCK of stock items are to be increased.
  b. Using advice notes to provide numbers by which the QUANTITY IN STOCK of stock items are to be decreased.
(both (a) and (b) may happen).

28.16 The changes to stock recorded in the delivery notes and advice notes are called **"transactions"** and the collection of advice notes and delivery notes is an **unsorted transaction file.**

28.17 The update of the master file will be more straight forward if
  a. the master file is in sequential order eg. in ascending sequence of STOCK NUMBER
and b. the transaction file is sorted into the same sequential order prior to the up-date.

28.18 Use the specimen delivery note and advice note of figure 28.3 to update the record in figure 28.1. Details of the whole file update will follow shortly.

```
┌─────────────────────────────┐   ┌─────────────────────────────┐
│      STEPIT SHOES LTD.       │   │      STEPIT SHOES LTD.       │
│                             │   │                             │
│  Delivery Note              │   │  Advice Note    Till Number ___ │
│                             │   │                             │
│  ┌──────────┐  ┌──────────┐ │   │  ┌──────────┐  ┌──────────┐ │
│  │Stock Number│ │Number Delivery│ │  │Stock Number│ │Number Sold │ │
│  │ □□□□□ │  │          │ │   │  │ □□□□□ │  │          │ │
│  └──────────┘  └──────────┘ │   │  └──────────┘  └──────────┘ │
└─────────────────────────────┘   └─────────────────────────────┘
              a.                                b.
```

```
┌─────────────────────────────────┐
│        STEPIT SHOES LTD.         │
│                                 │
│  Batch Control Slip   From Till Number ___ │
│                                 │
│  Number of Documents    ____    │
│                                 │
│  Date __ __ / __ __ / __ __   Initials _____ │
└─────────────────────────────────┘
                 c.
```

28.3. Some Specimen Documents.

MASTER FILE MAINTENANCE
28.19 The master file may need to be altered in other ways from time to time. There are three cases of this file maintenance to consider in this example:-
  a. When a new item of stock is introduced a new record is added to the master file.
  b. When a stock item is to be discontinued a "D" is placed in the reorder-indicator field of the stock master record. When the stock level falls to zero the record is removed from the file.
  c. When details of a stock item need to be changed eg. an increase in price, the appropriate field is changed.

28.20 Assume that these details are sent by post from head office and are recorded on suitable advice notes.

28.21 The maintenance of the master file can be accomplished in a similar fashion to an update and the two processes, update and maintenance, may be combined into one operation if doing so is desirable.

COMPUTERISATION
28.22 The stock control system described so far is a simple manual one. Manual systems vary greatly in size and complexity but very large stock control systems become unmanageable to deal with manually and have to be handled by computer. Many large chains of department stores and supermarkets rely heavily on computers for their stock control.

28.23 Whenever the use of a computer is considered for a particular application the costs of the computer (both purchase and running costs) must be compared with the benefits it will provide. Unless the computer can pay for itself in increased profits, savings or better service etc., it should not be used. In the following paragraphs we shall assume that costs and benefits have been considered and that a *small* computer system is introduced to aid the branch stock control system.

COMPUTERISED MASTER FILE

28.24 The computerised version of the master record in figure 28.1 differs slightly from the manual version and must be very clearly defined. It should be noted that computerisation frequently involves the complete redesign of all files and documents and also requires many changes in procedures. In this case the computer record has the same fields as the manual record. The definition of the computerised master file is shown in figure 28.4.

28.25 A specimen computerised master file is shown in figure 28.5.

28.26 Computerised transaction records. The data on the delivery notes and advice notes in figure 28.2 will be entered into the computer and placed in a transaction file, which will initially be unsorted. Once sorted this transaction file can be used to update the master file. The transaction file records have the format shown in figure 28.6

FIELD NUMBER	FIELD NAME	FIELD DESCRIPTION
1	STOCK-NUMBER	A 5 digit number.
2	STYLE-NAME	A 10 character name.
3	CUSTOMER-TYPE-CODE	A two character code of which the first character is `A' for Adult or `C' for child. `A' can be followed by `M' for man or `W' for woman. `C' can be followed by `B' for Boy `G' for girl or `I' for infant.
4	SIZE	This will be one of the set of values 1, 1 , 2, 2 . . . 15 except that childrens sizes stop at 13 .
5	WIDTH	A single character from the set A, B, C, D, E, F, G
6	SHOE-TYPE	A two character code. (See figure 28.1).
7	COLOUR-CODE	A two character code eg. GY for grey, (See figure 28.1).
8	MANUFACTURER-CODE	A single letter from A . . . Z.
9	RETAIL-PRICE	Expressed in pounds and pence. (Never more than £99.99).
10	QUANTITY-IN-STOCK	Never more than 99.
11	REORDER-LEVEL	Never more than 99. If the number in stock falls below this level it is time to reorder more.
12	REORDER-QUANTITY	Never more than 99. This is the number of items to be reordered.
13	REORDER-INDICATOR	A single character, normally a space, but set to ``R'' when goods are reordered so that they are not reordered twice. Also set to ``D'' if the item is to be discontinued.

Figure 28.4. The Computerised Master File.

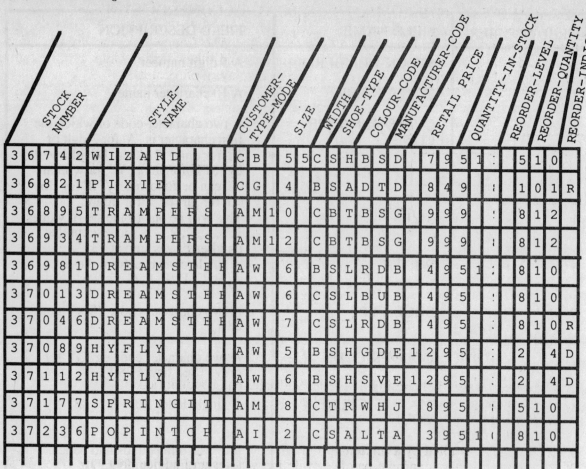

Figure 28.5. A Specimen Computerised Master File in Sequential Order.

Transaction file format.

FIELD NUMBER	FIELD NAME	FIELD DESCRIPTION
1	RECORD-TYPE	A single character: - A : Add to stock (A delivery) T : Take from stock (A sale)
2	STOCK-NUMBER	A 5 digit number.
3	UPDATE-QUANTITY	A 2 digit number corresponding to the number of items delivered or sold.

Note: i. The delivery note of figure 28.3a would be coded onto a transaction record as:
       |A|3|6|7|4|2|1|0|

      ii. The advice note of figure 28.3b would be coded onto transaction record as:
       |T|3|6|7|4|2| |5|

Figure 28.6 A Computerised Transaction File.

GENERAL VIEW OF THE COMPUTERISED STOCK CONTROL SYSTEM

28.27 An overview of the hardware is shown in figure 28.7. The VDU is used for all communications with the computer, including data entry. The floppy disks are used to store programs and files. The printer is used to print reports and other details which require hard copies (ie. printed copies on paper) rather than screen displays (soft copies)

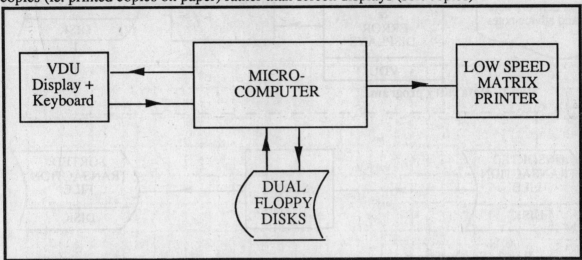

Figure 28.7. Hardware Overview.

28.28 Three main stages in handling deliveries and sales can be identified:-
    a. Data entry
    b. Sorting
    c. Master file update
    Each stage is handled by a separate program

28.29 Data entry. In this example batches of delivery notes and advice notes are typed in at the VDU. The user requests either a sale or a delivery input and the program sets up the appropriate record type: "A" OR "T". The program which takes in the data validates it by checking the following details:-
    a. The stock number typed in must be a 5 digit integer
        (ie. between 11111 or 99999 inclusive).
    b. The update quantity must be an integer between 1 and 99 inclusive.
        Thus the validation check deal with *data type* and *range*.

28.30 Errors are displayed on the VDU screen and corrected immediately. When the details of each transaction (delivery or sale) are correct the transaction record is written onto the transaction file on disk. When all transactions have been entered the unsorted transaction file is complete.

28.31 Sorting. A program is used to sort the transaction file into the sequential order of the master file ie. in ascending stock number sequence.

28.32 Master file update. The sorted transaction file is used to update the master file. (Fig 28.8). More details will be given later.

28.33 This flow of data and sequence of processing can be summarised in a flowchart called a **System Flowchart.** System flowcharts have been used in an informal, self explanatory way already but consult appendix IV for details. (See figure 28.8).

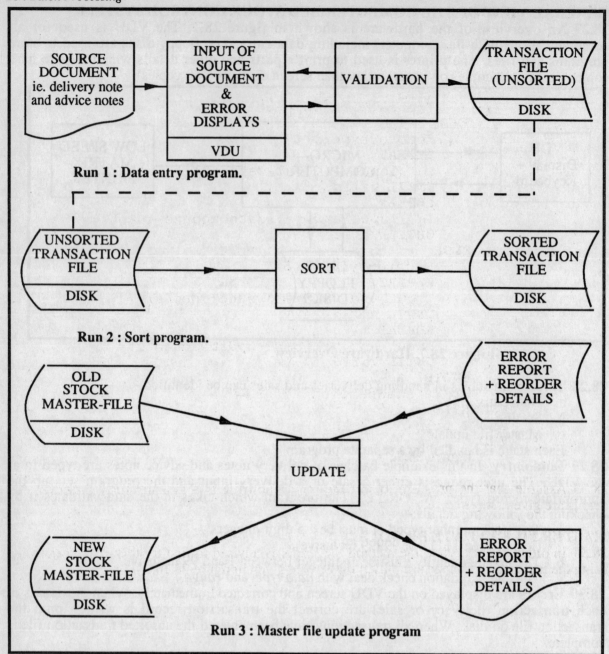

Run 1 : Data entry program.

Run 2 : Sort program.

Run 3 : Master file update program

Figure 28.8. System Flowchart.

DATA ENTRY PROGRAM DETAILS
28.34 The data entry program is described in figure 28.9. Full details of the validation are omitted in the interests of clarity.

```
BEGIN
OPEN the file called "TRANSACTION"
WHILE
    More transactions to input
DO
    IF
        Transaction is a delivery
    THEN
        Record-type := "A"
        REPEAT
            Input and validate stock number
        UNTIL valid
        REPEAT
            Input and validate update quantity
        UNTIL valid
    ELSE
        Record-type := "T"
        REPEAT
        Input and validate stock number
        UNTIL valid
        REPEAT
        Input and validate update quantity
        UNTIL valid
    ENDIF
    Write transaction record
ENDWHILE
CLOSE file
END
```

Figure 28.9.

28.35 Assume that the program to sort the transaction file is a system utility program. No details are given therefore.

MASTER FILE UPDATE DETAILS
28.36 In order to understand the method the reader is advised to first try this manual exercise using the transaction file and simplified master file given in figure 28.10.

429

SIMPLIFIED MASTER FILE				
Stock Number	Quantity-In Stock	Reorder Level	Reorder Quantity	Reorder Indicator
36742	11	05	10	
36821	08	10	15	R
36895	09	08	12	
36934	08	08	12	
36981	12	08	10	
37013	09	08	10	
37046	03	08	10	R
37089	01	02	04	D
37112	03	02	04	D
37177	08	05	10	
37236	10	08	10	

Figure 28.10a

SORTED TRANSACTION FILE		
Record-Type	Stock-Number	Update-Quantity
T	36742	02
A	36821	15
T	36934	01
T	37046	02
T	37089	01
T	37112	02
T	37120	02
T	37177	01
T	37177	02

Figure 28.10b.

28.37 The reader is advised to write out a copy of each of the records from the two files and use these copies in this exercise. Some blank records will also be needed on which to write the new master file. Use small strips of paper or cards for the records (ie. one piece per record).

28.38 Arrange the files on your desk in the way shown in figure 28.11 which imitates the way computer storage would be used.

28.39 The first old master record (STOCK NUMBER 36742) should be "read" into main memory, ie. place the record in the space provided. The first transaction record (STOCK NUMBER 36742) should also be read into main memory ie. placed into the record space provided. The update process is now set up.

28.40 The keys of the two records are compared. In this case they are equal. This means that the data on the transaction record should be used to update the master record. (A copy of the old master record is made to form a new master record). However the quantity in stock will be 9 ie. (11-2) since the quantity in stock on the new master record must be updated. 9 is above the reorder level of 5 and so the first transaction record is finished with.

28.41 The next transaction record is read into memory and replaces the previous one. Its STOCK-NUMBER (36821) is greater than the stock number of the master file record so the new master file record may be output and another old master file record may be input.

28.42 This process continues until all records have been processed. You will find if you work through the data of figure 28.10, that there are a number of different cases to deal with. You may wish to try this out for yourself and decide what action should be taken in each case. Now examine the details in figure 28.12. **Note** that in figure 28.12 "EOF" means End of File, and KEY ( ) means the key of the file whose name is given in parentheses.

431

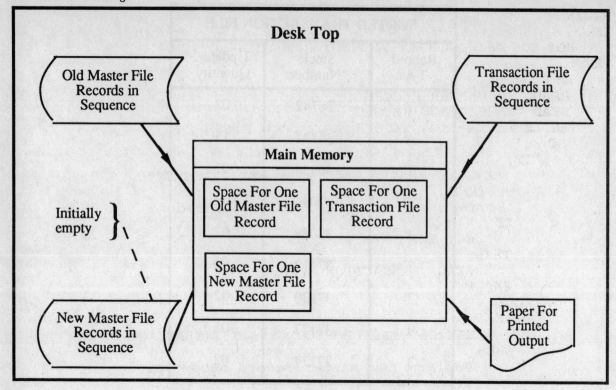

Figure 28.11. Manual Exercise.

FILE MAINTENANCE

28.43 The file maintenance described in paragraph 28.19 can be performed on the computerised file in a similar way to the update. In fact it is common practice to combine update and maintenance into one process. It is achieved by having a greater number of transaction record types than those used for the update (figure 28.10). Further transaction records types might be "N" for new records, "D" for deletions and "C" for changes. These records would each have an appropriate format.

FILE INTERROGATION

28.44 In a batch processing system, answers to queries concerning a master file can be obtained by running an appropriate program. Such programs usually produce printed reports.
28.45 Suppose that the manager required a list containing details of all boots produced by a particular manufacturer with style names in alphabetical order. This requires a *selection* from the master file to produce a file of selected records copies from the master file. The selected file must be sorted into the required sequence and then the *report* can be printed. This is summarised in figure 28.13.

432

```
BEGIN
IF
    NOT EOF(OLD-MASTER) AND NOT EOF(TRANSACTION)
THEN
    /*  Set up */
    READ OLD-MASTER RECORD
    READ TRANSACTION RECORD
    WHILE THERE IS A RECORD FROM EACH FILE
     DO
        IF
           KEY(OLD-MASTER RECORD) = KEY(TRANSACTION RECORD)
             THEN
           Perform master record update procedure
        IF
              NOT EOF(TRANSACTION)
        THEN
              READ TRANSACTION RECORD
        ENDIF
      ELSE
        IF
              KEY(OLD-MASTER RECORD) < KEY(TRANSACTION RECORD)
        THEN
              Perform new master record output procedure
              IF
                 NOT EOF(OLD-MASTER)
              THEN
                 READ OLD-MASTER RECORD
              ENDIF
        ELSE
              Perform transaction record error procedure
              IF
                 NOT EOF(TRANSACTION
              THEN
                 READ TRANSACTION RECORD
              ENDIF
          ENDIF
      ENDIF
   ENDWHILE
```

continued...

```
        IF
            EOF (TRANSACTION)
        THEN
            perform new master record output procedure
            WHILE
                NOT EOF (OLD-MASTER)
            DO
                READ OLD-MASTER RECORD
                new-master-record := old-master-record
                WRITE new-master-record
            ENDWHILE
        ELSE
            perform transaction-record error procedure
            WHILE
                NOT EOF (TRANSACTION)
            DO
                READ TRANSACTION RECORD
                perform transaction-record error procedure
            ENDWHILE
        ENDIF
    ELSE
        PRINT "ONE FILE EMPTY - NO PROCESSING"
    ENDIF
END
```

Further details.

i.   "Perform master record update procedure". This
     procedure must deal with both transaction record types
     and with reordering.

ii. "Perform new master record output procedure".
     This procedure copies appropriate details across from
     the old master record and outputs the new master
     record, *except* in the case where the master record
     required deletion.

iii. "Perform transaction record error procedure". This
     procedure deals with printing an error message when
     a transaction record has no matching master record eg.
     T 37 12002

Figure 28.12.

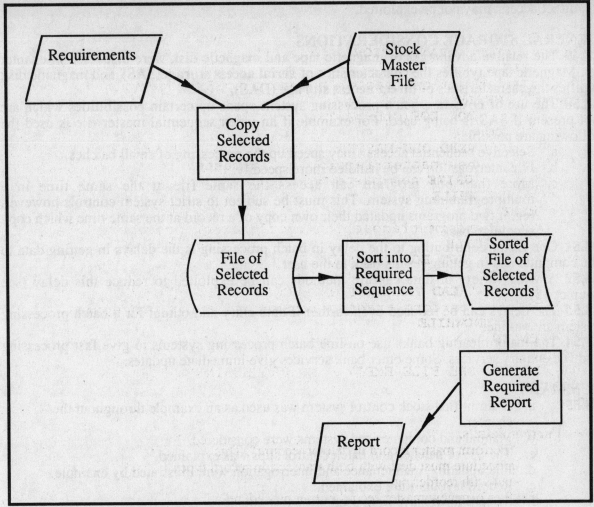

Figure 28.13. File Interrogation to Produce a Report.

SOME GENERAL POINTS

28.46 The examples given in this chapter have illustrated various aspects of batch processing in order to emphasise the important characteristics of batch processing which are:-

    a. The accumulation of transactions into batches.

    b. The transactions are sorted and then processed

    c. There is some degree of *delay*.

    d. The results of processing a particular data item are not known until the whole batch has been processed.

28.47 Batch processing is an important method of manual and computerised data processing. The batching of documents helps to keep control over document handling and reduces the risk of document loss (see paragraph 28.13).

28.48 In the case of computerised batch processing systems the older systems tended to involve data input by punched cards (now obsolete) and the use of magnetic tape files. Modern batch processing tends to involve direct data entry or PC based entry to create transaction files. Interactive computing is often used at this stage in order to aid and speed validation. These days the files used on a batch systems are usually held on disk although all features of the disk, eg. direct access, may not be exploited.

GENERAL STORAGE CONSIDERATIONS

28.49 The relative advantages of magnetic tape and magnetic disk were discussed in chapter 15. Magnetic tape typifies the characteristics of **serial access** storage(SAS) and magnetic disk typifies the characteristics of **direct access storage (DAS)**.

28.50 The use of DAS in a batch processing system opens up certain possibilities which are not present if SAS is being used. For example if an index sequential master file is used the following are possible:-

    a. Selective sequential access may speed up the processing of small batches.

    b. File interrogation can be handled more speedily.

    c. More than one program can access the same file at the same time in a multiprogramming system. This must be subject to strict system controls however. (eg. if two programs updated their own copy of a record at the same time which copy should go back?)

28.51 One factor contributing to the delay in batch processing is the delays in getting data to the computer and in getting results back to the user.

28.52 A wide variety of data capture methods can be exploited to reduce this delay (see chapter 13).

28.53 The delays can be reduced even further if data entry and output for a batch processing system are on-line.

28.54 The major clearing banks use on-line batch processing systems to give fast processing and file enquiry services. Some other bank services give immediate updates.

SUMMARY

28.55
    a. A simplified stock control system was used as an example throughout the chapter.

    b. Manual and computerised systems were considered.

    c. The use of batches and batch control slips was explained.

    d. File updating, maintenance and interrogation were illustrated by example.

    e. Record layouts were explained.

    f. System flowcharts were used.

    g. The use of different record types was explained.

    h. The main characteristics of batch processing were explained.

POINTS TO NOTE

28.56
    a. Batch processing is often the most appropriate method to use even when interactive on-line processing is available.

    b. Batch processing **should not** just be associated with more traditional media. It can be equally appropriate when using VDUs and floppy disks. The processing requirements will determine the method and the media.

    c. A small scale batch processing system has been used in this chapter so as to make practical class work easier to conduct. Batch processing is equally suited to larger systems.

QUESTIONS A *(With answers)*

1.   What is the aim of the stock control system?

2.   Give two advantages of placing documents into batches.

3.   What is a batch control slip?

4.   What is a system flowchart?

5.   Name four general characteristics of batch processing systems.

QUESTIONS B *(Without answers)*

1. ·   *The reader should set up his or her own files and documents for the stock control system described in this chapter and work through the system as a manual exercise.*

29 Interactive processing

INTRODUCTION

29.1 When the inherent delays of batch processing are unacceptable and there is a need to have data up to date and directly accessible, then interactive systems are required. The interactive processing methods provided on such systems are normally an alternative to batch processing rather than a replacement. This chapter concentrates on some practical examples of interactive processing.

INTERACTIVE STOCK CONTROL

29.2 An alternative approach to the batch processing methods described in the previous chapter would be to process all transactions when they occur and to allow direct interrogation of individual data items on the master file.

29.3 Using this method for this application *would probably be an expensive and inappropriate use of resources* but the example is continued here so as to highlight the differences. The method would be very appropriate for large on-line ordering or booking systems involving multi-access.

THE SYSTEM

29.4 A hardware overview is given in figure 29.1.

29.5 The stock master file is held on disk. In order to provide facilities for random and sequential processing the master file is held as an index sequential file.

FILE UPDATING, MAINTENANCE AND INTERROGATION

29.6 **File updating** can take place from VDU's A, B and C. VDUs A and B, in the shop, will be used to enter sales. VDU C, in the stock room, will be used to enter deliveries.

29.7 **File maintenance** can take place in the office by using VDU D. Details of new stock items, changes or discontinued liens can be entered.

29.8 **File interrogation** can also take place in the office by using VDU D enquiries about single items can be handled directly at the VDU from which a printed copy of details can be requested. Larger reports can be produced by batch processing.

MENU DRIVEN SYSTEMS

29.9 For many modern interactive on-line applications all communication between the terminal user and the computer are handled by means of "MENUS". This means that a number of alternative actions are displayed on the VDU screen and the user merely makes a selection by pressing an appropriate key. A menu enables the user to control the system without the need to learn complicated details concerning monitor commands.

29.10 Systems which operate by means of user menu selections are said to be "**menu driven**". Since such systems are easy to use they are said to have "user friendly" features. Some of the most "user friendly" computer applications are computer games!

29.11 The main menu for the system being considered in this chapter is shown in figure 29.2.

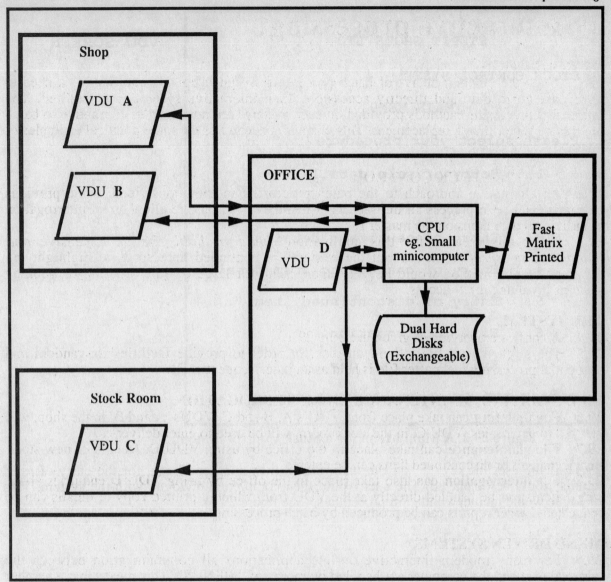

Figure 29.1. Hardware Overview.

```
┌────────────────────────────────────────────────────────┐
│                                                        │
│               STEPIT  SHOES  LTD.        VDU  SCREEN   │
│                                                        │
│  STOCK CONTROL SYSTEM                                  │
│                                                        │
│                  MAIN  MENU                            │
│                                                        │
│  Please select your procedure                         │
│                                                        │
│       1.    Entry of sale details.                    │
│                                                        │
│       2.    Entry of delivery details.                │
│                                                        │
│       3.    Entry of new items details.               │
│                                                        │
│       4.    Entry of changes to item details          │
│                                                        │
│       5.    Entry of discontinued item.               │
│                                                        │
│       6.    File interrogation.                       │
│                                                        │
│       7.    Exit at end of day.                       │
│                                                        │
│  PLEASE HIT KEY 1, 2, 3, 4, 5, 6, or                  │
└────────────────────────────────────────────────────────┘
```

Figure 29.2. A Main Menu for a Stock Control System.

29.12 If the user hit key "1" on the main menu, then another screen, for the entry of sales details would be displayed. The user would then complete a dialogue with the system. This dialogue would include validation procedures. (See figure 29.3).

VDU SCREEN

```
┌─────────────────────────────────────────┐
│         ENTRY OF SALES DETAILS           │
│                                          │
│                                          │
│   STOCK NUMBER = ? 36742                 │
│                                          │
│   NUMBER SOLD  = ? 5                     │
│                                          │
│                                          │
│                                          │
│                                          │
│                                          │
│                                          │
│   ARE THESE DETAILS CORRECT? (Y/N)       │
│                                          │
└─────────────────────────────────────────┘
```

NB.

i. Data typed by the user is in plain type. Data displayed by the computer is in bold type.
ii. Each data item input is terminated by the user pressing the "RETURN KEY".
iii. Once the entry is complete the system returns to the main menu having first updated the file.

Figure 29.3.

29.13 Details of the random file update associated with figure 29.3 are given in figure 29.4. A System Flowchart is given in figure 29.5.

```
BEGIN
Display headings
REPEAT
    REPEAT
        Input and validate Stock number
    UNTIL valid
    REPEAT
        Input and validate number sold
    UNTIL valid
    confirm details
UNTIL details correct
seek record
IF
    record found
THEN
    get record
    update record
    put updated record back on disk
ELSE
    Displays display error
ENDIF
END
```

Figure 29.4. A Random Stock Record Update.

Please note the following points regarding figure 29.4.

    i.   The validation of the stock number involves checking for an integer in the range 11111 to 99999.

   ii.   The validation of the number sold involves checking for an integer in the range 1 to 99.

  iii.   Details of getting records from random files are omitted in the interests of clarity

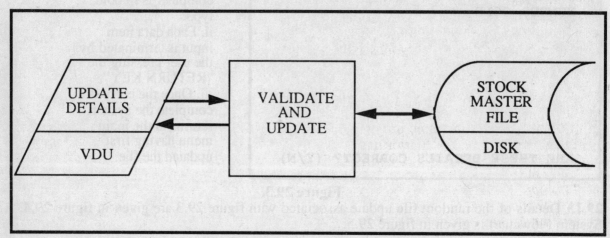

Figure 29.5 Systems Flowchart.

29.14 In the interests of clarity details of file security were not included in the last example. For details of file security on disk see figure 14.14.

29.15 In a multi-access system, steps have to be taken by the operating system to prevent two users from trying to modify the same record at the same time.

29.16 Other file processing activities for update, maintenance and interrogation are handled in a similar way to the example given in figure 29.4.

SOME GENERAL POINTS

29.17 The interactive on-line example presented in this chapter contrasts with the batch processing example of the last chapter. In this multi-access system the delays associated with batch processing are eliminated to the extent that each transaction is carried out straight away. The main characteristics are:-

    a.   Transactions can be dealt with individually.

    b.   Random access is used to access individual records.

    c.   Delay can be largely eliminated.

    d.   The results of processing each data item are available once the data item has been processed.

29.18 On a multi-access timesharing system, delays may still be experienced by users. These delays are caused by the "load" on the system caused by other users. For some applications even these delays may be unacceptable and real-time response may be required. Interactive multi-user real-time systems dealing with the updating, maintenance and interrogation of single files or databases are called **Transaction Processing Systems.**

TRANSACTION PROCESSING SYSTEMS

29.19 In practical terms you could say that in a real-time system a single transaction becomes a batch which is processed immediately on demand. If the transaction involves input, validation, updating or maintenance the system is a **Transaction Processing System.** Other real-time systems may have greater emphasis placed on file interrogation or data retrieval than on updating and maintenance.

29.20 Applications. Areas in which transaction processing may be exploited are:-

    a. Airline booking systems.

    b. Data retrieval systems used by the Police, fire services and hospitals.

    c. Systems used in the control of processes such as automated processes and production control in factories.

    Airline booking is described in further detail in order to give a clearer practical picture of real-time applications.

29.21 Airline booking system. Records of seat availability on all its planes will be kept by an airline on a central computer. The computer is linked via terminals to a world-wide system of agents. Each agent can gain access to the flight records and within seconds make a reservation in respect of a particular flight. This reservation is recorded *immediately* so that the next enquiry for that flight (following even microseconds after the previous reservation) finds that particular seat or seats reserved. Notice the computer records reflect an accurate picture of the airline's seating load at all times because there is no time lag worth mentioning. The computer would then output information for the production of the customer's ticket and flight instructions, on confirmation of the booking by the customer.

29.22 System requirements. Large transaction processing systems require large quantities of hardware to support them eg. large and fast main and backing storage plus efficient communications equipment. They also need sophisticated operating systems able to support a reliable and secure system with good response times.

29.23 Such systems prove very costly and cannot often be justified, although they have become more popular in recent years because of reductions in hardware costs.

OTHER INTERACTIVE APPLICATIONS

29.24 There are many different kinds of interactive on-line applications in use today. Many small computer systems operate in this manner although delays may be experienced because of the limits to the speed of operation.

SUMMARY

29.25 a. Most of this chapter has been devoted to a simplified interactive multi-user stock control system.

    b. File updating, maintenance and interrogation were discussed.

    c. A "menu driven" system was discussed.

    d. General characteristics of interactive systems were discussed.

    e. Transaction processing systems were introduced.

POINTS TO NOTE

29.26 a. There are many possible types of interactive systems. The examples given in this chapter are intended to contrast the differences between batch processing and interactive systems rather than to give a comprehensive set of examples of interactive systems.

b. An "on-line batch processing system" with fast turn around time may have a performance comparable to a slow interactive system. The "on-line" part of such a system is the data entry and job submission.

QUESTIONS A *(With answers)*

1. *What facilities does interactive processing give which are not available by batch processing?*

2. *What is a "menu driven system"?*

3. *Give four characteristics of interactive on-line systems.*

QUESTIONS B *(Without answers)*

1. *The reader is advised to work through his or her own version of the practical exercise given in this chapter.*

30 Control and Manufacturing

INTRODUCTION

30.1   In this chapter we look at how computers may be used to control things and how this ability can be used in manufacturing. The basic ideas will be introduced by a series of simplified examples based upon applications which the reader should already have general knowledge of. However, the use of computers for the activities described include very many other applications than those described here. Indeed, the scope for this kind of computer use is very broad indeed. The reason for not taking the topic any further is that the subject matter can require technical knowledge which is too advanced for this level of study.

30.2   We start the chapter by looking at a simplified example of how a microcomputer could be used to control a simple automatic washing machine. Although the example is greatly simplified and deliberately avoids a number of technical issues it is based upon something that does happen in practice. There are washing machines for sale today which are controlled by microcomputers and there is an increasing number of electrical products controlled in this way.

THE WASHING MACHINE

30.3   In fig 30.1 you can see a diagram of an automatic washing machine. At first sight it may look rather complicated but if you spend a few minutes looking at it carefully you will find that really it is not.

30.4   The washing machine has the usual drum into which clothes can be placed via the glass door at the front. From the back we can see that the drum can be rotated by a drive belt running from the electric motor to the drum. Clean water can enter the drum via a pipe. The flow of this water is regulated by an inlet valve which can be on, to let the water in, or off. Waste water can be pumped out through another pipe. The pump can either be on, to pump out water, or off. There is an electric heater inside the drum which is used to heat the water. Again, this heater can either be on or off. There are two water level detectors fitted inside the drum which is used to heat the water. The one at the bottom detects when the drum is empty and the one near the top detects when the drum is sufficiently full. The detectors switch on when the water level inside the drum rises above them and switch off if the water level falls below them. There is an electric thermometer towards the bottom of the drum which can be used to detect how cold or hot the water is. It is only a simple thermometer and is only able to distinguish between four temperature bands: cold, warm, very warm and hot. The electric motor control box is able to switch the motor to one of these four states: off, slow speed, slow spin speed and fast spin speed. The control panel at the front of the washing machine has seven buttons to start machine washes. There is one button for each of seven separate types of wash.

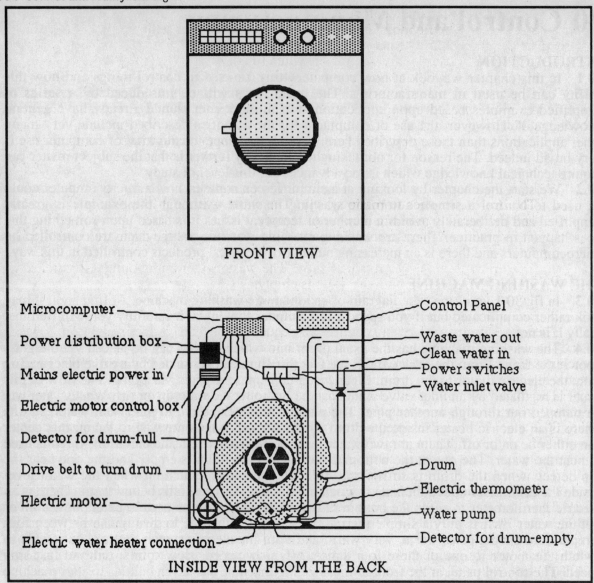

FRONT VIEW

Microcomputer

Power distribution box

Mains electric power in

Electric motor control box

Detector for drum-full

Drive belt to turn drum

Electric motor

Electric water heater connection

Control Panel

Waste water out

Clean water in

Power switches

Water inlet valve

Drum

Electric thermometer

Water pump

Detector for drum-empty

INSIDE VIEW FROM THE BACK

Figure 30.1.

30.5   The microcomputer has a program in ROM memory which it uses to control the washing machine. As soon as the washing machine is switched on this program begins execution. The input and output devices of this computer are specialised but quite simple:

    a. Inputs to the microcomputer
          i.   Control panel
          ii. Detector for drum-empty
          iii. Detector for drum-fill
          iv. Thermometer reader

  b.   Outputs from the microcomputer
        i.   Electric motor control box switch (one of four settings).
        ii.   Electric heater power switch (on or off)
        iii. Water inlet valve power switch (on or off).
        iv.   Water outlet pump power setting (on or off).

30.6   To illustrate what happens when the washing machine is used we will take as an example the wash provided by pressing button number one (for "hot wash"). The wash proceeds in the following order.

  a.   The drum starts rotating slowly and cold water enters the drum until the drum is full.
  b.   The drum continues to rotate slowly. The heater is switched on and stays on until the water in the drum is hot.
  c.   The drum continues to rotate slowly for fifteen minutes.
  d.   The drum continues to rotate slowly. The waste water out-let pump is switched on and continues to run until the drum is empty.
  f.   The drum continues to rotate slowly. Cold water enters the drum until the drum is full.
  g.   The drum continues to rotate at slow. The waste water outlet pump is switched on and continues to run until the drum is empty.
  h.   The drum rotates at a fast spin speed for two minutes.
  i.   The drum stops and the wash is completed.

30.7   The microcomputer is able to control this sequence of events. It does so by keeping track of the current state of the machine, for which it makes use of its input devices, and by switching things on and off at the right time, for which it makes use of its output devices and an internal clock.

30.8   The following table shows how the input and output data may be represented. We will assume that the computer inputs and outputs data using the binary representations shown in tables 30.2 and 30.3. For example, the microcomputer sends the output 01 to the electric motor control box when it wants the motor to start running at slow speed. It receives the data 11 from the thermometer when the water in the drum is hot.

30.9   The computer program which controls each wash follows a sequence of steps along the lines of those listed in paragraph 30. 6. For example, step (a) would be as outlined in fig 30.4.

30.10 The other stages in the program would be along the same lines as the example just given and therefore there is no need for us to go through the details of the rest of them. You might like to do them as an exercise. For stages involving timekeeping, such as stage (c) you may assume that there is a procedure called WAIT which can be used to time delays, eg. using WAIT (2) for a delay of two minutes.

30.11 By now you should have a good idea of how a computer can be used to control things. All manner of devices can be controlled in a similar way to this. The control of robots would be a relatively simple example.

MANUFACTURING

30.12 We will now turn to the use of computers in manufacturing. There are lots of different ways in which computers can be used in manufacturing. The example given here is intended to highlight a number of these ways.

30.13 A manufacturer of computer equipment has one factory production line dedicated to the manufacture of VDUs. The VDUs made on this line are all basically the same but extra features can be added by placing additional components in the basic model. For example, the basic model only works in black and white but an alternative screen and associated circuits can be included instead to make it a colour model.

30.14 Assembling a VDU is rather like making a kit or Do-It-Yourself product in that it starts with a tray full of components and proceeds in a series of ordered steps until the job is completed. The main difference is that several of the steps require specialist equipment and specially trained staff. Another difference in this case is that rather than have one person assemble a whole VDU, different people work on it at each stage.

30.15 You have probably noticed that in this example the manufacturing process is not totally automated. The VDUs are not made by an army of robots! However, computers are used to control some of the equipment on the production line, using methods not so very different from those used in the washing machine described earlier. Computers are used in other ways too.

30.16 The department responsible for the VDU production line receives orders for its VDU's from other parts of the company. There is a constant demand, so the production line runs every day, but each VDU is made to order. The department uses its own computer to deal with these orders and with the production line. The system works in the following way.

30.17 Orders are fed into the computer when they arrive. These orders specify exactly which models are required and how many of each. In the future the company hopes to have a computer network which allows these orders to be sent electronically.

DEVICE	POSSIBLE STATES	REPRESENTATION IN BINARY
1. Control Panel	No button pressed	000
	Button 1 pressed	001
	Button 2 pressed	010
	Button 3 pressed	011
	Button 4 pressed	100
	Button 5 pressed	101
	Button 6 pressed	110
	Button 7 pressed	111
2. Detector for drum-empty	empty	0
	not-empty	1
3. Detector for drum-full	not full	0
	full	1
4. Thermometer	cold	00
	warm	01
	very warm	10
	hot	11

Figure 30.2. Input Representations.

DEVICE	POSSIBLE STATES	REPRESENTATION IN BINARY
5. Electric motor switch	off slow speed slow spin speed fast spin speed	00 01 10 11
6. Electric heater switch	off on	0 1
7. Water inlet valve	off on	0 1
8. Water outlet pump	off on	0 1

Figure 30.3. Output Data Representations.

```
BEGIN
/** start motor at slow speed */
SEND 1 TO DEVICE 5
/** open water inlet valve **/
SEND 1 TO DEVICE 7
/** Wait for drum to fill **/
REPEAT
    /** check if drum is full **/
    GET Fullstatus FROM DEVICE 3
UNTIL
    /** drum is full **/
    Full Status = 1
/** close water inlet valve **/
SEND 0 TO DEVICE 7
END
```

Note: i.   Program comments are enclosed between /* and */
ii. In SEND and GET statements all data is in decimal
rather than the binary form given in figs 30.2 and 30.3

Figure 30.4. Part of a Control Program.

30.18 The computer is able to determine which components are required for each VDU model from data it has in its files. It feeds these requirements through to an automated stockroom in which components held in boxes are removed from the shelves and placed on special trays. Each tray contains the components for one VDU.

The special device which removes the boxes from the shelves is controlled by computer. It is not actually a robot because it has no control over its own actions but it has two metal arms which can clip onto handles on the boxes and it can move up and down and to and fro across the front of the boxes selecting those that it needs.

30.19 Trays from the automated stockroom are deposited on the front of the production line. Each tray has a label on it, which has been printed by the computer. The label specifies which model VDU is to be produced and contains a list of a number of things which must be checked and signed at various stages along the production line. These checks are used to make sure that the work done at each stage has been completed properly so that when the VDUs arrive at the end of the production line they are all undamaged and in proper working order. If at any stage a VDU is found to be faulty it is removed from the production line to be dealt with separately. We will not go into the details here.

30.20 The label on the tray also contains a bar coded strip. As the tray completes each stage in assembly its code is read on a bar code reader connected to the department's computer. This information enables the computer to keep track of the production process. This information is required by those in charge of the production line. They need to be able to use a computer terminal to gain up to date information of how work is progressing and they also need to be able to get the computer to print out reports containing tables and statistics about what production has taken place.

30.21 At some stages along the production line it is necessary to test the VDU electronically to see that each circuit have been properly fitted. To do this the VDU is connected up to the microcomputer which can carry out a series of tests automatically. The computer not only indicates whether or not the partly assembled VDU has passed the test it also diagnoses the nature of any faults so that they can be corrected.

30.22 When the VDU arrives at the end of the production line it is turned on and run for a number of hours. During this test it is connected to another computer which makes it perform in a variety of ways to test its functions. Some visual checks are done manually.

30.23 Finally, after the very last inspection, the VDU is placed in its box onto which is stuck a label for its destination. This label has a bar coded strip on it which is used in the automated warehouse prior to dispatch.

30.24 The system in the warehouse assembles orders for dispatch in a similar way to the system which assembles the tray of components. The individual boxes are loaded onto shelves as they come off the various production lines. The machine which does this looks rather like an unmanned fork lift truck on rails and is controlled by computer. Once all boxes for an order have arrived in the warehouse the machine removes the required boxes from the shelves, where it placed them previously, and places them in the loading bay connected to the computer. Delivery notes are printed out for each order which is deposited in the loading bay.

30.26 That concludes the description of the manufacturing system. The description was not complete in every detail but it should have given you an idea of how computers can be used in manufacturing. Some of the things mentioned, such as the automated warehouse, can be found in other applications so some aspects of this example are quite general.

30.27 Notice how the computer was used for the following kinds of tasks:

a. Maintaining and providing information, eg. about components and orders.

b. Monitoring events, eg. what stage a VDU had reached.

c. Controlling activities, eg. the production process.

d. Controlling machinery, eg. the warehouse machine.

e. Monitoring and testing, eg. testing VDU circuits.

30.28 The computer was able to give a number of benefits in the manufacturing process. For example, it was able to keep such accurate information and tight control on the stock and production process that the amount of stock which needed to be held could be reduced thus making savings. Also, it reduced labour costs because of the automation, it made savings because it was able to diagnose faults, and it helped to improve quality by aiding the monitoring and control process. Using a computer for things like the automated test equipment also meant that the equipment could continue to be used even if the design of the VDUs changes because the computer could be reprogrammed with new tests.

30.29 Of course the computer does not provide all the answers. Automation of production seldom pays off unless the numbers of things being manufactured are quite large and what is being produced is fairly standard. The computer can also create problems, particularly if automation leads to job losses. This point will be discussed in a later chapter. However, it should be noted that computers can do relatively few jobs which humans can do, only the repetitive and boring ones in fact, and therefore they pose little threat to jobs provided we have a society which finds appropriate ways of employing people. The computer industry is also a source of many jobs.

SUMMARY

30.30 a. The use of a computer to control things was illustrated by an example of an automatic washing machine.

b. Some of the uses of computers in manufacturing were illustrated by an example based upon a production line on which VDUs were made.

c. The computer is very well suited to monitor and control mechanised processes in which the same or very similar tasks are done repeatedly many times and where the decision making necessary is easy to reduce to simple rules.

POINTS TO NOTE

30.31 Both examples in this chapter are simplified versions of what actually takes place in practice. You are advised to gain first hand experience of real computer applications of this kind if you possibly can.

QUESTIONS A *(With answers in appendix 2)*

1. A computerised petrol pump has four buttons for selecting the grade of petrol. Suggest a suitable way of representing these four grades as input data to the computer controlling the pump.

2. In what ways can computers be used in manufacturing?

3. Write a control program like the one in fig 30.4 to deal with stages c and d of paragraph 30.6.

QUESTIONS B *(Without answers)*

1. What advantages are there in using computers to test equipment such as electronic circuit boards?

ASSIGNMENTS

1. Gather information about computerised domestic products and summarise your findings.

2. Complete the program outlined in paragraph 30.6.

31 The development of applications

INTRODUCTION
31.1 This chapter takes an introductory look at some of the methods associated with developing computer applications with the emphasis on stages which take place *before* programs are written. Later, in chapter 32, these methods will be put into the context of the organisation. The reader is not expected to master the methods introduced here but should have no trouble being able to follow the notation used.

METHODOLOGIES
31.2 As should already be clear to the reader from the earlier discussions about programming, the development of computer applications needs to be carried out in a methodical way. Just as programming needs suitable notations (eg pseudocode) applications development also requires the right notations for representing such things as designs or specifications. The work is also made easier by the use of computerised "tools", just as programming is aided by tools such as editors. If all these elements are present and work together as a whole then the developer may be said to be using a **methodology** for systems development. In short, a **development methodology** is **an orderly and integrated collection of various methods, tools and notations used for systems or applications development.**

STRUCTURED METHODS
31.3 Many of the modern techniques of systems development not only use new notations, often in the form of specialist chart, they also fit together into a overall methodology. For this reason, these modern methodologies are also sometimes called "**structured methods**". The term structured is borrowed from "structured programming", partly because this give the desired impression, but also because they do genuinely impose a *structure* on the design.

BASIC PRINCIPLES
31.4 Although it is very important to be familiar with the latest methods, and to be able to use them properly, it must also be recognised that most methods become dated eventually. Therefore, it is important to recognise any basic principles which apply whatever the method. In fact, there must be dozens of principles which apply to the process of systems development.
31.5 Here are some important ones expressed as a set of recommendations.
  - a. Make sure you understand the problem.
  - b. Fully identify the requirements and get them agreed by the client.
  - c. Clearly document all work as you do it.
  - d. Have all work checked to an agreed standard of quality at every stage.
  - e. Be systematic.
  - f. Be creative but make sure it works.
  - g. Allow for future changes.
  - h. Make sure that all users find the system usable.
  - i. Break the problem down into manageable tasks and carry them out in a planned and methodical way.
  - j. Make sure that the final system is all there, in full working order and does what it's supposed to do, **before** you say it's ready.

The reader should see that these principles can be applied to programming. The important point to recognise is that they apply to the whole development process not just programming.

PROPRIETARY METHODOLOGIES
31.6 A considerable number of methodologies are in use today and, although many are described in specialist texts generally available to the public, they are mostly sold as products comprising manuals, specialist training, consultancy services and automated aids. Among the better-known methodologies are:

- a. Structured Analysis and Design by Yourdon.
- b. Structured Systems Analysis by Gane and Sarson.
- c. Information Engineering from James Martin.
- d. Jackson Systems Development (JSD) by Michael Jackson.
- e. SSADM, originally produced by LBMS for the CCTA.

31.7 It is **not** the purpose of this text to describe any one of these methodologies in any detail. Each methodology has its own overall method within which the various activities fit. All of the methods make use of **charting techniques** whereby particular properties of the system are represented diagrammatically using an appropriate convention. It is some of these conventions which give rise to the term "structured".

31.8 An introduction to some of the more familiar techniques follows.

DATA MODELS
31.8 A **data model** is a representation of the properties of the data within an existing or proposed system. The complete process of constructing a data model from scratch is called **data analysis**.

31.9 **EAR models.** The EAR model is one of the most common and successful types of data model around. Its basic elements are called **Entities, Attributes** and **Relationships**, hence the name EAR model, or occasionally ER model.

31.10 This is what these elements are:

- a. **Entity.** An entity is anything about which data is to be stored. For example, if the system needs to store data about customers or products then the model would have customer or product entities.
  Note. Although the definition is stated in terms of what must be stored, in fact it is retrieval of the data which is the fundamental requirement.
- b. **Attributes.** The attributes of an entity are those facts which need to be stored about the entity. For example, the attributes of a customer might include the account number, name, address and credit limit.
- c. **Relationships.** Relationships exist between various entities within a system. For example, there may be a relationship between the customer and an order.

31.11 Various rules govern how a data model must be constructed, they are all based upon common sense ideas, although you might not think so sometimes when they are expressed in unnecessarily complicated ways. For example, each occurrence of an entity, such as each individual customer, must be uniquely identifiable by means of a key comprising one or more attributes. The customer's full name or account number might serve as a key, for example. Other attributes (non-key attributes) may be regarded as facts about what the key stands for (eg, facts about the customer). So given the key, other facts relating to the key can be obtained. For each entity in the final model every non-key attribute must be a fact about *the key, the whole key and nothing but the key*. Although these rules are straightforward it does take some time to master the methods associated with them. Again, the reader is reminded that it is not necessary to study this material in detail at this level.

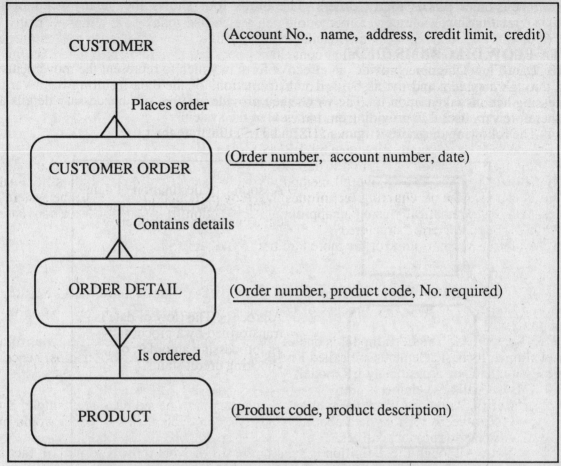

Figure 31.1 A EAR Data Model of an Ordering System.

31.12 To round off this description of data models here is a diagram of a simple EAR model concerning customers making orders for products (figure 31.1). In the diagram:

a. Entities are represented by round-cornered boxes.

b. Attributes are listed beside the entities. For example, the CUSTOMER entity has the attributes listed as
  "Account No. , name, address, credit limit, credit"
  and the CUSTOMER ORDER entity has the attributes listed as
  "Order number, account number, date"

c. Keys are underlined. Note that the "order detail" entity has a **composite key** , ie, a key formed from more than one attribute. The "customer order entity" would require the composite key "Order number, account number" if the same order number could be assigned to more than one customer. In other words the key must be a unique identifier, as indicated earlier.

d. Relationships are represented by lines between entities. The "birds' feet" at the end of the arrows are used to show the **degree** of the relationship. In the example, **one** customer places **many** orders. The bird's foot shows the "many" end of the relationship.

DATA-FLOW DIAGRAMS (DFDs)

31.13 Data-Flow Diagrams provide an effective form in which to represent the movements of data through a system and the associated transformations of the data resulting from various processing actions taken upon it. The views they provide are free of unnecessary details and are therefore very useful in providing an overview of the system.

31.14 The following diagrams (figures 31.2 and 31.3) illustrate their use.

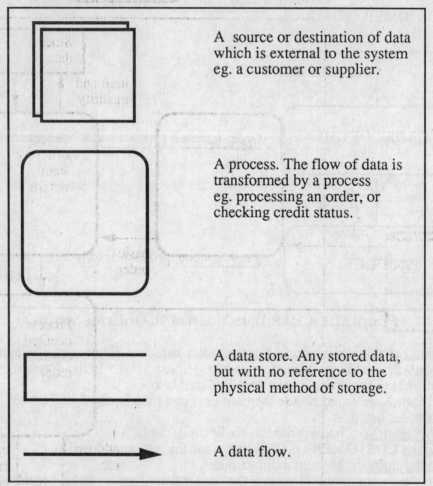

A source or destination of data which is external to the system eg. a customer or supplier.

A process. The flow of data is transformed by a process eg. processing an order, or checking credit status.

A data store. Any stored data, but with no reference to the physical method of storage.

A data flow.

Figure 31.2. Data-Flow Diagram Symbols

Figure 31..3. A Data-Flow Diagram of an Order Processing System.
FOLLOWS ON THE NEXT PAGE

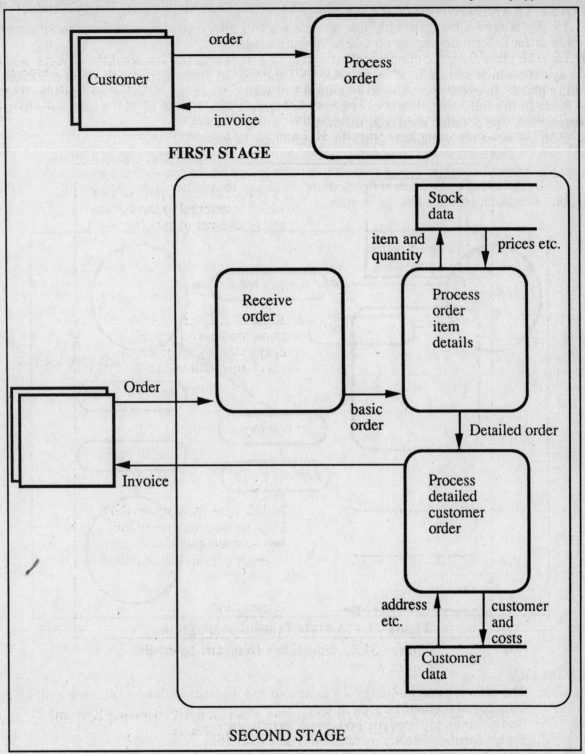

FIRST STAGE

SECOND STAGE

457

STATE TRANSITION DIAGRAMS

31.15 By way of a contrast with data models we will now consider state transition diagrams which differ in form depending on where they are used.

31.16 The ideas are quite simple and effective. It is first necessary to identify **objects** within the system which can each be in any one of a number of states depending upon the **events** taking place. An event gives rise to an **action** , or series of actions, which may cause a change of state. In the following simple example the operation of a simple object, a conveyor belt, is represented. The notation used is as follows.

   a. Circles represent states that the system may be in.

   b. Labelled arrowed lines from states signify events which give rise to actions.

   c. Round-cornered boxes represent actions to be taken when events happen.

   d. Arrowed lines from actions show a change to another state, or possibly a further action to be taken before a change in state.

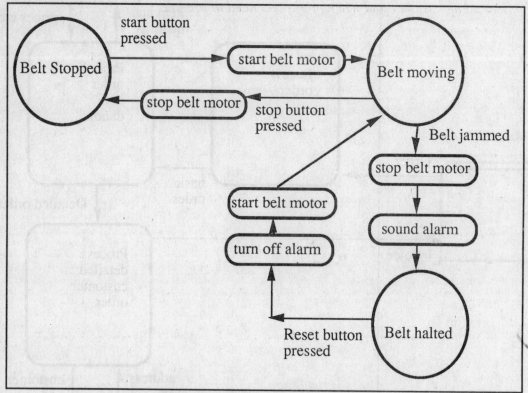

Figure 31.4 A State Transition Diagram.

SUMMARY

31.17 a. The idea of a **methodology** was introduced together with an explanation of what a **structured method** is.

   b. Some commonly used methods were introduced:

   i. Entity-Attribute-Relationship (EAR) data modelling.

   ii. The use of data-flow diagrams (DFDs).
   iii. The use of state transition diagrams.

POINTS TO NOTE

31.18 a.   Methods have been developed greatly over recent years. It is not necessary for you to learn these methods but you should be aware of their importance in improving the quality and effectiveness of applications and systems development.

QUESTIONS A *(With answers in appendix 2)*

1.   *What is a methodology?*

QUESTIONS B *(Without answers)*

1.   *What is a composite key and when might you need to use one.*

COMPUTERS IN PERSPECTIVE

1. In the introduction to the first Part of this book Computer Studies was described as a subject which deals with the features of computers and the ways and methods of using computers, so as to provide a basis for understanding the impact of computers on individuals, organisations and society. Having read this far the reader should be able to judge to what extent this introductory text has so far provided the expected information.

2. The final three chapters take a rather broader view of the subject than has been covered in previous chapters and place a greater emphasis on individuals, organisations and society.

3. Chapter 32 considers the ways computers are used within organisations. In particular, it looks at computer related jobs.

4. Chapter 33 takes an historical view of the subject and pays attention to the people and their ideas and innovations.

5. Chapter 34 considers social and economic matters including the economic and social effects of automation and issues such as data protection.

32 Computers in the Organisation

INTRODUCTION

32.1   All organisations have aims which they endeavour to achieve eg. making a profit or providing a service. To meet their aims organisations must use their resources effectively. These resources include people, equipment, money, buildings and information. Resources are only used effectively if they are properly managed and controlled.

32.2   This chapter looks at the way computer systems are developed in order to meet the needs of organisations. The chapter also looks at the ways in which computer staff and computer systems are managed and controlled.

SYSTEM LIFE CYCLE

32.3   New computer systems frequently replace existing manual systems. The process of replacing the old system by the new, happens in a series of stages, and the whole process is called the "**system life cycle**".

32.4   In outline the stages in the system life cycle are as follows:

a. **Preliminary survey.**

b. **Feasibility Study.** An initial study conducted by a team who produce a report of their findings .

c. **Investigation and fact recording.** Assuming that management decides to continue in the light of the feasibility study, a detailed study is conducted. The purpose of this study is fully to understand the existing system and to identify the information requirements.

d. **Analysis.** At this stage the results of the investigation are studied. This is part of a "**top-down**" process of analysis and design. The general flow of data and the information requirements are identified. The aim is to achieve *far more* than just converting every detail of the existing system into a computerised version. The analysis should make full use of the details of the investigation to produce a full analysis of the existing system. The result of this analysis will be a clear picture of the user's requirements and the basic function of the system. The analysis is done in a step by step fashion and by starting at a high level of generalisation no feasible alternative should be excluded. At the end of this study a report is produced which presents possible alternative systems which may be designed. For example a manual stock control system may be investigated and various alternative computerised versions suggested. One version may be selected for design and development.

e. **Design.** After all interested parties have been consulted a detailed design of the system is produced. The results of this design stage will be a **System Specification**. The system specification will include details of:

    i.   Documents produced earlier in the life cycle process

    ii. A statement of what the new system is supposed to do and what benefits it will provide.

    iii. A system description and specification (Hardware and Software).

    iv. Specifications of all details required by programmers and those developing any manual parts of the system ie.

        A. Data descriptions.

        B. Input/Output specifications

        C. Document specifications

    D. Storage specifications (eg. File design).

    E. Procedure specifications.

   v. Details of how the design is to be implemented ie:

    A. When the change over will happen

    B. How the change over will happen

   vi. Details of the users of the system.

 f. **Implementation.** This will follow the methods set out in the design. Activities included in this stage are:-

    A. Programming and testing

    B. Staff training

    C. Changing files and documents from the old system to the new.

The change over is usually done in parallel if possible ie. continuing to run the old system for a while when the new system is introduced so that the new system is fully operational before it has to be relied upon.

 g. **Review.** Once a system is implemented and in full operation it is examined to see if it has   met the objectives set out in the original specification. Unforeseen problems will need to be overcome. From time to time the requirements of the organisation will change and the systems will have to be examined to see if it can cope with the changes.

SYSTEMS ANALYSIS AND DESIGN (SAD)

32.5 The work associated with the various stages of the system life cycle is known as **Systems Analysis and Design (SAD)** or just simply **Systems Analysis.**

32.6 Systems analysis may be defined as the methods of determining how best to use computers, with other resources, to perform specific tasks.

32.7 A person engaged in Systems Analysis is called a "System Analyst". This title is rather misleading because a Systems Analyst does far more than just "analysing". Indeed the variety of skills and expertise required for Systems Analysis means that normally a team of analysts with differing expert knowledge work together on each project.

THE ORGANISATION OF COMPUTER DEPARTMENTS

32.8 The development maintenance and use of computer systems involve a number of different specialist staff. Already in this chapter the work of managers, analysts and programmers has been mentioned. Computer departments have to be properly organised in order to work efficiently. Figure 32.1 shows the organisation of a typical computer department, such a diagram is an example of an **"organisation chart".**

THE WORK OF COMPUTER STAFF

32.9 The following details should be read with reference to figure 32.1

32.10 Computer Manager. (Data Processing Manager in Commercial Organisations) The Computer Manager has overall responsibility for the computer department. He must ensure that the computer installation runs efficiently in satisfying the computing needs of the organisation which it serves.

32.11 Systems Analyst. (See paragraph 32.7). His or her main jobs are:-

 a. To examine the feasibility of potential computer applications.

 b. Analysis of existing systems with a view to their application to a computer

 c. Design of computer-based systems, their implementation, and review.

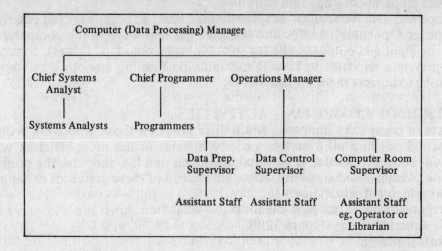

Figure 32.1. The Organisation of a Typical Computer Department.

32.12 It is very likely that systems analysts would work in project teams with a senior analyst in charge.

32.13 The chief systems analyst will work very closely with his counterparts in other sections and the computer manager, and will assist in forward planning and overall project control.

32.14 Programmers. Following the design process the job of programming begins. The programmer:-

    a. Encodes the procedures detailed by the analyst in a language suitable for the specified computer.

    b. Will liaise very closely with the analyst and the user to ensure logical correctness of programs.

32.15 Specialisation. In a large computer department programmers might specialise in certain areas of programming. These may be:-

    a. **Applications.** Applications programmers are the people who write the initial programs for each application.

    b. **Maintenance.** Once the programs written by the Applications programmer are operational they are handed over to a Maintenance programmer, whose job it will be to carry out any amendments or improvements that may be necessary. The applications programmer then moves on to fresh fields.

    c. **Systems software.** This programmer will specialise in writing "non-application" programs ie. systems software. These programs will supplement those supplied by the manufacturer.

32.16 In smaller installations, of course, a smaller team of programmers will have to turn their hands to any task that comes along.

32.17 Operations Manager. He or she is responsible to the Computer Manager for operation of the computer and ancillary equipment. Also under his control will be:-

    a. Data control section - dealing with manual control of documents used with the computer.

    b. Data preparation. - eg. data entry .

    c. Tape and disk library/ies - off-line storage must be organised and controlled.

32.18 Computer Operator handles and operates the hardware in the computer room. He or she handles the input and output media (eg. placing tapes onto tape drives), communicates with the operating system and tries to keep the installation running smoothly by stepping in when things go wrong to correct them immediately.

THE CONTROL OF COMPUTING ACTIVITIES

32.19 The use of computers imposes certain disciplines on those who work with them. Work has to be carried out in a uniform and orderly manner in the most efficient way. Staff and equipment will be well regarded if work is completed quickly and with the minimum of error or interruption. Well defined standards allow the control of these activities to happen naturally.

32.20 Factors which aid control are:-

    a. **Organisation.** ie. all staff should know what their duties are and where they fit in the general picture (Figure 32.1).

    b. **Staff training.**

    c. **Supervision and working to plans.**

    d. **The use of documentation** to guide and assist work.

    e. **Clear procedures** for individuals to follow.

DATA SECURITY

32.21 One important aspect of control is the control of data to prevent its loss, misuse or disclosure. This type of control is called "data security".

32.22 Data security is the protection of data. In some situations data security will be concerned with preventing the loss of data eg. in the file security method used during updates. In other situations data security will be concerned with preventing the misuse or unwanted modification of data eg. due to access by unauthorised persons. A third situation is the prevention of disclosure of data to unauthorised persons eg. where the data is important to national security.

32.23 Various measures can be taken to ensure all three types of security. Here are some common methods.

    a. The use of back up copies of tapes or disks eg. in conjunction with generations of files.

    b. Physical prevention eg.

        i. Write permit rings and similar devices.

        ii. Restricting the access of personnel.

        iii. Keeping data under lock and key.

    c. The use of passwords to prevent unauthorised use of computer terminals or unauthorised   access to on-line files.

    d. Constant checks of security.

32.24 People often demand higher standards of security from computer systems than they demand from manual systems. The reader might consider which is most secure, a folder of printed documents or a floppy disk holding the same information. A floppy disk can easily be damaged by dust or scratches so that its data is lost. On the other hand specialist equipment and software will be needed to read its data, thus the data is more secure from those not trained in its use.

SUMMARY

32.25 a. The system life cycle was described:-

       i. Preliminary survey.

      ii. Feasibility study.

     iii. Investigation and fact recording.

     iv. Analysis

      v. Design

     vi. Implementation

    vii. Review

  b. Systems Analysis and Design (SAD) was discussed.

  c. The organisation of a computer department was described and the work of its staff was explained:

       i. Computer Manager.

      ii. Systems Analysts

     iii. Programmers

     iv. Operations Manager

      v. Operators

  d. The control of computing activities was discussed.

  e. Data Security was defined and ways of achieving data security were described.

POINTS TO NOTE

32.26 a. Computer systems can only give good service if they are properly developed and then managed and controlled correctly. When these points are ignored all manner of silly and serious system faults can occur.

QUESTIONS A *(With answers)*

1. List the stages in the system life cycle.

2. Define "Systems Analysis"

3. Draw an organisation chart for a typical computer department. What difference in computer staffing would you expect to find in a small organisation.

4. Describe the work of a computer operator.

5. Describe the work of a systems analyst.

6. Name four factors which aid the control of computer activities.

7. Define "Data security".
Identify three different types of data security.

8. Give three basic methods of ensuring the data security of a computer system.

9. A GP is considering putting his patients' records onto a small computer system but is concerned about the security of the data which would contain confidential information.

Briefly outline the points you would make to reassure him on this matter.

QUESTIONS B *(Without answers)*

1. *Why is thorough investigations, fact recording and analysis so important in systems analysis and design? What dangers are there in attempting to design a system before the analysis is complete?*

2. *A **small** firm uses a microcomputer based system, with keyboard, VDU, dual floppy disks and matrix printer, to handle a small stock control system. A master file is updated and used for enquiries and reports everyday. The file fits onto one floppy disk.*

   What security precautions would you advise the firm to adopt for this system?
   What computer staff would you expect them to have?

33 The Origins of Modern Computers

INTRODUCTION

33.1   The manager of a modern computerised warehouse has only to press a few keys on a computer's VDU to see displayed in front of him the details of how many items he has in stock. The herdsman of ancient times had only to place his hand into a pocket and draw out a handful of pebbles to know how many sheep he had: one for each pebble.

These two examples lie at opposite ends of the history of computer technology. It is the story of the application of changing technology to the increasingly sophisticated methods used in activities such as record keeping and calculating. There are several interwoven strands to the story which begins with early methods of counting and recording numbers. This chapter tells that story.

EARLY DEVICES AND METHODS

33.2   The concepts of number and counting are believed to have been developed first by the herdsmen of ancient times, who sought methods to avoid animal losses. For example, every morning as the sheep left the fold the herdsman would drop one pebble into his pocket as each sheep passed out of the fold gate. On the animals' return in the evening they could all be accounted for by reversing the process until no pebbles were left in the pocket. Each pebble left in the pocket represented a lost sheep and action could be taken to find the animal.

These simple methods were later used to count other possessions, and alternatives to pebbles such as sticks or scratches on stone were employed. The latter may well have led the way to the idea of using stylized pictures or symbols to represent objects and numbers so that simple inventories could be kept.

These symbolic representations preceded the use of symbols for written language, which through the developments of engraved stones, papyrus, scrolls, modern letter symbols, paper, manuscripts, the printing press, books, the typewriter etc. have led to the major libraries and paper filing systems for information storage and retrieval. The long reign of paper as the primary medium for information storage may be nearing its end as the realm of computer applications extends. A catch phrase for the next generation of computerised offices is "paperless office".

Returning for a moment to the simple methods of counting using pebbles, sticks etc., it is helpful to consider the use of counting on the fingers. A "digit" is a finger or toe, and counting on one's fingers is a "digital operation". The term "digital operation" has been extended to cover any operation on distinct values which is carried out in steps eg. Switch lights on is a digital operation, operating a radio's volume control is not. The vast majority of computers in use today are "**electronic digital computers**" and as their name suggests they carry out their work by performing high speed digital operations on data. The first electronic digital computers were built in the mid 1940s, their fore runners were a number of digital devices of which the **abacus**, itself the successor of counting with pebbles, was the earliest.

THE DEVELOPMENT OF CALCULATING DEVICES

33.3   **The Abacus** is a mechanised pebble counter which has been in use in a variety of forms over the last 2,000 years or so, and is still in use today in parts of Asia. Beads are strung on wires or strings held in a frame. The beads are slid along the wires when counting, adding etc. A very simple form is shown in Figure 33.1. which has separate bead columns for the units, tens, hundreds etc.

A Simple Abacus

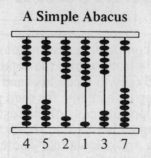

Figure 33.1.

33.4   Napier's Bones. John Napier a Scottish mathematician did a considerable amount of work on aids to calculation, the most notable of which was the invention of logarithms in 1614. He also devised a set of rods for use as multiplication aids. These rods were carved from bone and are often called "Napier's Bones". You can easily make a set for yourself by copying the multiplication tables onto cards as shown in Figure 33.2 which also shows how to use the rods once you have cut them out.

33.5   The Slide Rule. In 1620, just six years after the invention of logarithms, **William Oughtred** invented the slide rule, which is a calculating device which uses the principles of logarithms. A simple slide rule consists of two graduated scales, one of which slips upon the other. The scales are devised so that suitable alignment of one scale against the other makes it possible to obtain products, quotients or other functions by inspection. See Figure 33.3.

The slide rule is an example of an **analog** device, which is unlike a digital device in that readings can be taken in a smooth continuous scan along the scale, instead of stepping along a set of distinct values.

33.6   Pascal's Arithmetic Machine. In 1642 Blaise Pascal, a French mathematician devised the first true calculating machine, reputedly to help his father who was a tax collector! Numbers were entered by dialling a series of numbered wheels, and a series of toothed wheels transferred the movements to a results dial. A ratchet "carry" mechanism was incorporated. Addition and subtraction were straightforward. The method of subtraction used "number complements" an important method used in electronic computers. Number complements will be dealt with later. Pascal's machine could only perform multiplication by repeated addition, and division by repeated subtraction. Despite these limitations the machine established the practicability of calculating machines and paved the way for further developments. In the late 1960's a new computer programming language was developed by Professor **Niklaus Wirth** in Zurich, and was named PASCAL in recognition of Pascal's contribution to computing.

33.7   Leibniz' Calculating Machine. In 1671 **Gottifried von Leibniz,** a German Mathematician, invented a calculating machine which was able to perform true multiplication and division. He wrote "It is unworthy of excellent men to lose hours like slaves in the labour of calculation ....", a statement which would no doubt endear him to many Maths pupils. Leibniz' machine depended on the same principles of intermeshed toothed wheels used by Pascal, but incorporated an important new feature, a series of sliders forming a **shift** mechanism. The shift mechanism mimics the actions in manual multiplication and division where one works in stages moving from column to column. The move left or right is a shift. One version of Leibniz' machine was produced, but at that time sufficient accuracy in manufacture was not possible to achieve a reliable product.

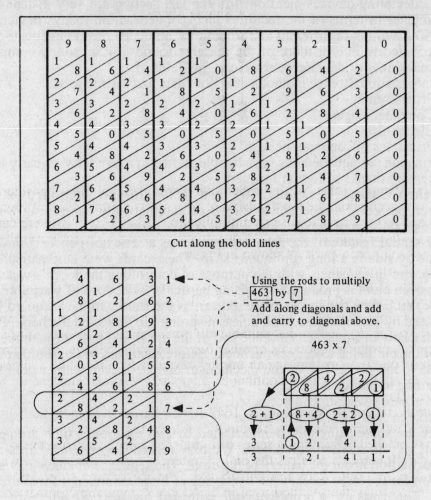

Figure 33.2. Napier's Bones.

A SECTION OF A SIMPLE SLIDE RULE

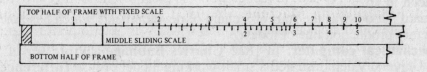

The middle scale has been positioned with the "1" against the "2" of the top scale so that multiples of 2 can be read off along the scale. Alternatively the scale shows divisions giving quotients of 2.

Figure 33.3.

FROM MECHANICAL CALCULATORS TO MODERN ELECTRONIC DESIGN

33.8 The calculating devices mentioned in the last section are very distant ancestors of the modern computer in terms of the facilities incorporated within todays devices. In the period 1800 to 1950 a number of different and sometimes unrelated developments took place each of which contributed to one or more of the features found in almost any computer built since 1950. The main areas of development were in the fields of:-

a. Information Storage methods - for both data and instructions.

b. Programming

c. Computer Logic.

d. Electronics

e. Principles of computer design.

Information storage methods for example started to move forward early in the nineteenth century thanks to Joseph Jacquard.

33.9 Punched Cards. Between 1802 and 1804 **Joseph Jacquard** a French textile manufacturer, perfected a mechanical means of automatically controlling weaving looms to facilitate the production of woven cloth with complex patterns.

An essential feature of the Jacquard loom was a series of punched cards strung tightly together side by side in a long continuous strip. These cards were automatically fed through a loom mechanism in sequence, with the purpose of controlling the loom's weaving action. The pattern in woven cloth is produced by raising particular selections of warp threads (those fixed to the frame) each time the shuttle is passed across the frame. In the Jacquard loom each warp could be raised by an individual hook unless a sprung pin deflected the hook. If the sprung pin aligned with a hole in a punched card one end of the pin would pass through the hole so that the other end of the pin failed to deflect the hook. Before each pass of the shuttle the next card was moved close to the pins. Then as the mechanism operated, each warp would be raised or not raised according to the rule:-

Hole in card - warp thread not raised.

No hole in card - warp thread raised.

There are some principles demonstrated by this example which are applied in a very fundamental way in modern computers. We may regard the punched cards as a **media for storing information** about the pattern of the cloth. The sequence of cards may also be regarded as a **program** for the loom mechanism consisting of **instructions in a form directly usable by a machine.** The cards use a primitive code with *just two possible alternative:* Hole = Warp thread not raised and No hold = Warp thread raised. This is an example of **binary** coding, which is used extensively in modern computers. Binary means two numbered just as Bicycle means two wheeled cycle.

The first person known to have used binary codes for number representations was **Francis Bacon** in 1623.

Jacquard's loom was the start of a chain of developments which has reached to the robot operated factory production line of today.

33.10 A mechanical computer. In 1822 **Charles Babbage** a Professor of Mathematics at Cambridge University demonstrated a small working model of his "**Difference Engine**" to the Royal Society. The demonstration won government backing for Babbage who wished to produce a larger machine able to generate reliable astronomical and mathematical tables containing values accurate to 20 decimal places. The machine was never completed because of mechanical difficulties. However, Babbage's researches led him to develop the concept of an "**Analytic Engine**", essentially a general purpose automatic calculator, which he designed in

1834. Its design owed much to Jacquard's invention and incorporated many features present in modern computers:-

 a. Data and program instructions fed in via a device using a suitable medium (punched cards).
 b. Storage facilities for data and instructions.
 c. A mechanised unit for calculation - a "mill"
 d. A suitable output device.

Lady Ada Lovelace, an amateur mathematician and friend of Babbage produced supporting material for the analytic engine in the form of programs and explanatory documentation. One programming language "ADA" was named after her.

33.11 Computer Logic. An important theoretical development occurred between 1847 and 1854 as **George Boole,** an English Logician, devised an algebraic system, now called "Boolean Algebra", for representing and manipulating logical expressions. The full significance of these developments was not realised at the time. Boole's work applied to those kinds of problems where there are statements and answers which can be one of either TRUE or FALSE. It was the binary nature of these true/false problems which made the link with computer developments.

33.12 Hermann Hollerith. Dr. Hermann Hollerith was a census statistician at the U.S. census bureau in the mid 1880's. At that time the bureau was still trying to count results from the 1880 census and saw little prospect of completing the count before the next census which was scheduled for 1890. Hollerith proposed a mechanised solution to the problem which was based upon equipment handling punched cards. His idea was to 'code' the data by representing it by punched hole combinations on the cards. Some equipment was used to punch holes in the card. Other equipment was able to process the data by detecting holes in the cards. Electrical contacts brushed the cards and made through holes in the cards as the cards passed through the device. These devices were called tabulators. Tabulators were also used for the semi-automatic selection and sorting of cards.

The impact of Hollerith's methods was very striking. Whereas the census of 1880 on 50 million citizens had taken over 7 years to complete, the census of 1890 on 63 million citizens took only 3 years to complete.

These ideas were exploited further by the development of devices rather like difference engines fed with cards which could perform calculations like those desired by Babbage. Other developments continued in the commercial application of these machines.

Hollerith set up his own company, "The Computing Tabulating REcording Company" which later became the International Business Machine Corporation (**IBM**) which today is by far the largest computer manufacturer in the world.

33.13 Recording Devices, Valves & Switching Circuits. In 1900 **Valdemar Poulson** was developing recording devices which used media consisting of tapes and drums coated with thin films of magnetic material. These were the fore runners of a host of recorders, Video cassette recorders, and of particular interest, computer data storage devices, including several versions also using magnetic tape. An even more significant technological advance took place in 1906 when **Lee de Forest** invented the **thermionic valve.** A valve resembles a squat cylindrical light bulb glowing dimly, into which has been inserted a number of additional wires and metallic plates. Valves are able to amplify or switch electrical signals electronically ie. without the movement of electrical or mechanical parts. **Electronic Switching** is a vital feature within modern digital computers, and valves were the first devices to be employed for that purpose. Valves have since been superseded by newer and better alternatives.

33.14 The use of Electronic Switching Circuits in computers is largely due to the fact that such circuits can be employed to perform logic and arithmetic. This fact was established in 1938 by **Claude Shannon,** an electrical engineer. Shannon showed how the hitherto theoretical Boolean Algebra could be applied to practical problems of circuit design.

33.15 Another important theoretical step took place one year before Shannon's discovery when in 1937 **Alan Turing,** a British Mathematician, showed how *any* problem having a logical solution can be reduced to a solution based upon a small set of simple instructions. Modern computers are therefore able to solve very complex problems by the rapid application of a relatively small set of inbuilt operations.

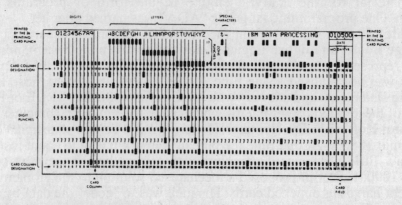

Courtesy of IBM

Note. Each character is represented by holes punched in a column of the card. Note that:-

a. Numeric 'digits' have one hold punched.
b. Alphabetic characters have two holes punched. (one "zone" plus one other).
c. Special characters may have one, two or more holes punched.
d. The characters printed across the top of the card make the card "human-sensible" and punched holes also make the card "machine-sensible".

Figure 33.4. A Punched Card.

NB. Punched paper tape was based upon the same basic principles as punched cards.

Figure 33.5. Punched Paper Tape.

33.16 From Electrical Machines to Electronic Machines.

a. **The Automatic Sequence Controlled Calculator (ASCC)** - Also called the **Harvard Mark 1.**

The ASCC was a fully automatic electrically driven machine. Its development was started at Harvard University USA in 1937 by Professor **Howard Aiken** in conjunction with IBM.

Hollerith cards containing data or instructions were fed into the machine a few at a time and results were output onto punched cards or an electric typewriter. Aiken also developed punched paper tape as an input medium. The machine was completed in 1944 and was used until 1959.

b. **Early special purpose electronic machines.**

    i. During the second world war electronic valve based calculating machines called **Z3** and **Z4**, were produced in Germany by **Konrad Zuse.** They are known to have been used for a time in 1941, and to have used stored programs to perform calculations, but they were later destroyed by Allied bombing.

    ii. In Britain at the same time another valve based machine called **COLOSSUS** was produced at the British Intelligence Establishment at Bletchley Park. **Alan Turing** was a member of staff on the project. The machine was used in 1943 to break a top secret German code called ENIGMA.

c. **Electronic Numerical Integrator and Calculator (ENIAC).** This machine was developed by **J Presper Eckert** and **John Mauchly** at Pennsylvania University and was completed by 1946. It was the electronic equivalent of the ASCC and contained some 18,000 valves. It could perform 5000 additions per second, an astonishing feat at the time, but consumed 150 kilowatts of power, which would be enough to heat a mansion, and needed to be water cooled.

33.17 The Von Neumann Report. In what is now an historic report **John Von Neumann** in 1946 set out a summary of the design requirements for the modern computer. The main points were:-

a. Binary codes should be used for the representation of Data and Instructions in a way which would make no distinction between them, [this will be explained later] and allows them to be stored together and share the same storage space within the computer.

b. The computer should be able to process both data and instructions. This includes the modification of programs by programs.

These two principles contain within them the possibilities for the controlled modification and manipulation of data and instructions under one automatic process.

COMPUTER GENERATIONS WITH CHANGING TECHNOLOGY

33.18 The First Generation. The "first generation" computers were valve based machines based upon Von Neumann's design principles. Starting with the first they included:-

a. **Electronic Delay Storage Automatic Computer (EDSAC).** This machine was built at Cambridge University by **M.V. Wilkins** and first ran in May 1949.

b. **Electronic Discrete Variable Automatic Computer (EDVAC).** This machine was built at Pennsylvania University, the home of ENIAC, and was completed in 1950.

c. **Automatic Computer Engine (ACE).** This was built at the National Physics laboratory in 1951.

  d. **Lyons Electronic Office (LEO).** This was the *first commercial computer* and it was produced in 1951 by **M.V. Wilkes.**
  e. **UNIVAC - 1.** This machine was produced by UNIVAC (Universal Accounting Company) in 1951. The company was set up by Eckert and Mauchly.

33.19 The Transistor was invented in 1948 by a team of scientists headed by **William Shockley** at the Bell Laboratories in America. Transistors are made from materials called **semiconductors** principally silicon (the main element in sand and rock), and germanium. A transistor is produced by 'doping' layers of crystal with impurities which drastically alter the electrical properties of each layer (See Appendix IV).

Transistors are able to perform similar operations to valves eg. amplification or switching, but they are simpler to manufacture less prone to failure, cheaper, smaller, consume less power and have a longer life. They have replaced valves in all but a few specialist applications. Transistors and developments from them are often called **solid-state devices.**

Simple transistor circuits called **bistables** (two stable states) or **flip-flops** are of particular importance. They can be built to flip from one state to the other and back again in a clock like fashion, or built to hold either state until switched to the other by a single electrical pulse. These bistable states suggest the possibilities for storing binary coded data. In fact bistable (two-stage) circuits are the basis of the internal binary operation and storage of electronic digital computers.

33.20 The Second Generation. "Second generation" computers used transistors instead of valves. The use of transistors reduced size, manufacturing costs and running cost, and improved reliability and processing power. Early second generation models were the IBM 7000 series and LEO mark III. In 1962 Manchester University completed what was probably the best known second generation machine, the **ATLAS.** ATLAS used **magnetic disc storage** and exploited the features of disc storage very well. Magnetic disks resemble gramophone records. Data is recorded on their surfaces magnetically in invisible concentric rings.

During the second generation manufacturers moved towards making computers of **modular construction.** A suitable combination of processing, storage, input and output units could be assembled from a range of possible modules in order to meet the particular needs of each customer.

Also at that time there were major advances in computer languages away from codes directly usable by the machine (like those on punched cards (and towards the 'natural' languages of English and Mathematics. The first of the **"high level languages"** called **FORTRAN** (FORmula TRANslation) was released in 1957. Over the next few years many other new languages appeared.

33.21 Integrated Circuits. After the invention of the transistor it was realised that the properties of semiconductors would allow the production of entire electronic circuits within single crystals. The name **Integrated Circuit (IC)** was adopted for such units. The first IC was patented by **Harwick Johnson** of RCA in 1953. Later developments resulted from;
  a. the application of photo engraving to IC manufacture
  b. the use of layers of silicon oxide insulation in order to build up multiple layers of crystal circuitry.

The latter of these two methods is often referred to as **MOS technology** (Metal-Oxide-Semiconductor).

An entire Integrated Circuit is effectively one electrical component in manufacture. The development of ICs allowed further advances in miniaturisation, reliability and the reduction of manufacturing costs of electronic devices.

33.22 Integrated circuits with the equivalent of more than 100 components are called **LSI** (Large Scale Integration) and those with more than 1000 components are called VLSI (Very Large Scale Integration).

33.23 Modern ICs are built on wafer thin slices of extremely purified silicon crystal called **CHIPS.** Chip manufacture takes place in scrupulously clean conditions and involves a series of processes including silicon refining, crystal growing, computerised photoengraving, oxidisation, doping and high temperature gas etching.

Some chips have been developed specifically for the purpose of data storage. Many of these "memory" chips are produced using **CMOS** technology (Complementary Metal Oxide Semiconductors), an improvement over MOS technology.

33.24 The Third Generation. "Third generation" computers using integrated circuits were first released onto the market in 1964. Two of the successful first series of third generation computers were the IBM 360 series and the ICL 1900 series. The computers being manufactured today are also third generation machines, but advances in design and performance continue to take place at quite a pace. Third generation machines can be classified under the following broad headings:-

a.   **Mainframes.** These are large general purpose computers with extensive processing, storage and input/output capabilities. The IBM 360 and ICL 1900 were classified as mainframes but more recent and more powerful examples are the IBM 370, ICL 2900 and   DEC10.

b.   **Minicomputers.** These are physically small compared with mainframes and tend to be used for special purposes or small scale general purpose. Advances in circuitry mean that many modern minicomputers can out-performance older mainframes of the 60s. Examples of minicomputers are the Digital PDP 11 and Vax range, and the Data General range.

c.   **Microcomputers.** One remarkable line of IC development has been the production of IC's which have the equivalent of the whole of a computer's processing circuitry on a single silicon chip. They have quite naturally been called **microprocessors.** By adding additional circuitry to the microprocessor it is possible to build a complete **micro-computer.** Many microcomputers are built for special purpose eg. for use in watches, clocks and cameras. Other **microcomputers** are built to provide scaled down versions of minicomputers in which case they should strictly speaking be called **microprocessor based systems.** The first microprocessor was the model 4004 produced by the Intel corporation in 1972.

SUMMARY

33.25 a.   This chapter has traced the origins of modern computers and introduced various types of computers in the process.

b.   The origins of numbers of important concepts and terms have been traced.
Digital Operation. One performed in steps on distinct values (eg. counting).
Analog Operation. One performed in a continuous action instead of stepwise.
Binary Code. A code based on items with two possible states only one of which is possible at any one time.
Silicon Chips. IC's (integrated circuits) built on wafer thin slices of silicon crystal.
Micro processor. A computer's processing circuitry built on a single silicon chip.

c.   The work of a number of computer pioneers was described. Here is a checklist of names:- John Napier, William Oughtred, Blaise Pascal, Niklaus Wirth, Gottfried Von Leibniz, Joseph Jacquard, Francis Bacon, Charles Babbage, Ada Lovelace, George Boole, Hermann Hollerith, Valdermar Poulson, Lee de Forest, Claude Shannon, Alan Turing, Howard Aiken, Konrad Zuse, J Presper Eckert, John Mauchly, John Von Neuman, William Shockley and Harwick Johnson.

d. Various classifications of computers have been introduced:-
   i. Analog or Digital.
   ii. First Generation (Valve based), Second Generation (Transistor based), Third Generation (IC based).
   iii. Mainframe, Minicomputer, Microcomputer based system.

POINTS TO NOTE
33.26 a. This book is mainly concerned with modern third generation digital computers.

QUESTIONS A *(Answers in Appendix II)*

1. *Describe, briefly, two uses of punched cards prior to the year 1900.*

2. *What were the main areas of technological development which contributed to the design and use of modern computers?*

3. *What is the Von-Neuman Report and what does it say?*

4. *What is a microprocessor? Distinguish between a microprocessor based computer system and a mainframe computer system.*

QUESTIONS B *(Without answers)*

1. *List and describe briefly 5 aids to calculation used before Pascal invented his arithmetic machine.*

2. *What technological developments distinguish the first, second and third generations of computer?*

3. *Write brief notes on the achievements of each of the following people.*
   i. *Howard Aiken,*
   ii. *Claude Shannon*
   iii. *Alan Turing,*
   iv. *Lee de Forest.*

34 The Social and Economic Aspects

INTRODUCTION

34.1 The role of computers in society is a large subject to consider and this chapter merely highlights some important issues. Computers are just one example of automation although they have many special features. In a society which relies heavily on all forms of automation and on the automated handling of information computers are bound to be very important. Issues related to jobs and privacy are particularly significant.

COMPUTERS IN INFORMATION TECHNOLOGY

34.2 It is generally recognised that we live in an industrial society in which the efficiency of production of wealth depends heavily on various kinds of automation. Computers are special in that they *automate many methods of processing information*. Computers are also playing an ever increasing role in many other forms of automation.

34.3 Computers, telecommunications equipment, and other technologies associated with automation, come under the general heading of **Information Technology (IT).** Information Technology is having an impact on individuals organisations and society. Various aspects of this impact will be discussed in the remainder of this chapter. Particular reference will be made to computers, and some key issues, notably privacy and employment.

THE GENERAL BACKGROUND

34.4 Prior to industrialisation approximately 90% of the labour force was engaged in agriculture, ie. society was agrarian. Methods of communication were limited and a very small proportion of the labour force was involved with the processing storage and retrieval of information, which in any case merely involved manual paper based methods or word of mouth.

Industrialisation produced a major shift in the labour force, with the proportion involved in agriculture falling below 10% in the UK. With industrialisation came the beginning of Information Technology and the start of a series of IT developments taking us right up to the present day:- Telegraph, Telephone, Radio/TV, Computes, Microelectronics etc.

34.5 These new forms of IT, and other developments, produced new forms of work. The larger scale of organisations has given rise to large administrative structures in which there are large numbers of clerical workers and people with technical and managerial skills collectively known as "**white collar workers**". Computerisation has mainly affected white collar work so far.

34.6 In addition to changes in the type of work there has been an increase in the number of organisations involved in activities other than manufacture. Some such organisations, for example those in the power industries, contribute to manufacturing and provide a general service. As a result of this change only 25% of the labour force remained in organisations directly involved in the manufacture of goods. For a number of reasons, not particularly related to IT, that 25% has fallen to 20% in the last few years and levels of unemployment have risen.

34.7 The fact that so few remain in manufacture, although manufacturing continues to generate most wealth, has lead to society today being called "Post Industrial Society".

34.8 Looking at the whole of the national and international community, and at the way organisations are run, highlights the fact that modern society is heavily dependent on the communication, processing and storage of information. It is claimed by some, that we are moving towards an "information Society" in which the majority of the labour force will be engaged in Information Processing and the use of "Information Technology".

34.9 It is a mistake to imagine that technological innovation is what causes such changes. Such changes are the collective results of actions taken by those people able to control and influence the use and distribution of resources, within their own organisations, or within society at large. The uses of resources are determined by the goals which are being pursued. The next section looks at these issues.

ORGANISATIONS

34.10 The uses of computers in various kinds of organisations have been discussed in a number of earlier chapters. The term "organisation" was used fairly informally. However, it is possible to be more formal in defining what an organisation is and doing so highlights some significant points.

34.11 An organisation is a human group which has been deliberately constructed with the aim of seeking specific goals. An organisation will be reconstructed, from time to time, so that it can continue to seek its goals effectively.

34.12 The goals sought will depend on the organisation.

Examples.

a. The owners of commercial organisations may have profit as their goal with themselves as the main beneficiaries eg. in private or public companies.

b. The goals of many organisations are to provide "*services*" to their clients or the general public eg. medical services, schools and colleges.

c. Other organisations have the mutual benefits of their members as goals eg. clubs or trade unions.

34.13 Any organisation needs to be controlled and coordinated and to be able to plan ahead. To do so it will need information and facilities to communicate. An example of this is provided by the stock control system of chapter 28.

34.14 In most organisations and particularly in large ones, Information Technology can aid in the processing of information and thereby help the organisation to meet its goals. Whether or not an organisation uses such technology will depend on its evaluation of the technology in relation to its own goals.

EVALUATION OF INFORMATION SYSTEMS

34.15 There are many methods for evaluating new methods and technologies. In the area of computerisation the main methods are those used in Systems Analysis. A proposed computer system is evaluated in terms of how well it can meet objectives which will enable the organisation to meet goals such as profit, service or optimum use of resources.

34.16 The results of such evaluations determine whether organisations invest in computers. This in turn promotes or limits technological developments.

34.17 Large organisations such as government bodies or large corporations can have a major influence in this way. For example the US government attached a high importance to micro-electronics and silicon chip technology because of the goals of providing national defence that depended on having miniaturised electronic circuitry in rockets, planes etc. The necessary research and development costs were provided from the defence budget.

COMPUTERISATION AND WORK

34.18 When computers are introduced into organisations because of the benefits they can provide it usually affects the work of staff within the organisation. Some jobs are changed, some may be created and some may be lost. This creates a demand for training and retraining.

34.19 Any loss of jobs due to computerisation can give rise to alarm, particularly at a time of high unemployment. However such job "losses" probably signify yet another shift in the work of the general labour force as has happened many times in the past.

34.20 Only a very small proportion of the current level of unemployment is directly attributable to new technology. In certain particular applications jobs are likely to be lost, notably:-

    a. Some office jobs eg. caused by Word Processing.

    b. Factory production where industrial robots may replace production line works.

34.21 Whether these job losses will result in permanent unemployment is another matter. It depends on the process of redeployment of labour and labour retraining. It may help to consider an example at this stage.

34.22 In the USA in the early 1970s there were proposals to introduce bar coded POS equipment into supermarkets. This appeared to be an attractive proposition because a saving of $100 million could be achieved if such equipment was introduced into 5000 stores.

34.23 Initially there was alarm from the trade unions who predicted 20% job losses by 1975, the date at which implementation was due to be completed.

34.24 These fears were unfounded for two reasons. Firstly the rate at which the new technology was introduced was much slower which allowed staffing changes to be dealt with by redeployment and natural wastage. By 1979 only 803 stores had equipment installed. Very different from the predicted 5000 by 1975. The trade unions were also able to negotiate an automation deal with their employers. This protected their jobs. The store owners were still able to make large savings by the introduction of the equipment, and to redeploy staff in ventures which improved and extended company activities. (In Britain the banks have also used automation to allow them to redeploy staff in broader and better services).

34.25 Since these early difficulties were overcome the introduction of the equipment has continued smoothly in the USA and at an increasing rate. In Britain its introduction has been straightforward.

PRIVACY

34.26 Another consequence of higher levels of computerisation is the increase in the use of computer based equipment to store large quantities of data about individuals. Some of this data is of a particularly personal or private nature and there is a natural concern that it should not be misused. There is also concern that individuals may have personal information stored about them without their knowledge or control, and that it may be hard or impossible to find out whether such information is accurate.

34.27 In 1975 a government white paper considered this issue and in 1976 a committee was set up chaired by Sir Norman Lindop. The idea was that systems dealing with records containing personal details should be controlled.

34.28 The Lindop report appeared about two years later and was well received. It established a number of principles eg. that stored data should only be used for the purpose for which its use was originally authorised and intended. The report suggested that a **Data Protection Authority (DPA),** should be set up which would enforce codes of conduct for different types of systems.

34.29 At about the same time, the Council of Europe set up a "Convention for the Protection of Individuals with regard to Automatic Processing of Personal Data". Each country signs twice, once to agree to legislate and the second time when it has legislated. Britain had only signed once by early 1982 and computer organisations such as the BCS (British Computer Society) and CSA (Computer Services Association) have expressed fears and delays could cost the UK dearly in terms of lost international contracts through failure to introduce legislation.

34.30 Such legislation is the primary responsibility of the Home Office, itself an important user of computer data banks of an unusual kind, eg. those concerned with police records like those held on the Police National Computer at Hendon (North London).

34.31 A further government white paper appeared early in 1982. It only covered some aspects of data protection. In April 1983 a bill began its passage through Parliament but ran into trouble over the issue of confidentiality. The bill was lost when the general election was called but was reintroduced in a slightly modified form becoming an act in 1984.

THE 1984 DATA PROTECTION ACT

34.32 The 1984 Data Protection act was intended "to regulate the use of automatically processed information relating to individuals and a provision of services in respect of such information." What is immediately apparent is that the act does not cover manual records. This fact is not only a disappointment to those concerned with freedom of information by may also be a discouragement to the use of computers for some applications.

34.33 The act defines a number of terms including "Data" (information in a processable form), "Personal Data" (data relating to identifiable living individuals) and "Data Subject" (the living individual concerned).

34.34 The act requires those using personal data to register with the **Data Protection Register.** The end of April 1986 was set as the deadline for initial registrations for existing uses.

34.35 There are a number of general and specific exemptions. These exemptions are the subject of considerable controversy and practical difficulties. At the general level there are exemptions for a number of government departments for reasons stated to be related to national security and covering some aspects of criminal records, immigration, health and social security. More specifically, there are exemptions for work such as word processing, pensions, accounting and payroll. However, these exemptions are rather weak in that if the system under consideration carries out other tasks it may not be exempt. For example, if the payroll system is used for anything more than calculating and paying wages it will not be exempt.

34.36 An organisation may easily make a genuine mistake in interpreting these rules but will still be liable to criminal prosecution. Therefore, it is not surprising that many organisations have appointed an expert whose sole responsibility is to deal with matters concerned with the act. The title for such a post is normally that of **Data Protection Officer.**

34.37 In future, it will be important for all staff involved in Data Processing to have an awareness of what the act covers so that they know when to consult a Data Protection Officer for specific advice.

34.38 The main points covered by the act which need to be born in mind are:
  a. Data about individuals which is held for processing must have been obtained fairly for a specified lawful purpose.
  b. The data must only be used for the specified purpose and may only be disclosed in accordance with the specified purpose.
  c. Data must not be excessive for the purpose but merely adequate and relevant.
  d. Data must be accurate, up to date and kept no longer than necessary.
  e. The data must be protected and held securely against unauthorised access or loss but must be accessible to data subjects on request.

THE FUTURE

34.39 The current rapid rate of computerisation and technical innovation has lead some people to talk of a "micro electronics revolution". To others these changes are merely viewed as another phase in the process of automation which started with the industrial revolution. Either way it seems reasonable to expect change and yet more change in the future.

34.40 The "fifth generation" supercomputers may well be here by the end of this century if current research and development programmers keep to schedule. Who can say whether these computers will cause delight or dismay? The answers do not rest in the technology.

SUMMARY
34.41 a. The place of computers in Information Technology was discussed.
  b. The general background to the current state of computerisation in society was given.
  c. Organisations were defined and their role in computerisation was discussed.
  d. Computerisation and its impact on employment was discussed.
  e. Privacy and recent development in data protection were discussed.
  f. The future was considered briefly.

POINTS TO NOTE
34.42 a. Computerisation is not just a matter of technological innovation and development, it is a process which involves individuals, organisations and society in general.

QUESTIONS A *(With answers)*

1. *What is an organisation?*
   Give examples of different kinds of organisations.

2. *In what way do organisations promote or limit technological developments?*

3. *Will computerisation lead to long term unemployment?*

4. *What is a DPA?*

ASSIGNMENT

1. Use this chapter as the basis for class discussion.

APPENDICES

Four appendices are provided here. They are:

Appendix   I   Revision test questions with and without answers.

Appendix   II   Answers to questions at chapter ends and to revision test questions.

Appendix   III   Coursework and Projects (Including assignments suitable for BEC courses).

Appendix   IV   Details omitted from the text in the interests of clarity.

Appendix I. Revision test questions with and without answers.

This appendix is divided into two sections, A and B. The answers to section A are given in Appendix II but no answers are given to questions set in section B. (See preface for further details).

SECTION A (With answers)

1. Define the following terms.

    a. Computer
    b. Program
    c. Hardware and Software
    d. Parity
    e. Bit
    f. BCD and Pure binary
    g. Identifiers constants and variables
    h. Data structure
    i. Subscript
    j. Computer file
    k. Operation, Operand, Operator
    l. Validation and verification
    m. RAM and ROM
    n. Physical record and logical record
    o. Key-to-Disk
    p. OMR, OCR, MICR
    q. Dot matrix impact character printer
    r. Viewdata, Videotex, teletex, teletext
    s. Byte and Word
    t. Fixed and variable length records
    u. Exchangeable disk
    v. Machine language, low level language and high level language.
    w. Logic operator, logic element and logic network
    x. Assembler, compiler and interpreter
    y. Batch processing, real-time and time-sharing
    z. word processor

2. Explain clearly and in detail, in the correct sequence, the stages in the preparation of a program, from the first idea to the production of useful results; in your explanation show where errors may occur, what their effects would be on the subsequent stages, and how you would detect them.

[20]
(Oxford 1979)

3. a. Choose **one** of the following types of backing store and explain how data is stored and retrieved referring to speed, capacity and cost.
    Magnetic Tape; Floppy Disc; Magnetic Bubble store. [8]
    b. Using suitable examples explain how the following are stored in computers: [4]
    i. numbers used for arithmetic purpose, [4]
    ii. characters [4]
    c. Give **two** methods of data validation [4]

(AEB 1980)

4. Give an account of the principal methods of data capture used in TWO of the following application areas
   a. Banks
   b. Supermarkets
   c. Clothing and Footwear retailing.

)

   (10 *marks for each part chosen*

   (RSA Stage II 1980)

5. Describe the work done by:
   a. Systems analyst;   [10]
   b. a junior programmer   [10]
   (Oxford 1980)

6. Write an account of the use of magnetic tape for the storage of files. In your account describe
   a. how data is organised on magnetic tape,   [7]
   b. how magnetic tape files are created and how updated,   [5, 4]
   c. how their security is ensured.   [4]
   (Oxford 1980)

7. A major reason for errors in input data is the transcription process. Describe those devices and systems which are available to bypass this process, and identify their relative advantages and disadvantages.

   (20 *marks*)
   (RSA Stage II 1979)

8. Complete the truth table for the circuit shown in Figure 1.

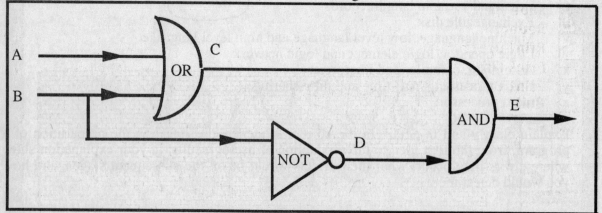

Figure 1.

484

A	B	C	D	E

[5]

10. In diagram 1 you see a screen display as viewed by a user of a **computer graphics** program with the trade name Macpaint used on an Apple Macintosh Computer. There is a **window** on the screen in which the user can draw with the aid of a **mouse**. The mouse button is currently being pressed while the arrow on the screen points to the word **"File"**. This causes the **menu** of items from "New" to "Quit" to be displayed. The arrow can be pulled down the menu to the required position and the mouse button is then released. This is an example of what is called a WIMPs (**Windows, Mice, Icons** and Pull down **Menus**) system.

Explain the words printed in bold letters in diagram 1 below.

Diagram 1

SECTION B (Without answers)

1. COM (Computer output on microfilm) : Bar Codes Graphical Displays: Subroutine:
   ROM (Read only memory).
   Choose **three** of the above and for each one:
   a. outline what it is,
   b.   give a brief description of an application in which it can be used.   [20 marks]
   (AEB 1981)

2. Using standard symbols, draw a flowchart to express the logic of the following
   instructions given to an order clerk:
   "On receipt of an order, check to see if the cash has been received with it. If so, check that
   the cash is correct. If not correct, investigate the discrepancy and report accordingly to the
   manager. If cash has not been received, check to see if the customer is allowed credit and
   if not, reject the order. If credit is allowed, check that the value of the order is within the
   amount of credit allowed, taking into account any existing balance. If credit is adequate,
   pass the order, otherwise, reject the order."   (12 *marks*)

   b.   Describe any other technique, other than narrative, which might be used to express
   the logic of a particular procedure   (8 *marks*)
   (RSA Stage II 1980)

3. The following computer print-out, listing the numbers of the houses to which each paper is
   to be delivered, is designed to assist a newsagent in sorting his morning papers.

   ```
   ROSE   GARDENS
      FULCHESTER

   MAIL  3, 6, 8, 9
   SUN   2, 5, 6, 7, 7, 11
   TELEGRAPH  1, 4, 9
   GUARDIAN  3, 8, 12
   EXPRESS   7, 10

   PRIMROSE WALK
      FULCHESTER

   MAIL  2, 3, 5, 6
   SUN   4, 7, 9
   TELEGRAPH  5, 6, 7
   GUARDIAN  1, 2, 9, 10
   EXPRESS  1, 8, 9, 12
   ```

a. Give two reasons why this information in this format is not very helpful to the paper boy. [4]

b. Redraw the print-out in a format more useful to the paper boy explaining why you have used that format. [6]

c. Using the data above described an algorithm to convert the data into the new format suitable for the paper boy. [10]

(AEB 1980)

4. a. What do WAN and LAN stand for and what is the difference between a WAN and a LAN?

b. Explain the terms:
  i. Fourth Generation Computer.
  ii. Fourth Generation Language.

5. A computerised library system has been designed so that when a book is borrowed, the borrower's code number and the code numbers of the books have to be recorded onto the computer's files.

a. Suggest, with reasons, a suitable method of data capture.

b. Explain why the data validation techniques used will depend upon whether or not the recording device is on-line to a computer system which has direct access to the borrowers file and the book file.

c. State one way in which a computerised library system might affect the privacy of a borrower. [9 marks]

(London 1981)

6. a.i. Describe a system you might use for representing alphabetic characters in binary so that they can be stored in a computer. [3 marks]

  ii. Similarly describe a system you might use for representing two digit integers in binary. [3 marks]

b. Postal codes are made up in any of the following formats:
  L25 2RD, SH5 7TN, EH5 12RY, SWW6 4BH, NW1X 3QR

  i. Suggest a way in which the above postal codes could be encoded in binary in an economic manner (ie. using as few bits as possible). [9 marks]

  ii. Using the method you have described in (b(i)) encode the following:
  NW1X 14ZQ [5 marks]

(AEB 1981)

7. A clothing warehouse keeps a list of its contents on index cards. The information consists of:

Item Number	(6 digit integer)
Item Name	(up to 20 characters)
Manufacturer Code	(5 characters)
Location Code	(6 digits)

The information is to be stored on magnetic backing storage media, so that it becomes part of an on-line Stock Control Computerised system.

a. Devise a suitable data capture form for this information. [6]

b. Describe the data in terms of fields and records [4]

c. Which backing storage media would be most suitable and why? [3]

d. What other field is normally added when such a system is computerised? [4]

e. What other information relevant to this application could be stored on the backing storage? [3]

(AEB 1980)

8. The **Central Processing Unit** of a certain computer contains an **accumulator,** an **index register** and a **program counter (instruction counter),** and the main store has 4096 **words** each of 18 **bits.**
    Each word can contain one machine code instruction which has an **operation code,** 1 bit for reference to the index register, and the **absolute address** of a word in the main store.
    a. Explain each of the underlined terms.   [2 x 8]
    b.i. How many bits are needed for a unique absolute address for each word in the main store?   [2]
      ii. If this number of bits is used for the address part of the instruction, how many bits are available for the operation code?   [1]
      iii. How many different operation codes are there?   [1]
                                                                              (Oxford   1979)

9. A certain computer uses the following instruction code:
    Bn: Copy contents of location n to the accumulator
    Cn: Copy contents of accumulator to location n
    Jn: If contents of Acc = O go to location n for next instruction

    Gn: If contents of Acc > 0 go to location n for next instruction
    Kn: If contents of Acc < 0 go to location n for next instruction.
    Pn: Go to location n for next instruction
    On: Output the contents of location n.
    In: Input a data value into location n
    Sn: Subtract the contents of location n from Acc leaving result in Acc
    Dn: Subtract one from location n
    Z: Halt
    Using the above code write a program for the flowchart opposite.
    The first instruction will be stored in location 100.
    The first items of data will be stored in locations 500, 501
    The first two items of data will be 1000, 0
    Each line of your program should have the format:

Instruction location	Instruction Code	Location address
120	B	510

                                                                              (AEB 1980)
                                                                                     [20]

10. a. Explain the difference between a program file and a a data file.
    b.   What is a concentrator and where might it be used?

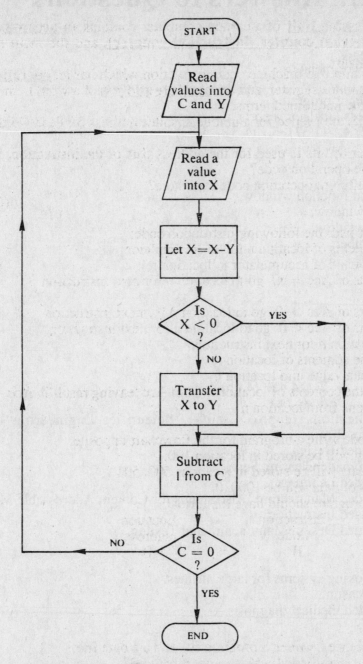

FLOWCHART FOR QUESTION NUMBER 9

Appendix II. Answers to Questions

Chapter 1
1. a   (1.15)
    b.i. output display of menu
       ii. input of data
       iii. storage of data or programs
       iv. printing address labels or reports.
2. (1.17)   **3.** (1.22) **4.** (1.37) **5.** (1.31 – 1.33)

Chapter 2
1. (2.3)
2. a.   Command and function window.
    b.   Spreadsheet window.
    c.   Current cell window.
3. (3.27), person-number

Chapter 3
1. (3.6)

Chapter 4
No questions.

Chapter 5
1.   (4.2)   **2.** (4.4a) (4.4b)
3.   (4.6)   **4.** (5.6c)
5. Commercial applications (approx' 80%), Scientific, Engineering and Research applications (approx' 20%).
6. a.   Computer Aided Design.
    b.   Bankers' Automatic Clearing Services.
    c.   Computer Aided Learning.
    d.   Computer Aided Manufacture [Also stands for Content Addressable Memory].
    e.   Computer Aided Instruction.
    f.   Computer Aided Design Manufacture and Testing.
7.   Hybrid
8.   eg.
    a.   Real-time booking systems for large airlines.
    b.   Weather forecasting.
    c.   Computer aided medical diagnosis.

Chapter 6
1. (6.5)
2. (6.22) In an even parity system, as i n fig 6.5, "B" has 3 bit spots and requires a check bit but "C" has 4 bit spots and does not.
3. (6.3) (6.4)   **4.** 3625, 3, 5

Chapter 7
1.

	i.	ii.	iii.	iv.	v.	vi.
a.	22	32	54	62	157	255
b.	10010	11010	101100	110010	1101111	10101101
c.	12	1A	2C	32	6F	AD

	vii	viii	ix	x	xi	xii
a.	304	354	452	513	576	1003
b.	11000100	11101100	100101010	101001011	101111110	1000000011
c.	C4	EC	12A	14B	17E	203

2.

	i	ii	iii	iv	v	vi
a	39	53	85	136	157	350
b	27	35	55	88	9D	15E
c.	100111	110101	1010101	10001000	10011101	101011110

3.

	i.	ii	iii	iv	v
Decimal	13	228	328	432	491
Octal	213	344	510	660	753

4. 3352653_8, $DD5AB_{16}$

5.   i. 0.625   ii. 0.8125   iii. 0.1875
         iv. 5.375   v. 11.9375   vi. 13.3125

6.   i. 0.11   ii. 0.1011   iii. 0.10101
         iv. 11.111   v. 1101.0111   vi. 10.011001100.....

7. a.i. 0.001101011   ii. 0.110111010
        iii. 0.100 000 101
        b.i. 0.1000 0111 0010   i. 0.1010 0011 1110
        iii. 0.1011 1111 1101

8. a.i. 100 010   ii. 101 000 101   iii. 10 001
        b.i. 0011 0100   ii. 0011 0010 0101
        iii. 0001 0111

Chapter 8

1.   a.True   b.True.   c.False   d.False   e.True   f.False,

2.   (8.9),

3.   **REPEAT loop.** This is performed at least once and a test occurs at the end of each loop to determine whether or not another repetition is required.
          WHILE loop. This loop has a test at the beginning of the loop and may not even be processed once if in the initial test the required condition is met.

5.
BEGIN
Use a knife to spread a slice of bread with butter.
Cover the buttered slice with a layer of sliced cheese.
Use a knife to spread a second slice of bread with butter.
Place the second slice of bread, buttered side down, on top of the first slice.
Cut across the top slice with a knife and cut right through to the bottom of the bottom slice.
END

6.

> **BEGIN**
> Use a knife to spread a slice of bread with butter.
> Enquire of person eating whether ham or cheese is required.
> **IF**
>   Answer is "Ham"
> **THEN**
>   Cover the buttered slice with a layer of sliced ham.
> **ELSE**
>   Cover the buttered slice with a layer of sliced cheese.
> **ENDIF**
> Use a knife to spread a second slice of bread with butter.
> Place the second slice of bread, buttered side down, on top of the first slice.
> Cut across the top slice with a knife and cut right through to the bottom of the bottom slice
> **END**

7. NB. A REPEAT loop has been used here. A WHILE loop could have been used and would be better if there was any chance that the initial loaf could be thinner than one slice.

> **BEGIN**
> Place loaf on the bread board.
> **REPEAT**
>   Cut a slice of bread from the loaf using the breadknife.
>   Examine the thickness of the remaining loaf.
> **UNTIL**
>   Remaining loaf thickness > Thickness of one slice
> **END**

8. In answering this question you should have identified the need to record data on the quantity, cost and price of each item. Quantities will need to be recorded at regular intervals, as will total sums of money paid and received. Activities considered should have been included. Examining quantities in order to determine what items need to be repurchased and examining money to determine profit or loss.

8.   a. True   b. False   c. False   d. True

9.   (8.31)

10.   (8.36)

11.   a. 7.   b. 8   c. 9   d. 8   e. 9   f. 6
The procedure finds the largest value and prints it.
If A = B = C there is no largest number but C is printed.

12.   2, 4, 8, 16, 32, 64, 128, 256, 512, 1024. Power = 10 at the end. 2^{10} = 1024.

13. a . P := O
   b.   Number > 5000
   c.   Print Number, Print P

14.   One possible solution
                    BEGIN
                    Input Mark
                    IF
                        Mark > 60
                    THEN
                        PRINT "CREDIT"
                    ELSE
                        IF
                            Mark > 40
                        THEN
                            PRINT "PASS"
                        ELSE
                            PRINT "FAIL"
                        ENDIF
                    ENDIF
                    END

Three items of test data are needed eg. 25, 45, 65.
NB. A better solution will include checks that the mark is between 0 and 100
inclusive   and will test more cases eg. Mark = 60, Mark = 40, Mark = 0,
Mark < 0, Mark = 100, Mark > 100.

15.   **BEGIN**
                    Input mark
                    WHILE
                        Mark <> 999
                    DO
                        IF
                            Mark > 60
                        THEN
                            PRINT "CREDIT"
                        ELSE
                            IF
                                Mark > 40
                            THEN
                                PRINT "PASS"
                            ELSE
                                PRINT "FAIL"
                            ENDIF
                        ENDIF
                        INPUT mark
                    ENDWHILE
                    END

Test data as for question 14 but with 999 as final data value.

Chapter 9

1.	(9.1)	**2.**	(9.8), (9.15)	**3.**	(9.20)
4.	(9.26)	**5.**	(9.29)	**6.**	(9.30)
7.	(9.32)				

8. Assuming the postal charge data is stored as CHARGE =

5	8	12	26	50
2	3	6	15	28

and MASSARRARY = (100   150   200   1000   2001)

ONE POSSIBLE SOLUTION
> **BEGIN**
> **INPUT** Mass
> **INPUT** Class
> Posn := 1
> **WHILE** ((Posn) <5) **AND** (MASS > MASS ARRAY(POSN))
> **DO**
>> Pos := Posn + 1
>> **PRINT** "CHARGE", CHARGE (CLASS, POSN), "E"
> **END**

NB. A better solution would test the range and validity of Mass and class

Chapter 10
1. ii., iii, v, vi.
2. The operation is addition. The operator is "–". The operands are 8 and 5.
3. a. >, b. < or < =, c. <>, d. > or > =, e. =, f. <
4. a, b, c, f.
5.

A	B	a.	b	c	d	e
0	0	0	0	1	1	1
0	1	1	0	0	0	1
1	0	0	1	0	0	1
1	1	0	0	0	0	0

f. A	B	C	(A AND C) OR (B AND C)
0	0	0	0
0	0	1	0
0	1	0	0
0	1	1	1
1	0	0	0
1	1	0	1
1	1	0	0
1	1	1	1

Chapter 11
1.
a. Random Access Memory
b. Large Scale Integration.
c. Micro Processor Unit
d. Computer Output on Microfilm.
e. Read Only Memory
f. Point of Sale
g. Charged Coupled Devices.
h. Very Large Scale Integration.
i. Arithmetic and Logic Unit
j. Central Processing Unit.
2. (11.3).
3. a.(11.9)   b. (11.7)   c. (11.8)   d. (11.7)
4. On-line, connected to the computer and under its control eg. fixed disk unit.

Off-line, away from the computer and not under its control eg. a magnetic tape in its case.
5.   (11.25)b. e

Chapter 12
1.   (12.15)
2.   (1.12)(12.15)
Chapter 13
1.   (13.6)
2.   (11.17)(11.18)
PRINT3. (13.9)
4.   (13.11)
5.   (13.33)
6.   Fig. 11.13
7.   (13.54)
8.   a.(12.7) b. (12.9) c. (12.8) d. (12.9)
9.
    a.   A daisy wheel printer
    b.   A graph plotter
    c.   Thermal or ink-jet printer.
    d.   An impact line printer
    e.   A dot matrix impact character printer.

Chapter 14
1.   Immediate Access Storage (14.2).
2.   (14.5), (14.9), (14.9), (14.8), (14.10).
3.

4.   (14.18)
5.   (Figure 14.2) (143.29)
6.   (Figure 14.8) (14.34)
7.   (14.36)
8.   (14.49)
9.   (Figure 14.14) (14.54)

Chapter 15
1.   (15.2) (15.3)
2.   Relative advantages:

VDU	PRINTER TERMINAL
Economical in terms of no paper consumed.	Produces permanent copies
Faster maximum speeds	Not limited to length of
Quieter than most printers	screen when viewing
Very reliable: No moving	output.
parts except keyboard.	Nicer to read.

3. eg.
   a. OCR or MICR
   b. OM
   c. Voice data entry.
   d. Tags eg. Kimball tags.
   e. Bar coding and reader
   f Daisywheel printer.
   g. Laser printer.
   h. COM
   i. ROM
   j. Exchangeable disk
   k. Winchester disk. (NB. but dusty environments should be avoided)
   l. Magnetic tape
4. Optical disk (14.58)

Chapter 16
1. a.(16.5)   b. (16.6)
2. a.(16.36)   b. (16.38)   c. (16.33)   d. (16.34)
3. (16.18)
4. (16.11) Optical fibre is able to transfer data faster than coaxial cable
5. (16.24)

Chapter 17
1.

HEXADECIMAL ADDITION TABLE

1	0	1	2	3	4	5	6	7	8	9	A	B	C	D	E	F
0	0	1	2	3	4	5	6	7	8	9	A	B	C	D	E	F
1	1	2	3	4	5	6	7	8	9	A	B	C	D	E	F	10
2	2	3	4	5	6	7	8	9	A	B	C	D	E	F	10	11
3	3	4	5	6	7	8	9	A	B	C	D	E	F	10	11	12
4	4	5	6	7	8	9	A	B	C	D	E	F	10	11	12	13
5	5	6	7	8	9	A	B	C	D	E	F	10	11	12	13	14
6	6	7	8	9	A	B	C	D	E	F	10	11	12	13	14	15
7	7	8	9	A	B	C	D	E	F	10	11	12	13	14	15	16
8	8	9	A	B	C	D	E	F	10	11	12	13	14	15	16	17
9	9	A	B	C	D	E	F	10	11	12	13	14	15	16	17	18
A	A	B	C	D	E	F	10	11	12	13	14	15	16	17	18	19
B	B	C	D	E	F	10	11	12	13	14	15	16	17	18	19	1A
C	C	D	E	F	10	11	12	13	14	15	16	17	18	19	1A	1B
D	D	E	F	10	11	12	13	14	15	16	17	18	19	1A	1B	1C
E	E	F	10	11	12	13	14	15	16	17	18	19	1A	1B	1C	1D
F	F	10	11	12	13	14	15	16	17	18	19	1A	1B	1C	1D	1E

2. a.i. 101110_2 ii. 1010001_2 iii. 10001010_2

     iv. 110010_2 v. 1100.0000_2 vi. 1011.1000_2

    b.   i. 476_8 ii. 400_8 iii 1072_8

     iv. 1112_8

    c.i. $4C_{16}$ ii. $F5E_{16}$ iii. $1C7A_{16}$

     iv. $1A51_{16}$

3.

```
     Sign
     bit                 Point
     ^                   ^
  a  0  0  0  1  0  1  1  0
  b  1  1  1  0  0  0  1  0
  c  0  0  1  0  0  1  0  1
  d  1  1  0  0  1  1  0  0
  e  1  0  1  1  0  1  0  1
  f  0  1  0  1  1  0  0  0
  g  1  0  0  1  1  1  1  1
  h  1  0  0  0  0  0  1  1
```

4. a.

```
   0  0  0  0  1  1  0  0     +12₁₀
   1  1  1  1  0  0  1  1     ones
   1  1  1  1  0  1  0  0     + 1 giving – 12₁₀
   0  0  0  1  1  0  0  1     + 25₁₀ Add
 1 0  0  0  0  1  1  0  1     Result + 13₁₀
```

b.

```
   0  0  0  1  1  0  1  0     + 26₁₀
   1  1  1  0  0  1  0  1     ones
   1  1  1  0  0  1  1  0     + 1 giving – 26₁₀
   0  0  1  0  0  0  1  1     + 35 Add
 1 0  0  0  0  1  0  0  1     Result + 19₁₀
```

c.

```
   0  0  1  0  0  0  0  1     + 33₁₀
   1  1  0  1  1  1  1  0     ones
   1  1  0  1  1  1  1  1     + 1 giving – 33₁₀
   0  0  0  1  1  1  0  0     + 28 Add
   1  1  1  1  1  0  1  1     Result twos complement (–5)
```

d.

```
   0  0  0  1  0  1  0  1     21₁₀
   1  1  1  0  1  0  1  0     ones
   1  1  1  0  1  0  1  1     + 1 giving – 21₁₀
   0  0  0  1  1  1  0  0     + 28 Add
 1 0  0  0  0  0  1  1  1     Result + 7₁₀
```

5. a. Largest 0111 1111 1111 1111$_2$, $(2^{15} - 1)_{10}$ = 32767$_{10}$

    b   Most negative 1000 0000 0000 0000 2, $-2^{15}{}_{10}$ = 32768$_{10}$

6. (17.46), (17.47)

7. The least significant bits are dropped. 0.9 is a recurring binary fraction so it will not be represented to full precision in a word of finite length.

8.   24 is   00011000
           3 right shifts give: 00000011   (value 3)
           2 left shifts give: 01100000 (value 96)

Chapter 18
1. a. Exclusive or (NEQ)
        b.   NAND

2.

A	B	C	D	E	F	G
0	0	1	1	0	0	0
0	1	1	0	0	1	1
1	0	0	1	1	0	1
1	1	0	0	0	0	0

$E = A.\bar{B}$, $F = B.\bar{A}$, $G = (A.\bar{B}) + (B.\bar{A})$

NB. G is NEQ

3. a.

X	Y	X.Y	$\overline{X.Y}$ = A
0	0	0	1
0	1	0	1
1	0	0	1
1	1	1	0

b.

X	Y	Z	$\bar{X}$	$\bar{Y}$	$\bar{Y} + Z$	$\bar{X}.(\bar{Y} + Z)$ = A
0	0	0	1	1	1	1
0	0	1	1	1	1	1
0	1	0	1	0	0	0
0	1	1	1	0	1	1
1	0	0	0	1	1	0
1	0	1	0	1	1	0
1	1	0	0	0	0	0
1	1	1	0	0	1	0

c.

X	Y	Z	$\bar{Y}$	$\bar{Y}.X$	Y.Z	$(\bar{Y}.X) + (Y.Z)$ = A
0	0	0	1	0	0	0
0	0	1	1	0	0	0
0	1	1	0	0	0	0
0	1	1	0	0	1	1
1	0	0	1	1	0	1
1	0	1	1	1	0	1
1	1	0	0	0	0	0
1	1	1	0	0	1	1

4.   (18.30)

5. a.

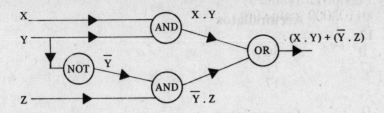

b.

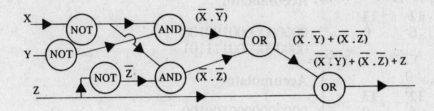

6. (18.31), (18.32)
7. (18.38), (18.37)
8. (18.40), (18.41)

Chapter 19
1. (19.7), (19.10), (19.12), (19.13), (19.20), (19.22)
2. (19.40), (19.40), (19.41), (19.42) (19.43), (19.44)
3. **In outline the answer is:-**
FETCH
The contents of the sequence control register are used to determine the address of the next instruction.
The next instruction is loaded into the current instruction register from memory.
The sequence control register has its contents increased by 1 immediately after its contents have been used to provide the address of the next instruction.
EXECUTE
The instruction in the current instruction register is decoded by the control unit which then selects and controls the appropriate operations.
Some instructions will require data to be accessed from memory or placed into memory.
Some instructions will not require memory access.
Conditional jump instructions may cause the contents of the sequence control register contents to be changed thus altering the instruction sequence. Unconditional jump instructions will always cause the sequence control register contents to be changed.

Chapter 20
1. a (20.,6)   b. (20.8)   c. (20.9)
        d. (19.42)   e. (19.43)
2.   (19.17)

3. (20.13)

4. a.

Locations				Accumulator
10	**11**	**12**	**13**	
36	25	6	0	36
			17	11
				17

b.

Locations				Accumulator
10	**11**	**12**	**13**	
36	25	6		36
37				3

c.

Locations				Accumulator
10	**11**	**12**	**13**	
36	25	6	0	0000000000100100
				0000000000111101

d.

Locations				Accumulator
10	**11**	**12**	**13**	
36	25	6	0	0000000000100100
		25	4	0000000000000100
				1111111111111011
				0000000000 011001

5. The program outputs "CAT". to device number 3.

6. Dry Run

Accumulator Contents	Sequence Control Register Contents	Output To Device 4
68 ie. "D"	20	"D"
	21	
22	22	
79 ie. "O"	20	
	21	"O"
33	22	
71 ie. "G"	20	
	21	"G"
25	22	
46 ie. "."	20	
	21	"."
0	22	

The program outputs "DOG." to device 4 by taking in characters and outputting them one by one until it reaches an input\".".

Chapter 21

1. a.i. (21.5)

ii. (21.6)

b. They are a standardised, efficient and economical method of connecting modular components together.

2.   (21.8c)
3.   (21.11)
4.   (21.19)
5.   a.   (21.22)
     b.   (21.23)
     c.   (21.24)
     d.   (21.26)
6.   (21.30)

Chapter 22

1.   (22.2)
2.   (22.6), (22.9)
3.   (22.7), (22.8)
4.   (22.12 – 22.24)
5.   a.(22.63j)   b. eg. (22.60)

Chapter 23

1.   a.   (23.3)
     b.   (23.7)
     c.   (23.9)
2.   (23.22)
3.   (Figure 23.3)
4.   (23.35). Second part of question:- With reference to 23.28 you would need a, b, c, d, h, i. A readable self documenting program would be particularly helpful.
5.   (23.32)
6.   (23.39)
7.   Very simply by changing "STUDNO > CAND (POSN)" to "STUDNO < CAN(POSN)"
8.   Dry run:

NUM	TOT	POSN	OUTPUT
6	1	1	1209 65
	2	2	1215 46
	3	3	1226 52
		4	
		5	
	4	6	1253 49
		7	

9. Make these changes to figure23.10
    a.   1st instruction before low 1 should be Input Number.
    b.   Next instruction should test condition Number > 1.
    e.   Change all cases of "19" to "Number".
    f.   Change all cases of "approx3" to "approx2".

Chapter 24

1.   (24.12),   (20.4) (24.4)
2.   (24.17)   (Figure 24.5)
3.   a. 24_{10}
     b.   8, 11, 17

c. The program adds the number N1, N2 and N3 and places their sum in SUM

4.   a.   10, 11, 12, 13

b.   The table given below shows values only when they change

N1	N2	N3	SUM	DIF	SCR	Decimal	Binary
							Accumulator
3	8				14	3	0 0 0 0 0 0 0 0 0 0 0 0 0 0 1 1
					15	11	0 0 0 0 0 0 0 0 0 0 0 0 1 0 1 1
			11		16		
					17	3	0 0 0 0 0 0 0 0 0 0 0 0 0 0 1 1
					18	15	1 1 1 1 1 1 1 1 1 1 1 1 1 0 1 1
				–5	19		
					20		

c. The program performs $SUM := N1 + N2$ and $DIF := N - N2$.

5.   The program subtracts N2 from N1 and stores the result in X. It uses the method of (18.18).

6.   Missing instructions:
```
LDA      L
IOP,  0,  3
IOP,  0,  3
LDA,  0
IOP,  0,  3
```
Note: There is no need to load "L" twice.

7.   Possible test data sets [N1 = 8, N2 = 5], [N1 = 5, N2 = 8] [N1 = N2 = 8]
The program outputs the larger number of N1 and N2 to device number 5. N2 is output if both numbers are equal.

8.   It outputs the ASCII character "A", "B", "C"...."Z"   to device number 5 by performing a loop in which the ASCII code is increased in steps of 1 from 65 to 90.

9.   The program fails to print the last letter, "R". It can be corrected in a number of possible ways eg:-

a.   change   LOP: JAZ
     to   LOP: JAG

b.   change   ACC, C
     to   BC: ACC, C
     and change   ACC, S, 7
     to   ACC, S, 8
     and change   LDA, I, R
     to   LDA, I, BC

10.   A possible solution:
```
BEGIN
CHI :
CH2 :
        IOP, I, 2
        STA  CHI1
        IOP, I, 2
        STA  CH2
        SUB  CH1
        JAL  ELS
        LDA  CH1
```

502

```
                IOP, O, 3
                LDA CH2
                IOP, O, 3
                JPU XIT
        ELS:    LDA CH2
                IOP, O, 3
                LDA CH1
                IOP, O, 3
        XIT:    HLT
        .END
```

11.   A possible solution:

```
        .BEGIN
                ACC, L, 57
                SAI
                ACC, C
                ACC, S, 9
        LOP:    JAG XIT
                SAI
                IOP, O, 7
                ACC, S, 1
                SAI
                ACC, A, 1
                JPU LOP
        XIT:    HLT
```

Chapter 25
1.   (25.2 – 25.4)
2.   (25.6 – 25.21)
3.   (25.33)
4.   (25.33)
5.   (25.18)

Chapter 26
1.   a. (26.15) b. (26.15) c. (26.17) d. (26.24) e. (26.15)
2.   (26.37)

Chaper 27
1.   (27.2 – 27.6)
2.   (27.10)
3.   Job Control Language (27.22)
4.   (27.18)
5.   (27.23 – 27.27)
6.   (27.30 – 27.32)
7.   (27.33)
8.   (27.10h) (27.33 – 27.34)
9.   (27.33 – 27.36)
10.   (27.37 – 27.48)

Chapter 28
1. (28.5)
2. eg. Control to prevent document loss and a more controlled and organised method of processing.
3. (28.13)
4. (Appendix IV.5)
5. (28.46)

Chapter 29
1. (29.1)
2. (29.9)
3. (29.17)
4. (29.21)

Chapter 30
1. 00, 01, 10, 11
2. 30.27
3.
```
            BEGIN
                WAIT(15)
                (*start pumping out the water*)
                SENT 1 TO DEVICE 8
                (*wait for the drum to empty*)
                REPEAT
                    (*check if drum is full*)
                    GET Empty Status FROM DEVICE 2
                UNTIL
                    (*drum is empty*)
                    Empty Status = 0
                (* stop the pump*)
                SEND 0 to DEVICE 8
            END
```

Chapter 31
1. (31.2)

Chapter 32
1. (32.4)
2. (32.6)
3. (Figure 32.1). A small organisation would have fewer staff and each member would therefore need to deal with different types of work.
4. (32.18)
5. (32.11)
6. (32.20)
7. (32.22)
8. (32.23)
9. The points raised would include those of (32.23) and (32.24) with particular stress on (32.23b ii) (32.23b iii) and (32.23c).

Chapter 33
1. (33.12) and (33.9)   2. (33.8)
3. (33.17)   4. (33.24)

Chapter 32
1. (34.11) (34.12)
2. (34.16)
3. Not necessarily. See (34.20 and 34.21).
4. a. Data Protection Authority (34.28)

ANSWERS TO APPENDIX 1 SECTION A
1. a. (1.43) b. (1.42) c. (1.44)
    d. (6.20) e. **Binary digit**
    f. Binary Coded Decimal (7.17), (7.18)
    g. (8.30) h. (9.1) i. (9.9)
    j. (9.26) k. (10.3) l (11.8), (11.7)
    m. (11.24), (11.25) n. (12.6)
    o. (11.22) p. (13.12, 13.15, 13.18) q. (3.39)
    r. (16.36 – 16.38) s. (14.9)
    t. (Figure 14.2) u. (14.39)
    v. (24.2)(25.5) w. (18.2)(18.10)(18.17)
    x. (22.14)(22.17) y. (27.10)
    z. (29.26)
2. (8.9 – 8.16)
3. a. Magnetic tape (11.31) (Figure 11.8)
        (6.15) (6.16)
        Floppy Disk (11.33) (Figure 11.9) (Figure 14.11)
        Bubble Store (11.33)
Author's note. The above references are there to help you find the answers to the question. Time is always limited in an examination so answer *each* point in the question quickly and concisely eg. for magnetic tape deal with the fact it is a magnetic medium, bits as magnetic spots, binary character codes, characters written and read in blocks on a serial medium, magnetic tape unit with read/write heads, fast *transfer* speed, capacity approx. 40 Mbytes, cost approx £25.
    b.i. Pure binary
    ii. eg. 14.12 or 14.13 + explanation
    c.(10.7) eg: data type check (alphabetic or numeric) range check (on numeric).
4. a. MICR (12.21)
    b. Bar coded EAN's (13.24)
    c. Tags eg. Kimball tags (13.23)
5. i. (32.11)
    ii. See (32.14) but a junior programmer will probably liaise with the senior programmer rather than an analyst, will only be concerned with parts of programming projects and will be less involved with high level design if at all.
6. i. (14.29)
    ii. eg. (14.33)
    iii. (Figure 14.7) 14.8
7. (See 10.12) eg. OMR, OCR, BAR-CODING, MICR (Figure 14.1)
8.

A	B	C	D	E
0	0	0	1	0
0	1	1	0	0
1	0	1	1	1
1	1	1	0	0

9.   Computer graphics (12.4)
         window (12.16)
         mouse (12.3g)
         file (9.27)
         menu (12.16)
         Icon (12.9)

Appendix III. Coursework and Projects (Including assignments suitable for BTEC courses)

INTRODUCTION

1. Many of the examination courses for which this book is a preparation require students to undertake a considerable amount of coursework throughout the course. Sometimes, this takes the form of **course assignments,** as in the case of **BTEC,** and in other cases it may take the form of practical programming work as part of the final examination, as in the case of many **GCSE** examinations.

2. This appendix provides some notes for guidance, and a number of assignments primarily intended for BTEC students, but probably of use to other readers as coursework exercises, projects etc.

APPROACHING COURSEWORK AND PROJECTS

3. You may find the following ideas useful.
   a. Try to relate your practical work, or coursework, to the theory you have covered so far, (ie. turn principle into practice).
   b. You can often build on earlier work or experience so look for:
   i. A pattern in problem.
   ii. Similarities and differences between the present problem and those done earlier. (This helps you to build up a set of general problems solving skills).
   c. Keep you work in a suitable folder and in sufficient order that you can understand it later eg. keep a diary or log.
   d. Refer to the appropriate sections in this book, and to your notes before you tackle each piece of work.

4. **Programming Projects.** (If possible choose real problems with *real* data but don't be over ambitious).
   a. Plan ahead and keep to deadlines as you prepare the project.
   b. It is easier to develop a project which has been clearly defined in terms of objectives at each stage and an overall aim.
   c. Don't get sidetracked into trivial work which may make your program look nice, when you should be tackling programming problems. The examiner will not be fooled by pages of printout which hide a lack of substance in the work.
   d. The examiner has to be able to understand your project when he reads it. He can only mark what you give him, and may miss some of what you have submitted if it is not clearly presented.
   e. The required contents of a project are usually specified for each examination. Make sure you include every section. In particular, projects should make sense to possible other users.

5. **General Study.**
   a. Visits to installations near your home can give you an insight into current practice.
   b. Reading occasional articles in weekly computer magazines can give you details of modern ideas and developments and sometimes provide case studies which act as a framework for examination answers. Some newspapers, such as the Guardian run regular features on computers.
   c. Many hobby magazines eg. Personal Computer World, Practical Computing etc. contain regular features and advertisements which may give you handy illustrations of some modern computer technology.

6.   Course Assignments.

a. Course assignments are intended to test that you have achieved some objectives, eg. that you can use a method, or that you can describe and compare two specified items etc.

b. Your aim is to provide evidence of your ability, by presenting an answer which displays what you can do, clearly and concisely, and does not hide what knowledge you have in tiresome waffle.

c. *Always read questions fully and carefully.* If for example a question asks you to *compare* two things, you have *not* answered the question if you describe each of the two things separately, and make no comparisons.

d. Always go back and check through the question and your answer, *before* you hand your work in to be marked.

e. Many of these points apply equally well to examination questions. If you get into good habits with your coursework it will help you to pass your examination.

ASSIGNMENTS

the following assignments are primarily intended for use on BTEC options in Elements of Data Processing or Computer Studies. they may well prove useful in other courses.

ASSIGNMENT 1
REFERENCE MATERIAL

A computer terminal manufacturer supplies a printer at discount prices which depend on the number purchased to date. The discounts allowed are summarised below.

Number of terminals ordered (to date) (including present order)	Price £
1 - 4	1250
5 - 19	1150
20 - 49	1000
50 -	850

Example

An order of 4 more printers from a customer who has previously brought 2 printers makes the total to date = 6. The price for the 4 will therefore be 4 x £1150 = £4600. This customer's first order would have been at the higher price, ie. 2 printers at £1250 = £2500. If this customer were to subsequently order 15 printers these would be priced at £1000 each as the order to date would then be 21.

A card is kept for each customer on which is listed each order and the number purchased to date.

QUESTIONS

1. *Assuming that the invoice for each order is produced manually.*

   a. *Use pseudocode showing the procedure that the clerk should adopt in handling each nvoice.*

   b. *What aids could you give the clerk producing this invoice?*

   c. *Apply the procedure in (a) to an order of 15 printers from a customer who has previously purchased 10 printers.*
   It may not be possible for you to perform each step in the procedure but indicate any stage at which this occurs).

2. *Assuming that the invoice for each order is produced by computer.*

    a. *Produce pseudocode, which gives the procedure for calculating the correct charge to be made (Let N be the number of printers ordered in the current order. Let P be the number purchased previously. Let C be the charge to be made in pounds).*
    b. *Test your pseudocode with suitable values of N and P.*

ASSIGNMENT 2
REFERENCE MATERIAL

Machine operators in a small "jobbing" firm record their work on cards which they hand in at the end of each working day. These cards (one per employee per day) contain the following information:

    a. Date;
    b. Department (one of three);
    c. Employee (one of 26)
       (a) to (c) appear just once on each card.
    d. Number of jobs worked on (A 6 digit number)
    e. Operation performed (ie. which machine used - no more than 9 machines in any department).
    f. Time taken (to the nearest half hour).
    g. Material cost (never more than £999.99)
       (d) to (g) may appear several times on each card showing data for different jobs.

QUESTIONS

1. *Suggest reasons why such data (as that given on these cards) is needed.*
2. *Design a card for the employees (machine operators) to use.*
   The card should be designed so as to facilitate the easy production of records for computer input by a keyboard device (on-line or off-line)
   The size of fields should be compressed by using suitable 'coding' where possible. Explain any coding which you use.
3. *What advantage might 'batching' have in handling cards each day?*
4. *Code this data using the card of your design:-*

```
15th October 1990,  Smith, Fabrication Dept.
  Job 637482,  Operation 5,  2 1/4 hours,  £56.38.
  Job 584372,  Operation 6,  5 hours  10 mins., $340.

15th October 1990,  Brown,  Assembly  Dept.
  Job 584216,  Operation 1,  1 hour 18 mins.,  £112.15.
  Job 268249,  Operation 2,  6 hours 12 mins.,  £412.92.

15th October 1990,  Jones,  Checking Dept.
  Job 168340,  Operation  8,  2 hours  20 mins.
  Job 198347,  Operation  9,  4 hours 10 mins
  Job  209832  Operation  7,  2 hours.
```

ASSIGNMENT 3
REFERENCE MATERIAL

For this assignment you must use a library. Look through recent specialist computer or business magazines and select an article on computer input devices or methods. Alternatively examine a number of advertisements for computer input devices.

QUESTIONS

1. a. List the devices or methods mentioned.
   b. State one important advantage of each device or method.
   c. State one limitation of each device or method.
2. Name three output devices which you have seen advertised and suggest a possible commercial application of each one.
3. Describe the features, characteristics and uses of a particular backing storage device which you have seen in use for commercial purposes. (This may require you to visit a computer installation). Why is this device being used instead of other backing storage devices?

ASSIGNMENT 4
REFERENCE MATERIAL

These questions draw upon your knowledge of files and file processing. Read any sections in this book that you feel you need to read once you have read the questions. Your answer must not just reproduce material from this book, because to answer the question you must *apply* what you have learnt.

QUESTIONS

1. A *manufacturer's products master file* is processed daily to update the production figures and is processed weekly to give a production report. At other times the file may be referenced in order to answer management enquiries about particular products or products of a particular type. The file is stored as an INDEX SEQUENTIAL file on disk.
   a. Why is a disk used for this application?
   b. For many applications files are arranged in sequential order. What advantages are obtained by this practice?
   c. **Use this example** to explain the advantages of using index sequential files. (Refer to the organisation of the file and the means of access to it.)
2. A transaction file is produced at the end of each day for the purpose of updating the products masters file.
   Departments send in a document with details for each product giving product number and production figures for each product. These documents are input onto a floppy disk by means of a PC. **Refer to this example** when you answer the following questions:-
   a. What errors might arise during the recording and transcription of transaction file data? (name each type of error and give an example).
   b. How can these errors be (i) reduced, (ii) avoided?
   NB. In answering part b be prepared to consider alternative methods and media.
3. If a production manager requires a report about a particular product, what procedures might be adopted for him to obtain it? What facilities (eg. Hardware, Software, Staff) will be needed in order to deal with enquiries of this type?

ASSIGNMENT 5
QUESTIONS

1. A firm which already has a computer installation has decided to transfer its manual stock control system to the computer. The choice is between having the programmes written by its own staff and using a software package.
   a. In what circumstances would you expect them to buy a package?
   b. How would the firm obtain and implement a suitable package.
2. Produce a short report (**not** an essay) about a software package you have used. Divide your report into numbered sections, give it a title, an index, numbered paragraphs, a

summary and a conclusion. Consider how well or badly the package covers the following points:-

a. Specification of what the package does and of what its limitations are.
b. Instructions to the user of the package.
c. Ease of use eg. for input, output, selections of commands etc.
d. Providing "foolproof" methods of operation.

ASSIGNMENT 6
REFERENCE MATERIAL

Most shops keep constant checks on their stock holdings in order to deal with stock needing reordering and stock which is not selling too well. It is becoming more common to computerise this problem even in the case of individual stores. Visit a variety of shops and stores and look for evidence of the use of data collection methods suited to or used in a computerised stock control system. Do not in any way interfere with the work of the shop or store, or with its stock. It is advisable and courteous to speak to a member of the staff first to explain the purpose of your visit and to ask permission.

QUESTIONS

1. a. Draw up a table which shows the methods you observed, the name of the store in which you observed them, and the type of store eg. Supermarket, department store etc.
   b. Draw some conclusion from the information you have gathered regarding the way computers are used in these kinds of retailing.
2. Compare the case of computerised stock control for A) a small grocery shop with B) a supermarket chain.
   Tabulate your answers under these headings:-
   a. Dp requirements:-
      i. Hardware;
      ii. Software.
   b. Sources of data
   c. Personnel used.
   d. Data collection, transmission and processing

ASSIGNMENT 7
REFERENCE MATERIAL

Assume that you go to visit a friend's house and discover that your friend's parents, who have their own small business, have decided to buy a microcomputer based system of a particular make and model, together with a small applications package. They have had the system and package on trial and are satisfied that it meets their requirements.

However, they also require another small program for one of their own specialised applications. The computer supplier has offered to write the program for them.

QUESTIONS

1. Why is it important for your friend's parents to specify carefully the nature of their program requirements?
2. What documentation would you advise them to ask the supplier to provide with the program?
3. Your friend's parents have some sales literature about computers which contains the statement "The thing which distinguishes a computer from a calculator is the computer's use of stored programs". Explain in simple terms what this statement means.

4. *The same sales literature claims that a particular computer has a "High level language" which is "particularly suited to handling commercial programming problems". What features and facilities would you expect such a language to have?*

ASSIGNMENT 8
REFERENCE MATERIAL

The computerisation of payroll has become a standard data processing application. For some years, most large companies and institutions have used computers for this purpose, in one way or another. More recently, there has been a trend towards smaller organisations using computers to handle this application.

A typical procedure is for documents to be passed to the "computer unit" on a weekly/monthly basis. The final outcome is for employees to receive a payslip along with their payment at the appropriate time. Payment is issued by the wages department, in the case of wage earners receiving weekly payments. Other employees including salaried staff, paid on a monthly basis, receive payment by cheque or bank draft via the finance/treasurer's department.

QUESTIONS

Answer one of the following two questions.

1. *Assume that you are to consider the provision of a computerised payroll for a small organisation eg. approximately 100 employees.*

    a. *Give a full account of the hardware and software, which you think would need to be available within the organisation, if it was to handle its own computerised payroll.*

    b. *A small organisation may only be able to employ one or two specialist computer staff. What experience, knowledge and skills will they look for in trying to obtain people to fill such a post?*

    c. *Suggest suitable procedures and documents, which could be used to collect the data and complete its input to the computer. Justify your choice of methods and documents.*

    d. *Draw an outline system flowchart to describe this payroll system.*

    e. *Outline an alternative way of providing for the firm's payroll needs, which would use external services instead of the firm's own computer and computer staff. Suggest reasons why this alternative method might be preferable.*

2. *Assume that you are to consider the provision of a computer payroll for a large organisation such as a national corporation, local authority etc.*

a. Assuming that the payroll is only one of several systems handled by the computer services department, explain how the hardware and software requirements would be provided. Consider the possibility of either centralised or distributed computer resources.

b. Explain in diagrammatic form how the staff might be organised within the computer services department. Give a brief outline of the work done on a payroll system by each of three members of staff shown in your diagram.

c. Specify the main controls which should be built into each stage of data collection, and what   precautions should be taken to safeguard the security of stored information.

d. Assume that there is one masterfile which contains records for all employees. Give pseudocode which gives the procedure for reading this file and producing two new ones. The first file should contain all wage earners, the second should contain all salary earners. State any assumptions that you make.

Appendix IV. Details omitted from the text in the interests of clarity

THE TRANSISTOR (see 33.19)

1. A transistor is produced by "doping" layers of crystal with impurities which drastically alter the electrical properties of each layer. Common impurities used in silicon transistors are arsenic and antomony. The doped crystal is either called **n-type** semiconductor crystal because of its **N**egative electric charge characteristics or **p-type** semiconductor crystal because of its **P**ositive electric charge characteristics.

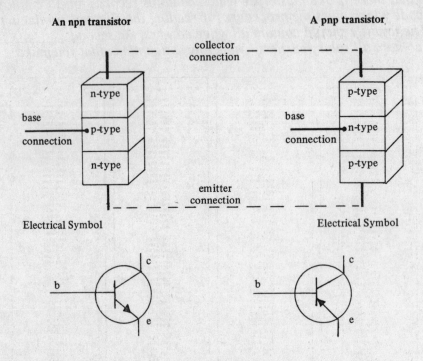

The base layer is typically about one hundred thousandth of one meter!

SIMPLE PROGRAMMING LANGUAGE EXAMPLES

2. a. The following examples are parts of programs which print the whole numbers from 1 to 10.

    b. **BASIC**
```
10 FOR 1 = 1 TO 10
20    PRINT 1
30 NEXT 1
```

    c. **COBOL**
```
PARA 1.
    PERFORM PARA 2 VARYING PRINT-NUMBER
    FROM 1 BY 1 UNTIL PRINT-NUMBER > 10.
    STOP RUN
PARA 2.
    WRITE PRINT-NUMBER BEFORE ADVANCING
    ONE LINE.
```

d. **FORTRAN**
   DO 81 = 1, 10, 1
   WRITE 95) I
   8 CONTINUE

e. **PASCAL**
   const last-number = 10;
   var a-number = integer;
   begin
      for a-number : = 1
      to last-number
      do writeln (a-number)
   end.

ASCII AND EBCDIC CODE
3.

ASCII AND EBCDIC CODE (see 4.13)

3.

EBCDIC	Bit Configuration	ASCII-8	EBCDIC	Bit Configuration	ASCII-8	EBCDIC	Bit Configuration	ASCII-8	EBCDIC	Bit Configuration	ASCII-8
NUL	0000 0000	NUL		0100 0101	E		1000 1010			1101 1111	
SOH	0000 0001	JOH		0100 0110	F		1000 1011		}	1101 0000	
STX	0000 0010	STX		0100 0111	G		1000 1100		J	1101 0001	
ETX	0000 0011	ETX		0100 1000	H		1000 1101		K	1101 0010	
PF	0000 0100	EOT		0100 1001	I		1000 1110		L	1101 0011	
HT	0000 0101	ENQ	¢	0100 1010	J		1000 1111		M	1101 0100	
LC	0000 0110	ACK		0100 1011	K				N	1101 0101	
DEL	0000 0111	BEL	<	0100 1100	L		1001 0000		O	1101 0110	
GE	0000 1000	BS	(	0100 1101	M	j	1001 0001		P	1101 0111	
RLF	0000 1001	HT	+	0100 1110	N	k	1001 0010		Q	1101 1000	
SMM	0000 1010	LF			0100 1111	O	l	1001 0011		R	1101 1001	
VT	0000 1011	VT				m	1001 0100			1101 1010	
FF	0000 1100	FF	&	0101 0000	P	n	1001 0101			1101 1011	
CR	0000 1101	CR		0101 0001	Q	o	1001 0110			1101 1100	
SO	0000 1110	SO		0101 0010	R	p	1001 0111			1101 1101	
SI	0000 1111	SI		0101 0011	S	q	1001 1000			1101 1110	
				0101 0100	T	r	1001 1001			1101 1111	
DLE	0001 0000	DLE		0101 0101	U		1001 1010				
DC1	0001 0001	DC1		0101 0110	V		1001 1011			1110 0000	
DC2	0001 0010	DC2		0101 0111	W		1001 1100			1110 0001	
TM(DC3)	0001 0011	DC3		0101 1000	X		1001 1101		S	1110 0010	
RES	0001 0100	DC4		0101 1001	Y		1001 1110		T	1110 0011	
NL	0001 0101	NAK	!	0101 1010	Z		1001 1111		U	1110 0100	
BS	0001 0110	SYN	S	0101 1011	\				V	1110 0101	
IL	0001 0111	ETB	*	0101 1100	)		1010 0000		W	1110 0110	
CAN	0001 1000	CAN		0101 1101		~	1010 0001		X	1110 0111	
EM	0001 1001	EM	;	0101 1110		s	1010 0010		Y	1110 1000	
CC	0001 1010	SUB		0101 1111		t	1010 0011		Z	1110 1001	
CU1	0001 1011	ESC				u	1010 0100			1110 1010	
IFS	0001 1100	FS		0110 0000	`	v	1010 0101			1110 1011	
IGS	0001 1101	GS	/	0110 0001	a	w	1010 0110			1110 1100	
IRS	0001 1110	RS		0110 0010	b	x	1010 0111			1110 1101	
IUS	0001 1111	US		0110 0011	c	y	1010 1000			1110 1110	
				0110 0100	d	z	1010 1001			1110 1111	
DS	0010 0000	SPACE		0110 0101	e		1010 1010				
SOS	0010 0001	!		0110 0110	f		1010 1011		0	1111 0000	
FS	0010 0010	"		0110 0111	g		1010 1100		1	1111 0001	
	0010 0011	=		0110 1000	h		1010 1101		2	1111 0010	
BYP	0010 0100	$		0110 1001	i		1010 1110		3	1111 0011	
LF	0010 0101	'	!	0110 1010	j		1010 1111		4	1111 0100	
ETB	0010 0110	&		0110 1011	k				5	1111 0101	
ESC	0010 0111	'		0110 1100	l		1011 0000		6	1111 0110	
	0010 1000	(		0110 1101	m		1011 0001		7	1111 0111	
	0010 1001	)	>	0110 1110	n		1011 0010		8	1111 1000	
SM	0010 1010	*	?	0110 1111	o		1011 0011		9	1111 1001	
CU2	0010 1011	+					1011 0100		LVM	1111 1010	
	0010 1100	,		0111 0000	p		1011 0101			1111 1011	
ENQ	0010 1101	-		0111 0001	q		1011 0110			1111 1100	
ACK	0010 1110	.		0111 0010	r		1011 0111			1111 1101	
BEL	0010 1111	/		0111 0011	s		1011 1000			1111 1110	
	0011 0000	0		0111 0100	t		1011 1001		EO	1111 1111	
	0011 0001	1		0111 0101	u		1011 1010				
SYN	0011 0010	2		0111 0110	v		1011 1011				
	0011 0011	3		0111 0111	w		1011 1100				
PN	0011 0100	4		0111 1000	x		1011 1101				
RS	0011 0101	5		0111 1001	y		1011 1110				
UC	0011 0110	6	=	0111 1010	z		1011 1111				
EOT	0011 0111	7		0111 1011	{						
	0011 1000	8	#	0111 1100	}		1100 0000				
	0011 1001	9	@	0111 1101	}	A	1100 0001				
	0011 1010	:		0111 1110	\	B	1100 0010				
CU3	0011 1011	;		0111 1111	DEL	C	1100 0011				
DC4	0011 1100	<				D	1100 0100				
NAK	0011 1101	=		1000 0000		E	1100 0101				
	0011 1110	>	a	1000 0001		F	1100 0110				
SUB	0011 1111	?	b	1000 0010		G	1100 0111				
			c	1000 0011		H	1100 1000				
SPACE	0100 0000	@	d	1000 0100		I	1100 1001				
	0100 0001	A	e	1000 0101			1100 1010				
	0100 0010	B	f	1000 0110			1100 1011				
	0100 0011	C	g	1000 0111			1100 1100				
	0100 0100	D	h	1000 1000			1100 1101				
				1000 1001			1100 1110				

NB. ASCII is a 7 bit code, but IBM use an expanded 8-bit version on their system/370 for the purpose of Input/Output. EBCDIC is used as an internal code on the system/370 (4.26).

Configurations, Extended Binary Coded Decimal Interchange Code (EBCDIC) and American National Standard Code for Information Interchange (ASCII).

This diagram Courtesy of IBM.

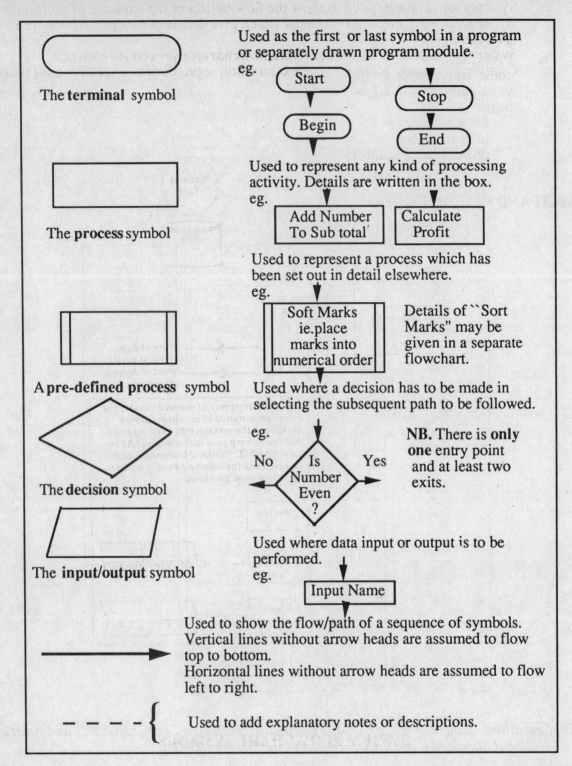

The **terminal** symbol

Used as the first or last symbol in a program or separately drawn program module.
eg.

Start

Begin

Stop

End

The **process** symbol

Used to represent any kind of processing activity. Details are written in the box.
eg.

Add Number To Sub total

Calculate Profit

A **pre-defined process** symbol

Used to represent a process which has been set out in detail elsewhere.
eg.

Soft Marks ie.place marks into numerical order

Details of ``Sort Marks'' may be given in a separate flowchart.

The **decision** symbol

Used where a decision has to be made in selecting the subsequent path to be followed.
eg.

No   Is Number Even ?   Yes

NB. There is **only one** entry point and at least two exits.

The **input/output** symbol

Used where data input or output is to be performed.
eg.

Input Name

Used to show the flow/path of a sequence of symbols. Vertical lines without arrow heads are assumed to flow top to bottom.
Horizontal lines without arrow heads are assumed to flow left to right.

Used to add explanatory notes or descriptions.

SYSTEM FLOWCHARTS

5.   a.   System flowcharts are used to show the flow of data or the sequence of procedures, in contrast with program flowcharts which give details of how procedures are to be carried out.

      b.   System flowcharts are also called **data flowcharts** or **procedure charts.**

      c.   **Common symbols** (Consult your examination regulations to see which ones to use).

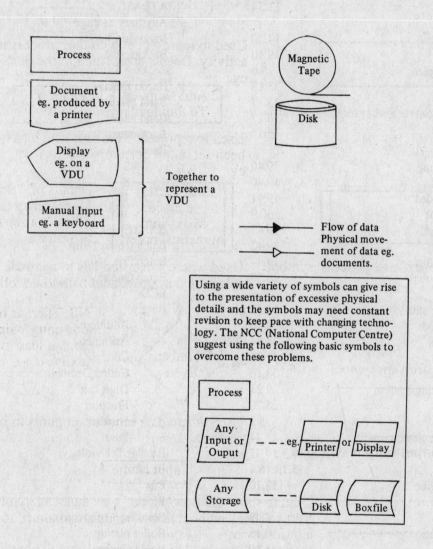

SYSTEM FLOWCHART SYMBOLS

Index

COMPUTING
An Active-Learning Approach
PM Heathcote

The aim of this book is to provide the **classroom support material** needed on **Advanced Level Computing** and BTEC courses.

There are many excellent textbooks on computing at this level (including *Computer Science* by CS French) which give valuable support and wider reading/reference for the student **outside** classroom time.

This book, however, has been designed as an interactive teaching and learning aid, eliminating the need for hand outs or copious note taking. It incorporates the following features:

- concise explanation of principles

- questions at **appropriate points** within the text (with space allowed for student to fill in answers) to enable the student to test and broaden knowledge and understanding, develop ideas, supply discussion points and test application of principles.

Teachers can explain each part of a topic in whatever way they like and use the concise explanations as the 'skeleton' of the classroom work. Students take an active part in the learning process via the questions interspersed throughout the text.

Apart from its value **during** the course, this is also an ideal book around which each student can build his/her revision programme.

CONTENTS:

Introduction to Computers and Business Data Processing • Databases • Internal Organisation of Computers • Programming in Pascal • Data Structures • Machine Languages and Assemblers • Systems Development • Programming Languages • Operating Systems • Communications • Peripherals • Computer Applications and Social Implications.

Free Lecturers' Supplement

The lecturers' supplement enables the book to be incorporated easily into lesson plans. It provides tips on implementation of the course and outline answers to all in-text questions and chapter-end exercises/exam questions.

ISBN: 1 870941 86 1

Date: June 1991

Edition: 1st

Extent: 400 pp

Size: 275 × 215 mm

COMPUTER SCIENCE
3rd Edition
CS French

This book provides a simplified approach to the understanding of Computer Science. In this latest edition the following topics are given greater emphasis: methods used in the various stages of systems development; computer languages; applications packages; databases and Human Computer Interfaces (HCIs).

COURSES ON WHICH THIS BOOK IS KNOWN TO BE USED:
A Level Computing; BTEC National and HNC/D Computer Studies; City & Guilds; BCS; AS Level Computer Science; BSc Applied Science Computing.

CONTENTS:

Foundation Topics • Introduction to Computers & Computer Science • Data Representation & Transmission • Number Bases • An Overview of Hardware • An Overview of Software • **Storage** • Main Storage • Backing Storage • **Input & Output** • Terminals & Workstations • Output devices • Data Capture & Data Entry • Human Computer Interfaces • **Computer Systems Organisations I** • Computer Systems Architecture • Data Communications & Networks • **Programming I** • Operations on Data • Program Structures • Program Design • Program Specification • **Files & File Processing** • Computer File Concepts • Magnetic Tape • Magnetic Disk • Processing Sequential Files • Processing Non-sequential Files • **Logic & Formal Notations** • Boolean Algebra • Machine Logic • Formal Notations • **Computer Arithmetic** • Arithmetical Procedures • Fixed-point & Floating-point Arithmetic • Errors & Accuracy • **Computer Systems Organisation II** • Machine Language • Low Level Language • Input-output Subsystem • Operating Systems • **Software** • Software Types • High Level Languages • Translators • Application Packages • **Programming II** • Further Data Structures • Further Methods • **Databases & 4GLs** • Database Architecture • Query Language & 4GLs • **Systems Development** • System Life-cycles • "Structured" Methods • Systems Design • Implementation & Post-implementation • Project Management • **Applications** • Applications Areas • Business Computing • Industrial Computing • Applications Organisation • **Computers in Context** • Evolution of Computer Systems • Computers in Society.

ISBN: 0 905435 83 4

Date: 1989

Edition: 3rd

Extent: 672 pp

Size: 245 × 187 mm

REVIEW COMMENTS:

'I think the presentation is superb and content perfect

Free Lecturers' Supplement

UNDERSTANDING COMPUTER SYSTEMS ARCHITECHTURE

Dr M Lacy

The aim of this book is to provide a course text for HNC/D and first or second year computing degree courses variously called 'Computer Systems', 'Computer Architecture' and 'Computer Technology'.

The many good reference texts on the subject can be too intimidating and off-putting to be useful for the students mentioned above. What is needed, and this book aims to satisfy that need, is a book which assumes a knowledge of computer hardware and software to approximately GCSE level and provides students with the knowledge and skills to consult with confidence the advanced texts on this topic. In doing so, the text covers in detail the key concepts which are central to understanding computer systems at HNC/D/degree level. An 'active learning' approach is integral to the book's structure.

CONTENTS:

THE PROCESSING UNIT - **Processor Basics:** A Simplified Processor • The Fetch/ Execute Cycle • Different Execute Sequences • **Towards Real Processors:** Multiplexer • Address Adder • General Purpose Registers • Flag Register • The Stack • **Microprocessors:** I8085 • Z80 • I8086 • THE PROCESSOR & DIGITAL LOGIC - **Logic Basics:** Gates • Physical Implementation • Combinational Circuits • Circuit Design • **Sequential Circuits:** Latches • Flip-flops • Sequencers • Circuit Design • **Components of the Processor:** Registers • ALU • Control Unit • THE COMPUTER AS A SYSTEM - **System Components:** Memory • Interfaces • Controllers • **Communication Between Components:** Programmed I/O • Interrupt-driven I/O • Delegated I/O • Autonomous Devices • **The User Interface:** Assembly Language • Assemblers • Loaders • Linkers • HIGHER PERFORMANCE SYSTEMS - **Increased Flexibility:** Microprogramming • **Developments within the von Neumann Framework:** Improved Technology • Memory Interleaving • Cache • Pipelining • CISC vs RISC • **New Directions:** Multiprocessor Classification • Interconnection Networks • Array Processors • Multiprocessor Systems • Software.

ISBN: 1 870941 81 0

Date: June 1991

Edition: 1st

Extent: 400 pp (Approx)

Size: 246 × 189 mm

Free Lecturers' Supplement

BASIC PROGRAMMING
3rd Edition
BJ Holmes

The text is useful for all computers that use BASIC. Particular emphasis, however, has been placed on the IBM PC and PC compatible computers, and the BBC model B and Electron computers.

A full coverage of the BASIC language is presented, with example programs being coded in Microsoft and BBC Basic. The book is packed with 47 documented worked examples and 121 questions complete with answers.

Notes on the Third Edition

In writing a new edition of this very popular book, the author has made the following changes:

Old dialects of the BASIC language have been removed, and much emphasis has been placed on writing programs for PC compatibles using Microsoft BASIC and BBC Basic on Model B computers.

All answers to the self-test questions are now available in Appendix I.

CONTENTS:

A Computer Model • Program Design • Elementary BASIC - A Sequence • Program Implementation • Selection • Repetition • Worked Examples • Further Input/Output • Subroutines and Procedures • Tables • String Processing • Mathematics • Sorting and Searching • Data Validation • Introduction to File Processing • Advanced File Processing • Process Control • Computer Graphics • Sound • Appendices: Answers to Questions; Suggested Programming Projects • BASIC Reserved Words Index.

ISBN: 1 870941 33 0
Date: 1990
Edition: 3rd
Extent: 288 pp
Size: 246 × 189 mm

Also available as ELBS edition in member countries

REVIEW COMMENTS:

'Computing is a subject which many people will regard with trepidation. If more books like this one are forthcoming that trepidation will soon disappear.'
"AUTA"

'Quite the best and most comprehensive book on BASIC I have seen - congratulations to author and publisher!' *Lecturer*

STRUCTURED PROGRAMMING IN COBOL
2nd Edition
BJ Holmes

This book is written around two themes: the design of structured computer programs based on the techniques from Jackson Structured Programming (JSP); and the methods available for coding these designs in the COBOL language.

Notes to the Second Edition

The contents of this edition have been reordered, with additional new chapters on *Computer Environment, Structured Design, Program Development, COBOL-85* and *JSP/COBOL – a design programming tool.*

The author has used Standard COBOL in the translation of JSP program designs into COBOL code. The programs in the text have been compiled using an ANS 1985 COBOL compiler. Because of the subset of language statements used, it is also possible to compile the programs using older compilers that conform to the ANS 1974 Standard.

COURSES ON WHICH THIS BOOK IS KNOWN TO BE USED:
Degrees in Computer Studies; BTEC National & Higher National Computer Studies; City & Guilds examinations in programming.

CONTENTS:
Computer Environment • Structured Design • Elements of COBOL • A Complete Program • Program Development • Picture Editing • Coding Data Files and Reports • Introduction to File Processing • Program Structures from File Structures • File Maintenance • Tables • Direct Access Files • COBOL 85 • Program Implementation Techniques • JSP/COBOL – A Design Programming Tool • Miscellaneous Features.

REVIEW COMMENTS:
'Good on Jackson's Structures ...' 'The author has brought together in a practical way the JSP philosophy with all the traditional areas of COBOL. At its price it offers unrivalled value for money.'
                                                                    Lecturers
'A number of texts were mentioned, but the most popular seems to be BJ Holmes, Structured Programming in COBOL ...'

**Report on COBOL on BTEC Higher
National Courses, Manchester Polytechnic**

Free Lecturers' Supplement
New! With the lecturers' supplement is a free (and copyright free) PC compatible disk incorporating all the illustrative programs in the text – saves keying in! Immediate use for demonstration and development purposes for lecturers and students.

Note:- The disk needs to be compiled using either an ANS 1985 or ANS 1974 COBOL compiler.

ISBN: 1 870941 82 9

Date: June 1991

Edition: 2nd

Extent: 400 pp (Approx)

Size: 240 × 190 mm

PASCAL PROGRAMMING
2nd Edition
BJ Holmes

PASCAL Programming can be regarded as a complete text on programming and the use of data structures. The aim of this book is to help the reader acquire and develop the skill of computer programming in a block-structured language and foster an understanding of the related topics of data structures and data processing.

Notes to the Second Edition
There are new chapters on recursion, sorting and searching, dynamic data structures, object-oriented programming and case studies. Chapters contain computer-generated illustrations to help explain the topics found in the text. Greater emphasis has been placed on the use of Turbo Pascal. To demonstrate the use of the Pascal language statements, the text contains seventy-five documented programs. There are one hundred and twenty questions, to which answers are supplied.

COURSES ON WHICH THIS BOOK IS KNOWN TO BE USED:
BTEC National and HNC/D Computer Studies; BCS Part 1; A Level Computing; First Year Undergraduate courses.

CONTENTS:

Computer Environment • Data • Instruction Sequence • Data Types • Selection • Repetition • Procedures • Program Development • Mathematics • Arrays • Sorting and Searching • Recursion • Text Files • Pointers • Dynamic Structures • Record Files • Common Extensions • Turbo Units • Object-oriented programming (OOP) • Case Studies in OOP.

REVIEW COMMENTS:

'...goes a lot further than other books on files.' '...good value ...'   *Lecturers*

ISBN: 1 870941 65 9
Date: Jan 1991
Edition: 2nd
Extent: 464 pp
Size: 240 × 190 mm

Free Lecturers' Supplement

NEW! With the lecturers' supplement is a free (and copyright free) PC compatible disk incorporating all the programs in the text — saves keying in! Immediate use for illustrative and development purposes for lecturers and students.

Note:- The programs on the disk need to be compiled using Borland Turbo Pascal compiler version 5.5 or later.

PASCAL BY ACTIVE LEARNING
Using the CORE Approach

Dr T Boyle & S Margetts

The aim is to provide an effective student-centred learning environment for PASCAL. This package allows students to be **active learners** of the language and so frees class tutors from extensive lecturing about language details.

An IBM PC-compatible disk with supporting booklet acts as a 'book substitute'. The CORE (Context, Objects Refinement, Expression) approach engages the student as an active learner from the very beginning. The central principle is to present concrete examples to be understood within an appropriate context rather than abstract rules to be learned by rote. This approach fosters natural curiosity and problem-solving skills within a clear supportive framework.

PASCAL by Active Learning covers the main language forms and data structures in PASCAL in nearly thirty learning blocks. Each learning block is structured as a guided discovery environment which culminates in the student writing or extending a program which incorporates the newly-acquired skills.

This method has been extensively tested at Manchester Polytechnic and Bury College and it has been very positively received by students. As one mature student exclaimed:

"Isn't it an easy way to learn?"

Using this CORE approach through open learning, students have proved able to learn PASCAL on a basis of less than 1 hour's lecturer contact per week.

COMPATIBILITY

1) **Hardware:** any IBM PC compatible micro-computers.
2) **Software:** PASCAL by Active Learning covers Standard PASCAL. The examples should work with any PASCAL compiler.

ISBN: 1 870941 76 4

Date: June 1991

Edition: 1st

Description:
   Disk and booklet

Sample material is available for lecturers' inspection/assessment

MODULA-2

BJ Holmes

This book develops language statements and programs in manageable steps. Examples and self-test exercises are simple enough to give the reader confidence at each stage of learning. Much emphasis is placed on the portability between computers, with programs being developed on a pc and ported, without modification, to a SUN workstation.

Within a single book there is enough information to provide a foundation for any reader who wishes to develop and implement a wide variety of systems in Modula-2.

COURSES ON WHICH THIS BOOK IS KNOWN TO BE USED:
BTEC National and HNC/D Computing; BTEC HNC/D Information Technology; BSc Computer Science; A Level Computing.

CONTENTS:

Computer Environment • Data • Instruction Sequence • Data Types • Selection • Repetition • Procedures • Program Development • Mathematics • Modules • Arrays • Sorting and Searching • Recursion • File Processing • File Maintenance • Pointers • Data Abstraction • Coroutines.

REVIEW COMMENTS:

'...will be switching to yours in the Autumn.' '...ideal for our BTEC Higher Computer Studies course.' '...its reasonable price, many examples, large answers section and complete coverage mean we will use it as a course text.' 'We found the Holmes' book on COBOL useful and this title is likely to be of the same value.'
Lecturers

Free Lecturers' Supplement

NEW! With the lecturers' supplement is a free (and copyright free) PC compatible disk incorporating all the programs in the text – saves keying in! Immediate use for illustrative and development purposes for lecturers and students.

Note:- The programs on the disk need to be compiled using 'JPI Top Speed Modula-2'

ISBN: 1 870941 31 4

Date: 1989

Edition: 1st

Extent: 352 pp

Size: 246 × 189 mm

Oliver and Chapman's
DATA PROCESSING AND INFORMATION TECHNOLOGY
8th Edition
Revised by CS French

This book provides a simplified approach to the understanding of data processing and information technology. It is intended for those with little or no knowledge of the subject.

The contents have been reorganised and extensively revised to provide a modern perspective. The text contains significant new material on work stations, structure methods, databases and 4GLs.

COURSES ON WHICH THIS BOOK IS KNOWN TO BE USED:
ACCA; CIMA; AAT; ICSA; IComA; City and Guilds; A Level Computing; BTEC National Computer Studies; BTEC HNC/D Business Studies; BSc Computer Studies; BSc Info Technology; IAM.

On reading lists of ACCA, AAT, IDPM, BCS and IComA

CONTENTS:

Introduction to Information Systems • Computer Storage • Computer Input and Output • Computer Systems Organisation • Computer Files • Software Development • File Processing • Software • Database Systems • Information Systems Development • Applications • Computer Sytems • Information Systems Management • The Social Aspect • Case Exercises.

REVIEW EXTRACTS:

'This new edition has some very useful changes from the previous one. The wider page format helps in presentation of the material (and reading the book). The order of the contents is more logical than the last edition and there are some useful additions in the areas of 4GL's, databases and workstations ... The book's strongest point is its coverage of computer technology and data processing. It has some very useful examples throughout the text and is as up-to-date as textbooks reasonably can be.'

"ACCA Students' Newsletter"

ISBN: 1 870941 39 X

Date: 1990

Edition: 8th

Extent: 432 pp

Size: 246 × 189 mm

Also avialable as ELBS edition in member countries

Free Lecturers' Supplement